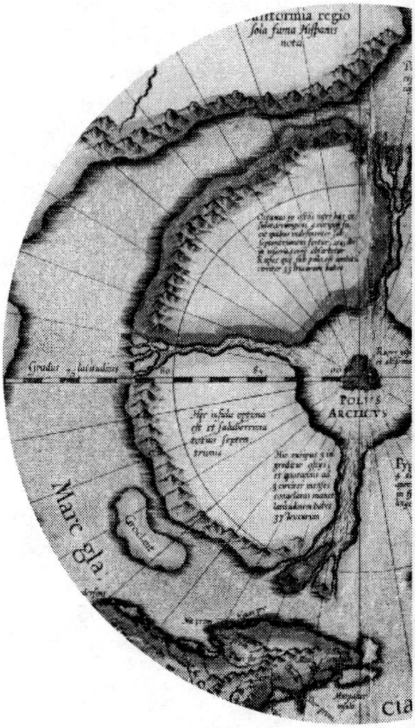

MERIDIANS
Sources in World History

History 115
World History to 1500
UMUC
Fall 2007

PEARSON
Custom Publishing

Director of Database Publishing: Michael Payne
Sponsoring Editor: Natalie Danner
Development Editors: Katherine R. Gehan and Katherine J. Thompson
Editorial Assistant: Laura Krier
Marketing Manager: Nathan Wilbur
Operations Manager: Eric M. Kenney
Production Project Manager: Jennifer M. Berry
Rights Editor: Francesca Marcantonio
Cover Designer: Renée Sartell

Cover Art: Courtesy of the Stapelton Collection/CORBIS.

Printed in the United States of America

Please visit our website at *www.pearsoncustom.com*
Attention bookstores: For permission to return any unsold stock, contact Pearson Custom Publishing at 1-800-777-6872.

ISBN-13: 978-0-536-24079-8   ISBN-10: 0-536-24079-5

PEARSON
Custom Publishing

PEARSON CUSTOM PUBLISHING
75 Arlington St., Suite 300
Boston, MA 02116

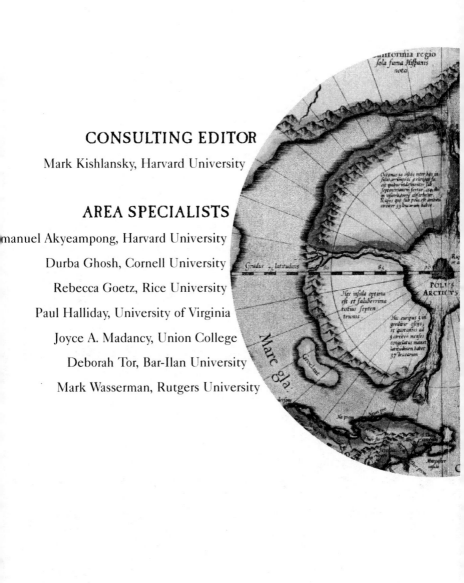

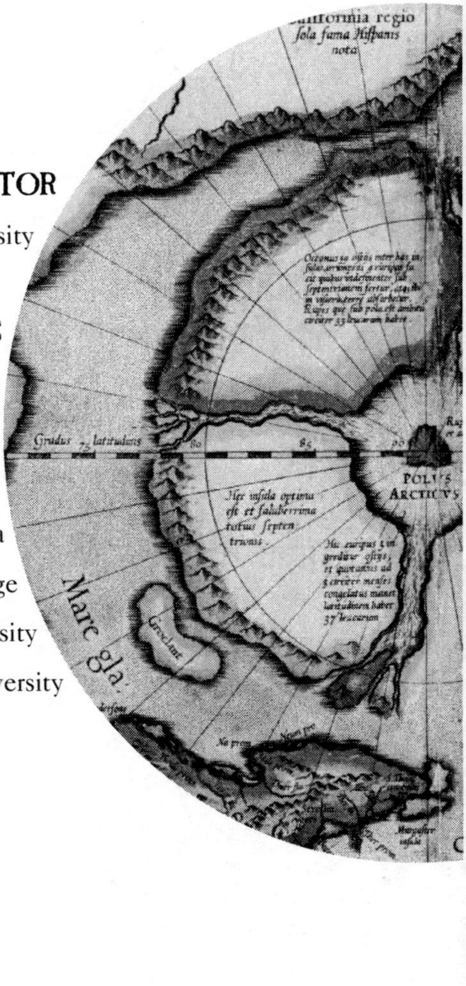

sola fama Hispanis
nota
Gradus
latitudinis
Marc gla.

CONTENTS

UMUC History Program Expectations and Requirements

Welcome. In order to assist you in preparing for this class, and in your overall efforts to plan your studies, the UMUC History program has prepared the following information about class expectations and requirements. Please take a moment to read this entire section closely. The procedures and program-specific directions contained here are standard in every UMUC History class, and you are expected to adhere to these instructions.

History Program Goals and UMUC Cross-Curricular Initiatives

This course has been designed to meet not only the specific course goals but also the educational goals of the History program as well as the UMUC cross-curricular initiatives. These objectives include:

- increasing your knowledge of information technologies and their uses
- enhancing your information literacy by offering models of critical analysis and appreciation
- improving your effective-writing skills
- broadening your historical and international perspective on human events

To meet these goals, the readings for this class have been carefully selected and the assignments carefully designed. Your successful completion of this course will indicate that you have demonstrated increased skills and knowledge in each of the above areas, as appropriate in a university class.

Advice for Student Success

As a general guideline, the assumption among teachers in higher education is that courses earning three credit hours require a minimum of three hours in the classroom each week and a minimum of six additional hours in preparation for weekly classroom participation. Courses with heavy reading assignments and papers often require more time. You should allow for those requirements in planning your study schedule. Courses such as this one also have higher expectations about the quality and quantity of student contributions, and grading standards are appropriately stringent.

Please always remember that the course is tied to an academic calendar, with weekly required activities, clear due dates for assignments, and an end to the semester. UMUC classes are not individual-study or self-paced classes: you are expected to participate in class discussions, regardless of class format, and to interact with your instructor and classmates in a timely manner.

Lower-level classes (numbered 100 through 299) provide the foundations for more advanced study, and provide you with the basic critical skills and discipline-specific knowledge needed to succeed in your studies. In order to do well in your studies, it is recommended that certain classes, such as ENGL 101 and LIBS 150, be taken as early in your course work as possible, and certainly within the first 15 credit hours, as required by UMUC. Additional intensive-writing classes are required of all students, and successful completion of those required classes will prove tremendously helpful in your history course work.

Upper-level classes (numbered 300 through 499) are recommended for advanced students who already possess a sufficient background both in critical skills and historical studies. You will discover that these classes have substantially higher expectations, not simply in the quantity of reading, writing, and participation required, but equally important in the quality of critical analysis and research sophistication exhibited in your work. Although very few history classes have official prerequisites, the assumption your instructors must work under is that students in advanced classes are aware of these requirements and have taken the necessary steps to meet them and thus ensure success. You should take a moment to honestly ask yourself if you have developed the necessary skills and possess the background knowledge that will enable you to successfully complete an upper-level class. If you are in need of guidance, please do not hesitate to contact your advisor or your instructor.

If you have enrolled in a distance-education class on WebTycho, this course may be the first online course experience for you. A certain amount of uncertainty and frustration is to be expected as you learn to use the technology during the first weeks. It's important you recognize that this online asynchronous classroom retains many of the requirements of the traditional classroom—such as lectures, class discussions, assignments, and required readings—while offering you greater control over your time as well as access to all the instructional resources available through the World Wide Web.

If your time is limited, you need to be very self-disciplined as a class member. Be prepared to visit the online classroom three times each week and to complete each of the activities assigned by your instructor. During your preparation time outside the classroom, study the readings carefully and engage in any additional research or writing activities assigned. And of course, avoid the temptation to procrastinate: not preparing for or attending class each week—or postponing that research project!—will almost certainly lead to unnecessary stress later and probably be reflected in your final grade.

Although online courses do retain many of the same schedules and requirements of classroom-based courses, there are some important differences. In asynchronous courses such as UMUC's WebTycho classes, class members may literally be scattered around the world, and instructors and students are not simultaneously logged on. The class discussions deserve your particular attention because you'll have the time to contribute in a thoughtful and reflective manner.

Your instructor will log in regularly to respond to e-mail and to grade submitted assignments as well as to upload course materials. He or she will inform you of the planned schedule for the semester and if any changes are necessary. Instructors are not available—either face to face or online—24 hours a day, seven days a week. Please remember that your instructor will need time to read and grade assignments before returning them to you. Please be patient, and any questions you might ask will be answered and your work graded.

Departmental Statement on Submission of Original Work

All work submitted must be written for this course during the term in which the course is being completed. Work from other courses or from other academic or non-academic settings, past or present, is not acceptable and will result in immediate failure for that assignment. No opportunities for resubmission or revision will be granted.

When assignments involve research, students may make reference to work originally submitted for other courses or other settings. If students wish to submit extensively revised or expanded work previously submitted in this or another course, they must obtain the approval of the class instructor in advance.

Plagiarism Prevention Assignment

Throughout every level of education in the United States there is increasing concern about standards of academic honesty and the rise in instances of plagiarism. The news media regularly report on these issues, and in several highly publicized cases, the failure to adhere closely to professional standards of documentation, citation, and ethics has embarrassed even some very respected scholars and widely published authors.

Teachers realize that, in most cases, incidents of plagiarism by students are accidental and may be attributable to insufficient training. Regardless, academic honesty is governed by clear policies that your teachers must uphold. Even inadvertent errors can lead to severe penalties. Please review the university's policy on academic dishonesty and plagiarism, which can be found in the Academic Policies section of your syllabus and in the Undergraduate Catalogue. Carefully review the definitions, procedures, and penalties set forth. Be aware that faculty are required to report incidents of possible plagiarism or academic dishonesty and that the sanctions that may be imposed can seriously affect your efforts to complete your education.

To help students avoid these problems, UMUC's Effective Writing Center offers advice and tutoring services, self-study tutorials, and other tools to support your educational success. A particularly useful tool is the self-study module, "How to Avoid Plagiarism," which can be found by following the Writing Resources link under Course Content on the left-hand menu in your WebTycho classroom, or by visiting the Effective Writing Center online at http://www.umuc.edu/prog/ugp/ewp_writingcenter/wc_selfhelp.html.

Since the fall 2002 semester, the History program requires each student in every history course to successfully complete the "How to Avoid Plagiarism" tutorial. Your first required assignment is to review this tutorial and to complete the self-examination at the end. When you successfully finish it, an online certificate of completion will appear.

After you have completed the "How to Avoid Plagiarism" tutorial and successfully taken the post-test, please be sure to submit a copy of your certificate to your instructor. To do this, follow the steps below.

1. Highlight all of the text in the certificate window with your cursor.
2. While the text is highlighted, right click and scroll down to "Copy" (or hold down the "Ctrl" key and press "C").

3. Use a common word-processing program (Microsoft Word is preferred), or other program that allows you to paste the copied certificate and then save it in .doc, .txt, or .rtf format. Save your certificate to your desktop or to an easily found folder on your computer.
4. Go to your assignment folder in your WebTycho classroom or to the WebTycho site that supplements your face-to-face class and follow the directions for submitting your certificate.

You must submit the certificate by the end of week two of your course. Your teacher will not grade any other submitted coursework without the posting of the certificate in the designated area. One point will be added to your final grade to acknowledge your successful completion of this assignment.

By working with you, the UMUC faculty wants to help you achieve academic success and excellence. If you have any questions about proper citation formats or doubts about when it is appropriate to document your information, your teacher and the staff of the Effective Writing Center are available to assist you.

Departmental Grading Standards

Students and faculty recognize that the grade the instructor gives is a professional judgment of the quality of the student's submitted work and that grades are based on shared assumptions and expectations. At the most basic level, we expect that assignments will be submitted to the instructor on time. Submitted assignments are to be clearly focused and organized, with a discernible thesis statement. Generalizations and conclusions are to be adequately supported and, when appropriate, research documentation is to be well integrated and effectively presented. A formal writing style is required, along with proper grammar, punctuation, and spelling.

It's important that students and faculty have shared expectations regarding the criteria for assignment grades. The following broad definitions are based on the suggestions of the UMUC Information Literacy and Writing Assessment Task Force and offer general criteria for grading. While these rubrics were written as guidelines for the grading of formal research essays, the same basic criteria will be used for the grading of essay examinations and other written assignments.

The grade of A reflects excellence. The A paper offers a well-focused and organized discussion appropriate to the instructor's assignment, reflects critical use of relevant materials, and demonstrates effective and formal writing requirements. Research papers must demonstrate outstanding efforts to identify varied pertinent sources, to employ those materials critically in the text of the papers, and to provide error-free citations of those resources.

The grade of B represents an effort beyond satisfactory and indicates the paper was completed in an appropriate and competent manner and, in general, demonstrates a strong attempt at original and critical analysis, writing, and research. The B paper may contain a number of minor errors of grammar or citation, and its thesis or its conclusions may be undeveloped or too weakly supported.

The grade of C indicates that the paper was done in a satisfactory or appropriate fashion and represents the average work expected for university courses. The presentation is organized around a central idea with arguments supported by relevant examples. The paper is structured into correctly written paragraphs and sentences. Although fulfilling the assignment, the C paper may exhibit one or more weaknesses including, but not limited to, errors of punctuation and grammar, imprecise or incorrect word use, inaccurate or uncritical use of materials, occasional inconsistency of organization or development, and lack of direct relevance of the selected research materials to the topic.

The grade of D indicates that the paper may have a poorly defined topic or thesis, lack clear focus or organization, and contain unsupported generalizations or conclusions. Research support is inadequate, not clearly relevant, or improperly documented. A less-than-minimal research effort is evident. The paper may also suffer from numerous or major formal writing errors.

The grade of F indicates that the paper is not clearly relevant to the assignment and that its topic and thesis are poorly focused or defined. The paper may display inadequate organization or development, unsupported generalizations, and nonstandard formal features (including language usage, sentence structure, paragraphing, and so on). Research support is absent, inadequate, or irrelevant to the assignment.

Using the *Chicago Manual of Style* for Papers

In your introductory English course, you were introduced to the fundamentals of term-paper writing and to different forms of bibliographic and note citation, for example MLA style, as developed by the Modern Language Association. Among historians, the preferred form is known as "University of Chicago" or "Chicago style." If you are interested, you can find all the detailed explanations for this form in *The Chicago Manual of Style*, a hardcover guide published by the University of Chicago Press.

Luckily, a more accessible and less costly guide to University of Chicago style is available in paperback—Kate Turabian's *A Manual for Writers of Term Papers, Theses, and Dissertations*. This work offers in a concise format all the information you will need for compiling notes and preparing bibliographies for your history courses. Using this well-known and respected resource along with the *UMUC Guide to Writing and Research* will help you improve your writing. For your convenience, you can find several basic guides to Chicago style on the Web, including one at http://umbc.edu/history/students/style.html.

What Is the EWC?

The Effective Writing Center (EWC) provides online services and resources for helping you to improve your writing.

How Do I Use the EWC?

You can submit any piece of writing to the EWC for feedback by a trained, experienced writing advisor.
You can e-mail writing-related questions to writingcenter@umuc.edu.
You can use the How to Avoid Plagiarism self-study module, developed by the EWC and the Center for the Virtual University. This module will help you manage research resources responsibly and correctly in your writing assignments. After completing the module, you can take a quiz to check your mastery of the material.
You can read UMUC's *Online Guide to Writing and Research*, which provides information on all aspects of researching and writing many kinds of course assignments.
You can complete additional self-study modules, in which you will learn about aspects of research and writing, and you can practice what you learn.

DOCUMENT

THE EPIC OF GILGAMESH

The Epic of Gilgamesh *is one of the oldest known human stories. The* Epic, *the oldest record—it dates to the second millennium B.C.E.—relates how Gilgamesh, legendary king of the third millennium B.C.E. Mesopotamian city-state of Uruk, goes on a quest for everlasting life after the death of his friend Enkidu has made him aware of human mortality. To this end, Gilgamesh seeks Utnapishtim "the faraway," the man who alone among humans was chosen by the gods to live forever and removed by them to the land of Dilmun, across the waters of death.*

The main part of this excerpt relates Gilgamesh's conversation with Utnapishtim after he has overcome all obstacles and the ferryman Urshanabi has taken him across the ocean and the waters of death, as well as the final outcome of Gilgamesh's quest.

PROLOGUE

Gilgamesh King in Uruk

O Gilgamesh, lord of Kullab, great is thy praise. This was the man to whom all things were known; this was the king who knew the countries of the world. He was wise, he saw mysteries and knew secret things, he brought us a tale of the days before the flood. He went on a long journey, was weary, worn-out with labour, and returning engraved on a stone the whole story.

When the gods created Gilgamesh they gave him a perfect body. Shamash the glorious sun endowed him with beauty, Adad the god of the storm endowed him with courage, the great gods made his beauty perfect, surpassing all others. Two thirds they made him god and one third man.

In Uruk he built walls, a great rampart, and the temple of blessed Eanna for the god of the firmament Anu, and for Ishtar the goddess of love. Look at it still today: the outer wall where the cornice runs, it shines with the brilliance of copper; and the inner wall, it has no equal. Touch the threshold, it is ancient. Approach Eanna the dwelling of Ishtar, our lady of love and war, the like of which no latter-day king, no man alive can equal. Climb upon the wall of Uruk; walk along it, I say; regard the foundation terrace and examine the masonry: is it not burnt brick and good? The seven sages laid the foundations.

. . .

4

The Search for Everlasting Life

Bitterly Gilgamesh wept for his friend Enkidu; he wandered over the wilderness as a hunter, he roamed over the plains; in his bitterness he cried, 'How can I rest, how can I be at peace? Despair is in my heart. What my brother is now, that shall I be when I am dead. Because I am afraid of death I will go as best I can to find Utnapishtim whom they call the Far-away, for he has entered the assembly of the gods.' So Gilgamesh travelled over the wilderness, he wandered over the grasslands, a long journey, in search of Utnapishtim, whom the gods took after the deluge; and they set him to live in the land of Dilmun, in the garden of the sun; and to him alone of men they gave everlasting life.

At night when he came to the mountain passes Gilgamesh prayed: 'In these mountain passes long ago I saw lions, I was afraid and I lifted my eyes to the moon; I prayed and my prayers went up to the gods, so now, O moon god Sin, protect me.' When he had prayed he lay down to sleep, until he was woken from out of a dream. He saw the lions round him glorying in life; then he took his axe in his hand, he drew his sword from his belt, and he fell upon them like an arrow from the string, and struck and destroyed and scattered them.

. . .

6

The Return

Utnapishtim said, 'As for you, Gilgamesh, who will assemble the gods for your sake, so that you may find that life for which you are searching? But if you wish, come and put it to the test: only prevail against sleep for six days and seven nights.' But while Gilgamesh sat there resting on his haunches, a mist of sleep like soft wool teased from the fleece drifted over him, and Utnapishtim said to his wife, 'Look at him now, the strong man who would have everlasting life, even now the mists of sleep are drifting over him.' His wife replied, 'Touch the man to wake him, so that he may return to his own land in peace, going back through the gate by which he came.' Utnapishtim said to his wife, 'All men are deceivers, even you he will attempt to deceive; therefore bake loaves of bread, each day one loaf, and put it beside his head; and make a mark on the wall to number the days he has slept.'

So she baked loaves of bread, each day one loaf, and put it beside his head, and she marked on the wall the days that he slept; and there came a day when the first loaf was hard, the second loaf was like leather, the third was soggy, the crust of the fourth had mould, the fifth was mildewed, the sixth was fresh, and the seventh was still on the embers. Then Utnapishtim touched him and he woke. Gilgamesh said to Utnapishtim the Faraway, 'I hardly slept when you touched and roused me.' But Utnapishtim said, 'Count these loaves and learn how many days you slept, for your first is hard, your second like leather, your third is soggy, the crust of your fourth has mould, your fifth is mildewed, your sixth is fresh and your seventh was still over the glowing embers when I touched and woke you.' Gilgamesh said, 'What shall I do, O Utnapishtim, where shall I go? Already the thief in the night has hold of my limbs, death inhabits my room; wherever my foot rests, there I find death.'

Then Utnapishrim spoke to Urshanabi the ferryman: 'Woe to you Urshanabi, now and for ever more you have become hateful to this harbourage; it is not for you, nor for you are the crossings of this sea. Go now, banished from the shore. But this man before whom you walked, bringing him here, whose body is covered with foulness and the grace of whose limbs has been spoiled by wild skins, take him to the washing-place. There he shall wash his long hair clean as snow in the water, he shall throw off his skins and let the sea carry them away, and the beauty of his body shall be shown, the fillet on his forehead shall be renewed, and he shall be given clothes to cover his nakedness. Till he reaches his own city and his journey is accomplished, these clothes will show no sign of age, they will wear like a new garment.' So Urshanabi took Gilgamesh and led him to the washing-place, he washed his long hair as clean as snow in the water, he threw off his skins, which the sea carried away, and showed the beauty of his body. He renewed the fillet on his forehead, and to cover his nakedness gave him clothes which would show no sign of age, but would wear like a new garment till he reached his own city, and his journey was accomplished.

Then Gilgamesh and Urshanabi launched the boat on to the water and boarded it, and they made ready to sail away; but the wife of Utnapishtim the Faraway said to him, 'Gilgamesh came here wearied out, he is worn out; what will you give him to carry him back to his own country?' So Utnapishtim spoke, and Gilgamesh took a pole and brought the boat in to the bank. 'Gilgamesh, you came here a man wearied out, you have worn yourself out; what shall I give you to carry you back to your own country? Gilgamesh, I shall reveal a secret thing, it is a mystery of the gods that I am telling you. There is a plant that grows under the water, it has a prickle like a thorn, like a rose; it will wound your hands, but if you succeed in taking it, then your hands will hold that which restores his lost youth to a man.'

When Gilgamesh heard this he opened the sluices so that a sweet-water current might carry him out to the deepest channel; he tied heavy stones to his feet and they dragged him down to the water-bed. There he saw the plant growing; although it pricked him he took it in his hands; then he cut the heavy stones from his feet, and the sea carried him and threw him on to the shore. Gilgamesh said to Urshanabi the ferryman, 'Come here, and see this marvellous plant. By its virtue a man may win back all his former strength. I will take it to Uruk of the strong walls; there I will give it to the old men to eat. Its name shall be "The Old Men Are Young Again"; and at last I shall eat it myself and have back all my lost youth.' So Gilgamesh returned by the gate through which he had come, Gilgamesh and Urshanabi went together. They travelled their twenty leagues and then they broke their fast; after thirty leagues they stopped for the night.

Gilgamesh saw a well of cool water and he went down and bathed; but deep in the pool there was lying a serpent, and the serpent sensed the sweetness of the flower. It rose out of the water and snatched it away, and immediately it sloughed its skin and returned to the well. Then Gilgamesh sat down and wept, the tears ran down his face, and he took the hand of Urshanabi; 'O Urshanabi, was it for this that I toiled with my hands, is it for this I have wrung out my heart's blood? For myself I have gained nothing; not I, but the beast of the earth has joy of it now. Already the stream has carried it twenty leagues back to the channels where I found it. I found a sign and now I have lost it. Let us leave the boat on the bank and go.'

After twenty leagues they broke their fast, after thirty leagues they stopped for the night; in three days they had walked as much as a journey of a month and fifteen days. When the journey was accomplished they arrived at Uruk, the strong-walled city. Gilgamesh spoke to him, to Urshanabi the ferryman, 'Urshanabi, climb up on to the wall of Uruk, inspect its foundation terrace, and examine well the brickwork; see if it is not of burnt bricks; and did not the seven wise men lay these foundations? One third of the whole is city, one third is garden, and one third is field, with the precinct of the goddess Ishtar. These parts and the precinct are all Uruk.'

This too was the work of Gilgamesh, the king, who knew the countries of the world. He was wise, he saw mysteries and knew secret things, he brought us a tale of the days before the flood. He went on a long journey, was weary, worn out with labour, and returning engraved on a stone the whole story.

7

The Death of Gilgamesh

The destiny was fulfilled which the father of the gods, Enlil of the mountain, had decreed for Gilgamesh: 'In nether-earth the darkness will show him a light; of mankind, all that are known, none will leave a monument for generations to come to compare with his. The heroes, the wise men, like the new moon have their waxing and waning. Men will say, "Who has ever ruled with might and with power like him?" As in the dark month, the month of shadows, so without him there is no light. O Gilgamesh, this was the meaning of your dream. You were given the kingship, such was your destiny, everlasting life was not your destiny. Because of this do not be sad at heart, do not be grieved or oppressed; he has given you power to bind and to loose, to be the darkness and the light of mankind. He has given unexampled supremacy over the people, in victory in battle from which no fugitive returns, in forays and assaults from which there is no going back. But do not abuse this power, deal justly with your servants in the palace, deal justly before the face of the Sun.'

The king has laid himself down and will not rise again,
The Lord of Kullab will not rise again;
He overcame evil, he will not come again;
Though he was strong of arm he will not rise again . . .

QUESTIONS

1. Why does Gilgamesh seek Utnapishtim?
2. How does Utnapishtim test Gilgamesh?
3. What does it reveal about Gilgamesh that he saves the plant of immortality for the old men of his city?
4. What is the significance of the fact that it is a snake that steals the plant?

DOCUMENT

ANCIENT MESOPOTAMIAN CHRONICLES

The ancient Near East was the world's first known literate society, and the home of the world's first human civilizations. The cultural heart of the very ancient world lay in Mesopotamia, where the superpowers of that age flourished. Fortunately, the people of the region left behind many surviving documents including letters, business documents, and religious and literary texts. These were written in the langauages of Sumerain or Akkadian, painstakingly inscribed in cuneiform writing on tablets. Another genre of cuneiform writing that has proven most valuable to historians is that of historiography, including both chronicles and king lists. These documents are especially interesting because, while some were obviously written upon royal command, others appear to have been composed on scribal initiative, or at the behest of powerful cultural organizations or individuals such as temple priests.

The first excerpt here is taken from a group of seven chronicles known as the Neo-Babylonian Chronicle series. This excerpt deals with a time of great toil in Babylon, 693 to 668 B.C.E. It opens with the revolt of the Babylonian king against Assyrian domination, describing the outcome and some of the consequences of that revolt, and ends with the ascension to the Babylonian throne of a son of King Esarhaddon of Assyria.

The second excerpt is taken from the Chronicle of Early Kings, *a work that relates some of the world's earliest historical events. The excerpt treats the reigns of two important kings: Sargon, king of Akkad from 2334 to 2279 B.C.E. and Shulgi (r. 2095 to 2047 B.C.E.), generally considered to have been the greatest and wisest of the rulers of Ur, in Sumer, although not by this chronicler.*

CHRONICLE 1

13. The first year of Mushezib-Marduk:[1] On the seventeenth (var. eighth) day of the month Ab
14. Kudur-(Nahhunte), king of Elam, was taken prisoner in a rebellion and killed. For ten months
15. Kudur-(Nahhunte) ruled Elam. Humban-nimea
16. ascended the throne
15. in Elam.
16. In an unknown year Humban-nimena
17. mustered
16. the troops of Elam (and) Akkad
17. and
18. did
17. battle against Assyria in Halule.[2]
18. He effected an Assyrian retreat.
19. The fourth year of Mushezib-Marduk: On the fifteenth day of the month Nisan
20. Humban-nimena, king of Elam, was stricken by paralysis and
21. his mouth was so affected that he could not speak.
22. On the first day of the month Kislev the city (i.e. Babylon) was captured. Mushezib-Marduk
23. was taken prisoner and transported to Assyria.
24. For four years Mushezib-Marduk ruled Babylon.
25. On the seventh day of the month Adar Humban-nimena, king of Elam, died.
26. For four years Humban-nimena ruled Elam.
27. Humban-haltash (I)[3] ascended the throne in Elam.
28. The eighth year of there not being a king in Babylon: On the third day of the month Tammuz
29. the gods of Uruk[4] went from [Ela]m into Uruk.
30. On the twenty-third day of the month Tishri Humban-[hal]tash (I), king of Elam,

31. became paralysed
30. at noon-hour
31. and died at [sun]set. For eight years Humban-haltash (I)
32. ruled Elam.
33. Humban-haltash the second, his [*son*], ascended the throne.
34. On the twentieth day of the month Tebet Sennacherib, king of Assyria.
35. was killed by his son (lit. his son killed him) in a rebellion. For [*twenty-four*] years Sennacherib
36. ruled Assyria.
37. The rebellion continued in Assyria
36. from the twentieth day of the month Tebet until
37. the second day of the month Adar.

21. In the month Kislev its booty entered Uruk.
22. On the fifth day of the month Adar the king's wife died.
23. The tenth year: In the month Nisan the army of Assyria marched to Egypt. (text) broken
24. On the third, sixteenth, (and) eighteenth days of the month Tammuz—
25. three times—there was a massacre in Egypt. (Var. adds: It was sacked (and) its gods were abducted.)
26. On the twenty-second day Memphis, the royal city, was captured (and)
27. abandoned by its king (lit. its king abandoned). His (the king's) son and bro[ther were taken pr]isoner.
28. (The city) was sacked, its inhabitants plundered, (and) its booty carried off.
29. The eleventh year: In Assyria the king put his numerous officers to the sword.
30. The twelfth year: The king of Assyria marched to Egypt (but)
31. became ill on the way and died on the tenth day of the month Marchesvan.
32. For twelve years Esarhaddon[5] ruled Assyria.
33. Shamash-shuma-ukin (and) Ashurbanipal, his two sons, ascended the throne in Babylon and Assyria respectively.
34. The accession year of Shamash-shuma-ukin: In the month Iyyar.
35. Bel[6] and the gods of Akkad

36. went out
35. from Libbi-ali (Ashur)
36. and on the *fourteenth/twenty-fourth* day of the month Iyyar they entered Babylon.
37. In that same year Kirbitu was t[aken] (and) its king captured.
38. On the twentieth day of the month Tebet Bel-etir, judge of Babylon, was taken prisoner and executed.
39. The first section, written according to the pattern-tablet, checked and collated.
40. Tablet of Ana-Bel-erish, son of Liblutu,
41. descendant of Kalbi-Sin. Written by Ea-nadin, son of
42. Ana-Bel-erish, descendant of Kalbi-Sin. Babylon,
43. the *sixth/sixteenth/twenty-sixth* [day of the month. . .], the twenty-second year of Darius,[7] king of Babylon and (all) lands.

CHRONICLE 20

1. Sargon, king of Agade,[8] came to power during the reign of Ishtar[9] and
2. he had neither rival nor equal.
3. He diffused
2. his splendour over the lands.
3. He crossed the sea in the east.
4. In his eleventh year he conquered the western land to its farthest point.
5. He brought it under one authority. He set up his statues in the west.
6. He sent their (the west's) booty into Amati.[10]
7. He stationed his court officials at intervals of five double hours and
8. ruled in unity the tribes of the lands.
9. He marched to Kazalla and turned Kazalla into a ruin heap
10. so that there was not even a perch for a bird left (lit. he destroyed the resting-place of a bird in it).
11. Afterwards, in his old age all of the lands rebelled against him and
12. surrounded him in Agade. Sargon went out to fight (lit. to arms) and brought about their defeat.
13. He overthrew them (and) overpowered their extensive army.

14. Afterwards, Subartu attacked (Sargon) in full force and called him to arms.
15. Sargon set an ambush and completely defeated them.
16. He overpowered their extensive army
17. and sent their possessions into Agade.
18. He dug up the dirt of the pit of Babylon and
19. made a counterpart of Babylon next to Agade.
20. Because of the wrong he had done the great lord Marduk became angry and
21. wiped out his people by famine.
23. They (his subjects) rebelled against him
22. from east to west
23. and he (Marduk) afflicted [him] with insomnia.
24. Naram-Sin, son of Sargon, [marched] to Apishal.
25. He made a breach (in the city wall) and
26. captured
25. Resh-Ad[ad],
26. king of Apishal, and the vizier of Apishal.
27. He marched to Magan and captured Mannudannu, king of Magan.
28. Shulgi, son of Ur-Nammu, provided abundant food for Eridu, which is on the seashore.
29. But he had criminal tendencies and
30. took away
29. the property of Esagil and Babylon
30. as booty. Bel caused . . . to consume his body . . . *killed him.*
31. Erra-imitti, the king,
32. installed
31. Enlil-bani, the gardener,
32. as substitute king on his throne.[11]
33. He placed the royal tiara on his head.
34. Erra-imitti[died] in his palace when he sipped a hot broth.
35. Enlilbani, who occupied the throne, did not give it up (and)
36. so was sovereign.

END NOTES

1. King of Babylon from 693 to 689 B.C.E.
2. In 689 B.C.E. Mushezib-Marduk, in alliance with the kingdom of Elam (located in today's southwestern Iran), led the Babylonians in revolt against Assyria and King Sennacherib.
3. Humban-haltash was king of Elam from 687–680 B.C.E.
4. First major city in Sumer, founded c. 3500; greatest and most populous (50,000) city in the world until the decline of sumer c. 2000 B.C.E. The modern name Irag is derived from Uruk (Biblical Erech).
5. King of Assyria from 681 to 669 B.C.E.
6. Bel, or Marduk (Ba'al in the Bible) was the ancient Near Eastern sun god.
7. King Darius I ("the Great") of Persia (r.521 to 486 B.C.E.). Famous for continuing his predecessor Cyrus's policy of restoring the Jewish state (the rebuilding of the Temple in Jerusalem was completed under his auspices in 515), and for his great defeat by the Greeks at the Battle of Marathon (490 B.C.E).
8. Chief city of the Mesopotamian kingdom of Akkad, founded by Sargon c. 2330 B.C.E. Sargon was king of Akkad from 2334 to 2279 B.C.E.
9. Most important ancient Sumero-Babylonian goddess.
10. Modern Hama, a city in northern Syria.
11. As part of the spring New Year celebration, the king would apparently appoint a mock king for a day, who would afterward be sacrificed to the gods in his stead. In this case, the real king died and the mock king remained on the throne for twenty-four years.

QUESTION

1. Why does the alliance between Babylon and Elam fall apart? What occurred as a result?
2. Who wrote down Chronicle 1?
3. What do the Assyrians do when they conquer Egypt?
4. The chronicler makes very explicit what his opinion of Sargon is. What evidence does he adduce in support of this view, and how do we reconcile the end of his account of Sargon with the beginning of his account of that ruler?

DOCUMENT

THE SIX DAYS OF CREATION

The Bible

The Bible is the most authoritative text in the Judeo-Christian tradition, and is still regarded by many Christians and Jews as divinely inspired. It is divided into two large parts: the Jewish Scriptures, known to Christians as the Old Testament; and the New Testament, containing twenty-seven books recognized as authoritative by Christians but not by Jews. In addition to the thirty-nine books of the Old Testament recognized by Protestant Christianity and by normative Judaism are another fifteen books or parts of books that were handed down with the Jewish Scriptures in Greek (known as the Septuagint). Most of these are accepted as canonical by the Roman Catholic Church and are referred to in its tradition as the "deuterocanonical" books.

The Old Testament contains a great variety of writings including myths, legends, legal codes, chronicles, edifying stories, poetry, prophecy, and wisdom literature. The original texts were compiled at various times between the twelfth and the second centuries B.C.E. *Almost all of them were written in classical Hebrew, except for a few short passages in Aramaic. The canon of the Hebrew scriptures (the so-called Massoretic text) was only established by Palestinian Jews toward the end of the first century* C.E. *and has remained substantially unchanged since that time. Greek Christians, however, made use of the Septuagint text, while Roman Catholic Christians in the Middle Ages used*

Reprinted from *The Revised English Bible.*

the Latin translation of St. Jerome (c. 342–420 C.E.) based on the Hebrew. Since the Reformation the customary practice in Protestant countries is to use vernacular translations based on the original Hebrew text.

In the first generations following the death of Christ (29/30 C.E.), Christians continued to use the Jewish Scriptures as sacred writings, interpreting them in the light of the teachings of Jesus and the apostle Paul. Gradually they assembled a body of their own writings, believed to be of apostolic origin. These were written in Greek during a seventy-five-year period between about 50 and 125 C.E. The first attested use of the expression "New Testament," however, comes in the writings of Tertullian around 200 C.E., and the first serious attempts by the Church to define the canon of the New Testament date only from the late fourth century C.E. The New Testament includes four early accounts of the life and teachings of Christ (the Gospels); a historical account of the early missions of the Church (the Acts of the Apostles); letters of various apostles; and a book of prophecies (Revelation) attributed to the apostle John. The letters of the apostle Paul are particularly significant statements of early Christian theology, and all the apostolic epistles contain instructions concerning morality and Church discipline.

The passage excerpted here, one of the most famous in the Bible, comes from the beginning of Genesis, the first book of the Bible, and describes God's creation of the world.

[1]In the beginning God created the heavens and the earth. [2]The earth was a
vast waste, darkness covered the deep, and the spirit of God hovered over
the surface of the water. [3]God said, 'Let there be light,' and there was light;
[4]and God saw the light was good, and he separated light from darkness.
[5]He called the light day, and the darkness night. So evening came, and
morning came; it was the first day.

[6]God said, 'Let there be a vault between the waters, to separate water
from water.' [7]So God made the vault, and separated the water under the
vault from the water above it, and so it was; [8]and God called the vault the
heavens. Evening came, and morning came, the second day.

[9]God said, 'Let the water under the heavens be gathered into one place,
so that dry land may appear'; and so it was. [10]God called the dry land
earth, and the gathering of the water he called sea; and God saw that it was

good. [11]Then God said, 'Let the earth produce growing things; let there be on the earth plants that bear seed, and trees bearing fruit each with its own kind of seed.' So it was; [12]the earth produced growing things: plants bearing their own kind of seed and trees bearing fruit, each with its own kind of seed; and God saw that it was good. [13]Evening came, and morning came, the third day.

[14]God said, 'Let there be lights in the vault of the heavens to separate day from night, and let them serve as signs both for festivals and for seasons and years. [15]Let them also shine in the heavens to give light on earth.' So it was; [16]God made two great lights, the greater to govern the day and the lesser to govern the night; he also made the stars. [17]God put these lights in the vault of the heavens to give light on earth, [18]to govern day and night, and to separate light from darkness; and God saw that it was good. [19]Evening came, and morning came, the fourth day.

[20]God said, 'Let the water teem with living creatures, and let birds fly above the earth across the vault of the heavens.' [21]God then created the great sea-beasts and all living creatures that move and swarm in the water, according to their various kinds, and every kind of bird; and God saw that it was good. [22]He blessed them and said, 'Be fruitful and increase; fill the water of the sea, and let the birds increase on the land.' [23]Evening came, and morning came, the fifth day.

[24]God said, 'Let the earth bring forth living creatures, according to their various kinds: cattle, creeping things, and wild animals, all according to their various kinds.' So it was; [25]God made wild animals, cattle, and every creeping thing, all according to their various kinds; and he saw that it was good. [26]Then God said, 'Let us make human beings in our image, after our likeness, to have dominion over the fish in the sea, the birds of the air, the cattle, all wild animals on land, and everything that creeps on the earth.'

[27]God created human beings in his own image;
in the image of God he created them;
male and female he created them.

[28]God blessed them and said to them, 'Be fruitful and increase, fill the earth and subdue it, have dominion over the fish in the sea, the birds of the

air, and every living thing that moves on the earth.' [29]God also said,
'Throughout the earth I give you all plants that bear seed, and every tree
that bears fruit with seed: they shall be yours for food. [30]All green plants
I give for food to the wild animals, to all the birds of the air, and to everything that creeps on the earth, every living creature.' So it was; [31]and God
saw all that he had made, and it was very good. Evening came, and morning came, the sixth day.
2 Thus the heavens and the earth and everything in them were completed.
[2]On the sixth day God brought to an end all the work he had been doing;
on the seventh day, having finished all his work, [3]God blessed the day and
made it holy, because it was the day he finished all his work of creation.

END NOTES

1:1–2 **In . . . earth was:** *or* When God began to create the heavens and the earth, [2]the earth was.
1:2 **the spirit . . . hovered:** *or* a great wind swept; *or* a wind from God swept.
2:2 **sixth:** *so some Vss.; Heb.* seventh.

QUESTIONS

1. What is the order in which God makes the various elements of the world?
2. What, in this account of creation, makes humans different from other creatures? How are they the same?
3. What words does God say? What is the relationship of language to divine power in this passage?
4. In what ways can we think of this passage as a kind of history?

DOCUMENT

THE WISDOM OF CONFUCIUS

Confucius

*It is unfortunate that the wisdom of Confucius (c. 551–c. 479 B.C.E.) has often been translated in such a way that his profound and often quite radical insights come across as simplistic. His thinking has had a deeper and more enduring impact on the structure of Chinese politics, economics, and social structure than perhaps any other man in history. Confucius lived in a very unsettled, violent time, and he and other philosophers struggled to develop ideologies that would generate and maintain social harmony. For Confucius, the answer was a highly structured society that stressed ethics above all, and advocated rule by the virtuous and well educated. Some scholars feel that Confucius's departure from the widely accepted notion that leadership should be accorded to those with military might and/or aristocratic birthright was nothing less than revolutionary. The Chinese civil service bureaucracy and the examination system through which access to those positions was attained trace their origins to Confucian ideology. Confucius himself was from an aristocratic family, but one that had seen better days by the time he was born, and his relative poverty might have had an impact on his thinking that goodness did not always go hand-in-hand with nobility and wealth. But all men could and should seek to become gentlemen (*junzi, chun-tzu*), something that is discussed at length in* The Analects.

It is not easy to condense Confucian ideology in this limited space, but in brief, an ideal Confucian society was structured by a hierarchy based on age, gender, and education. That hierarchy was reinforced by frequent and often elaborate rituals, usually accompanied by music. Family was the primary unit of society, and the cardinal virtue was filial piety, the heartfelt veneration of one's parents. Government was supposed to be benevolent, and a good ruler could govern simply by example. Goodness was within everyone's reach and it could be cultivated through education, particularly in the ways of the ancient sages of the Western Zhou (Chou) Dynasty (c. 1027–771 B.C.E.), particularly Confucius's idol, the Duke of Zhou. Of course, reality often differed considerably from the ideal, and part of the reason for the endurance of Confucianism is that it proved quite malleable in the hands of various dynasties and emperors.

The wisdom of Confucius has been conveyed through the ages through a collection of his sayings, conversations, and observations called The Analects (Lun Yu) *compiled by his students. (Confucius is referred to in that volume as The Master.) Although Confucius longed to offer his advice and services to a ruler and thus transform that ruler's state, he never held important government office and his most important accomplishment was his teaching.*

THE ANALECTS–LUN YÜ

BOOK I

2 Master Yu said, Those who in private life behave well towards their parents and elder brothers, in public life seldom show a disposition to resist the authority of their superiors. And as for such men starting a revolution, no instance of it has ever occurred. It is upon the trunk[1] that a gentleman works. When that is firmly set up, the Way grows. And surely proper behaviour towards parents and elder brothers is the trunk of Goodness?

3 The Master said, 'Clever talk and a pretentious manner' are seldom found in the Good.

BOOK II

1 The Master said, He who rules by moral force (*tê*) is like the pole-star, which remains in its place while all the lesser stars do homage to it.

2 The Master said, If out of the three hundred *Songs* I had to take one phrase to cover all my teaching, I would say 'Let there be no evil in your thoughts.'

3 The Master said, Govern the people by regulations, keep order among them by chastisements, and they will flee from you, and lose all self-respect. Govern them by moral force, keep order among them by ritual and they will keep their self-respect and come to you of their own accord.

4 The Master said, At fifteen I set my heart upon learning. At thirty, I had planted my feet firm upon the ground. At forty, I no longer suffered from perplexities. At fifty, I knew what were the biddings of Heaven. At sixty, I heard them with docile ear. At seventy, I could follow the dictates of my own heart; for what I desired no longer overstepped the boundaries of right.

5 Mêng I Tzu[2] asked about the treatment of parents. The Master said, Never disobey! When Fan Ch'ih[3] was driving his carriage for him, the Master said, Mêng asked me about the treatment of parents and I said, Never disobey! Fan Ch'ih said, In what sense did you mean it? The Master said, While they are alive, serve them according to ritual. When they die, bury them according to ritual and sacrifice to them according to ritual.[4]

6 Mêng Wu Po[5] asked about the treatment of parents. The Master said, Behave in such a way that your father and mother have no anxiety about you, except concerning your health.

7 Tzu-yu[6] asked about the treatment of parents. The Master said, 'Filial sons' nowadays are people who see to it that their parents get enough to eat. But even dogs and horses are cared for to that extent. If there is no feeling of respect, wherein lies the difference?

. . .

13 Tzu-kung asked about the true gentleman. The Master said, He does not preach what he practises till he has practised what he preaches.

. . .

20 Chi K'ang-tzu[4] asked whether there were any form of encouragement by which he could induce the common people to be respectful and loyal.

The Master said, Approach them with dignity, and they will respect you. Show piety towards your parents and kindness towards your children, and they will be loyal to you. Promote those who are worthy, train those who are incompetent; that is the best form of encouragement.

BOOK IV

16 The Master said, A gentleman takes as much trouble to discover what is right as lesser men take to discover what will pay.

17 The Master said, In the presence of a good man, think all the time how you may learn to equal him. In the presence of a bad man, turn your gaze within!

18 The Master said, In serving his father and mother a man may gently remonstrate with them. But if he sees that he has failed to change their opinion, he should resume an attitude of deference and not thwart them; may feel discouraged, but not resentful.

19 The Master said, While father and mother are alive, a good son does not wander far afield; or if he does so, goes only where he has said he was going.[7]

20 The Master said, If for the whole three years of mourning a son manages to carry on the household exactly as in his father's day, then he is a good son indeed.

BOOK V

15 Of Tzu-ch'an[8] the Master said that in him were to be found four of the virtues that belong to the Way of the true gentleman. In his private conduct he was courteous, in serving his master he was punctilious, in providing for the needs of the people he gave them even more than their due; in exacting service from the people, he was just.

BOOK VII

4 In his leisure hours the Master's manner was very free-and-easy, and his expression alert and cheerful.

. . .

8 The Master said, Only one who bursts with eagerness do I instruct; only one who bubbles with excitement, do I enlighten. If I hold up one corner and a man cannot come back to me with the other three, I do not continue the lesson.

9 If at a meal the Master found himself seated next to someone who was in mourning, he did not eat his fill. When he had wailed at a funeral, during the rest of the day he did not sing.

. . .

19 The Master said, I for my part am not one of those who have innate knowledge. I am simply one who loves the past and who is diligent in investigating it.

20 The Master never talked of prodigies, feats of strength, disorders[9] or spirits.

21 The Master said, Even when walking in a party of no more than three I can always be certain of learning from those I am with. There will be good qualities that I can select for imitation and bad ones that will teach me what requires correction in myself.

. . .

24 The Master took four subjects for his teaching: culture, conduct of affairs, loyalty to superiors and the keeping of promises.

25 The Master said, A Divine Sage I cannot hope ever to meet; the most I can hope for is to meet a true gentleman. The Master said, A faultless man I cannot hope ever to meet; the most I can hope for is to meet a man of fixed principles. Yet where all around I see Nothing pretending to be Something, Emptiness pretending to be Fulness, Penury pretending to be Affluence, even a man of fixed principles will be none too easy to find.

BOOK IX

4 There were four things that the Master wholly eschewed: he took nothing for granted, he was never over-positive, never obstinate, never egotistic.

. . .

7 The Master said, Do I regard myself as a possessor of wisdom? Far from it. But if even a simple peasant comes in all sincerity and asks me a question, I am ready to thrash the matter out, with all its pros and cons, to the very end.

. . .

22 The Master said, Respect the young. How do you know that they will not one day be all that you are now? But if a man has reached forty or fifty and nothing has been heard of him, then I grant there is no need to respect him.

. . .

24 The Master said, First and foremost, be faithful to your superiors, keep all promises, refuse the friendship of all who are not like you; and if you have made a mistake, do not be afraid of admitting the fact and amending your ways.

BOOK XII

1 Yen Hui asked about Goodness. The Master said, 'He who can himself submit to ritual is Good.' If (a ruler) could for one day 'himself submit to ritual', everyone under Heaven would respond to his Goodness. For Goodness is something that must have its source in the ruler himself; it cannot be got from others. . . .

2 Jan Jung asked about Goodness.[10] The Master said, Behave when away from home[11] as though you were in the presence of an important guest. Deal with the common people as though you were officiating at an important sacrifice. Do not do to others what you would not like yourself. Then there will be no feelings of opposition to you, whether it is the affairs of a State that you are handling or the affairs of a Family.[12]

. . .

7 Tzu-kung asked about government. The Master said, Sufficient food, sufficient weapons, and the confidence of the common people. Tzu-kung said, Suppose you had no choice but to dispense with one of these three, which would you forgo? The Master said, Weapons. Tzu-kung said, Suppose you were forced to dispense with one of the two that were left, which would you forgo? The Master said, Food. For from of old death has been the lot of all men; but a people that no longer trusts its rulers is lost indeed.

. . .

9 Duke Ai enquired of Master Yu, saying, It is a year of dearth, and the State has not enough for its needs. What am I to do? Master Yu replied, saying, Have you not got your tithes? The Duke said, Even with two-tenths instead of one, I still should not have enough. What is the use of talking to me about tithes? Master Yu said, When the Hundred Families[13] enjoy plenty, the prince necessarily shares in that plenty. But when the Hundred Families have not enough for their needs, the prince cannot expect to have enough for his needs.

. . .

11 Duke Ching of Ch'i[14] asked Master K'ung about government. Master K'ung replied saying, Let the prince be a prince, the minister a minister, the father a father and the son a son. The Duke said, How true! For indeed when the prince is not a prince, the minister not a minister, the father not a father, the son not a son, one may have a dish of millet in front of one and yet not know if one will live to eat it.[15]

BOOK XIII

1 Tzu-lu asked about government. The Master said, Lead them; encourage them! Tzu-lu asked for a further maxim. The Master said, Untiringly.

. . .

6 The Master said, If the ruler himself is upright, all will go well even though he does not give orders. But if he himself is not upright, even though he gives orders, they will not be obeyed.

. . .

9 When the Master was going to Wei, Jan Ch'iu drove him. The Master said, What a dense population! Jan Ch'iu said, When the people have

multiplied, what next should be done for them? The Master said, Enrich them. Jan Ch'iu said, When one has enriched them, what next should be done for them? The Master said, Instruct them.

10 The Master said, If only someone were to make use of me, even for a single year, I could do a great deal; and in three years I could finish off the whole work.

11 The Master said, 'Only if the right sort of people had charge of a country for a hundred years would it become really possible to stop cruelty and do away with slaughter.' How true the saying is!

12 The Master said, If a Kingly Man were to arise, within a single generation Goodness would prevail.

13 The Master said, Once a man has contrived to put himself aright, he will find no difficulty at all in filling any government post. But if he cannot put himself aright, how can he hope to succeed in putting others right?

. . .

15 Duke Ting asked if there were any one phrase that sufficed to save a country. Master K'ung replied saying, No phrase could ever be like that. But here is one that comes near to it. There is a saying among men: 'It is hard to be a prince and not easy to be a minister.' A ruler who really understood that it was 'hard to be a prince' would have come fairly near to saving his country by a single phrase.

Duke Ting said, Is there any one phrase that could ruin a country? Master K'ung said, No phrase could ever be like that. But here is one that comes near to it. There is a saying among men: 'What pleasure is there in being a prince, unless one can say whatever one chooses, and no one dares to disagree?' So long as what he says is good, it is of course good also that he should not be opposed. But if what he says is bad, will it not come very near to his ruining his country by a single phrase?

BOOK XV

33 The Master said, It is wrong for a gentleman to have knowledge of menial matters and proper that he should be entrusted with great responsibilities. It is wrong for a small man to be entrusted with great responsibilities, but proper that he should have a knowledge of menial matters.

. . .

37 The Master said, In serving one's prince one should be

Intent upon the task,
Not bent upon the pay.

BOOK XVI

4 Master K'ung said, There are three sorts of friend that are profitable, and three sorts that are harmful. Friendship with the upright, with the true-to-death and with those who have heard much is profitable. Friendship with the obsequious, friendship with those who are good at accommodating their principles, friendship with those who are clever at talk is harmful.

5 Master K'ung said, There are three sorts of pleasure that are profitable, and three sorts of pleasure that are harmful. The pleasure got from the due ordering of ritual and music, the pleasure got from discussing the good points in the conduct of others, the pleasure of having many wise friends is profitable. But pleasure got from profligate enjoyments, pleasure got from idle gadding about, pleasure got from comfort and ease is harmful.

6 Master K'ung said, There are three mistakes that are liable to be made when waiting upon a gentleman. To speak before being called upon to do so; this is called forwardness. Not to speak when called upon to do so; this is called secretiveness. To speak without first noting the expression of his face; this is called 'blindness'.

7 Master K'ung said, There are three things against which a gentleman is on his guard. In his youth, before his blood and vital humours have settled

down, he is on his guard against lust. Having reached his prime, when the blood and vital humours have finally hardened, he is on his guard against strife. Having reached old age, when the blood and vital humours are already decaying, he is on his guard against avarice.

8 Master K'ung said, There are three things that a gentleman fears: he fears the will of Heaven, he fears great men,[16] he fears the words of the Divine Sages. The small man does not know the will of Heaven and so does not fear it. He treats great men with contempt, and scoffs at the words of the Divine Sages.

9 Master K'ung said, Highest are those who are born wise. Next are those who become wise by learning. After them come those who have to toil painfully in order to acquire learning. Finally, to the lowest class of the common people belong those who toil painfully without ever managing to learn.

END NOTES

1. i.e. upon what is fundamental, as opposed to 'the twigs', i.e. small arts and accomplishments, which the gentleman leaves to his inferiors.
2. A young grandee of Lu, whose father sent him to study with Confucius. He died in 481 B.C.
3. A disciple.
4. Evidently by 'disobey' Confucius meant 'disobey the rituals'. The reply was intended to puzzle the enquirer and make him think. In *Mencius,* III, 1, II, 2, 'While they are alive . . .', etc., is given as a saying of Master Tsêng. Here and elsewhere 'sacrifice' means offerings in general and not only animal-sacrifice.
5. Son of Mêng I Tzu.
6. A disciple;
7. Particularly in order that if they die he may be able to come back and perform the rites of mourning.
8. Minister in the Cheng State; died 522 B.C.
9. Disorders of nature; such as snow in summer, owls hooting by day, or the like.
10. i.e. ruling by Goodness, not by force.
11. i.e. in handling public affairs.
12. A ruling clan, such as that of the Chi in Lu.
13. All the people.
14. Died 490 B.C. The last of a long line of powerful and successful dukes. The closing years of his reign were clouded by the intrigues of the Ch'ên Family, which menaced the security of the dynasty (the prince was no longer a prince; ministers, i.e. the leaders of the Ch'ên faction, were no longer content to be ministers); and by succession-squabbles among his sons (the father no longer had the authority of a father; the sons were not content to be sons).

15. Figure of speech denoting utter insecurity.
16. Probably the meaning here is 'morally great'; that is to say, people like Confucius

QUESTIONS

1. According to Confucius, what constitutes a gentleman? Good government?
2. After reading the excerpts from *The Analects,* how would you describe Confucius as a man?
3. What was it about Confucianism that made it such an appealing ideology to the Chinese state over the centuries?
4. Do you think it is feasible to run a state according to the advice of Confucius? Explain. What would government and society be like?

DOCUMENT

HAN FEIZI AND LEGALISM

Han Feizi

Although their ideas have had a profound impact on the organization of Chinese politics and society, very little is known about the life of many of China's ancient philosophers, including Han Feizi (Han Fei Tzu, c. 280–233 B.C.E.*). It is believed that Han Feizi was born a prince in the state of Han. Unlike fellow philosophers Confucius, Mencius, and Zhuangzi (Chuang Tzu) who came from aristocratic families that had fallen on hard times, Han Feizi was linked by blood to the Han ruling family. He apparently was also troubled by a terrible stutter, which impeded his career at a time when oratory was greatly respected and expected from philosophers and statesmen. That handicap, however, proved beneficial to historians, because the only way Han Feizi could effectively convey his ideas was through the written word. His work had a great impact on the man who would unify all of China under the Qin dynasty (221–206* B.C.E.*). Unfortunately, when the ruler of Han Feizi's state sent him to negotiate with the soon-to-be first emperor of the Qin Dynasty, Han Feizi's motives were questioned because of his allegiance to the Han state, and he was thrown in jail, where he died from drinking poison.*

The samples of Han Feizi's writings included here are typical of his advice to rulers. Like his teacher, Xunzi (Hsun Tzu, c. 310–215 B.C.E.*), Han Feizi was convinced that human nature was not good; he believed people tended to act in their own interest, and thus a ruler had to take that into account when governing. One of the best ways to ensure the behavior the ruler wanted was to impose an extensive system of laws to govern behavior through punishments* *and rewards. In Han Feizi's opinion, Confucianism was naïve, impractical, and hypocritical. He utterly rejected the Confucian notion of benevolent government, ridiculed the desire to return to a golden age of sage kings, scoffed at the concept of a trustworthy minister, and imparted the worst of motives to virtually everyone surrounding a ruler.*

Legalism on its own proved effective in uniting the fragmented warring kingdoms of China, but it was not geared toward winning the hearts and minds of the subjects of the Qin Dynasty. The First Emperor of the Qin is renowned for standardizing China's currency, axle lengths, and the written language to promote commerce and communication; for his huge public works projects, such as linking many of the unconnected pieces of the Great Wall; as well as for his extravagant tomb with its army of terra cotta warriors. However, he was also infamous for his persecution of Confucian scholars, which might explain in part why later histories penned by Confucian historians cast him in such a negative light. The Han dynasty (202 B.C.E.–220 C.E.) that overthrew the Qin owed much of its success to a subtle combination of Confucian principles and the authoritarianism (and detailed legal code) of the Legalist school. That combination proved so effective that it was adopted by many subsequent dynasties.

THE WAY OF THE RULER

Section 5

The ruler must not reveal his desires; for if he reveals his desires his ministers will put on the mask that pleases him. He must not reveal his will; for if he does so his ministers will show a different face. So it is said: Discard likes and dislikes and the ministers will show their true form; discard wisdom and wile and the ministers will watch their step. Hence, though the ruler is wise, he hatches no schemes from his wisdom, but causes all men to know their place. Though he has worth, he does not display it in his deeds, but observes the motives of his ministers. Though he is brave, he does not flaunt his bravery in shows of indignation, but allows his subordinates to display their valor to the full. Thus, though he discards wisdom, his rule is enlightened; though he discards worth, he achieves merit; and though he discards bravery, his state grows powerful. When the ministers stick to their posts, the hundred officials have their regular duties, and the ruler employs each according to his particular ability, this is known as the state of manifold constancy. . . .

If you do not guard the door, if you do not make fast the gate, then tigers will lurk there. If you are not cautious in your undertakings, if you do not hide their true aspect, then traitors will arise. They murder their sovereign and usurp his place, and all men in fear make common cause with them: hence they are called tigers. They sit by the ruler's side and, in the service of evil ministers, spy into his secrets: hence they are called traitors. Smash their cliques, arrest their backers, shut the gate, deprive them of all hope of support, and the nation will be free of tigers. Be immeasurably great, be unfathomably deep; make certain that names and results tally, examine laws and customs, punish those who act willfully, and the state will be without traitors. . . .

The enlightened ruler in bestowing rewards is as benign as the seasonable rain; the dew of his bounty profits all men. But in doling out punishment he is as terrible as the thunder; even the holy sages cannot assuage him. The enlightened ruler is never overliberal in his rewards, never overlenient in his punishments.

THE EIGHT VILLAINIES

Section 9

In dealing with those who share his bed, the enlightened ruler may enjoy their beauty but should not listen to their special pleas or let them come with personal requests. In dealing with his attendants, he should hold them personally responsible for their words and not allow them to speak out of turn. In dealing with his kin and elder statesmen, though he heeds their words, he should be careful to hand out the appropriate punishments or promotions afterwards, and should not let them advance to offices arbitrarily. As regards the buildings and possessions that delight and amuse the ruler, he should make certain that they are constructed and produced only on his order; the officials should never be permitted to present them as they please in an effort to ingratiate themselves with him. As regards the dispensing of favors and charity, all orders to disburse emergency funds or to open up the granaries for the relief of the people must come from the ruler; he should never allow his ministers to dole out charity on their own. As regards speeches and debates, he should be careful to discover the true ability of those whom the flatterers praise, and find out the true faults of those whom the slanderers denounce, and not allow the officials to plead on each other's behalf. In dealing with heroes and fighting men, the ruler should never hand out unduly large rewards to men who have won distinction in the army, and never pardon the offense of men who have taken up arms in a private quarrel. He must not allow the officials to use their funds to build up their own soldiery. As to the requests and demands of the feudal lords of other states, if they are lawful, he should grant them; if not, he should reject them.

PRECAUTIONS WITHIN THE PALACE

Section 17

It is hazardous for the ruler of men to trust others, for he who trusts others will be controlled by others. Ministers have no bonds of flesh and blood which tie them to their ruler; it is only the force of circumstance which compels them to serve him. Hence those who act as ministers never for a moment cease trying to spy into their sovereign's mind, and yet the ruler of men sits above them in indolence and pride. That is why there are rulers in the world who face intimidation and sovereigns who are murdered. If the ruler puts too much trust in his son, then evil ministers will find ways to utilize the son for the accomplishment of their private schemes. Thus Li Tui, acting as aid to the king of Chao, starved the Father of the Ruler to death.[1] If the ruler puts too much trust in his consort, then evil ministers will find ways to utilize the consort for the accomplishment of their private schemes. Thus the actor Shih aided Lady Li to bring about the death of Shen-sheng and to set Hsi-ch'i on the throne.[2] Now if someone as close to the ruler as his own consort, and as dear to him as his own son, still cannot be trusted, then obviously no one else is to be trusted either.

Moreover, whether one is ruler of a state of ten thousand chariots or of a thousand only, it is quite likely that his consort, his concubines, or the son he has designated as heir to his throne will wish for his early death.

How do I know this is so? A wife is not bound to her husband by any ties of blood. If he loves her, she remains close to him; if not, she becomes estranged. The saying goes, "If the mother is favored, the son will be embraced." But if this is so, then the opposite must be, "If the mother is despised, the son will be cast away." A man at fifty has not yet lost interest in sex, and yet at thirty a woman's beauty has already faded. If a woman whose beauty has already faded waits upon a man still occupied by thoughts of sex, then she will be spurned and disfavored, and her son will stand little chance of succeeding to the throne. This is why consorts and concubines long for the early death of the ruler.

THE FIVE VERMIN

Section 49

These are the customs of a disordered state: Its scholars praise the ways of the former kings and imitate their benevolence and righteousness, put on a fair appearance and speak in elegant phrases, thus casting doubt upon the laws of the time and causing the ruler to be of two minds. Its speechmakers[20] propound false schemes and borrow influence from abroad, furthering their private interests and forgetting the welfare of the state's altars of the soil and grain. Its swordsmen gather bands of followers about them and perform deeds of honor, making a fine name for themselves and violating the prohibitions of the five government bureaus. Those of its people who are worried about military service flock to the gates of private individuals and pour out their wealth in bribes to influential men who will plead for them, in this way escaping the hardship of battle. Its merchants and artisans spend their time making articles of no practical use and gathering stores of luxury goods, accumulating riches, waiting for the best time to sell, and exploiting the farmers.

These five groups are the vermin of the state. If the rulers do not wipe out such vermin, and in their place encourage men of integrity and public spirit, then they should not be surprised, when they look about the area within the four seas, to see states perish and ruling houses wane and die.

EMINENCE IN LEARNING

Section 50

When a sage rules the state, he does not depend on people's doing good of themselves; he sees to it that they are not allowed to do what is bad. If he depends on people's doing good of themselves, then within his borders he can count less than ten instances of success. But if he sees to it that they are not allowed to do what is bad, then the whole state can be brought to a uniform level of order. Those who rule must employ measures that will be effective with the majority and discard those that will be effective with only a few. Therefore they devote themselves not to virtue but to law.

If you depend on arrow shafts' becoming straight of themselves, you will never produce one arrow in a hundred generations. If you depend on pieces of wood's becoming round of themselves, you will never get a cartwheel in a thousand years. If in a hundred generations you never find such a thing as an arrow shaft that makes itself straight or a piece of wood that makes itself round, then how it is that people all manage to ride around in carriages and shoot down birds? Because the tools of straightening and bending are used. And even if, without the application of such tools, there were an arrow shaft that made itself straight or a piece of wood that made itself round, a good craftsman would not prize it. Why? Because it is not only one man who wants to ride, and not just one shot that the archer wants to make. And even if, without depending upon rewards and punishments, there were a man who became good of himself, the enlightened ruler would not prize him. Why? Because the laws of the state must not be ignored, and it is more than one man who must be governed. Therefore a ruler who understands policy does not pursue fortuitous goodness, but follows the way of certain success. . . .

You may admire the beauty of a lovely woman like Maoch'iang or Hsi-shih all you like, but it will not improve your own looks. If you apply rouge, powder, and paint, however, you may make yourself twice as attractive as you were to begin with. You may talk about the benevolence and righteousness of the former kings all you like, but it will not make your own state any better ordered. But if you make your laws and regulations clear and your rewards and punishments certain, it is like applying rouge, powder, and paint to the state. The enlightened ruler pays close attention to such aids to rule, and has little time for extolling the ancients. Therefore he does not talk about benevolence and righteousness. . . .

Nowadays, those who do not understand how to govern invariably say, "You must win the hearts of the people!" If you could assure good government merely by winning the hearts of the people, then there would be no need for men like Yi Yin and Kuan Chung[3]—you could simply listen to what the people say. The reason you cannot rely upon the wisdom of the people is that they have the minds of little children. If the child's head is not shaved, its sores will spread;[4] and if its boil is not lanced, it will become sicker than ever. But when it is having its head shaved or its boil lanced, someone must hold it while the loving mother performs the operation, and it yells and screams incessantly, for it does not understand that the little pain it suffers now will bring great benefit later.

Now the ruler presses the people to till the land and open up new pastures so as to increase their means of livelihood, and yet they consider him harsh; he draws up a penal code and makes the punishments more severe in order to put a stop to evil, and yet the people consider him stern. He levies taxes in cash and grain in order to fill the coffers and granaries so that there will be food for the starving and funds for the army, and yet the people consider him avaricious. He makes certain that everyone within his borders understands warfare and sees to it that there are no private exemptions[5] from military service; he unites the strength of the state and fights fiercely in order to take its enemies captive, and yet the people consider him violent. These four types of undertaking all insure order and safety to the state, and yet the people do not have sense enough to rejoice in them. . . . In appointing men, to seek among the people for those who are worthy and wise; in governing, to try to please the people—methods such as these are the source of confusion. They are of no help in ensuring good government.

END NOTES

1. "Father of the Ruler" was a title assumed by King Wu-ling of Chao when he abdicated in 291 B.C. in favor of his son, King Hui-wen. In 294 B.C. his palace was surrounded by soldiers headed by the high minister Li Tui, and after some three months of confinement he died of starvation. *Shih chi* 43.
2. Lady Li, a later consort of Duke Hsien of Chin, succeeded, with the aid of a court actor named Shih, in casting suspicion on the heir apparent, Shen-sheng, and forcing him to commit suicide in 656 B.C. Her own son by the duke, Hsi-ch'i, was then made heir apparent and succeeded to the throne in 651 B.C. *Kuo yü, Chin yü* 2.
3. For Yi Yin, see above, p. 94, n. 3; for Kuan Chung, see above, p. 33, n. 4, and p. 94, n.3.
4. Emending the *fu* in the text to the *fu* which means "increasingly."
5. Adding *she* after *chieh* and translating in accordance with the interpretation of Ch'en Ch'i-yu.

QUESTIONS

1. Judging from the documents included here, what are the main components of the Legalist philosophy?
2. What does Han Feizi think is the correct relationship between a ruler and his subjects? A ruler and his family? A ruler and his ministers? Why?
3. Why do you think this school of thought is called Legalism? Why do you think it is also called Realism?
4. Why do you think the Legalist philosophy could be appealing to rulers? What would be the disadvantages?

DOCUMENT

THE DAO DE JING

Laozi

Unlike the philosophy of Confucianism, which taught men about the importance of benevolence, ethics, and the conduct of ritual and ceremony in bringing harmony and order to the family and the state, Daoism encouraged individual expression and exploration. Confucianism sought order and hierarchy, while Daoists rejected such artificial constraints. Daoists also sought simplicity and rejected complex social and governmental systems. For Confucians, the Way was found in the words of the ancient sages of the Zhou Dynasty, while Daoists sought guidance in nature and the unceasing, unseen force at nature's core. Daoists delighted in the counter-intuitive, often using water as a metaphor for explaining what on the surface seems nonsensical. Water is soft and yielding, yet over time it can erode solid rock. And if one falls in the water, it is useless to flail and struggle; the best reaction is non-action, or floating.

Concrete information about both the text excerpted here and its presumed author is hard to find. The Dao De Jing (Tao Te Ching), *which literally means "The Classic of the Virtue of the Dao," is a collection of eighty-one chapters that are usually translated in verse form. As for Laozi, to whom the book is attributed, some scholars are even unwilling to concede that he actually lived. Others believe he was a contemporary of Confucius (c. 551 to c. 479 B.C.E.).*

The selections included here range from cryptic explorations of the meaning of the Dao, to more practical advice on effective government. The verses invite the reader to ponder the many possibilities of their meaning, and in doing so, perhaps find the Way.

ONE

The Tao that can be told is not the eternal Tao.
The name that can be named is not the eternal name.
The nameless is the beginning of heaven and earth.
The named is the mother of ten thousand things.
Ever desireless, one can see the mystery.
Ever desiring, one sees the manifestations.
These two spring from the same source but differ in name; this appears as darkness.
Darkness within darkness.
The gate to all mystery.

TWENTY

Give up learning, and put an end to your troubles.

Is there a difference between yes and no?
Is there a difference between good and evil?
Must I fear what others fear? What nonsense!
Other people are contented, enjoying the sacrificial feast of the ox.
In spring some go to the park, and climb the terrace,
But I alone am drifting, not knowing where I am.
Like a newborn babe before it learns to smile,
I am alone, without a place to go.

Others have more than they need, but I alone have nothing.
I am a fool. Oh, yes! I am confused.
Others are clear and bright,
But I alone am dim and weak.
Others are sharp and clever,
But I alone am dull and stupid.
Oh, I drift like the waves of the sea,
Without direction, like the restless wind.

Everyone else is busy,
But I alone am aimless and depressed.
I am different,
I am nourished by the great mother.

FORTY-FOUR

Fame or self: Which matters more?
Self or wealth: Which is more precious?
Gain or loss: Which is more painful?

He who is attached to things will suffer much.
He who saves will suffer heavy loss.
A contented man is never disappointed.
He who knows when to stop does not find himself in trouble.
He will stay forever safe.

FORTY-EIGHT

In the pursuit of learning, every day something is acquired.
In the pursuit of Tao, every day something is dropped.

Less and less is done
Until non-action is achieved.
When nothing is done, nothing is left undone.
The world is ruled by letting things take their course.
It cannot be ruled by interfering.

SIXTY

Ruling the country is like cooking a small fish.
Approach the universe with Tao,
And evil will have no power.
Not that evil is not powerful,
But its power will not be used to harm others.
Not only will it do no harm to others,
But the sage himself will also be protected.
They do not hurt each other,
And the Virtue in each one refreshes both.

SEVENTY-FIVE

Why are the people starving?
Because the rulers eat up the money in taxes.
Therefore the people are starving.

Why are the people rebellious?
Because the rulers interfere too much.
Therefore they are rebellious.

Why do the people think so little of death?
Because the rulers demand too much of life.
Therefore the people take death lightly.

Having little to live on, one knows better than to value life too much.

SEVENTY-SIX

A man is born gentle and weak.
At his death he is hard and stiff.
Green plants are tender and filled with sap.
At their death they are withered and dry.

Therefore the stiff and unbending is the disciple of death.
The gentle and yielding is the disciple of life.

Thus an army without flexibility never wins a battle.
A tree that is unbending is easily broken.

The hard and strong will fall.
The soft and weak will overcome.

EIGHTY

A small country has fewer people.
Though there are machines that can work ten to a hundred times
faster than man, they are not needed.
The people take death seriously and do not travel far.
Though they have boats and carriages, no one uses them.
Though they have armor and weapons, no one displays them.
Men return to the knotting of rope in place of writing.
Their food is plain and good, their clothes fine but simple, their
homes secure;
They are happy in their ways.
Though they live within sight of their neighbors,
And crowing cocks and barking dogs are heard across the way,
Yet they leave each other in peace while they grow old and die.

QUESTIONS

1. How can anyone learn the Way if it cannot be described?
2. According to the selections here, what are the best ways to find the Way?
3. Why do you think Daoists believe in the virtue of non-action?
4. Do you believe a country can be governed along Daoist principles? Why or why not?

DOCUMENT

ADMONITIONS FOR WOMEN

Ban Zhao

Ban Zhao (Pan Chao, 45–116 C.E.) lived during the Han Dynasty (221 B.C.E.–220 C.E.), the first dynasty to operate in a fundamentally Confucian manner and officially adopt Confucianism. The Han emperors promoted the Confucian ideal of government by merit, a radical concept at a time when military might and aristocratic blood more often determined the leaders of various warring states. Confucian values, such as filial piety (the veneration of one's parents), the maintenance of a patriarchal social hierarchy, and the reliance on ritual to reinforce one's place in that hierarchy were actively promoted in an attempt to maintain social harmony and loyalty to the state. Historians were extremely important in a Confucian government, because in a Confucian universe, history was a lesson in morality and ethics. History established heroes and villains, and justified dynastic ascension and decline.

Born to a family of scholars, Ban Zhao was notable for her unusual upbringing. When her parents, particularly her father, noted her academic interest and aptitude, they provided her with an education more suitable at that time for a son. That education did not go to waste. Ban Zhao unofficially served as historian to the imperial court, a post she assumed at the request of the emperor after the death of her brother Ban Gu (Pan Ku, 32–92 C.E.). Ban Gu was a renowned historian and court scholar who followed many of the historical conventions established by the legendary scholar Sima Qian (Ssu-ma Ch'ien, c. 145–c. 90 B.C.E.). While working at court after her brother's death, Ban Zhao was also asked to take on the responsibility of teaching the empress and her court ladies, and later when the empress served as regent, Ban Zhao

---

Reprinted by permission from *Pan Chao: Foremost Woman Scholar of China: Background, Ancestry, Life, and Writings of the Most Celebrated Chinese Woman of Letters.*

became one of her advisers. Her intellectual abilities and her access to the imperial court were paradoxical in light of her writings as a proponent of female subordination.

The selections here are from Ban Zhao's most famous work. Often called Admonitions for Women, *but translated here as* Lessons for Women, *it instructs women how to behave in the context of the most important relationships they were expected to develop.* Admonitions *has often been perceived as codifying the patriarchal structure of Confucian family life and society, and it became required reading for educated upper-class women for centuries. Ban Zhao herself did marry, but was widowed young and remained a paragon of virtue until her death.*

LESSONS FOR WOMEN[1]
INSTRUCTIONS IN SEVEN CHAPTERS FOR A WOMAN'S ORDINARY WAY OF LIFE IN THE FIRST CENTURY A. D.

Introduction

I, the unworthy writer, am unsophisticated, unenlightened, and by nature unintelligent, but I am fortunate both to have received not a little favor from my scholarly father,[2] and to have had a (cultured) mother and instructresses upon whom to rely for a literary education as well as for training in good manners. More than forty years have passed since at the age of fourteen I took up the dustpan and the broom[3] in the Ts'ao family. During this time with trembling heart[4] I feared constantly that I might disgrace my parents, and that I might multiply difficulties for both the women and the men[5] (of my husband's family). Day and night I was distressed in heart, (but) I labored without confessing weariness. Now and hereafter, however, I know how to escape (from such fears).[6]

Being careless, and by nature stupid, I taught and trained (my children) without system. Consequently I fear that my son Ku[7] may bring disgrace upon the Imperial Dynasty[8] by whose Holy Grace[9] he has unprecedentedly received the extraordinary privilege[10] of wearing the Gold and the Purple, a privilege for the attainment of which (by my son, I) a humble subject never even hoped. Nevertheless, now that he is a man and able to plan his own life, I need not again have concern for him. But I do grieve that you, my daughters,[11] just now at the age for marriage, have not at this time had gradual training and advice; that you still have not learned the proper customs for married women. I fear that by failure in good manners in other families you will humiliate both your ancestors and your clan. I am now seriously ill, life is uncertain. As I have thought of you all in so untrained a state, I have been uneasy many a time for you. At hours of leisure I have composed in seven chapters these instructions under the title, "Lessons for Women." In order that you may have something where-with to benefit your persons, I wish every one of you, my daughters, each to write out a copy for yourself.

From this time on every one of you strive to practise these (lessons).

CHAPTER I

Humility

On the third day after the birth of a girl the ancients[12] observed three customs: (first) to place the baby below[13] the bed; (second) to give her a potsherd with which to play;[14] and (third) to announce her birth to her ancestors by an offering.[15] Now to lay the baby below the bed plainly indicated that she is lowly and weak, and should regard it as her primary duty to humble herself before others. To give her potsherds with which to play indubitably signified that she should practise labor and consider it her primary duty to be industrious.[16] To announce her birth before her ancestors clearly meant that she ought to esteem as her primary duty the continuation of the observance of worship[17] in the home.

These three ancient customs epitomize a woman's ordinary way of life and the teachings of the traditional ceremonial rites and regulations. Let a woman modestly yield to others; let her respect others; let her put others first, herself last. Should she do something good, let her not mention it; should she do something bad, let her not deny it. Let her bear disgrace; let her even endure[18] when others speak or do evil to her. Always let her seem to tremble and to fear. (When a woman follows such maxims as these,) then she may be said to humble herself before others.

Let a woman retire late to bed, but rise early to duties; let her not dread tasks by day or by night. Let her not refuse to perform domestic duties whether easy or difficult. That which must be done, let her finish completely, tidily, and systematically.[19] (When a woman follows such rules as these,) then she may be said to be industrious.

Let a woman be correct in manner and upright in character in order to serve her husband. Let her live in purity and quietness (of spirit), and attend to her own affairs. Let her love not gossip and silly laughter. Let her cleanse and purify and arrange in order the wine and the food for the offerings to the ancestors.[20] (When a woman observes such principles as these,) then she may be said to continue ancestral worship.[21]

No woman who observes these three (fundamentals of life) has ever had a bad reputation or has fallen into disgrace. If a woman fail to observe them, how can her name be honored; how can she but bring disgrace upon herself?

CHAPTER II

Husband and Wife

. . . If a husband be unworthy then he possesses nothing by which to control his wife. If a wife be unworthy, then she possesses nothing with which to serve her husband. If a husband does not control his wife then the rules of conduct manifesting his authority are abandoned and broken.[22] If a wife does not serve her husband, then the proper relationship (between men and women) and the natural order of things are neglected and destroyed. As a matter of fact the purpose of these two (the controlling of women by men, and the serving of men by women) is the same.

Now examine the gentlemen of the present age. They only know that wives must be controlled, and that the husband's rules of conduct manifesting his authority must be established. They therefore teach their boys to read books and (study) histories. But they do not in the least understand that husbands and masters must (also) be served,[23] and that the proper relationship and the rites should be maintained.

Yet only to teach men and not to teach[24] women,—is that not ignoring the essential relation between them? According to the "Rites," it is the rule to begin to teach children to read at the age of eight years,[25] and by the age of fifteen years they ought then to be ready for cultural training.[26] Only why should it not be (that girls' education as well as boys' be) according to this principle?

CHAPTER III

Respect and Caution[27]

As *Yin* and *Yang* are not of the same nature, so man and woman have different characteristics.[28] The distinctive quality of the *Yang* is rigidity; the function of the *Yin* is yielding. Man is honored for strength; a woman is beautiful on account of her gentleness.[29] Hence there arose the common saying:[30] "A man though born like a wolf may, it is feared, become a weak monstrosity; a woman though born like a mouse may, it is feared, become a tiger."

Now for self-culture[31] nothing equals respect for others. To counteract firmness nothing equals compliance. Consequently it can be said that the Way of respect and acquiescence is woman's most important principle of conduct.[32] . . .

If husband and wife have the habit of staying together, never leaving one another, and following each other around[33] within the limited space of their own rooms, then they will lust after and take liberties with one another. From such action improper language will arise between the two. This kind of discussion may lead to licentiousness. Out of licentiousness will be born a heart of disrespect to the husband. Such a result comes from not knowing that one should stay in one's proper place.

Furthermore, affairs may be either crooked or straight; words may be either right or wrong. Straightforwardness cannot but lead to quarreling; crookedness cannot but lead to accusation. If there are really accusations and quarrels, then undoubtedly there will be angry affairs. Such a result comes from not esteeming others, and not honoring and serving (them).

(If wives) suppress not contempt for husbands, then it follows (that such wives) rebuke and scold (their husbands). (If husbands) stop not short of anger, then they are certain to beat (their wives). The correct relationship between husband and wife is based upon harmony and intimacy, and (conjugal) love is grounded in proper union. Should actual blows be dealt, how could matrimonial relationship be preserved? Should sharp words be spoken, how could (conjugal) love exist? If love and proper relationship both be destroyed, then husband and wife are divided.

CHAPTER IV

Womanly Qualifications

A woman (ought to) have four qualifications:[34] (1) womanly virtue; (2) womanly words; (3) womanly bearing; and (4) womanly work. Now what is called womanly virtue need not be brilliant ability, exceptionally different from others. Womanly words need be neither clever in debate nor keen in conversation. Womanly appearance requires neither a pretty nor a perfect face and form. Womanly work need not be work done more skilfully than that of others.

To guard carefully her chastity; to control circumspectly her behavior; in every motion to exhibit modesty; and to model each act on the best usage, this is womanly virtue.

To choose her words with care; to avoid vulgar language; to speak at appropriate times; and not to weary others[35] (with much conversation), may be called the characteristics of womanly words.

To wash and scrub filth away; to keep clothes and ornaments fresh and clean; to wash the head and bathe[36] the body regularly, and to keep the person free from disgraceful filth, may be called the characteristics of womanly bearing.

With whole-hearted devotion to sew and to weave; to love not gossip and silly laughter; in cleanliness and order (to prepare) the wine and food for serving guests, may be called the characteristics of womanly work.

These four qualifications characterize the greatest virtue of a woman. No woman can afford to be without them. In fact they are very easy to possess if a woman only treasure them in her heart. The ancients[37] had a saying: "Is Love[38] afar off? If I desire love, then love is at hand!" So can it be said of these qualifications.

CHAPTER V

Whole-hearted Devotion[39]

Now in the "Rites" is written the principle that a husband may marry again, but there is no Canon that authorizes a woman to be married the second time.[40] Therefore it is said of husbands as of Heaven, that as certainly as people cannot run away from Heaven,[41] so surely a wife cannot leave[42] (a husband's home). . . .

CHAPTER VI

Implicit Obedience[43]

Now "to win the love of one man is the crown of a woman's life; to lose the love of one man is her eternal disgrace.[44] This saying advises a fixed will and a whole-hearted devotion for a woman. Ought she then to lose the hearts of her father- and mother-in-law?[45] . . .

Whenever the mother-in-law says, "Do not do that," and if what she says is right, unquestionably the daughter-in-law obeys. Whenever the mother-in-law says, "Do that," even if what she says is wrong, still the daughter-in-law submits unfailingly to the command.

Let a woman not act contrary to the wishes and the opinions of parents-in-law about right and wrong; let her not dispute with them what is straight[46] and what is crooked. Such (docility) may be called obedience which sacrifices personal opinion. Therefore the ancient book, "A Pattern for Women," says: "If a daughter-in-law (who follows the wishes of her parents-in-law) is like an echo and a shadow,[47] how could she not be praised?"

CHAPTER VII

Harmony with Younger Brothers- and Sisters-in-law

In order for a wife to gain the love of her husband, she must win for herself the love of her parents-in-law. To win for herself the love of her parents-in-law, she must secure for herself the good will of younger brothers- and sisters-in-law. For these reasons the right and the wrong, the praise and the blame of a woman alike depend upon younger brothers- and sisters-in-law. Consequently it will not do for a woman to lose their affection. . . .

Modesty is virtue's handle;[48] acquiescence is the wife's (most refined) characteristic. All who possess these two have sufficient for harmony with others. In the "Book of Poetry" it is written that "here is no evil; there is no dart."[49] So it may be said of (these two, modesty and acquiescence).[50]

END NOTES

1. After this translation was made the writer noted that the title "Lessons for Women" had been given to this treatise by MacGowan (see *Imperial History,* second edition, Shanghai, 1906, p. 120, note).

   Pan Chao's successors in the field of moral writings have been so much more widely quoted than herself that modern China as well as the west has failed to appreciate the ethical value of this treatise. The classical style of the composition has likewise prevented a widespread knowledge of the contents except as interpreted through traditional teachings. Apparently it is these traditional interpretations which have been the sources for the so-called translations (see Cordier: *Bibliotheca Sinica,* Histoire, I, col. 675) in western literature. A detailed study of the text itself shows that it contains much which could be of permanent value to modern womanhood.
2. Pan Chao here alluded to her father as 先君 .
3. This expression for the marriage of the girl, 執箕帚 , is found in the *Han Shu* (*chüan* I, 高帝紀上) where the father of the future empress Lü, 呂后 , offered her to the future founder of the House of Han. Although the term was perhaps originally used to designate the duties of a girl in her husband's home, this could not be said to be true in the case of the empress Lü. It had become conventionalized, as an expression for the inferior position of the daughter-in-law in relation to her parents-in-law, see commentary on the passage.

   While according to tradition fifteen years was the age of marriage for girls, and Pan Chao was married at fourteen, twenty, and even twenty-three is given in the *Li Chi,* see Legge: *Li Ki, SBE,* XXVII, 479.
4. 戰戰兢兢 is translated by Legge (Book of Poetry, II, V, 2:6, *Classics,* IV, 333): "We should be apprehensive and cautious"——; and 而今而後 , 吾知免夫 . (Analects 8:3, same, I, 208), "Now and hereafter, I know my escape."

   In a note (same, IV, 333) is found 戰=恐 , "to be afraid," 兢=戒 , "to be cautious"; and (I, 209) 而=自 , "from."

   Legge (*Classics,* I, 252) noted that "懼 is fear when the troubles have arrived."
5. The husband's place is without, the wife's place is within, the home. Below, in Chapter VII (p. 89) of "Lessons"), Pan Chao used 外內 as well as 中外 .
6. Or such faults.
7. Fan Yeh in the biography of Pan Chao called the son Ch'êng, 成 . The commentator, Wang Hsien-ch'ien, wrote that while elsewhere it is recorded that the personal name of the son was Ch'êng, and the style Ku, 穀 , or Tzû-ku, 穀子 , it was strange for the mother to call her son by the style, 字 , rather than by the personal name, 名 (*San Fu Chüeh Lu, chüan* I, p. I, *Êrh-yu T'ang Ts'ung Shu,* 1821, cf. Chapter III, note 19.) See

also *Ch'ung-ting Wên Hsüan Chi P'ing, chüan 2,* 重訂文選集評 , 曹大家東征賦 (1778), by Yü Kuang-hua, 于光華 .

8. 清朝, "Pure Dynasty." This was chosen by the Manchus for the name of the recent dynasty, 1644–1911.
9. E. H. Parker ("The Educational Curriculum of the Chinese," *China Review,* IX [1880–1881], 5) wrote that as late as the Manchu dynasty the successful candidates for *hsiu-ts'ai,* 秀才 , at the graduation ceremony *kotow* thrice to his Majesty, and this is called 謝聖恩 .
10. "According to the *Han Shu* (*chüan* 19, 百官公卿表) this allowed two thousand piculs of grain, the gold seal, and the purple robe. See biography of Pan Chao, p. 41; the memorial in behalf of Pan Ch'ao. p. 74; *Tz'û Yüan,* 子 , p. 109, 戎 , p. 4.
11. "Not necessarily only her own daughters, but girls of her family. This term, 諸女 , seems to deny the assertion both of the French missionaries and of S. Wells Williams that these "Lessons for Women" were written to the empress who was a pupil of Pan Chao. In (*Hui-hsiang*) *Tung Han Yen-i* (*chiian* 4, 繪像東漢演義 , 第 ' 58 回) the writer had Pan Chao herself call her daughters into her presence for them to read these "Lessons," and for her to explain to them the difficult passages, and had Ma Rung to order the wives and daughters of his family to study with the daughters of Pan Chao. See p. 41.
12. Pan Chao does not indicate that any such custom existed in her time, it was the custom of ancients—people who were "ancient" more than eighteen hundred years ago.
13. That is: "on the floor, or the ground," cf. Maspero: same, pp. 128–129.
14. In the Book of Poetry (II, IV, 5:8–9, *Classics,* IV, 307) it is written that "Daughters shall be born to him——. They shall have tiles to play with." W. Scarborough ("Chinese Modes of Address," *Chinese Recorder,* X [1879], 267) wrote that "the birth of a daughter is (1879) politely spoken of as 弄瓦 ."

    S. Wells Williams ("Education of Woman in China," *Chinese Recorder,* IX [1880], 45) stated that "The tile is here used as an emblem of weaving, because women prepare the fibres of the nettle-hemp and grass-cloth for the loom by rubbing them on tiles, even to this day." (1880).

    Giles (*Adversaria Sinica,* p. 312) wrote of "'tiles as playthings for girls' from which it has been too hastily inferred that the Chinese have themselves admitted their absolute contempt for women in general. Yet this idea never really entered into the mind of the writer—the tile, so far from being a mere potsherd implying discourtesy was really an honorable symbol of domesticity, being used in ancient times as a weight for the spindle." See also B. Laufer: *Jade, A Study in Chinese Archaeology and Religion* (Chicago, 1912), p. 100.
15. Legge (*Classics,* I, 198 and 232) noted that 齋 means "to fast," or rather denotes "the whole religious adjustment enjoined before the offering of sacrifice, . . . Sacrifices presented in such a state of mind were sure to be acceptable."

    L. C. Hopkins ("Working the Oracle," *New China Review,* I [1919], 113) wrote that "Lo Chên-yü, 羅振玉 , in his *Yin Hsü Shu-ch'i K'ao-shih,* 殷虛書契考釋 , or 'Critical Interpretation of the Records of the Tumulus of Yin,' Introduction to the sixth section, on 'The Oracle Sentences,' says there are inquiries as to (1) the sacrifice known as *tsi,* 祭 (see below, note 17; (2) that known as *kao,* 告 , announcement——; and (4) ordinary journeys, literally 出入 , going out and entering."
16. Legge (Analects 13:19, *Classics,* I, 271) translated 執事敬 , "In the management of business, to be reverently attentive." Note the use of 執 above, note 3.
17. For women's place in the family group in the *Li Chi,* see Legge, *SBE,* XXVII and

XXVIII; in the Chou dynasty, see Maspero: same, pp. 120, 121, 123–128; in ancestral worship, same, p. 264.

In the *Chinese Repository* (I, 1832, 500) an observer wrote of "rites, performed at the tombs of ancestors, parents, and friends—(that) the practice is universal, and when the men are absent from their families, the women go to perform the rates." J. G. Andersson (*The Dragon and the Foreign Devils,* Boston, 1928, pp. 110–111) gives an account of a mother and her son making an offering to the memory of the lately deceased father of the family, who "had been the headman of his village, and as a mark of honor toward the deceased and his widow, the boy——had been made his father's successor in office with his mother as assistant."

S. Wells Williams ("The Perpetuity of Chinese Institutions," *Chinese Recorder,* XIII, 1882, 84) related that "Underlying these (Chinese national) characteristics is one general idea——. This is the worship and obedience due to parents and ancestors—(an) indirect result of which has been to define and elevate the position of the wife and mother. As there can be only one 'Illustrious consort' (of the father), 先妣 , named on the tablet, there is of course only one wife, 妻 , acknowledged in the family. There are concubines, 妾 ——but this acknowledged parity of the mother with the father, in the most sacred position she can be placed, has done much to maintain the purity and right influence of women."

L. C. Hopkins ("Working the Oracle," *New China Review,* I 1919, 249) stated that of "Various sacrificial services now known as *tsi*——Lo observes on the evidence of the Bone inscriptions that the word *tsi* or *chi* denoted only one of the total number of sacrificial ceremonies, and not, as it became later, the general term for all." See above, note 15.

18. 含垢 . Literally "Let her hold filth in her mouth, let her swallow insult."
19. 整理 . Pan Chao here used a term which in modern writings carries the reader from the concrete picture of a woman tidying up self and home as she goes about her tasks to the fact of the disorder in Chinese historical records calling for a scientific study of all source materials, see article by Hu Shih in 古史討論集, pp. 198 ff; as well as other articles in the same book. See preface by Liang Ch'i-ch'ao to his lectures (1925): same; also Ku Chieh-kang's *Ku Shih Pien,* Preface (pp. 1–103), pp. 30–59 ff. Hu Shih (*China Year Book,* 1924, p. 650) calls 整理國故 the "systematization of the national heritage."
20. G. Jamieson, "Translations from the *Lu-li,* or General Code of Laws," *China Review,* X (1881–1882), 97: "But the wife had special duties to perform in the periodical sacrifices. She was a sort of priestess assisting her husband, and ——. It was her duty to prepare the sacrificial cakes, the rice, the millet, and the fruits, and to see them served up upon the proper vessels."
21. Same, VIII (1879–1880), 197: "The 宗 , *Tsung,* correspond precisely to the group known as the Agnates (from the point of view of a woman) of the Civil Law, except they do not include adopted strangers by blood." For table of *Tsung,* see same, p. 200.

Legge (*Classics,* I, 271, in note 20) wrote that "宗族 is a designation for all who form one body having the same ancestor (note the use of the term in Introduction above)—being all of the same surname from the great-great grandfather to the great-great grandson—the circle of his relatives." For Chinese Family Nomenclature, see H. P. Wilkinson: *New China Review,* III ; (1921), 159–191. For a description of a clan, see P. G. von Möllendorf: "The Family Law of the Chinese," *JRAS, NCB,* XXVII (1892–1893), 170–171.

G. Jamieson (same, VIII [1879–1880], 201) noted that the custom of ancestral sacrifices is in harmony with the system of succession. "Every family has its own particular *sacra,* consisting of the ancestral tablets, which are handed down from father to son, increasing in number as one generation is added to another, and it is the duty of the eldest son or the adopted successor to take charge of these, and to perform the customary Rites with all due reverence."

The *Li-Chi, Hwan I,* Legge, *SBE,* XXVIII, 428) says that "The ceremony of marriage was intended to be bond of love between two (families of different) surnames, with a view, in its retrospective character, to secure the services in the ancestral temple, and in its prospective character, to secure the continuance of the family line."

G. Jamieson (same, X, 1881–1882, p. 97) quoted the following comment on the above passage from the *Li Chi:* "The superior man marries so that when he sacrifices to his ancestors he may—have some one to assist him in the worship—and when a wife is divorced the formula says, 'So-and-so is not intelligent. She is incompetent to assist me in serving up the offerings at the sacrifices.'"

Herbert Chatley ("Magical Practice in China," *JRAS, NCB,* XLVIII, 1917, pp. 16–17) wrote that "it is perfectly clear that the Chinese behave and have behaved for millennia as if the soul of each clan were a continuous organism, having an annual pulse, incarnate in the living descendants, transfusable into women brought into the clan by marriage and into children co-opted by adoption, immanent in all lives associated with the family, and present at the tombs, the ancestral temple, and the family altar." Confucius certainly believed that a worshipper should behave as if the ancestors were present (Analects 3: 12, Legge, I, 159).

For a modern scholar on ancestral rites, see E. T. C. Werner's translation of an article by Hu Shih, "Reform in Chinese Mourning Rites," *New China .Review,* II (1920), 225–247; *Hu Shih Wên Ts'un, chüan* 4, pp. 132 ff. (cf. Chapter IV, note II).

22. See the Book of Poetry, I, IV, 8, *Classics,* IV, 85.
23. Analects 20:3 (*Classics,* I, 354): 不知禮，無以立也, "Without an acquaintance with the rules of propriety, it is impossible for the character to be established." And note that this is from the section where the genuineness of the text is questioned, and thus would reflect the more Han Confucian thought.

    E. H. Parker ("The Philosopher Sün-tsz," fifth chapter, *New China Review,* IV, 1922, p. 14) translated 禮義, "courtesy and equity." Cf. Dubs: *Hsüntze,* Chap. VIII, *"Li:* The Rules of Proper Conduct."
24. The Analects (15:38, *Classics,* I, 305; cf. 275) records 有教無類, "The Master said, 'In teaching there should be no distinction of classes.'" Yet nowhere do Confucius' sayings show any interest in teaching women.

    The opening sentence of the "Doctrine of the Mean" is: 天命之謂性，率性之謂道 修道之謂教, which Legge (*Classics,* I, 383) translated: "What Heaven has conferred is called The Nature; an accordance with this nature is called The Path (of duty); the regulation of this path is called Instruction."

    Leonard Hsü of Yenching University, Peiping, translates this:

    "What God has endowed is nature;
    The pursuit of nature is the Way;
    The cultivation of the Way is education."
25. *Li Chi, chüan* 5, 內則: 八年出入門戶 (*SBE,* XXVII, 478.)
26. Legge (*Classics,* I, 196, note 4) translated 學, "liberal education." And in a note on Analects 1:6 (same, p. 140) he wrote that "after the performance of these things, 則以學文, 'he should employ them in polite studies'—not literary studies merely, but all the accomplishments of a gentleman also: ceremonies, music, archery, horsemanship, writing, and numbers." Cf. Maspero: same, p. 131.

27. The Analects (8:2) says that 慎而無禮則葸, which Legge translated (*Classics,* I, 208): "Carefulness without the rules of propriety becomes timidity."

The Analects (7:12) also says that 子之所慎, which Legge (*Classics,* I, 198) translated: "The things in reference to which the Master exercised the greatest caution.

28. See note 22 above.

The Chinese have a common expression, "Woman is woman; man is man"—the two being different, they are not comparable.

29. I. T. Headland ("Chinese Women from a Chinese Standpoint," *Chinese 'Recorder,* XXVIII, 1897, 14) quoting, translated this passage: "The *Yin* and *Yang,* like the male and the female, are very different principles; the virtue of the *Yang* is firmness; the virtue of the *Yin* is flexibility. So man's strength is his honor; woman's weakness is her beauty."

From the "Great Plan" of the Book of History, Legge (V, IV, 17, *Classics,* III, 333) translated that "for the reserved and retiring there is the strong, 剛, rule; for the lofty and intelligent there is the mild, 柔, rule."

In the hexagrams of the *I Ching,* 易經, the two elemental lines correspond to the two primordial substances *Yin* and *Yang,* and the unbroken lines are called "*Kang*" or "hard" lines, and the broken ones "*jou*" or "soft" lines, cf Maspero: same, p. 483.

Mencius (VII, II, 25:5, translated by Legge: *Classics,* II, 490) said that "He whose goodness has been filled up is what is called a beautiful man," 充實之謂美.

Huai-nan Tzû's 陰以柔爲用, (*chüan* 1, p. 10b), F. H. Balfour ("The Principle of Nature," *China Review,*" IX, 1880–1881, 288) translated 柔勝出 於己者其力不可量, "weakness can overcome what is far stronger than itself' See also same, p. 289, and Lao Tzû's *"Tao Tê Ching,"* Chap. 61, 謙德, P. Carus: *Lao Tsse's Tao-Teh-King* (Chicago, 1898), p. 128.

Giles (*Dict.,* no. 8139) translated 男以彊爲貴, "strength is the glory of man"; and (no. 8419) 女以弱爲美, "weakness is woman's charm."

30. Giles (*Dict.,* no. 8139) translated "if you have a son like a wolf, you still fear lest he should be a weakling"; and (no. 8419) "if your daughter is (timid) as a mouse, you still fear lest she should turn out a tigress."

31. The "Great Learning," translated by Legge (*Classics,* I, 359), says that "All must consider the cultivation of the person the root of everything besides." Cf. Mencius VI, I, 16; VII, I, 1–3, *Classics,* II, 419, 449–450.

This term, 修身, was used for the name of the ethics which was given a place with textbook even in the primary grades of the government schools of China for the first few years of the Republic.

32. Mencius (III, II, 2:2, *Classics,* II, 265) said: 以順爲正者, 妾婦之道也, "to look upon compliance as their correct course is the rule for women."

33. 周旋. Literally "follow around"; idiomatically, "to pay attention to."

34. *Li Chi,* Legge: *SBE,* XXVIII, 432; "she was taught here (three months before her marriage) the virtue (德), the speech (言), the carriage (容), and the work (功), of the wife." Cf. Maspero: same, p. 133.

35. In the Analects (14:14, *Classics,* I, 280) it is found that "My Master speaks when it is time to speak, and 人不厭其言, so men do not get tired of his speaking."

36. Legge (*Classics,* I, 284, note 22) wrote that "Properly, 沐, is to wash the hair with the water in which rice has been washed, and 浴 is to wash the body with hot water."

37. Analects 7:29, *Classics,* I, 204: 仁遠乎哉,我欲仁, 斯仁至矣. "The Master said: 'Is virtue a thing remote? I wish to be virtuous, and lo! virtue is at hand.'" This is the one place

where Pan Chao gave a direct quotation from the Analects or from Confucius without crediting it to its source.

38. On Analects 1:2, Legge (*Classics,* I, 139, note 2) stated that "仁 is explained as 'the principle of love,' 'the virtue of the heart.' 仁 is man,'—'benevolence' often comes near it."

    Léopold de Saussure, "On the Origin of Ideo-phonetic Characters," *New China Review,* III (1921), 392, note) wrote that "仁, *jên* (humanity), is merely a special meaning of the word 人, *jên* (man). Though deprived of accurate views on the etymological evolution, the Chinese scholars point out this phonetic identity in the saying: 仁者人也: 'Humanity is. man.'" Cf. *T'oung Pao* (1910), p. 244 (1913), p. 808; Dubs: same. Maspero (same, pp. 464–465) prefers "1'Altruisme," which must be distinguished from "1'Amour Universel" preached by. Mo Ti.

39. This is just the meaning of the western rime:

    "All that you do, do with your might,
    Things done by halves are never done right."

    Chapter V of "Lessons" applies this spirit in the broad field of the relationship of man and wife.

40. This sentence was written about the same time that the Corinthian Christians were asking Paul what his advice was about widows. Cf. *Li Chi* (Legge, *SBE,* XXVII, 439): "Once mated with her husband, all her life she will not change (her feeling of duty to him) and hence, when the husband dies she will not marry (again)."

41. Analects 3:13, Legge (*Classics,* I, 159): "He who offends against Heaven has none to whom he can pray."

42. Not even after the death of a husband does the worthy wife yet leave her husband's home.

43. See *Li Chi,* Legge: *SBE,* XXVIII, 430–431. M. F. C. ("The Chinese Daughter-in-law," *Chinese Recorder,* V [1874–1875], 207–214) aptly remarked that "Those who with native ability combine patience and shrewdness, adroitly manage the whole family, while seeming to be everyone's servant. They are so conciliating, and so winning, so wise, and yet so modest," that they win their way.

44. A repetition of the quotation above; see note 52.

45. Hu Shih ("The Social Message in Chinese Poetry," *Chinese Soc. and Polit. Science Review,* VII, 1923, 72) wrote that "in the Chinese family system where children are morally bound to live together under the same parental roof, there often arise troubles between the mother-in-law and the daughter-in-law, between sister-in-law and the younger brothers and sisters. There is in the Han literature of social problems a long poem entitled 'The Wife of Chiao Chung-ch'ing' (孔雀東南飛, *K'ung-ch'üeh Tung-nan Fei*) which tells the story of a faithful wife who was loved by her husband, but whose mother-in-law disliked her so much that she was forced to return to her own home." For translation of this poem see Waley: *The Temple,* pp. 113–125.

46. Analects 8:2 is translated by Legge (*Classics,* I, 208): 直而無禮則絞, "straightforwardness, without the rules of propriety, becomes rudeness."

47. This term, 影響 in modern usage has come to mean "influence."

48. In the Book of Changes, *Hsi Tz'û* (Legge: same, p. 397), is found: "*Li* shows us the foundation of virtue, *Ch'ien* its handle," 謙德之柄也 .

49. This quotation from the 周頌 section of the Book of Poetry differs from the text of Mao, 毛詩; see Legge (*Classics,* IV, 585) who translated as follows:

    在彼無惡 "There (in their States), not disliked;
    在此無斁 Here (in Chou), never tired of."

The Li Hsien commentary, 唐太子李賢註, of the T'ang dynasty, says that 射, instead of 斁, followed the Han text, 韓詩, one of the well-known texts of the Book of Poetry in the Han dynasty (see *Classics,* I, Prolegomena, 8–10).

50. In "Die Lebensgeschichte des Philosophen Mongtse" (*Chinesische Blätter für Wissenschaft und Kunst,* Veröffentlichung des China-Instituts zu Frankfurt am Main, I, 2, 1926, Darmstadt, Germany) Richard Wilhelm (died, 1930) included nine scenes from a scroll of a Sung painting (1101–1126 A.D.) illustrating Pan Chao's "Lessons for Women," which he also translated in part (pp. 83–87). These scenes were photographically reproduced (1913) from a scroll now in the possession of a former high official of the Chinese Government.

QUESTIONS

1. What are the most important values Ban Zhao wishes to convey to her daughters and all other young Chinese women, and why?
2. What responsibilities do Chinese men have to their wives, as described in this selection?
3. What do you think marriages were like in Ban Zhao's time? What did she think were the qualities that characterized a successful marriage? Why?
4. How are we to reconcile Ban Zhao's extreme modesty with her obvious literary merits and accomplishments? Do you think her *Admonitions* conceal resentment or does she seem genuinely committed to the patriarchal principles of Confucianism? Explain your answers.

DOCUMENT

The "DEVADATTA" *Chapter of the* LOTUS SUTRA

Kumārajīva

The Lotus Sutra, *an early Sanskrit Mahāyāna sūtra, or scripture, was likely compiled during the first and second centuries C.E. It has been an extremely popular sūtra, especially in East Asia where it was translated into Chinese six times. The source for this selection is a Chinese translation made by a Central Asian Buddhist scholar-monk named Kumārajīva in 406 C.E. Like the Sanskrit original, the Chinese version is written in a combination of prose and verse.*

The central teaching of the Lotus Sutra *is the universal accessibility of Buddhahood. Earlier Mainstream Buddhist schools had taught that the highest religious goal for most living beings was that of the arhat, or saint. Arhats are called "voice-hearers" in the* Lotus Sutra *because they attain nirvāna, or liberation, by listening to the teachings of Śākyamuni Buddha, the historical founder of Buddhism. The* Lotus Sutra, *and Mahāyāna tradition more broadly, rejects the arhat ideal in favor of the bodhisattva ideal, arguing that arhats seek only a personal nirvāna whereas bodhisattvas, who aspire to Buddhahood, seek the liberation of all living beings. According to Mahāyāna Buddhism, everyone is capable of achieving what Śākyamuni Buddha achieved. Hence these new Buddhists called themselves followers of the Mahāyāna, or Great Vehicle; they called everyone else followers of the Hīnayāna, or Lesser Vehicle.*

Ironically, the universalism of the Mahāyāna raised doubts about women's capacity for liberation, which Mahāyāna Buddhists define as Buddhahood. There are many examples of male as well as female arhats in

Mainstream and Mahāyāna Buddhist scriptures, but there are no female Buddhas in these scriptures. This fact caused some Mahāyāna Buddhists to question whether women can become Buddhas. The Lotus Sutra*'s answer is "yes" or at least that is how the sūtra is traditionally interpreted. In the Devadatta chapter of this sūtra, an eight-year-old dragon girl becomes a Buddha. (Dragons are serpent-like deities in Buddhist mythology.) Modern readers, however, are sometimes troubled by the fact that the dragon girl has to become a man before she becomes a Buddha.*

The dragon princess, who along with being female is also nonhuman and just eight years old, is not the only unlikely candidate for Buddhahood in this chapter. The chapter is named after Devadatta, an immoral monk who repeatedly tried to assassinate Śākyamuni Buddha so that he could take over the Buddhist monastic community. Surprisingly, Devadatta receives a prediction of his future Buddhahood in this chapter.

At that time the Buddha addressed the bodhisattvas, the heavenly and human beings, and the four kinds of believers, saying: "Immeasurable kalpas[1] in the past, I sought the Lotus Sutra without ever flagging. During those many kalpas, I constantly appeared as the ruler of a kingdom who made a vow to seek the unsurpassed bodhi.[2] His mind never wavered or turned aside, and in his desire to fulfill the six paramitas[3] he diligently distributed alms, never stinting in heart, whether the gift was elephants or horses, the seven rare articles, countries, cities, wife, children, maidservants, menservants, or his own head, eyes, marrow and brain, his own flesh and limbs. He did not begrudge even his own being and life. At that period the human life span was immeasurably long. But for the sake of the Law[4] this king abandoned his kingdom and throne, delegated the government to the crown prince, sounded drums and sent out proclamations, seeking the Law in four directions and saying, 'Who can expound the Great Vehicle for me? To the end of my life I will be his provider and servant!'

"At that time there was a seer who came to the king and said, 'I have a Great Vehicle text called the Sutra of the Lotus of the Wonderful Law. If you will never disobey me, I will expound it for you.'

"When the king heard these words of the seer, he danced for joy. At once he accompanied the seer, providing him with whatever he needed, picking fruit, drawing water, gathering firewood, setting out meals, even offering his own body as a couch and seat, never stinting in body or mind. He served the seer in this manner for a thousand years, all for the sake of the Law, working diligently, acting as a provider and seeing to it that the seer lacked for nothing."

At that time the World-Honored One, wishing to state his meaning once more, spoke in verse form, saying:

I recall those departed kalpas of the past
when in order to seek the great Law,
though I was the ruler of a worldly kingdom,
I was not greedy to satisfy the five desires
but instead struck the bell, crying in four quarters,
"Who possesses the great Law?
If he will explain and preach it for me
I will be his slave and servant!"
At that time there was a seer named Asita
who came and announced to this great king,
"I have a subtle and wonderful Law,
rarely known in this world.
If you will undertake religious practice
I will expound it for you."
When the king heard the seer's words
his heart was filled with great joy.
Immediately he accompanied the seer,
providing him with whatever he needed,
gathering firewood, fruit and wild rice,
presenting them at appropriate times with respect and reverence.
Because the wonderful Law was in his thoughts
he never flagged in body or mind.
For the sake of living beings everywhere
he diligently sought the great Law,
taking no heed for himself
or for the gratification of the five desires.[5]
Therefore the ruler of a great kingdom
through diligent seeking was able to acquire this Law
and eventually to attain Buddhahood,
as I will now explain to you.

The Buddha said to the monks: "The king at that time was I myself, and the seer was the man who is now Devadatta. All because Devadatta was a good friend to me, I was able to become fully endowed with the six paramitas, with pity, compassion, joy, and indifference, with the thirty-two features,[6] the eighty characteristics,[7] the purple-tinged golden color, the ten powers,[8] the four kinds of fearlessness,[9] the four methods of winning people,[10] the eighteen unshared properties,[11] and the transcendental powers and the power of the way. The fact that I have attained impartial and correct enlightenment and can save living beings on a broad scale is all due to Devadatta, who was a good friend."

Then the Buddha said to the four kinds of believers: "Devadatta, after immeasurable kalpas have passed, will attain Buddhahood. He will be called Heavenly King Thus Come One, worthy of offerings, of right and universal knowledge, perfect clarity and conduct, well gone, understanding the world, unexcelled worthy, trainer of people, teacher of heavenly and human beings, Buddha, World-Honored One. His world will be called Heavenly Way, and at that time Heavenly King Buddha will abide in the world for twenty medium kalpas, broadly preaching the wonderful Law for the sake of living beings. Living beings numerous as Ganges sands will attain the fruit of arhatship.[12] Immeasurable numbers of living beings will conceive the desire to become pratyekabuddhas,[13] living beings numerous as Ganges sands will conceive a desire for the unsurpassed way, will gain the truth of birthlessness, and will never regress. After Heavenly King Buddha enters parinirvana,[14] his Correct Law will endure in the world for twenty medium kalpas. The relics from his whole body will be housed in a tower built of the seven treasures, sixty yojanas[15] in height and forty yojanas in width and depth. All the heavenly and human beings will take assorted flowers, powdered incense, incense for burning, paste incense, clothing, necklaces, streamers and banners, jeweled canopies, music and songs of praise and offer them with obeisance to the wonderful seven-jeweled tower. Immeasurable numbers of living beings will attain the fruits of arhatship, numberless living beings will become enlightened as pratyekabuddhas, and unimaginable numbers of living beings will conceive a desire for bodhi and will reach the level of no regression."

The Buddha said to the monks: "In future ages if there are good men or good women who, on hearing the Devadatta chapter of the Lotus Sutra of the Wonderful Law, believe and revere it with pure hearts and harbor no doubts or perplexities, they will never fall into hell or the realm of hungry spirits or of beasts, but will be born in the presence of the Buddhas of the ten directions, and in the place where they are born they will constantly hear this sutra. If they are born among human or heavenly beings, they will enjoy exceedingly wonderful delights, and if they are born in the presence of a Buddha, they will be born by transformation from lotus flowers."

At that time there was a bodhisattva who was among the followers of Many Treasures World-Honored One from the lower region and whose name was Wisdom Accumulated. He said to Many Treasures Buddha, "Shall we return to our homeland?"

Shakyamuni Buddha said to Wisdom Accumulated, "Good man, wait a little while. There is a bodhisattva named Manjushri here whom you should see. Debate and discuss the wonderful Law with him, and then you may return to your homeland."

At that time Manjushri was seated on a thousand-petaled lotus blossom big as a carriage wheel, and the bodhisattvas who had come with him were also seated on jeweled lotus blossoms. Manjushri had emerged in a natural manner from the palace of the dragon[16] king Sagara in the great ocean and was suspended in the air. Proceeding to Holy Eagle Peak,[17] he descended from the lotus blossom and, having entered the presence of the Buddhas, bowed his head and paid obeisance to the feet of the two World-Honored Ones. When he had concluded these gestures of respect, he went to where Wisdom Accumulated was and exchanged greetings with him, and then retired and sat at one side.

Bodhisattva Wisdom Accumulated questioned Manjushri, saying, "When you went to the palace of the dragon king, how many living beings did you convert?"

Manjushri replied, "The number is immeasurable, incapable of calculation. The mouth cannot express it, the mind cannot fathom it. Wait a moment and there will be proof."

Before he had finished speaking, countless bodhisattvas seated on jeweled lotus blossoms emerged from the ocean and proceeded to Holy Eagle Peak, where they remained suspended in the air. These bodhisattvas had all been converted and saved by Manjushri. They had carried out all the bodhisattva practices and all discussed and expounded the six paramitas with one another. Those who had originally been voice-hearers[18] expounded the practices of the voice-hearer when they were in the air, but now all were practicing the Great Vehicle principle of emptiness.

Manjushri said to Wisdom Accumulated, "The work of teaching and converting carried out in the ocean was as you can see."

At that time Bodhisattva Wisdom Accumulated recited these verses of praise:

Of great wisdom and virtue, brave and stalwart,
you have converted and saved immeasurable beings.
Now those in this great assembly,
as well as I myself, have all seen them.
You expound the principle of the true entity,
open up the Law of the single vehicle,
broadly guiding the many beings,
causing them quickly to attain bodhi.

Manjushri said, "When I was in the ocean I constantly expounded the Lotus Sutra of the Wonderful Law alone."

Bodhisattva Wisdom Accumulated questioned Manjushri, saying, "This sutra is very profound, subtle and wonderful, a treasure among sutras, a rarity in the world. Are there perhaps any living beings who, by earnestly and diligently practicing this sutra, have been able to attain Buddhahood quickly?"

Manjushri replied, "There is the daughter of the dragon king Sagara, who has just turned eight. Her wisdom has keen roots and she is good at understanding the root activities and deeds of living beings. She has mastered the dharanis,[19] has been able to accept and embrace all the storehouse of profound secrets preached by the Buddhas, has entered deep into meditation, thoroughly grasped the doctrines, and in the space of an instant conceived the desire for bodhi and reached the level of no regression. Her eloquence knows no hindrance, and she thinks of living beings with compassion as though they were her own children. She is fully endowed with blessings, and when it comes to conceiving in mind and expounding by mouth, she is subtle, wonderful, comprehensive and great.

Kind, compassionate, benevolent, yielding, she is gentle and refined in will, capable of attaining bodhi."

Bodhisattva Wisdom Accumulated said, "When I observe Shakyamuni Thus Come One, I see that for immeasurable kalpas he carried out harsh and difficult practices, accumulating merit, piling up virtue, seeking the way of the bodhisattva without ever resting. I observe that throughout the thousand-millionfold world, there is not a single spot tiny as a mustard seed where this bodhisattva failed to sacrifice body and life for the sake of living beings. Only after he had done that was he able to complete the bodhi way. I cannot believe that this girl in the space of an instant could actually achieve correct enlightenment."

Before his words had come to an end, the dragon king's daughter suddenly appeared before the Buddha, bowed her head in obeisance, and then retired to one side, reciting these verses of praise:

He profoundly understands the signs of guilt and good fortune
and illuminates the ten directions everywhere.
His subtle, wonderful pure Dharma body[20]
is endowed with the thirty-two features;
the eighty characteristics
adorn his Dharma body.
Heavenly and human beings gaze up in awe,
dragons and spirits all pay honor and respect;
among all living beings,
none who do not hold him in reverence.
And having heard his teachings, I have attained bodhi—
the Buddha alone can bear witness to this.
I unfold the doctrines of the Great Vehicle
to rescue living beings from suffering.

At that time Shariputra said to the dragon girl, "You suppose that in this short time you have been able to attain the unsurpassed way. But this is difficult to believe. Why? Because a woman's body is soiled and defiled, not a vessel for the Law. How could you attain the unsurpassed bodhi? The road to Buddhahood is long and far-stretching. Only after one has spent immeasurable kalpas pursuing austerities, accumulating deeds, practicing all kinds of paramitas, can one finally achieve success. Moreover, a woman is subject to the five obstacles. First, she cannot become a Brahma heavenly king.[21] Second, she cannot become the king Shakra.[22] Third, she cannot become a devil[23] king. Fourth, she cannot become a wheel-turning sage king.[24] Fifth, she cannot become a Buddha. How then could a woman like you be able to attain Buddhahood so quickly?"

At that time the dragon girl had a precious jewel worth as much as the thousand-millionfold world which she presented to the Buddha. The Buddha immediately accepted it. The dragon girl said to Bodhisattva Wisdom Accumulated and to the venerable one, Shariputra, "I presented the precious jewel and the World-Honored One accepted it—was that not quickly done?"

They replied, "Very quickly!"

The girl said, "Employ your supernatural powers and watch me attain Buddhahood. It will be even quicker than that!"

At that time the members of the assembly all saw the dragon girl in the space of an instant change into a man and carry out all the practices of a bodhisattva, immediately proceeding to the Spotless World of the south, taking a seat on a jeweled lotus, and attaining impartial and correct enlightenment. With the thirty-two features and the eighty characteristics, he expounded the wonderful Law for all living beings everywhere in the ten directions.

At that time in the saha world[25] the bodhisattvas, voice-hearers, gods, dragons and others of the eight kinds of guardians, human and non-human beings all from a distance saw the dragon girl become a Buddha and preach the Law to all the human and heavenly beings in the assembly at that time. Their hearts were filled with great joy and all from a distance paid reverent obeisance. Immeasurable living beings, hearing the Law, understood it and were able to reach the level of no regression. Immeasurable living beings received prophecies that they would gain the way. The Spotless World quaked and trembled in six different ways. Three thousand living beings of the saha world remained on the level of no regression. Three thousand living beings conceived a desire for bodhi and received prophecies of enlightenment. Bodhisattva Wisdom Accumulated, Shariputra and all the other members of the assembly silently believed and accepted these things.

END NOTES

N. B. Definitions of terms taken from the glossary by Burton Watson.

1. *Kalpa:* An extremely long period of time.
2. *Bodhi:* Enlightenment or Buddhahood.
3. *Paramitas:* The Sanskrit word *paramita* means "perfecton" or "having reached the other shore," that is, having crossed over from the shore of delusion to that of enlightenment. According to Mahāyāna Buddhism, bodhisattvas must cultivate six perfections: generosity; morality; forbearance or bearing up patiently under opposition and hardship; heroic effort; meditation; and wisdom.
4. *Law:* Dharma or Truth as taught in Buddhism.
5. *Five desires:* The desires that arise from the contact of the five sense organs—eyes, ears, nose, tongue, and body—with their respective objects. Sometimes the five desires are defined as the desire for wealth, sex, food and drink, fame, and sleep.
6. *Thirty-two features:* Remarkable physical characteristics possessed by great beings such as Buddhas and wheel-turning kings. They are flat soles; markings of the wheel of the Law on the soles; long slender fingers; broad flat heels; webbed feet and hands; extremely flexible limbs; protuberant insteps; slender legs like those of a deer; hands that extend past the knees even when standing; concealed genitals; body height equal to arm span; body hair that turns upward; one hair growing from each pore; golden skin; light radiating from the body; thin, pliant skin; well-developed muscles in hands, feet, shoulders, nape of the neck; well-developed muscles below armpits; dignified torso like that of a lion; large straight body; substantial shoulders; forty teeth; even teeth; four white fangs; full cheeks like those of a lion; unexcelled sense of taste; long, broad tongue; voice that can reach to the Brahma heaven; eyes the color of blue lotus blossoms; long eyelashes like those of a cow; protuberant knot of flesh like a topknot on crown of head; tuft of white hair between the eyebrows curling to the right.
7. *Eighty characteristics:* Extraordinary features that only Buddhas and bodhisattvas possess. There are various explanations of the eighty characteristics; some of the characteristics duplicate the thirty-two features.
8. *Ten powers:* The powers of a Buddha, namely, the power of knowing what is true and what is not; power of knowing the karmic causality at work in the lives of all beings past, present and future; power of knowing all stages of concentration, emancipation and meditation; power of knowing the life-condition of all people; power of judging all people's understanding; power of discerning the superiority or inferiority of all people's capacity; power of knowing the effects of all people's actions; power of remembering past lifetimes; power of knowing when each person will be born and die and in what realm that person will be reborn; power of eradicating all illusions.
9. *Four kinds of fearlessness:* Four aspects of a Buddha's fearlessness in preaching. A Buddha is fearless in declaring that he is enlightened to the truth of all phenomena; fearless in proclaiming he has extinguished all desires and illusions; fearless in teaching that desires and karma can be obstacles to enlightenment; and fearless in teaching that one can overcome all sufferings by practicing Buddhism.
10. *Four methods of winning people:* Four methods employed by bodhisattvas to attract others to their teachings. They are to give alms and expound the Law; to speak in a kindly manner; to work to benefit others; and to share their hardships and cooperate with them.
11. *Eighteen unshared properties:* Properties possessed by a Buddha and not shared by others. These are: freedom from illusions; eloquence; absence of attachments; impartiality; constant concentration of mind; knowledge of all things; untiring intention to

lead people to salvation; incessant endeavor; consistency of teachings with those of other Buddhas; perfect wisdom; perfect emancipation; perfect insight; consistency of deeds with wisdom; consistency of words with wisdom; consistency of mind with wisdom; knowledge of the past; knowledge of the future; and knowledge of the present.

12. *Arhatship:* The state of being an arhat, one who has attained the personal nirvana of Mainstream Buddhism.
13. *Pratyekabuddha:* A "self-enlightened" being, one who has won an understanding of truth through his or her own efforts but makes no effort to enlighten others.
14. *Parinirvana:* A term similar to nirvana, it is used in reference to the apparent passing away of the physical body of a Buddha.
15. *Yojana:* A unit of measurement in ancient India, equal to the distance that the royal army could march in a day.
16. *Dragon:* (Sanskrit: *nāga*) One of the eight kinds of nonhuman beings who protect Buddhism and appear frequently in the *Lotus Sutra.*
17. *Holy Eagle Peak* (Gridhrakuta): Mountain northeast of the city of Rajagriha where Shakyamuni Buddha is said to have preached the *Lotus Sutra* and other teachings.
18. *Voice-hearers:* The term originally referred to Shakyamuni Buddha's first generation of disciples. In the *Lotus Sutra* it refers to those monastics who follow Buddhist teachings leading to the goal of arhatship rather than full Buddhahood.
19. *Dharanis:* A spell or formula said to protect the one who recites it and benefit the person by virtue of its mystic power.
20. *Dharma body:* A term open to considerable interpretation. It can refer to anything ranging from a body constituted by the qualities, or *dharmas,* of a Buddha; to a kind of formless and imperishable body equated with ultimate reality, which is the Dharma, or Truth, itself.
21. *Brahma heavenly king:* A king of the Brahma heaven, a deity who has attained supremacy in a particular universe.
22. *Shakra:* Originally, the god of thunder in Indian mythology, he was later incorporated into Buddhism as a protective deity.
23. *Devil:* In this passage the term refers to Māra, a Buddhist deity associated with desire, death, and rebirth.
24. *Wheel-turning sage king:* An ideal ruler in Indian mythology. In Buddhism the wheel-turning kings are kings who rule by justice rather than force.
25. *Saha world:* The present world, which is full of sufferings to be endured.

QUESTIONS

1. Like many Buddhist scriptures, the *Lotus Sutra* delivers mixed messages about women's religious capacities. The issue is further complicated by the fact that the dragon girl claims to have attained bodhi, or Buddhahood, prior to her physical transformation. Just when does she become a Buddha? Does she really have to become a man first?
2. What makes it possible for the dragon girl and Devadatta to attain Buddhahood? To answer this question, readers will need to pay attention to the claims the sūtra makes about its own miraculous and liberating powers. Such claims are typical of Mahāyāna sūtras.

3. What kinds of inspiration are Manjushri and Devadatta supposed to provide? How do they compare?
4. What is the role of the physical body in attaining Buddahood? Are the descriptions of one's physical self meant to be literal?

DOCUMENT

LAWS OF MANU

The Laws of Manu *achieved an important place in the juridical and legal framework of colonial and postcolonial India when it was translated into English in the late eighteenth century by British scholars. It is best known as the foundation of a code of laws for those who were identified as Hindu in the colonial period. But the* Laws of Manu *or* Manusmriti, *in Sanskrit, was also a guidebook of teachings that explained good conduct for those who belonged to the upper castes. Compiled in the period around the start of the common era, the* Laws of Manu *had no single author. Its aim was to reform a society that had fallen away from its Vedic roots, which had ended just a few centuries earlier. In many ways* Manu *was a response to those who had turned toward other forms of devotion, such as Buddhism or Jainism, which relied more on individual prayer and devotion than on a class of priests to facilitate one's relationship to God. Its edicts were largely religious, advising readers of their religious duties and obligations, but the advice it offered spilled into the domain of politics and good kingship, as well as into community and family relationships. It discussed how a society should deal with debts, gifts, animal sacrifice, bride price, and personal and community hygiene.*

This selection of verses explains the responsibilities of the householder, or the second stage of a pious and auspicious life. In the first stage of life, one is required to become a disciple or student and learn the Vedas *from one's guru. In the second, one becomes a householder and establishes a family and household that enables the reproduction of society. In the third and final stages, one gradually removes oneself from worldly concerns in preparation for death and*

---

reincarnation. This chapter from the Laws of Manu *details whom a man should marry, how he should treat his wife, and how he should perform his daily prayers and rituals.*

[1] The vow for studying the three Vedas with a guru is for thirty-six years, or half of that, or a quarter of that, or whenever the undertaking comes to an end. [2] When, unswerving in his chastity, he has learned the Vedas, or two Vedas, or even one Veda, in the proper order, he should enter the householder stage of life. [3] When he is recognized as one who has, by fulfilling his own duties, received the legacy of the Veda from his father, he should first be seated on a couch, adorned with garlands, and honoured with (an offering made from the milk of) a cow.[1]

[4] When he received his guru's permission and bathed and performed the ritual for homecoming according to the rules, a twice-born man should marry a wife who is of the same class and has the right marks.[2] [3] A woman who is neither a co-feeding relative on her mother's side nor belongs to the same lineage (of the sages) on her father's side, and who is a virgin, is recommended for marriage to twice-born men.[3] [6] When a man connects himself with a woman, he should avoid the ten following families, even if they are great, or rich in cows, goats, sheep, property, or grain: [7] a family that has abandoned the rites, or does not have male children, or does not chant the Veda; and those families in which they have hairy bodies, piles, consumption, weak digestion, epilepsy, white leprosy, or black leprosy.

[8] A man should not marry a girl who is a redhead or has an extra limb or is sickly or has no body hair or too much body hair or talks too much or is sallow; [9] or who is named after a constellation, a tree, or a river, or who has a low-caste name, or is named after a mountain, a bird, a snake, or has a menial or frightening name, [10] He should marry a woman who does not lack any part of her body and who has a pleasant name, who walks like a goose or an elephant, whose body hair and hair on the head is fine, "whose teeth are not big, and who has delicate limbs.[4] [11] A wise man will not marry a woman who has no brother or whose father is unknown, for fear that she may be an appointed daughter or that he may act wrongly.[5]

[12] A woman of the same class is recommended to twice-born men for the first marriage; but for men who are driven by desire, these are the women, in progressively descending order: [13] According to tradition, only a servant woman can be the wife of a servant; she and one of his own class can be the wife of a commoner; these two and one of his own class for a king; and these three and one of his own class for a priest. [14] Not a single story mentions a servant woman as the wife of a priest or a ruler, even in extremity. [15] Twice-born men who are so infatuated as to marry women of low caste quickly reduce their families, including the descendants, to the status of servants. [16] A man falls when he weds a servant woman, according to Atri and to (Gautama) the son of Utathya, or when he has a son by her, according to Śaunaka, or when he has any children by her, according to Bhṛgu.[6] [17] A priest who climbs into bed with a servant woman goes to hell; if he begets a son in her, he loses the the status of priest. [18] The ancestors and the gods do not eat the offerings to the gods, to the ancestors, and to guests that such a man makes with her, and so he does not go to heaven.[7] [19] No redemption is prescribed for a man who drinks the saliva from the lips of a servant woman or is tainted by her breath or begets a son in her.

[20] Now learn, in summary, these eight ways of marrying women, that are for all four classes, for better and for worse, here on earth and after death: [21] the marriages named after Brahmā, the gods, the sages, the Lord of Creatures, the demons, the centaurs, the ogres, and, eighth and lowest, the ghouls. [22] I will explain to you all about which one is right for each class, and the virtues and vices of each, and their advantages and disadvantages for progeneration. [23] It should be understood that the first six, as they are listed in order, are right for a priest, the last four for a ruler, and these same four, with the exception of the ogre marriage, for a commoner or a servant. [24] The poets say that the first four are recommended for a priest, only one, the ogre marriage, for a ruler, and the demon marriage for a commoner and a servant. [25] But here, three of the (last) five are right, while two—those of the ghouls and the demons—are traditionally regarded as wrong and are never to be performed.[8] [26] Two of the marriages mentioned above, those according to the centaurs and the ogres, are traditionally regarded as right for rulers, whether they are used separately or combined.

[27] It is said to be the law of Brahmā when a man dresses his daughter and adorns her and he himself gives her as a gift to a man he has summoned, one who knows the revealed canon and is of good character. [28] They call it the law of the gods when a man adorns his daughter and, in the course of a sacrifice, gives her as a gift to the officiating priest who is properly performing the ritual. [29] It is called the sages' law when he gives away his daughter by the rules, after receiving from the bridegroom a cow and a bull, or two cows and bulls, in accordance with the law. [30] The tradition calls it the rule of the Lord of Creatures when a man gives away his daughter after adorning her and saying 'May the two of you together fulfil your duties.'

[31] It is called the demonic law when a man takes the girl because he wants her himself, when he has given as much wealth as he can to her relatives and to the girl herself. [32] It is to be recognized as a centaur marriage when the girl and her lover join with one another in sexual union because they want to, out of desire.[9] [33] It is called the rule of the ogres when a man forcibly carries off a girl out of her house, screaming and weeping, after he has killed, wounded, and broken.[10] [34] The lowest and most evil of marriages, known as that of the ghouls, takes place when a man secretly has sex with a girl who is asleep, drunk, or out of her mind.[11] [35] For priests, the gift of a girl with (a libation of) water is the best (marriage); but for the other classes (the best is) when they desire one another.

[36] Listen, priests, while I tell you fully about all the qualities of these marriages that Manu has proclaimed. [37] If a son born to a woman who has had a Brahmā marriage does good deeds, he frees from guilt ten of the ancestors who came before him, ten later descendants, and himself as the twenty-first. [38] A son born to a woman who had a marriage of the gods (frees) seven ancestors and seven descendants, a son born to a woman who had a marriage of the sages (frees) three (of each), and a son born to a woman who had a marriage of the Lord of Creatures (frees) six (of each). [39] The sons born from these four marriages, in order beginning with the Brahmā marriage, are filled with the splendour of the Veda and are esteemed by educated men. [40] Beautiful and endowed with the quality of lucidity, rich and famous, enjoying life to the fullest, most religious, they live for a hundred years, [41] But from those (four) other remaining bad marriages are born cruel sons, liars who hate the Veda and religion.

[42] Out of blameless marriages with women come blameless progeny. Blameworthy progeny come to men from blameworthy (marriages); therefore one should avoid the blameworthy ones.

[43] The transformative ritual of taking the bride by the hand is prescribed for women of the same class; know that this (following) procedure is for the marriage ritual with women of a different class. [44] When a woman marries a man of superior class, a woman of the ruler class must take hold of an arrow, a commoner girl a whip, and a servant woman must grasp the fringe of (his) garment.

[45] A man should have sex with his wife during her fertile season, and always find his satisfaction in his own wife; when he desires sexual pleasure he should go to her to whom he is vowed, except on the days at the (lunar) junctures.[12] [46] The natural fertile season of women is traditionally said to last for sixteen nights, though these include four special days that good people despise.[13] [47] Among these (nights), the first four, the eleventh, and the thirteenth are disapproved; the other ten nights are approved. [48] On the even nights, sons are conceived, and on the uneven nights, daughters; therefore a man who wants sons should unite with his wife during her fertile season on the even nights. [49] A male child is born when the semen of the man is greater (than that of the woman), and a female child when (the semen) of the woman is greater (than that of the man); if both are equal, a hermaphrodite is born, or a boy and a girl; and if (the semen) is weak or scanty, the opposite will occur.[14] [50] A man who avoids women on the (six) disapproved nights and on eight other nights is regarded as chaste, no matter which of the four stages of life he is in.

[51] No learned father should take a bride-price for his daughter, no matter how small, for a man who, out of greed, exacts a bride-price would be selling his child like a pimp. [52] And those deluded relatives who live off a woman's property—her carriages, her clothes, and so on—are evil and go to hell. [53] Some say that the cow and bull (given) during the (wedding) of the sages is a bride-price, but it is not so. No matter how great or small (the price), the sale amounts to prostitution. [54] Girls whose relatives do not take the bride-price for themselves are not prostituted; that (gift) is merely honorific and a mercy to maidens.

[55] Fathers, brothers, husbands, and brothers-in-law who wish for great good fortune should revere these women and adorn them. [56] The

deities delight in places where women are revered, but where women are not revered all rites are fruitless. [57] Where the women of the family are miserable, the family is soon destroyed, but it always thrives where the women are not miserable. [58] Homes that are cursed by women of the family who have not been treated with due reverence are completely destroyed, as if struck down by witchcraft. [59] Therefore men who wish to prosper should always revere these women with ornaments, clothes, and food at celebrations and festivals.

[60] There is unwavering good fortune in a family where the husband is always satisfied by the wife, and the wife by the husband. [61] If the wife is not radiant she does not stimulate the man; and because the man is unstimulated the making of children does not happen. [62] If the woman is radiant, the whole family is radiant, but if she is not radiant the whole family is not radiant. [63] Through bad marriages, the neglect of rites, failure to study the Veda, and transgressing against priests, families cease to be families.

[64] By (making a living from) crafts or business or from cows, horses, and carts, by begetting children only with servant women, by farming the land, by serving a king, [65] by sacrificing for those who are unfit for the sacrifice, and by denying the doctrine of the effects of past actions, families who are bereft of Vedic verses quickly perish. [66] But families rich in Vedic verses join the highest rank of families and cultivate great fame even if they have little property.

[67] In the fire set at the time of marriage, the householder should perform the domestic rituals and the five (great) sacrifices in accordance with the rules, and do his everyday cooking. [68] A householder has five slaughter-houses, whose use fetters him: the fireplace, the grindstone, the broom, the mortar and pestle, and the water jar.[15] [69] The great sages devised the five great sacrifices for the householder to do every day to redeem him from all of these (slaughter-houses) successively. [70] The study (of the Veda) is the sacrifice to ultimate reality, and the refreshing libation is the sacrifice to the ancestors; the offering into the fire is for the gods, the propitiatory offering of portions of food is for the disembodied spirits, and the revering of guests is the sacrifice to men.[16] [71] The man who does not neglect these five great sacrifices as long as he is able to perform them is not defiled by the stains of the slaughter-houses, even while he lives as a householder. [72] But who-

ever scatters no propitiatory offering to the five—the gods, guests, dependants, ancestors, and the self—breathes but does not (truly) live.[17] [73] These five sacrifices are [also] known as 'the not-offered-in-the-fire', 'the offered-in-the-fire', 'the offered-by-scattering', 'the offered-to-priests', and 'the eaten'.[18] [74] 'The not-offered-in-the-fire' is chanting (the Veda), 'the offered-in-the-fire' is the offering into the fire, 'the offered-by-scattering' is the propitiatory offering to the disembodied spirits, 'the offered-to-priests' is the reception of priests (as guests), and 'the eaten' is the refreshing libation to the ancestors.

[75] The man in this (stage of life) should be regularly engaged in the daily personal study (of the Veda), and also in rituals for the gods; for the man who is diligently engaged in rituals for the gods maintains this (whole universe), moving and unmoving. [76] An offering cast properly into the fire approaches the sun; rain is created from the sun, from rain comes food, and from that, progeny. [77] Just as all living creatures depend on air in order to live, so do members of the other stages of life subsist by depending on householders. [78] Since people in the other three stages of life are supported every day by the knowledge and the food of the householder, therefore the householder stage of life is the best.[19] [79] It must be carried out with zeal by the man who wants to win an incorruptible heaven (after death) and endless happiness here on earth, but it cannot be carried out by men with feeble sensory powers.[20]

[80] The sages, ancestors, gods, disembodied spirits, and guests expect things from householders, which the understanding man should do for them. [81] He should honour the sages with the private recitation of the Veda, the gods with offerings into the fire in accordance with the rules, the ancestors with the ceremonies for the dead, men with food, and the disembodied spirits with the ritual of the propitiatory offering. [82] Day after day at the ceremony for the dead he should offer what gives pleasure to the ancestors: food, or water, or milk, roots, or fruits. [83] He should feed a priest, even if it is only one, as a means of pleasing the ancestors during the ritual that is part of the five great sacrifices; but he should not feed any twice-born (priest) at this time for the purposes of fulfilling the ritual to the All-gods.[21]

[84] Every day, a priest should take (a portion) of the sanctified (food) for the ritual to the All-gods prepared according to the rules and make an

offering in the household fire to the following deities:[22] [85] first to Fire, then to Soma, and then to both of them together, and then to the All-gods and Dhan-vantari;[23] [86] and then to the goddesses of the new-moon day and the full-moon day, to the Lord of Creatures, to the earth and sky together, and finally to Fire of the Perfected Offering.[24]

[87] And when he has offered the oblations properly in this manner, he should distribute the propitiatory offering in all the cardinal directions, in clockwise order: one each to Indra, Death, the lord of the Waters, and the Moon, together with their attendants.[25] [88] He should put down (a portion) at the door while saying 'To the Maruts,' and one in some water while saying 'To the waters.' Saying 'To the Lord of the Trees,' he should offer (one) on the mortar and pestle.[26] [89] He should make a propitiatory offering at the head to the goddess of Good Fortune, and at the foot to the Benevolent Dark Goddess, and in the centre of the house to ultimate reality and the Lord of the House.[27] [90] He should toss up into the air a propitiatory offering to the All-gods, and one to the disembodied spirits who roam in the daytime and also one to the disembodied spirits who roam at night. [91] In the upper part of the house he should make a propitiatory offering for the Spirit of All Food, and all the remainder of the propitiatory offering should be put towards the south for the ancestors.[28] [92] And he should placidly scatter a propitiatory offering on the ground for the dogs, for those who have fallen, for 'Dog-cookers', for those whose evil deeds have made them ill, for birds, and for worms.[29] [93] A priest who in this way constantly honours all the disembodied spirits takes on a physical form of brilliant energy and attains the supreme condition by the straightest route.

[94] When he has performed this ritual of the propitiatory offering, he should first feed a guest and, in accordance with the rules, give alms to a beggar and to a chaste student of the Veda. [95] By giving alms, the twice-born householder wins a reward for merit which is the same as the reward for merit won by giving a cow to the guru in accordance with the rule.[30] [96] He should present alms, or even just a vessel of water that has first been ritually prepared, to a priest who knows the true meaning of the Veda. [97] The offerings that ignorant men make to the gods and ancestors are lost if the donors give them by mistake to priests who have become dead ashes.[31] [98] An offering offered in the fire which is the

mouth of a priest rich in learning and inner heat rescues (the sacrificer) from an unfortunate fate and a great offence.

[99] He should offer a guest, as soon as he arrives, a seat, some water, and food that has first been ritually prepared and perfectly cooked, to the best of his ability. [100] If a priest stays (as a guest) and is not honoured, (when he departs) he takes away all the (credit for) good deeds even of someone who lives by gleaning (corn) and gathering (single grains), even of someone who makes regular offerings in five fires.[32] [101] Grass (laid down for a resting place), space (to rest), water, and pleasant conversation—these four things never run out in the house of good people. [102] A priest who stays even one night is traditionally regarded as a guest, for he stays (*sthita*) not all the time (*anitya);* thus he is called 'a guest' (*atithi,* 'not staying'). [103] A convivial priest who lives in the same village should not be regarded as a guest, even when he comes to a house where there are a wife and (sacrificial) fires.[33] [104] Stupid householders who live off other people's cooked food become because of that, after death, the livestock of those who have given them food.[34]

[105] A guest who comes with the setting sun in the evening should not be turned away by the householder who is a sacrificer; whether he arrives at a convenient time or an inconvenient time, he should not be allowed to stay in his house without eating. [106] (The householder) should not himself eat anything that he does not feed to his guest. The revering of guests wins wealth, a good reputation, long life, and heaven. [107] He should present the best seat and room, the best bed, the best farewell and the best service to guests of the highest status, inferior ones to those of inferior status, and middling ones to those whose status is the same as his. [108] And if another guest should come after the ritual to the All-gods is finished, he should give him, too, whatever food he can, but he should not distribute the propitiatory offering (again).

[109] A priest should not drop the name of his family and his lineage (of the sages) in order to get a meal, for wise men call a man who invokes them in this way to get a meal 'an eater of regurgitated food'.[35] [110] A ruler is not called a guest in the house of a priest, nor is a commoner, a servant, a friend, a relative, or one's guru. [111] But if a ruler comes to the house as a guest, (the householder) may feed him, too, if he wants to, after the priests have been fed. [112] If even commoners and servants have

arrived at the house as guests, in a show of his mercy he may feed them along with his dependants. [113] Others, too, such as friends who have come to the house in the spirit of good will, he may feed with natural food along with his wife, to the best of his ability. [114] He may without hesitation feed newlywed women, small girls, people who are ill, and pregnant women, right after the guests. [115] The fool who eats first, without giving anything to these people, does not know that because he is eating he himself is devoured by dogs and vultures.[36]

[116] Now, when the priests, the members of the family, and the dependants have eaten, the husband and wife may later eat what is left over. [117] The householder should eat the leftovers only after he has revered the gods, the sages, humans, ancestors, and the household deities. [118] The person who cooks only for himself eats nothing but error, for the food left over from the sacrifice is the food intended for good men.

[119] With the honey-mixture he should honour a king, an officiating priest, a Vedic graduate, a guru, close friend, father-in-law, or maternal uncle who has come again after a year (since the last visit).[37] [120] He should also honour with the honey-mixture a king or a priest who knows the Veda by heart if they arrive when a sacrifice is being performed, but not if there is no sacrifice—that is the fixed rule.

[121] In the evening, the wife may make the propitiatory offerings from the sanctified food, although without reciting any of the Vedic verses, for what is called the ritual of the All-gods is prescribed for both the morning and the evening.

END NOTES

1. The offering made from a cow is the *madhuparka,* the honey-mixture, referred to in 3.119–20.
2. The period of Veda study culminates in the homecoming ritual discussed at 2.245–6.
3. In Vedic times, and to some extent in present-day India among certain priests, men traced their descent through a ritual lineage (*gotra*) to one of the seven mythical sages or *ṛṣis* to whom the Veda was first revealed.
4. The goose (*haṃsa*) and elephant (*vārana*) walk with a rolling gait that ancient Indian poets considered a sign of beauty in a woman.
5. If she has no brothers, her father may 'appoint' her to raise sons to be his heirs, and so her sons would be her father's heirs instead of her husband's. If her father is not known, her natural parents may turn out to be related to the bridegroom too closely (i.e. wrongly, involving *adharma*).

6. Here Manu argues with the authors of other *dharmaśāstras*. The fall may be from caste or into hell.
7. A man can make certain sacrifices only with the assistance of a wife of the proper class. Offerings of oblations in the sacrificial fire to the gods, of water to the ancestors, and of food from the family's meal to priests who are guests comprise three of the five obligatory daily 'great sacrifices' of the householder. The other two are the propitiatory sacrifice of rice-balls placed on the ground for the disembodied spirits and the sacrifice to the *brahman* or ultimate reality, which is the study and recitation of the Veda. See 3.69–83.
8. 'Here' means 'in this text'. The three marriages that are right (*dharmya*) among the last five are those of the Lord of Creatures, centaurs, and ogres.
9. The centaurs (*gandharvas* in Sanskrit, possibly cognate with the Latin *centaurus*) are celestial patrons of music, horses, and sexual love. The term 'Gandharva marriage' became a euphemism in Sanskrit literature for an otherwise unsanctioned sexual union, i.e. one witnessed only by these creatures.
10. The verse does not specify the object of this mayhem. Some commentators suggest that it is the people of the house who try to oppose the ogre bridegroom; others suggest that the first two verbs (kill and wound) apply to such people, while the last applies to the house itself, which is broken into.
11. The first is the Brahmā marriage (3.27), and the second is the centaur (*gandharva*) marriage (3.32).
12. The lunar junctures are the *parvans,* the new- and full-moon days (and, sometimes, the eighth and fourteenth day of each lunar fortnight; see 4.113–14). Traditionally, in Vedic ritualism, the sacrificer and his wife prepared themselves for the performance of the new- and full-moon sacrifices by various kinds of observances, including sexual abstinence.
13. The special days are the first four after the beginning of her menstrual period.
14. The final instance would be a child with no sexual organs at all, or a miscarriage, or no conception at all.
15. These are slaughter-houses because small creatures are, often inadvertently, killed through their use.
16. The propitiatory offering to the disembodied spirits (*bhūtas*) is the *balli* offering of portions of food scattered on the ground.
17. The observant reader will note that this list of five differs from that given directly above. The dependants may be those whom he is bound to support, such as servants or aged relatives or animals, or the disembodied spirits (*bhūtas*) referred to in previous verses.
18. These compounds roughly translate the technical terms in Sanskrit: the *ahuta,* the *huta,* the *prahuta,* the *brāhmyahuta,* and the *prāśita.*
19. Knowledge (*jnāna*) here refers to the daily recitation of the Veda.
20. 'Feeble sensory powers' (*durbalendriya)* may refer to general weakness or to the failure to control the sense organs. 'Incorruptible', in the seventeenth-century sense, seems the best word to capture the meaning of *akṣaya,* literally 'not-decaying', with the added meaning of transcending the inevitable dissolution of worldly things.
21. The ritual to the All-gods (*vaiśvadeva*) is an offering of food to the gods that is to be performed daily at sunrise, noon, and sunset. The verse indicates that these two rituals are to be kept separate, and hence one should not feed the two sets of priests at once.
22. The household fire (*gṛhyāni*) is the fire set at the time of marriage (see 3.67), the fire in which the householder performs the domestic rituals and the five great sacrifices, as well as ordinary cooking. It should be distinguished from the householder's fire (*garhapatyāgni*) (2.231).

23. Fire and Soma together form the dual deity to whom the *agniṣṭoma* is offered. Dhanvantari is the physician of the gods.
24. Kuhu is the goddess of the new-moon day, Anumati the goddess of the full-moon day, and Agni Sviṣṭakṛt is the Fire of the Perfected Offerings.
25. The offering is made clockwise, literally 'to the right' (*pradakṣiṇam),* proceeding from the east to the south (the south being called *dakṣiṇa).* The deities thus honoured are Indra in the east, Death (Antaka, 'The Ender', more often called Yama) in the south, the Lord of the Waters (Āppati, more often called Varuṇa) in the west, and the Moon (Indu, more often called Soma) in the north.
26. The Maruts are storm gods, servants of Indra.
27. The 'head' and 'foot' are most likely the top and bottom of the house, in contrast with the centre mentioned in the next part of the verse; but commentators suggest that these terms may refer to the head and foot of the marriage bed, or to the place where the Lord of the House (Vāstospati, the benevolent spirit of the dwelling place) puts his head and foot. Śrī is the goddess of fortune, and Bhadrakālī a benevolent form of Kālī (the Dark Goddess).
28. The spirit of All Food is Sarvānnabhūti; some manuscripts read Sarvātmabhūti, Spirit of All Souls.
29. 'Dog-cooker' is generally a term of opprobrium for Untouchables; Manu uses it to designate a particular caste of Untouchables (9.19, 51–6). The evils that make a man ill may have been committed in this life or a previous life; smallpox and leprosy are particularly indicated in this way.
30. The rule is that a student should give his guru a present (a *gurudakṣiṇā*), preferably a cow, at the end of his period of study of the Veda. See 2.246.
31. See 3.168 for the metaphor of the priest whose sacrificial fire has been extinguished.
32. That is, the mistreated guest takes away the bad host's good credit for good past actions (and, as is stated in other texts, he transfers to that host his own bad credit for bad past actions). The one who makes offerings in five fires is the *āhitāgni.*
33. The term translated as 'convivial' (*sāṅgatika*) may rather designate someone who comes on business or is a member of one's own group. The house with a wife and sacrificial fires is the home of a householder who has established his sacrificial hearth.
34. That is, in the other world, or in their next birth, they are reborn as animals who will be thus eaten.
35. The name of the family is the *kula,* and the lineage of the sages is the *gotra.*
36. He will be eaten like this after his death, or in the other world.
37. The honey-mixture is the *madhuparka,* an offering of honey and milk given to certain guests.

QUESTIONS

1. What are the requirements of a properly auspicious and pious life? Why is there so much detail on how one might achieve such a life?
2. How important is a wife to the householder?
3. Are there contradictions in this text? How are these contradictions resolved? What do these contradictions suggest about this society?
4. Are there hierarchies in this society? What benefits do those on the top of this hierarchy enjoy? What responsibilities do they have?

DOCUMENT

THE MAHABHARATA

Of the two major Sanskrit epics, (the other is the Ramayana*), the* Mahabharata *is vastly longer. Comprising over a hundred thousand verses, it is seven times longer than the Greek epics the* Iliad *and the* Odyssey *combined. Written between 400 B.C.E. and 400 C.E., the* Mahabharata *emphasizes the importance of sons, the necessity of dharma, the obligations of kingship, the benefits of right action and of ascetic practice, and the integral relationship between one's own happiness and the happiness of others. Many of the characters featured in the* Mahabharata *are named or alluded to in earlier sacred texts such as the Yajur Veda, the Satapatha Brahmana, and the Chandogya Upanisad.*

Unlike the idealized characters of the Ramayana, *the* Mahabharata's *characters are portrayed as being victims of typically human flaws: greed, jealousy, pride, lust for revenge, and lack of sound moral judgment. The epic chronicles the lives, adventures, and misfortunes of several kings and sages, queens and fair maidens, but its central story is the battle between two sets of cousins, the Pandavas and the Kauravas, which takes place at Kurukshetra. The Pandavas emerge victorious with the help of the god Krishna, who appears in this story as an avatar, or incarnation, of Vishnu. Krishna serves as the charioteer and counselor of the Pandava prince Arjuna. Arjuna, the son of King Pandu's wife Kunti (who has been taught by a sage how to invoke the gods to obtain children), is identified as the son of Indra. Arjuna despairs at having to shed the blood of his own relatives, and hesitates to engage in battle. His dilemma and Krishna's advice is the central story of the* Bhagavad Gita, *the eighteenth book of the Mahabharata, which has become immensely*

Reprinted by permission from *The Mahabharata*, translated by Chakravarthi V. Narasimhan.

popular in its own right and is often printed separately from the longer epic. While the Mahabharata *may seem preoccupied with violence and aggression, its message ultimately promotes peace and reconciliation.*

VII

. . . In due course Śakuni, the son of the king of Gāndhāra, brought his sister, endowed with great wealth, to the Kurus, and gave her away in the proper manner to Dhṛtarāṣṭra. He then returned to his own capital. The beautiful Gāndhārī pleased all the Kurus by her exemplary conduct and respectful attentions.

One day Gāndhārī pleased Vyāsa, who had arrived at the palace hungry and fatigued. He granted her a boon, and she expressed her desire to have one hundred sons like her husband. Some time afterwards, she became pregnant, but bore the burden in her womb for two years without being delivered, and was therefore much afflicted with grief.

Meanwhile she heard that Pāṇḍu's queen Kuntī had borne a son, bright as the morning sun. She could not help feeling that in her case the time of bearing the child in the womb was too long. Deprived of reason by her grief, she struck her womb with force, without the knowledge of Dhṛtarāṣṭra. Thereupon she brought forth a hard mass of flesh like an iron ball which had been in her womb for two years. On learning this, Vyāsa, best of ascetics, soon came to her and saw that mass of flesh. He asked Gāndhārī, "What have you done?" She revealed the truth to him, saying "Having heard that Kuntī had first given birth to a prince, bright as the sun, I struck at my womb in grief. You gave me the boon that I should bear one hundred sons. But only this ball of flesh has emerged instead."

Vyāsa said, "O Gāndhārī, it shall be as I said. I have never uttered a lie even in jest. Let one hundred jars, filled with ghee, be brought quickly and let cool water be sprinkled on this ball of flesh." The ball of flesh, being thus cooled with water, split into parts, each about the size of a thumb. These were then placed in the jars, which were stationed in a concealed spot and carefully watched. The holy one bade Gāndhārī open the lids of the jars only after two years. Having given these instructions and made these arrangements, the holy and wise Vyāsa went to the Himālaya mountains to perform penance.

It was thus that Prince Duryodhana was born. According to the order of birth, however, Yudhiṣṭhira, the eldest son of Pāṇḍu, was senior to him. As soon as a son had been born to him, Dhṛtarāṣṭra said: "Summon the Brāhmaṇas, as well as Bhīṣma and Vidura. The prince Yudhiṣṭhira is the eldest of our line. There is no doubt that he should succeed to the kingdom in his own right."

At that time beasts of prey, jackals, and crows made ominous noises everywhere. Seeing these frightful portents, the assembled Brāhmaṇas and the wise Vidura said to Dhṛtarāṣṭra, "It is clear that your son will be the exterminator of your race. The peace of the family depends upon his being abandoned. There will be great calamity in keeping him." Though he was thus adjured by Vidura and by all those learned Brāhmaṇas, the king did not heed their advice, because of his natural love for his son. There were born within a month one hundred sons to Dhṛtarāṣṭra, and also a daughter, Duḥśalā.

VIII

The chief of the Yadus, named Śūra, had a son, Vasudeva, and a daughter, Pṛthā, whose beauty was matchless on earth. As had been promised, Śūra gave Pṛthā in adoption to his childless cousin and close friend, the high-souled Kuṅtibhoja. Hence she also came to be known as Kuṅtī. In her adopted father's house Kuṅtī's duties were to worship the family deities and look after the guests.

One day, by her solicitude, she pleased the terrible and notoriously short-tempered sage Durvāsa, who was learned in the mysteries. Through his foresight, Durvāsa could see that Kuṅtī would have difficulty in conceiving sons. He therefore taught her an invocatory spell, saying to her, "Through the radiance of those celestials whom you invoke by this spell, you will obtain progeny."

After a while the virtuous Kuṅtī out of curiosity tried the spell and invoked the sun god. That brilliant deity the Sun, who sees everything in the world, immediately appeared before her, and the beautiful Kuṅtī was overcome by astonishment at this wondrous sight. The light of the universe, the Sun, got her with child. Thus was born the hero of divine ancestry, known all over the world by the name of Karṇa, the foremost of warriors. He was born wearing armour and earrings. Thereafter the Sun restored Kuṅtī's maidenhood and returned to heaven.

Afraid of her friends and relatives, Kuṅtī resolved to hide her transgression. She accordingly threw her handsome son into the river, from which he was rescued by a charioteer. He and his wife Rādhā brought up the infant as their own son, giving him the name of Vasuṣeṇa, because he was endowed with wealth even at birth, namely armour and earrings. Vasuṣeṇa grew up to be very strong and energetic, and adept in the use of all weapons. He used to worship the Sun until the afternoon sun scorched his back. When he was thus engaged in worship, the heroic, truthful, and high-souled Vasuṣeṇa would give away to the Brāhmaṇas anything on earth which they requested of him.

Once Iṅdra, the protector of all living things, came to him for alms, adopting the guise of a Brāhmaṇa, and asked him for his armour and the earrings. Perplexed though he was at Iṅdra's request, he cut off the armour from his body, and also his earrings from his ears, and gave them, dripping with blood, to Iṅdra with joined hands. Greatly surprised at his generosity, Iṅdra gave him the Śakti weapon, saying, "Be your foe a celestial, asura, human being, Gaṇdharva, Nāga, or Rākṣasa, if you hurl this missile at him, it will certainly kill him." The son of Sūrya, who till then was known by the name of Vasuṣeṇa, came to be called Karṇa [the cutter] after this act of unequalled generosity.

IX

Kuṅtibhoja held a svayaṁvara for his beautiful and virtuous daughter. There she saw that tamer of lions and elephants, the mighty Pāṇḍu, in the midst of all the kings present. She chose him for her husband, even as Paulomī chose Iṅdra.

Bhīṣma also obtained for Pāṇḍu, in exchange for much wealth, the daughter of the king of Madra, Mādrī, who was famous for her beauty in all the three worlds, after which he solemnized the marriage of the high-souled Pāṇḍu.

One day, while roaming in the forest, Pāṇḍu saw two deer in the act of mating, and hit both of them with five sharp and swift arrows, embellished with golden feathers. They were an ascetic, the son of a sage, and his wife, with whom he was thus disporting in the form of a deer. "I am the sage Kiṅdama, without equal in austerity," said the deer. "You have killed me in the act of mating in the form of a deer, a form I have assumed out of modesty. Though you will not be visited with the sin of killing a Brāhmaṇa, since you did not know who I was, you shall however be punished similarly: when you are overcome by desire in the company of your wife, you shall also die!"

Thus cursed, Pāṇḍu returned to his capital, and explained his predicament to his queens, after which he said to Kuṅtī: "At my request, you should have children endowed with all good qualities by the grace of a Brāhmaṇa who is a great sage; if you do so, I shall go the same way as those with sons." To this request, Kuṅtī, ever interested in her husband's welfare, replied to Pāṇḍu, "O king, since you so desire, I shall invoke a god as taught me by Durvāsa, so that we may have issue." Pāṇḍu said: "Among the gods Dharma is the one who bestows spiritual merit. Hence I request you to invoke the god Dharma this very day."

Gāṅdhārī had been pregnant for a year when Kuṅtī invoked the eternal Dharma for progeny, worshipping him and repeating in the proper form the invocation which Durvāsa had taught her. She was then united with Dharma in his spiritual form and, in time, gave birth to a fine boy. As soon as the child was born, a voice with no visible source said: "This child will certainly be virtuous. He will be known as Yudhiṣṭhira; he will be famous over the three worlds. He will be splendid, determined, and renowned."

Having been blessed with this virtuous son, Pāṇḍu bade Kuṅtī ask for a son of great physical strength, since the Kṣatriyas were the foremost in strength. In response to her husband's request, Kuṅti invoked Vāyu, who begot the mighty Bhīma, of great strength. On his birth, the supernatural voice said: "This child will be the greatest of all strong men." Duryodhana was born on the very day on which Bhīma was born.

Thereafter the illustrious Pāṇḍu consulted with the great sages and asked Kuṅtī to observe certain vows for one full year. At the end of the period Pāṇḍu said, "O beautiful one, Iṅdra the king of the celestials is pleased. Invoke him and conceive a son." In response, the illustrious Kuṅti invoked Iṅdra, the lord of the celestials, who came to her and begot Arjuna. As soon as the prince was born, a supernatural voice boomed over the whole sky with a loud and deep roar, saying: "O Kuṅti, this child will be as strong as Kārtavīrya and Śibi, invincible in battle as Iṅdra himself. He will spread your fame everywhere, and will acquire many celestial weapons."

After the birth of Kuṅtī's sons, and those of Dhṛtarāṣṭra, Mādrī privately spoke to Pāṇḍu thus, "It is my great grief that, though we are of equal rank, my husband should have sons by Kuṅti alone. If the princess Kuṅti will arrange that I may have sons, she will do me a great kindness, and it will also be of benefit to you."

Thereupon Pāṇḍu again spoke to Kuṅtī privately. He said, "O blessed lady, give me some more sons, and ensure the funeral oblations for myself and my ancestors. O blameless one, aid Mādrī, as though with a raft across the river, by helping her to obtain progeny. Thus you will obtain great renown."

Kuṅtī then said to Mādrī, "Think of some celestial by whose grace you may obtain worthy offspring." Thereupon Mādrī reflected a little and invoked the twin Aśvins. Both of them came to her and sired twin sons, namely Nakula and Sahadeva, unmatched for beauty on earth. On their birth, the supernatural voice said: "The twins will be handsome and good, and will excel all men in beauty, energy, and wealth. They will glow with splendour."

The sages living in Śataśṛṅga[1] invoked blessings on the princes and performed their birth rites with devotion. They named the eldest of Kuṅti's sons Yudhiṣṭhira, the second Bhīmasena, and the third Arjuna. Mādrī's twin sons they named Nakula and Sahadeva. The five sons of Pāṇḍu and the hundred sons of Dhṛtarāṣṭra, the ornaments of the Kuru race, bloomed like lotuses in a lake.

One day Pāṇḍu saw Mādrī adorned with jewels, and his desire was aroused. But as soon as he touched her, he died. Thereupon Mādrī ascended Pāṇḍu's funeral pyre, asking Kuṅtī to bring up her children with kindness and love. Then Vidura, King Dhṛtarāṣṭra, Bhīṣma, and other relatives performed the last rites of Pāṇḍu and Mādrī and offered the funeral oblations.

Thereafter the sons of Pāṇḍu were brought by the citizens to Hastinapura. There the Pāṇḍavas performed all the purifying rites prescribed in the scriptures. They grew up in royal style in their father's house, sporting with the sons of Dhṛtarāṣṭra, whom they excelled in all the boyish games. Bhīma vanquished all the sons of Dhṛtarāṣṭra in various feats. Seeing his extraordinary strength, Duryodhana, the mighty son of Dhṛtarāṣṭra, conceived a lasting enmity towards him.

X

Once the great sage Bharadvāja happened to see the beautiful nymph Dhṛtācī in the sacrificial place, when her dress was accidentally blown aside by the wind. Aroused by this sight, the sage dropped his seed in a vessel [droṇa], in which the wise Droṇa was born. He read all the Scriptures.

Bharadvāja had a royal friend, named Pṛṣata, who had a son named Drupada. Prince Drupada went every day to Bharadvāja's hermitage, where he played and studied with Droṇa. When Pṛṣata died, the mighty Drupada succeeded to the kingdom of the Northern Pāñcālas.

At about the same time the illustrious Bharadvāja also passed away; thereupon, in accordance with his late father's wishes, and being desirous of offspring, Droṇa married Kṛpī, the daughter of Śaradvata. Ever engaged in sacrifices and penance, the pious Kṛpī bore Droṇa a son, named Aśvatthāmā. As soon as he was born, he neighed like a horse. Thereupon a voice from the skies said, "As this child neighed like a horse and could be heard over a great distance, he will be known by the name of Aśvatthāmā [the horse-voiced]."

Droṇa, who was extremely pleased at having a son, then became deeply interested in the study of archery. He heard that the great-souled Paraśurā ma was giving away all his wealth to Brāhmaṇas. Seeing Paraśurāma as lie was leaving for the forest, Droṇa said, "Know me to be Droṇa, best of Brāhmaṇas, who has come to you seeking wealth."

Paraśurāma said, "O treasury of penance! I have already given away to the Brāhmaṇas my gold and whatever wealth I had." "O Paraśurāma," said Droṇa, "give me then all your arms and weapons, and teach me the secrets of launching and withdrawing them." Paraśurāma said: "So be it!" He gave away all his weapons to Droṇa and taught him the science of arms and all its secrets. Droṇa, considering himself amply rewarded and feeling well pleased, went to see his dear friend Drupada.

In due course approaching Drupada, the son of Pṛṣata, Droṇa said, "Know me as your friend." Drupada said: "Our former friendship was based on the bonds of skill; but time, that erodes everything, wears out friendship too." Thus rebuffed by Drupada, the mighty Droṇa was filled with wrath. He reflected for a moment, while he made up his mind as to his course of action, and then went to Hāstinapura, the city of the foremost of the Kurus.

XI

Anxious to give his grandsons a superior education, Bhīṣma inquired about tutors who were brave and well skilled in the science of arms. He decided that the preceptor of the Kurus should be strong, intelligent, and illustrious, and complete master of the science of arms.

When he heard that a stranger had arrived [in Hāstinapura], Bhīṣma knew that this must be Droṇa and decided that he was the right tutor for his grandsons. Welcoming Droṇa, he asked him why he had come to Hāstinapura. Droṇa told him everything. Bhīṣma then appointed Droṇa as the preceptor and gave him various gifts. He presented his grandsons, including the sons of Pāṇḍu, according to custom, and handed them over to Droṇa, who accepted them all as his pupils.

Droṇa called them aside when they saluted him, and said privately to them: "O princes, in my heart I have one special yearning; promise me that you will fulfil it when you have become proficient in arms." To these words the Kuru princes made no reply. Arjuna, however, gave his promise.

Thereupon Droṇa taught Arjuna how to fight from the back of a horse, on an elephant, on a chariot or on the ground, in single combat or in a crowd. He taught him how to fight with the club, the sword, the spear, and the dart. Two of Droṇa's pupils, Duryodhana and Bhīma, became highly proficient in club fighting; Aśvatthāmā surpassed the others in the mysteries of the science of arms; the twins Nakula and Sahadeva outshone everybody in swordsmanship; Yudhisthira was first among car-warriors.

Arjuna reigned supreme in every field; he excelled all in intelligence, in concentration, in strength, and in zest, and was famous unto the limits of the ocean as the foremost of car-warriors. He was unequalled not only in the use of arms but also in his love and regard for his preceptor. Though all the royal pupils received the same instruction, yet the mighty Arjuna by his excellence became the only Atiratha among all the princes. The wicked sons of Dhṛtarāṣṭra became jealous of Bhīma's strength and Arjuna's many accomplishments.

When the sons of Dhṛtarāṣṭra and Pāṇḍu had thus become proficient in arms, Droṇa said to King Dhṛtarāṣṭra, "O king, your sons have completed their studies. Permit them to display their skill." The king replied, with joy in his heart: "O Droṇa, O best of Brāhmaṇas, great is your achievement!" By order of the king, the masons built a huge arena according to the rules, with a grandstand for the king and the royal ladies. Then, with Yudhiṣṭhira at their head, the heroic princes followed each other in the order of their age and began to display their wonderful skill in arms.

At the command of the preceptor, the youthful Arjuna, equipped with leather protector for the finger, his quiver full of arrows, bow in hand, and wearing golden armour, performed the initial rites of propitiation and entered the arena like the evening cloud reflecting the rays of the setting sun. His very entrance caused a stir among the spectators. When they had calmed down a little, Arjuna displayed before his preceptor his easy mastery of arms and his great skill in the use of the sword, the bow, and the club.

While the spectators were watching Arjuna's feats in wide-eyed wonder, that conqueror of hostile cities, Karṇa, entered the spacious arena. The entire assembly of people remained motionless staring at the newcomer. Curious to know his name, they asked one another in agitation, "Who is he?" Then, in a voice deep as thunder, Karṇa, foremost of eloquent men, said to Arjuna, whom he did not know to be his brother: "O Arjuna, I shall repeat before these spectators all that you have just done. Do not be surprised." Thus challenged, Arjuna was abashed and angry, but Duryodhana was touched with affection for the challenger. With the permission of Droṇa, the powerful Karṇa, ever fond of battle, duplicated all the feats that Arjuna had displayed a little earlier.

Thereupon Duryodhana with his brothers embraced Karṇa with joy and spoke to him thus: "O mighty hero, welcome to you! Your arrival is our good fortune. The entire Kuru kingdom and I myself are at your service." Karṇa replied, "I desire only your friendship."

Karṇa then challenged Arjuna to a duel. When the two heroes were ready with their great bows, Kṛpī, the son of Śaradvata, who knew all the rules governing such duels, said: "O mighty hero, tell us of your father and mother, of your family, and of the royal line which you adorn. It is only after knowing your lineage that Arjuna can decide whether or not to fight with you." Duryodhana announced, "O preceptor, it is said that royalty may be claimed by three classes of men, namely, by a person of noble birth, by a hero, and by a leader of soldiers. If Arjuna is unwilling to engage in a duel with one who is not a king, I shall install Karṇa at once as the king of Aṅga."

Without delay the mighty car-warrior Karṇa was seated on a golden seat, and crowned as the king of Aṅga by those learned in the rites, with unhusked rice, flowers, waterpots, gold, and much wealth. When the cheers subsided, Karṇa said to the Kaurava king, Duryodhana, "What can I give you compared with your gift of a kingdom? O great king, I shall do your bidding." Duryodhana replied, "I seek only your friendship." Then Karṇa said, "So be it!" They thereupon joyfully embraced each other and felt very happy.

Having obtained Karṇa, Duryodhana forgot his fears aroused by Arjuna's skill in arms. The heroic Karṇa, accomplished in arms, spoke words of comfort to Duryodhana. Yudhiṣṭhira too was impressed with the conviction that there was no bowman on earth like Karṇa.

XII

One day the preceptor Droṇa called his pupils together and asked for his dakṣiṇā[1] from them all. He said, "I want you to capture the king of Pāñcāla, Drupada, in battle and bring him securely to me. That will be the most precious dakṣiṇā you can give me." Saying "So be it!" and armed with quivers of arrows, the princes mounted their cars and went with Droṇa to win wealth for their preceptor. They attacked the Pāñcālas and killed them, and then besieged the capital of the famous Drupada. Successful in capturing Drupada, along with his ministers, they brought him to Droṇa.

Droṇa, remembering his former enmity towards Drupada, now humiliated, bereft of wealth, and completely subdued, spoke thus to him, "I have quickly laid waste your kingdom and your capital. Do you wish to renew our old friendship and to receive your life at my hands?" Smiling, he added, "O king, be not afraid for your life. We Brāhmaṇas are lenient. I seek your friendship again. I shall grant you one half of your kingdom. You may rule the territory lying to the south of the Gaṅgā, and I shall rule the northern part. O king of Pāñcāla, if it pleases you, know that I am your friend from now on." Drupada said, "O Brāhman, such generosity is not surprising in men of noble soul and great strength. I am pleased to accept your friendly offer and I desire your eternal friendship."

Then Droṇa released Drupada, and with a pleased heart he bestowed upon him half the kingdom. Drupada, however, was unable to recover his peace of mind, being obsessed by his hatred of Droṇa. He knew he could not hope to avenge his defeat by superior force, nor by spiritual power, in which too he was aware of being weak. Hence King Drupada desired the birth of a son, who would be the instrument of his revenge.

XIII

Meanwhile the wicked-minded Duryodhana continued to nurse his jealousy of Bhīma's superior strength and Arjuna's many accomplishments, and Kama, Śakuni, and many other followers of Duryodhana plotted to kill the Pāṇḍavas. The Pāṇḍavas came to know all this, being in the confidence of Vidura, and were able to protect themselves.

One day, on the instructions of Dhṛtarāṣṭra, some clever courtiers depicted the charms of the city of Vāraṇāvata. They referred to the festival of Paśupati [Śiva] which had begun in that city of Vāraṇāvata and described the concourse of people gathered there as the most splendid in the world. The king, noticing that the Pāṇḍavas' interest had been aroused, said to them, "O my sons, if you wish to attend the festival of Vāraṇāvata, go there with your friends and followers, and enjoy yourselves for some time. You may then return to Hāstinapura."

When the king thus spoke to the high-minded Pāṇḍavas, the wicked Duryodhana became very happy. Summoning Purocana, one of the ministers, privately, he said, "On the suggestion of Dhṛtarāṣṭra the Pāṇḍavas are going to Vāraṇāvata, where they will participate in the festival for some time. Go there before them, and erect a splendid quadrangular palace similar to an armoury. In erecting that house, use hemp, resin, and any other inflammable material that is available; but do it in such a way that the Pāṇḍavas and others may not suspect you or examine the structure and find out that it is made of inflammable stuff. After completing the house, invite the Pāṇḍavas with a great show of respect to live in it with Kuntī and all their friends. When they have relaxed and begun to enjoy themselves in the city of Vāraṇāvata, and when they are sleeping in that house without suspicion or fear, set fire to its gateway." Purocana, who was ever in Duryodhana's confidence, repaired speedily to Vāraṇāvata and carried out the prince's instructions faithfully.

Meanwhile the Pāṇḍavas got ready to depart for Vāraṇāvata. They got into their cars, yoked with fine horses fleet as the wind. When ascending their chariots, they felt uneasy and touched the feet of Bhīṣma, of King Dhṛtarāṣṭra, of the high-souled Droṇa, Kṛpa, and Vidura, and of all the other elders. When everyone else had left, the learned Vidura, conversant with all aspects of virtue, privately warned Yudhiṣṭhira and made him aware of the dangers ahead, after which he bade them farewell and returned to his house. The Pāṇḍavas then left for Vāraṇāvata, and were greeted by the people of the town on their arrival.

Welcomed by the citizens and greeting them in return, the Pāṇḍavas entered the populous and decorated city. When they had lived there for ten days, Purocana spoke to them about the house, called "Śiva" [blessed], though it was in truth the very opposite. Visiting that house, and smelling the odour of fat mixed with ghee and lac products, Yudhiṣṭhira observed to Bhīma that the building was made of inflammable materials. "If this house is known to be a fire-trap" said Bhīma, " then let us return to the safe place where we lived first." Yudhiṣṭhira said, "I think we should live here, without showing any suspicion; but we must seek some sure means of escape. Let us excavate in all secrecy, this very day, an underground exit. If we can keep it secret, then the fire will not consume us."

Just then a friend of Vidura, well skilled in excavation work, came and spoke thus to the Pāṇḍavas in private. "I have been sent by Vidura; I am an expert in excavation. Tell me what work you desire me to perform." Yudhiṣṭhira replied: "O friend, I know you to be a dear friend of Vidura, pure, true, and ever devoted to him. There is no predicament of ours which the learned Vidura does not know. The danger anticipated by Vidura is now very near. Deliver us from this without Purocana's knowledge." The miner replied, "So be it!" He began carefully and secretly the work of excavation, and soon he had made a big underground passage leading out of the house.

A full year came and went. Seeing them living cheerfully and without suspicion, Purocana was very pleased, and thought the time had come. Observing Purocana in such a frame of mind, Yudhiṣṭhira said to Bhīma, Arjuna, and the twins Nakula and Sahadeva, "The pitiless and sinful Purocana thinks that we are unsuspecting, and he has thus been completely taken in. I think that now is the time for our escape."

One night, on the occasion of an almsgiving, Kuṅtī invited a large number of Brāhmaṇas and also a number of ladies to dinner. They ate and drank and enjoyed themselves to their heart's content. And late in the night they all returned home with Kuṅtī's leave. The same night, impelled by fate, a Niṣāda woman with her five sons came for food, and she too enjoyed herself thoroughly. Then she went to sleep there along with her five sons.

When all the citizens had gone to bed and a strong breeze was blowing, Bhīma set fire to the house, in which Purocana too was sleeping. Thereupon the fire began to blaze with intensity and with a mighty roar which awoke the people of the city. Suspecting what was afoot, the people said, "The wicked Purocana built this house under the directions of Duryodhana, and he has now set fire to it. That evil man has burnt those best of men, the innocent and unsuspecting Pāṇḍavas, and has himself been burnt to death, as decreed by fate." Meanwhile the sorrowful Pāṇḍavas emerged with their mother out of the underground passage and left unnoticed. Bhīma, endued as he was with great speed and strength, carried his mother and all his brothers.

In the morning all the people of the city came to the spot to see what had happened to the Pāṇḍavas. When they put out the fire they saw that the house was made of lac and that the minister Purocana had been burnt to death. They then began to look for the Pāṇḍavas. Seeing the innocent Niṣāda woman who had been burnt to death with her five sons, and taking them to be Kuṅtī and the five Pāṇḍavas, the citizens then informed Dhṛtarāṣṭra that the Pāṇḍavas as well as the minister Purocana had been burnt to death.

When he heard the very unpleasant news of the death of the Pāṇḍavas, King Dhṛtarāṣṭra displayed great sorrow. The other Kauravas also loudly bemoaned the fate of the Pāṇḍavas. Only Vidura showed little grief, for he knew the truth. Meanwhile, leaving the city of Vāraṇāvata, the Pāṇḍavas proceeded speedily in a southern direction. Guiding themselves in the dark by the stars, they soon reached a dense forest where they slept that night.

XIV

Close to the place where the Pāṇḍavas slept, a rākṣasa named Hidiṃba lived in a śāla tree. Scenting the presence of human beings, that huge man-eating monster spoke thus to his sister: "It is a long time since my favourite food has come my way. My mouth waters in anticipation. I shall overpower the man, cut his throat, and drink my fill of hot, fresh, and frothy blood. Go and find out who is lying asleep in this forest."

The rākṣasī, whose name was also Hidiṃbā, went as her brother had bidden her to the place where the Pāṇḍavas were resting. There she saw the Pāṇḍavas and Kuṅtī fast asleep, while the invincible Bhīma sat awake, keeping watch. Seeing him who resembled a śāla tree and who was uniquely handsome, the rākṣasī was filled with desire. As she was capable of taking on any form, she assumed an excellent human shape and slowly approached the mighty Bhīma.

She said: "O divine creature, I have been sent here on a scouting expedition by my brother of evil disposition, the rākṣasa, who has the intention of eating your flesh. I tell you truly, however, after seeing you, radiant as a celestial, I do not desire anybody else but you as my husband. O mighty-armed hero, let me save you from the rākṣasa, my brother, who eats human flesh. O sinless one, become my husband, and let us live in mountain caves."

Bhīma replied: "O rākṣasī, I desist from fighting your wicked brother only because I am afraid of awakening my mother and brothers who are fast asleep. O you with beautiful eyes, know that no one, be he rākṣasa or yakṣa, Gaṇdharva or human, is capable of overpowering me.

As his sister had been away for a long time, the king of the rākṣasas, Hidiṁba, got down from his tree and came to the spot where the Pāṇḍavas were sleeping. He saw his sister in human form, her head adorned with garlands of flowers and her face radiant as the full moon. The man-eater, guessing why she had assumed that charming human form, became very angry. He said to her, "I shall even now kill you along with all those on whose behalf you are trying to betray me."

Seeing that the rākṣasa was so annoyed with his sister, Bhīma smiled and said, "O Hidiṁba, why do you disturb these people who are sleeping peacefully? O wicked rākṣasa, fight me first, without loss of time. When I have killed you, men frequenting this forest will no longer be bothered by you, and can walk here in peace."

Hidiṁba readily accepted Bhīma's challenge. Fighting like two large and full-grown elephants mad with rage, they pulled down the trees and tore off the creepers that grew around. The clash between the two awakened the sleeping Pāṇḍavas. Rising from sleep, those best of men and their mother Kuṅtī were amazed on seeing the extraordinary beauty of the rākṣasī Hidimbā. They also saw Bhīma and the rākṣasī Hidiṁba already engaged in combat, dragging each other to and fro, and eager to overwhelm each other, like two strong lions. Arjuna said, "O Bhīma, let me finish off the rākṣasa since you are tired and may need some rest." When Arjuna said these words, Bhīma was overcome by anger. He dashed Hidiṁba to the ground with all his might and killed him like a beast.

Thereafter Bhīma said to the rākṣasī Hidiṁba, "I know that rākṣasas avenge themselves on their foes by alluring deceptions. Therefore, O Hidiṁbā, begone!" Thereupon, respectfully saluting Kuṅtī and Yudhiṣṭhira with joined hands, the rākṣasī Hidiṁbā said to them, "O respected lady, you are aware of the pangs that the god of love makes women suffer. O blessed lady, I am suffering them on account of Bhīma. Think of me as a fool or a devotee or a follower, but let me have your son as my husband. Let me go away at will, taking this handsome hero with me. Trust me, O blessed lady. I promise to bring him back."

Yudhiṣṭhira said, "O lady with the speed of fancy! You two may sport as you will during the day, but you must always bring him back every night." Having promised this by saying, "So be it!", the rākṣasī Hidiṁbā took Bhīma with her and went away. Assuming a most beautiful form, and wearing many ornaments, she sported with Bhīma.

In course of time, the rākṣasī Hidiṁbā bore Bhīma a mighty son with terrible eyes, large mouth, pointed ears, copper-like lips, sharp teeth, and fearful appearance. His mother remarked that his head was bald, like a pot, and accordingly they gave him the name of Ghaṭotkaca. He was deeply devoted to the Pāṇḍavas, and became a great favourite of theirs—almost one of them. In time it was to be seen that Ghaṭotkaca had been created by the illustrious Iṅdra for the destruction of the matchless Karṇa, and in order to counteract the Śakti weapon that Iṅdra had given him.

XV

The heroic Pāṇḍavas resumed their wanderings and moved from forest to forest, continuing to study the scriptures, namely the Vedas, the Vedāñgas, and all other moral sciences. At last they saw their grandsire Vyāsa. Respectfully greeting the illustrious Vyāsa, they stood, along with their mother, with joined hands before him. Vyāsa said, "Not far from here is a beautiful city, where you will be safe. There you may live in concealment until my return." Vyāsa then comforted them and Kuṅtī too, and took them to the city of Ekacakra, where they lived for a while in the house of a Brāhmaṇa.

After many days had passed, a Brāhmaṇa of great austerity came to live in the house of the Pāṇḍavas' host. Kuṅtī and her sons asked the Brāmaṇa if he would tell them about his experiences. Toward the end of his narrative, he spoke to them of the wonderful svayaṁvara of Draupadī, the Pāñcāla princess. He also spoke of the birth of Dhṛṣṭadyumna, of Śikhaṇḍī, and of Draupadī, who was born of no woman, but emerged from the fire in the great sacrifice of Drupada. Questioned further, the Brāhmaṇa related in detail the circumstances of the birth of Draupadī, as follows:

Unable to forget his defeat at Droṇa's hands, King Drupada wandered among the hermitages of many Brāhmaṇas in search of experts in sacrificial rites. He was dissatisfied with the children and relatives that he already had and was always despondent; his only thought was of revenging himself on Droṇa.

When he met two sages named Yaja and Upayaja, who were studious and self controlled, Drupada requested Yaja to perform a sacrifice by which he could obtain an invincible son able to kill Droṇa in battle. As a reward, he offered Yaja ten million kine. Yaja agreed to perform the sacrifice for the destruction of Droṇa, and began to collect the various ingredients for the sacrifice. In view of the importance of the sacrifice he sought the assistance of Upayaja, who coveted nothing for himself.

King Drupada set about making the preparations needed to ensure the success of the sacrifice, which was begun in due course. When Yaja poured the sanctified libation on the fire, there emerged from the flame a boy who looked like a celestial, and was as bright as the fire from which he had arisen. He wore a crown and excellent armour, and was armed with a sword and a bow and arrows; and he roared frequently.

From the same sacrificial fire emerged a daughter, blessed with good fortune, who was called Pāñcālī. Though her complexion was dark, she was captivating and beautiful, with eyes like lotus petals and curly blue hair. She appeared like a veritable celestial damsel in human form, and her body was redolent with the sweet fragrance of the blue lotus. In sum, no maiden on earth could compare with her in appearance.

The Brāhmaṇas said, "As this son of Drupada possesses confidence and courage, and as he was so brilliant at birth, let him be called Dhṛṣṭadyumna. Since this daughter is dark in complexion, let her be called Kṛṣṇā."[3] Thus were born in the great sacrifice the son and daughter of Drupada.

After hearing the Brāhmaṇa's narrative, Kuṅtī became restless. She said, "O Yudhiṣṭhira, we have spent many nights in the Brāhmana's house and passed our lives very pleasantly in this beautiful city, living on charity. We have now heard that alms are to be had easily in Pāñcāla and that King Drupada is devoted to the Brāhmaṇas. It is my view that one should not stay too long in one place. Therefore, O son, if you agree, we may now move to Pāñcāla." She spoke similarly to Bhīma, Arjuna, and the twins Nakula and Sahadeva, and they all said, "So be it!" Then Kuṅtī and the Pāṇḍavas saluted and thanked the Brāhmaṇa who had been their host at Ekacakra and started for the beautiful city of the high-souled Drupada.

XVI

The Pāṇḍavas at last arrived in the Pāñcāla country. After seeing the city, they took up their residence in a potter's shed. King Drupada had always cherished a secret desire to give his daughter Draupadī in marriage to Arjuna, the son of Pāṇḍu, but he never spoke of it. Having Arjuna in mind, the Pāñcāla king caused a very rigid bow to be made. He then erected a device in the sky and set up above it a golden target.

King Drupada made the following announcement: "Whoever is able to string this bow and then with these arrows to shoot the mark above the device will obtain my daughter." This proclamation of Drupada's was published far and wide, and in response to it all the kings came there, including Duryodhana and the Kurus, accompanied by Karṇa. There came also many illustrious sages desirous of seeing the svayaṁvara.

Seated in the arena along with the Brāhmaṇas, the Pāṇḍavas observed the unequalled prosperity of the Pāñcāla king. When the arena became absolutely quiet, Dhṛṣṭadyumna stood in the centre of the stage and said in a majestic voice, "Hearken, O ye assembled kings—here is the bow, these are the arrows, and there is the target. You have to shoot the target through the aperture in the device with these fine and sharp arrows. Truly I say, whosoever, being of noble birth, handsome, and strong, performs this difficult feat shall obtain today for his bride my sister Draupadī; I do not speak falsely." After giving this pledge to the assembled kings, Dhṛṣṭadyumna turned to his sister, and informed her of the names, the lineage, and the accomplishments of the assembled kings.

"O blessed girl!" said Dhṛṣṭadyumna. "All the Kṣatriyas celebrated in the world have gathered here on your account. These heroes will try to shoot the target for you. Among them, O fortunate girl, you shall take as your husband him who is able to shoot the target."

Meanwhile the young princes present, decked with earrings, bragged to one another; and each of them, believing himself to be the most skilled in arms, stood up arrogantly flaunting his weapons. But when they tried to perform the prescribed feat, those mighty princes were unable to bend that rigid bow and were all tossed to the ground where they lay motionless. Their bracelets shattered and their earrings crushed, they gave vent to exclamations of woe, having lost their hope of obtaining Draupadī.

When all the kings had failed in their attempts to string the bow, the large-hearted Arjuna rose from the midst of the Brāhmaṇas. While the assembled Brāhmaṇas were talking among themselves, Arjuna came to the bow and stood there like a mountain. He first walked round the bow in due form. Then, bowing his head, he lifted the bow and strung it in an instant. He took up the five arrows, shot the target through the aperture, and felled it to the ground. Thereupon a great tumult rose in the sky and also a great clamour in the arena, while the celestials showered divine flowers on Arjuna's head.

King Drupada was delighted at the feat of the unknown Brāhmaṇa, and desired to assist him with his army. When he announced his wish and intention of bestowing his daughter on that high-souled Brāhmaṇa, the assembled kings, all filled with rage, exchanged glances. Those powerful princes, with arms like iron maces, rose in a body and rushed upon Drupada with their weapons to kill him. Seeing all those princes surging towards him in anger and armed with bows and arrows, Drupada sought refuge with the Brāhmaṇas. Bhīma and Arjuna at once arose to resist the kings advancing upon Drupada like mad elephants, and fought them fearlessly. In the course of the fight Bhīma overcame Śalya in single combat. Seeing that feat of Bhīma, the Lord Kṛṣṇa surmised that both of them were the sons of Kuṅtī. He persuaded the princes to desist, saying, "She has been won fairly." Those heroes among men, Bhīma and Arjuna, who had been severely injured by their enemies, at last emerged from the crowd, looking resplendent, and followed by Draupadī.

Meanwhile, at home, Kuṅtī began to fear various evils that might have befallen her sons, since they did not return even though it was past the time for alms. Out of her love for her sons, Kuṅtī thought that something terrible must have happened to them.

It was late in the afternoon when Arjuna, attended by many Brāhmaṇas and with a Brāhmana preceding him, entered the humble potter's shed, like the sun emerging from the clouds. Those best of men, Bhīma and Arjuna, then came to their mother, and represented Draupadī to her as the "alms" they had obtained that day. Kuṅtī, who was inside the room, did not see her sons or Draupadī. She therefore replied from within, "Share equally, all of you, whatever you have got." A moment later she came out, saw the maiden, and exclaimed, "Alas! what have I said?"

XVII

Kṛṣṇa and Balarāma, who had a shrewd suspicion that the heroes of the svayaṁvara were the Pāṇḍavas, now came to the potter's shed where the Pāṇḍavas were living. Yudhiṣṭhira, foremost of the Kuru race, made kind inquiries about Kṛṣṇa's welfare, and said, "O Vāsudeva, how were you able to trace us, living as we are in hiding?" Kṛṣṇa smilingly replied, "O king, even if a fire is hidden, it can be traced. Who else among men, save the Pāṇḍavas, can perform such feats?" He then blessed them, took leave of them, and went away, accompanied by Balarāma.

Meanwhile Drupada had sent his priest with a message to the Pāṇḍavas. The priest said, "A goodly feast has been prepared for the bridegroom's party by King Drupada to celebrate his daughter's wedding. After completing your daily observances, please join him without delay, along with Draupadī. These splendid cars, adorned with golden lotuses and drawn by swift horses, are truly fit for kings and are at your disposal. I request you all kindly to mount them and drive to the palace of King Drupada." The Pāṇḍavas accepted the invitation of the king. They sent away the priest and, having seated Kuntī and Draupadī on one of the cars, they ascended those splendid vehicles and drove to the palace. As befitted a royal banquet, well-dressed waiters and waitresses and accomplished cooks served excellent dishes on plates made of gold and silver.

After dinner King Drupada addressed Prince Yudhiṣṭhira as if he were a Brāhmaṇa. Cheerfully he asked that illustrious son of Kuntī, "How should we treat you, as Kṣatriyas or Brāhmaṇas?" Yudhiṣṭhira replied: "O king, we are Kṣatriyas, sons of the famous Pāṇḍu. I am the eldest of the sons of Kuntī and these two are Bhīma and Arjuna, who won your daughter in the svayaṁvara. The twins Nakula and Sahadeva are standing near Draupadī. So banish the sorrow weighing on your mind, for we too are Kṣatriyas. This your daughter is like a lotus which has been transplanted from one lake to another." On hearing this, King Drupada was filled with delight. His eyes showed his pleasure and for some time he could not answer Yudhiṣṭhira.

Drupada said, after a while, "O hero, take the hand of my daughter in holy wedlock with all due rites, or give her hand to whomsoever you think best." Yudhiṣṭhira replied: "O king, Draupadī shall be the queen of us all, as ordained by our mother." Drupada then said, "O descendant of Kuru, I know it is permissible for a husband to have many wives, but a wife has never been allowed to have more than one husband. Pure as you are, and acquainted with the moral code, do not commit a sinful act that is against both the scriptures and usage."

Yudhiṣṭhira replied: "O great king, morality is subtle and we do not know its ways. Let us therefore tread the path of our illustrious predecessors." Thereupon they all discussed this matter; and at that very time Vyāsa came there by chance. King Drupada welcomed the great sage with due rites, after which he sought the views of that illustrious man on the subject of the marriage of Draupadī.

Vyāsa replied: "Once upon a time, there lived in a hermitage the daughter of an illustrious sage. She was beautiful and chaste, but she did not get a husband. She propitiated the god Śiva by her strict penance. The Lord appeared before her and said, 'Ask of me whatever you wish.' In reply, she repeatedly said to the Lord, the giver of boons, 'I desire to have a husband endowed with all good qualities.' Śiva gave her the boon with a joyful heart and said, 'You shall have five husbands.'

"She said again, 'O Śiva, I desire to have only one accomplished husband.' The god of gods, well pleased with her, then replied in these auspicious words, 'You have asked me five times, "Give me a husband." O blessed one, it shall therefore be as you have asked. All this will come to pass in one of your future incarnations.'

Vyāsa continued, "O Drupada! That maiden of celestial grace was reborn as your daughter. The faultless Draupadī of the Pṛṣata family was predestined to be the wife of five men. After severe penances, the divine Lakṣmī herself emerged from the great sacrifice as your daughter, for the benefit of the Pāṇḍavas. O king, that beautiful goddess, on whom all the celestials attend, becomes the wife of five husbands, impelled by her own destiny. She was created by Brahmā for this very purpose. Now, knowing all this, do as you desire."

Drupada then said, "I now understand that in her former life Draupadī asked the Lord five times, 'Give me a husband.' The Lord granted her boon accordingly, and he himself knows the propriety of this." Thereupon King Drupada and his son Dhṛṣṭadyumna made preparations for the marriage. The king gave away his daughter Draupadī, duly bathed and adorned with many gems. Then those mighty car-warriors, the ornaments of the Kuru race, took Draupadī's hand day by day in succession. When the wedding celebrations were over, the Pāṇḍavas passed their days happily in the capital of the Pāñcāla king Drupada.

. . .

XXI

Lingering in that hall, Duryodhana inspected it at leisure along with Śakuni. He saw many unique things such as he had never beheld in the city of Hāstinapura. Once he reached a transparent surface and, mistaking it for water, drew up his clothes and went around the hall; when he discovered his error he felt ashamed and unhappy. Then he mistook a pond with crystal-clear water, adorned with lotuses, for land and fell into the water fully clothed. The servants laughed at this, but provided him with dry clothes at the royal command of Yudhiṣṭhira. The mighty Bhīma, Arjuna, the twins, and everybody else laughed at Duryodhana's discomfiture.

Duryodhana could not forgive their derision but, to save appearances, he ignored it. He then took leave of the Pāṇḍavas, but having witnessed the wonderful opulence displayed at the great rājasūya sacrifice, he returned to the city of Hāstinapura sad at heart. On his return, Śakuni said, "O Duryodhana, why are you going about sighing like this?" Duryodhana replied, "O uncle, I have observed the whole world brought under the sovereignty of Yudhiṣṭhira by the great Arjuna's skill in the use of arms. I have also seen the great sacrifice of Yudhiṣṭhira, which can be compared only to that performed by the glorious Indra among the gods. Because of this, I am filled with envy which burns me day and night, and I feel dried up like a small pond in the summer."

"O Duryodhana," said Śakuni, "you should not envy Yudhiṣṭhira. After all, the Pāṇḍavas are enjoying their own good fortune." This was no consolation to Duryodhana, who replied: "If you will let me do so, I shall conquer them with your help and that of the great car-warriors who are our allies. Then the world will be mine, including that opulent assembly hall of great wealth, while all the kings will do me homage." Śakuni said, "The Pāṇḍavas cannot be defeated in battle even by the gods; they are great car-warriors, expert bowmen, learned in the science of arms, and eager for battle. But I know how Yudhiṣṭhira can be overcome."

Duryodhana's spirits picked up on hearing this. He said, "O uncle, tell me how they can be defeated without risk to our friends." Śakuni said, "Yudhiṣṭhira is fond of gambling, though he is no expert at throwing the dice. If he is invited to a game, he will not be able to resist the temptation. I am an expert gambler, without equal in the three worlds. Therefore ask

Yudhiṣṭhira to play a game of dice. But, Duryodhana, you must inform the king, your father, about this. With his permission, I shall defeat Yudhiṣṭhira without a doubt."

Duryodhana readily agreed to this plan. Śakuni then went up to Dhṛtarāṣṭra and said, "O great king, you should know that Duryodhana has become pallid, wasted, weak, and absent-minded." Dhṛtarāṣṭra sent for his son and said to him, "O my son, why are you so sad? If you can confide in me, tell me why." "O king," replied Duryodhana, "I am unhappy on seeing the boundless wealth of the enemy. I am obsessed with this thought, so that I cannot obtain any peace of mind."

Śakuni then said, "O king, listen to the stratagem by which you can gain the matchless wealth of Yudhiṣṭhira which you have seen. I am adept in the art of throwing the dice. Yudhiṣṭhira likes to gamble, though he does not know how to throw the dice. If invited to play, he will surely respond. Therefore, ask him to a game." Dhṛtarāṣṭra said, "The wise Vidura is my adviser on whose counsel I act. I shall first consult him and I shall then know how to decide this issue." Duryodhana said, "If Vidura is consulted, this plan will not go through, and, O king of kings, if you stop this, I shall certainly commit suicide."

On hearing these sad words of his beloved son, Dhṛtarāṣṭra ordered his servants, "Let the masons quickly build a commodious and beautiful hall with a thousand pillars and a hundred doors. It must be well built and easily accessible, adorned with gems all over and provided with dice. Let me know when the hall is completed."

When the hall was ready, King Dhṛtarāṣṭra said to Vidura, his chief adviser, "Go to Prince Yudhiṣṭhira and request him on my behalf to come here quickly, along with his brothers, to see this wonderful assembly hall of mine, adorned with costly jewels and furnished with luxurious couches. We shall also have a friendly game of dice."

Vidura said, "O king, I do not like your message. Do not act thus. I apprehend the destruction of the family, for I fear there will soon be a quarrel amongst the brothers." Dhṛtarāṣṭra said, "O Vidura, if fate so ordains, such a quarrel will not trouble me. This world does not act on its own, but only at the will of the Creator and under the influence of fate. Therefore, go to the king as I have directed, and quickly fetch here the invincible Yudhiṣṭhira."

Thus Vidura was forced by Dhṛtarāṣṭra to go to fetch the wise Pāṇḍavas. When he reached Yudhisthira, the latter said, "I can see that you are unhappy. Vidura, is your mission one of peace? Are the sons of Dhṛtarāṣṭra behaving well? Are the subjects docile?" Vidura replied sorrowfully, "The king is well, as are his sons, but he is obstinate and selfish, and bent on self-aggrandisement. The king of the Kurus asked me to tell you, having first made kind enquiries after your happiness and welfare, 'This hall matches yours in appearance, my son; so come and visit it along with your brothers. In it, O Yudhiṣṭhira, have an enjoyable game of dice with your brothers. We will be delighted if you can come, and so will all the Kurus assembled here.'"

After giving this message, Vidura continued, "You will see gamblers and cheats placed there by King Dhṛtarāṣṭra. I have come to give you this message. Do as you think fit." After considering the situation, Yudhiṣṭhira replied, "Terrible cheats and deceitful gamblers will be there. But we all have to submit to fate and. the will of the Creator. I do not wish to play with cheats, and I am reluctant to gamble with Śakuni unless that insolent one challenges me in the hall. If challenged, however, I shall never disregard it. This is my firm vow."

Having said this to Vidura, Yudhiṣṭhira quickly ordered everybody to get ready to depart. The next day he started for Hāstinapura with his family and servants, and also the ladies, led by Draupadī. Having reached Hāstinapura, they spent the night happily. Then, early the next morning, they all completed their daily rites and entered the splendid hall full of gamblers.

XXII

Śakuni said, "O king, here are people gathered to capacity in this hall and ready to play. O Yudhiṣṭhira, now is the time to cast the dice and to agree on the rules of the game." "I have vowed that I shall not refuse to play if I am challenged," replied Yudhiṣṭhira. "O king, destiny is powerful and I am in its grip. Tell me, whom should I take on in this assembly? Who among these players can match my stakes? Answer me, and then let the game begin."

Duryodhana said, "O king, I shall furnish the gems and riches needed for stakes and my uncle Śakuni will play on my behalf." Yudhiṣṭhira replied, "It seems to me that it is wrong for one to play for another. I am sure even you will accept that. However, let it be as you wish." He continued," O king, this expensive chain, rich with gems and adorned with the finest gold, and obtained from the ocean, this is my stake. What is the stake with which you will match it? I am going to win this stake." So saying, he cast the dice. Then Śakuni, who knew the secret of gambling, grabbed the dice. He cast them and then said to Yudhiṣṭhira, "I have won."

Yudhiṣṭhira said, "You won that stake by cheating. Fie on you, O Śakuni! Let us play staking thousands. I now stake these hundred jars, each filled with a thousand gold coins." They played, and again Śakuni claimed, "I have won." When the game had gone on for a while and Yudhiṣṭhira had lost again and again, Śakuni said, "O Yudhiṣṭhira, you have lost the greater part of the wealth of the Pāṇḍavas. Tell me if you have any assets left." Yudhiṣṭhira said, "O king, my city, my kingdom, my lands, the property that does not belong to the Brāhmaṇas, and the subjects who are not Brāhmaṇas—these are my remaining assets. With this as my stake, O king, I shall now play against you." Once more Śakuni cheated when casting the dice and said to Yudhiṣṭhira, "I have won."

Having lost all his wealth, Yudhiṣṭhira said, "This dark young man with crimson eyes, who looks like a lion and is endowed with mighty shoulders, Nakula, is now my stake." Thereupon, Śakuni cast the dice again and claimed that he had won. Yudhiṣṭhira then said, "Sahadeva dispenses justice and has earned a reputation for wisdom throughout the world; though he does not deserve this and is dear to me, I shall stake him." Again Śakuni cheated when casting the dice, and told Yudhiṣṭhira, "I have won."

"O king," said Śakuni, "I have won both the sons of Mādrī, who are dear to you. Apparently Bhīma and Arjuna are even dearer to you, since you do not wish to stake them." Thus taunted, Yudhiṣṭhira said, "I shall now stake Arjuna who enables us to sail through a battle like a boat, who is the conqueror of enemies, who is a vigorous prince and the hero of the world." Having heard this, Śakuni again cheated when casting the dice, and told Yudhiṣṭhira, "I have won."

"O king," Yudhiṣṭhira said, "I shall now offer as my stake Bhīma, our leader, who leads us singlehanded in battle, who has straight eyes and close-set eyebrows, who has the shoulders of a lion and who never forgives an insult, whose strength is unmatched among humans, who is foremost among club-fighters, and who destroys his enemies." Śakuni, cheating while casting the dice, again said to Yudhiṣṭhira, "I have won."

Yudhiṣṭhira then said, "The only person left is myself, dear to my brothers. If I, too, am won we shall accept our misfortune and the lot of the vanquished." Having heard this, Śakuni cheated again when casting the dice, and told Yudhiṣṭhira, "I have won."

Śakuni then said, "There is one stake left that has not been won as yet—your beloved queen. Stake Draupadī, the daughter of the Pāñcāla king, and win back freedom along with her." "O wretch," replied Yudhiṣṭhira, "I shall now stake the slender-waisted and beautiful Draupadī, the princess of Pāñcāla, and play with you." When Yudhiṣṭhira said these words, the assembled elders voiced their disapproval. But, flushed with victory and mad with conceit, Śakuni cast the dice once more and said, "I have won."

Duryodhana said, "O Vidura, go and fetch Draupadī, the beloved spouse of the Pāṇḍavas. Let her clean this house and be one of our servant maids." Vidura said, "O fool, you cannot see that by these words you are binding yourself with cords. You do not realize that you are hanging on a precipice. You do not know that you are behaving like a child, like a deer rousing tigers."

Drunk with pride, Duryodhana ignored this warning, saying, "Fie on Vidura." He noticed Prātikāmī in the hall and told him, in the midst of the venerable assembly, "Prātikāmī, fetch Draupadī here, since you are not afraid of the Pāṇḍavas. Vidura speaks in fear, and he never wished us well."

Accordingly, Prātikāmī went to the Pāṇḍavas' residence and told Draupadī of his errand. Draupadī then said, "O son of a charioteer, go and ascertain from the gambler in the hall whether he lost himself, or me, first. When you have this information, return to me and then lead me there." When Prātikāmī returned with this message from Draupadī, Duryodhana said, "O Duḥśāsana, this son of my charioteer is weak-minded and afraid of Bhīma. Go yourself to Draupadī and seize and bring her here. What can these husbands of hers do, having lost their freedom?"

XXIII

His eyes red with anger, Prince Duḥśāsana rose at his brother's words, and entered the residence of those great car-warriors, the Pāṇḍavas. There he said to the Princess Draupadī, "Come, O Pāñcālī, you have been won. Discard your shyness and look at Duryodhana. O lady whose eyes are like lotus petals, respect the Kurus, who have won you fairly, and enter the hall." On hearing these words, the miserable Draupadī rose up in sorrow and, covering her pale face with her hands, she ran to the ladies' quarters in the palace of the old king. Thereupon Duḥśāsana ran after her in hot pursuit, roaring in anger, and caught hold of her by her long blue wavy tresses. He roughly dragged the defenceless Draupadī by her hair to the hall, while she quivered pitiably like a plantain tree in a storm.

With her hair dishevelled and her dress in disarray, the bashful Draupadī said deliberately, in anger, "O shame! The moral standards of the Bhāratas and of the Kṣatriya code have perished. In this hall everybody assembled looks on while the bounds of virtue are transgressed." So saying, she looked at her helpless husbands. While she was thus invoking virtue, Duḥśāsana shook her with even greater force, repeatedly calling her a slave and laughing aloud. Except for Duryodhana, Duḥṣāsana, Śakuni, and Karṇa, all those present felt very sad on seeing Draupadī thus dragged into the hall.

Bhīma then said to Yudhiṣṭhira, "All the tribute and other wealth you took from the king of Kāśī, all the gems the other kings presented to you, our chariots, our armour and weapons, our kingdom, and even our own selves, have all been lost in gambling. None of this provoked my anger, since you are our lord. But I think you went too far when you played with Draupadī as a stake."

Meanwhile, the evil Duḥśāsana began to pull at Draupadī's clothes, intending to disrobe her by force in the middle of the hall.[4] But as her clothes were thus being pulled off, many similar clothes appeared in their place. There were loud acclamations from all the kings who saw that most miraculous spectacle.

Even as Duḥśāsana was engaged in his effort to remove Draupadī's clothing by force, she remembered that the great sage Vasiṣṭha had taught her a long time ago to meditate upon the Lord when she was in great peril.

She began to recall again and again in her mind Lord Kṛṣṇa, in his various manifestations, as Goviṇda, as Nārāyana, as the denizen of Dvāraka, beloved of the cowherdesses. In her mind she appealed to him for succour even as she was being shamed by the Kauravas. Without revealing his presence, Kṛṣṇa saved Draupadī from humiliation. As one piece of cloth was stripped, another piece of cloth covered her, and hundreds of cloths of different colours littered the floor. The royal personages present in the hall were astonished by this miracle. They applauded Draupadī, and condemned the action of Duḥśāsana.

Then Bhīma swore in a loud voice in the presence of those kings, with his lower lip trembling in anger, and squeezing one hand in the other, "O kings, O men, listen to these my words which have never yet been uttered by any man and which will never be said by anyone else. If I do not drink the blood of this sinful, lowborn wretch Duḥśāsana in battle after rending apart his chest, let me forego the path of my ancestors!" Hearing his vow, which astonished everybody, many in the hall acclaimed Bhīma vigorously and condemned Duḥśāsana. When finally a mass of clothes was heaped in the midst of the assembly, Duḥśāsana, tired and abashed, gave up his evil design and sat down.

Draupadī then said, "I, who was seen only in the svayaṁvara arena by the assembled kings, and was never seen elsewhere in public, have been brought by force to the assembly hall today. I think that these are evil times when the Kurus allow their daughter-in-law to be thus tormented. O Kauravas, say whether this wife of Yudhiṣṭhira, born like him of a royal family, is a slave or not. I shall accept your verdict."

Upon this, Duryodhana said to Yudhiṣṭhira, "Bhīma, Arjuna, and the twins are subject to your command. Reply to Draupadī's question, whether you deem her won or not." Having said this, and with the purpose of encouraging Karṇa and annoying Bhīma, before Draupadī's very eyes Duryodhana bared his left thigh. Bhīma then vowed, "Let me forego the regions of my ancestors if I do not break that thigh of yours in the great battle that is to come."

Meanwhile, thoroughly abashed by Draupadī's appeal, Dhṛtarāṣṭra said, "O Pāñcālī, ask any boon you wish of me. Virtuous and devoted to Dharma as you are, I regard you as the foremost of my daughters-in-law." Draupadī said, "O best of the Bhāratas, if you would give me a boon, I pray that the ever dutiful Yudhiṣṭhira may be set free." Dhṛtarāṣṭra granted her wish and said, "O blessed one, my heart goes out to you. You deserve more than one boon. I wish to give you a second boon; ask of me whatever you want." Draupadī then said, "Let Bhīma and Arjuna, Nakula and Sahadeva be given their chariots and bows: this is my second wish."

Dhṛtarāṣṭra then said, "Ask of me a third boon, for two boons are not enough for you. Truly you are the most virtuous and illustrious of my daughters-in-law." Draupadī said, "O best of kings, avarice kills virtue; I do not wish to be greedy and I do not deserve a third boon. These my husbands, having been rescued from the miserable state of slavery, will win prosperity by their good deeds."

"O king," said Yudhiṣṭhira, "command us and tell us what we should do, for you are our lord. We wish to obey your commands at all times." Dhṛtarāṣṭra said, "O Yudhisthira, I wish you everlasting prosperity! I give you leave to go in safety and rule your own kingdom with all your wealth intact." Then Yudhiṣṭhira saluted and took leave of everybody, and left with his brothers. Accompanied by Draupadī, they mounted their cars, and with happy minds they left for the most splendid of cities, Iṅdraprastha.

XXIV

After the departure of the Pāṇḍavas, Duḥśāsana said to Duryodhana, Karṇa, and Śakuni, "O great car-warriors, the old man has ruined what was achieved with so much effort and difficulty. The wealth has returned to the enemy." Then Duryodhana said to Dhṛtarāṣṭra, "O father, having got back their weapons and cars, the Pāṇḍavas will kill us like angry serpents. O best of the Bhāratas, there is only one solution: we should again gamble with the Pāṇḍavas, the penalty for the losers being exile to the forest, and we shall thus be able to control them. Either one of us, having lost at dice, shall enter the thick forest, dressed in skins, and live there for twelve years. In the thirteenth year the losers shall live in hiding amid the people. If recognized during this period, they shall return to the forest for another twelve years.

"One or the other of us shall live in this way," Duryodhana continued. "Therefore let the game commence once more. Let the dice be cast, and let the Pāṇḍavas be invited again to play. O king, this is our most important task. You know that Śakuni is skilled in the art of gambling. O king, if at the end of the thirteenth year the Pāṇḍavas return after having kept the vow, we can easily conquer them. By then we will be firmly established in our kingdom, and meanwhile we shall have gained allies and built up a strong, big, and invincible army. O destroyer of foes, consider this." Dhṛtarāṣṭra said, "Ask the Pāṇḍavas quickly to come back, even if they have gone some distance. Let them return and play again."

Prātikāmī was then dispatched to invite Yudhiṣṭhira to come and play again. Prātikāmī said, "O King Yudhiṣṭhira, the assembly is gathered and your father has asked me to invite you again to come and play at dice." "All creatures receive good or evil at the command of the Creator," said Yudhiṣṭhira. "If I have to play once more, it is inevitable. I know that this command of the king, this fresh invitation to a game of dice, will cause desolation all round. But even so, I am not able to disregard it." So saying, he returned to the gambling hall.

Śakuni then said, "The old king returned your wealth, and that is truly commendable. But listen to me carefully, for I am going to propose another very high stake. If you defeat us at dice we shall be exiled in the forest for twelve years, clad in deerskins, and shall live in hiding during the thirteenth year. If recognized during this period, we shall go into exile in the forest for another twelve years. On the other hand, if we defeat you, you shall likewise live in exile in the forest for twelve years, dressed in deerskins, and accompanied by Draupadī. At the end of the thirteenth year, one or the other shall regain his own kingdom. O Yudhisthira, with this compact between us, cast the dice for the game, and let us play."

"O Śakuni," said Yudhisthira, "how can a dutiful king like me refuse to accept such a challenge? I shall play with you." Thereupon Śakuni, casting the dice again, said to Yudhiṣṭhira, "I have won."

Then the defeated Pāṇḍavas prepared to go to the forest. They wore upper garments of deerskin, according to the compact. When the Pāṇḍavas were leaving the hall the foolish Duryodhana imitated the gait of Bhīma who walked like a lion. Bhīma said, "I shall kill Duryodhana, and Arjuna shall slay Karṇa, while Sahadeva will kill the deceitful Śakuni. I shall kill the evil Duryodhana in a club-fight. I shall stand with my foot on his head while he lies on the ground. Like a lion I shall drink the blood of the sinful Duḥśāsana, who is brave only in words."

When the Pāṇḍavas were getting ready to leave, Vidura said: "It is not right that the revered Princess Kuṅtī should go to the forest. She is delicate and aged, and should ever be comfortable. The blessed Kuṅtī will live in my house as an honoured and welcome guest. Know this, O Pāṇḍavas, and I bless you that you may always be safe!"

As she was about to depart, Draupadī was oppressed by sadness. She took leave of the illustrious Kuṅtī and the other ladies there. Kuṅtī, also greatly disturbed on seeing Draupadī ready to leave, spoke a few sad words with difficulty. "Good women are never worried about the future," she said. "Your great virtue will protect you and you will soon gain prosperity." Having consoled the weeping Kuṅtī and saluted her, the unhappy Pāṇḍavas left for the forest. When they had gone, King Dhṛtarāṣṭra's mind was overcome with worry. He asked Vidura to join him immediately.

BHĪṢMA PARVA

XLVIII

Before the fighting began, the Kurus, the Pāṇḍavas, and the Somakas entered into certain covenants regarding the different kinds of combat. Thus it was agreed that a car-warrior should fight only with a car-warrior. He who rode on an elephant could fight only with another such combatant. A horseman might fight with a horseman and a foot soldier with a foot soldier. It was also agreed that a combatant who was engaged in fighting with another, one seeking refuge, one retreating, one whose weapon was broken, and one who was not clad in armour should never be attacked. Likewise charioteers, animals, men engaged in carrying weapons, drummers, and conch-blowers should not be attacked.

When the two armies were ready for battle, the holy Vyāsa, foremost of all learned men, grandfather of the Pāṇḍavas and the Kurus, who was gifted with divine vision, spoke in private to Dhṛtarāṣṭra, who was distressed by the evil policy of his sons. "O king," said Vyāsa, "the last moments of your sons and of other kings have come. They have gathered to fight and they will kill one another. If you wish to witness the fighting, I shall bestow sight on you."

Dhṛtarāṣṭra replied, "O foremost of sages! I have no desire to see the slaughter of my kinsmen. Through your grace, however, I would like to hear a full account of this battle." Thereupon Vyāsa bestowed a boon on Sañjaya, saying, "O king, Sañjaya will give you an account of this great battle. He will be able to see everything that takes place over the entire battlefield."

Vyāsa then made a last appeal for peace. He said, "O king, Death himself has been born in the form of your son, Duryodhana. Slaughter is never praised in the Vedas. It can never produce any good. Save your good name and fame, and your virtue. Let the Pāṇḍavas have their kingdom and let the Kauravas have peace. You will thereby assure yourself of a place in heaven." Having made this final and fruitless appeal, Vyāsa went away, while Dhṛtarāṣṭra reflected in silence.

Meanwhile both sides prepared to give battle. When the troops were arrayed according to rule, Duryodhana said to Duḥśāsana, "O Duḥśāsana, let chariots be quickly directed so as to assure the protection of Bhīṣma. Make haste in urging all our troops to advance. What I have been wishing for a number of years has at last come to pass: the clash of the Pāṇḍavas and the Kurus at the head of their respective armies."

At sunrise the next day, the armies of the Kurus and the Pāṇḍavas completed all their arrangements. The eleventh division of the Kuru army stood in advance of all others; at the head of these troops stood Bhīṣma. On one side were the eleven splendid divisions of the Kaurava army. On the other side were the seven divisions of the Pāṇḍavas army, protected by the foremost of men. The two armies facing each other looked like two mighty oceans agitated by fearful makaras.

Sañjaya reported to Dhṛtarāṣṭra: "When placed in battle array, the two armies, full of elephants, cars, and horses, looked like two woods in blossom. Both of them seemed as if they could conquer the very heavens. Both of them were commanded by excellent men. The Kaurava armies stood facing the west while the Pāṇḍavas stood facing the east—all ready for battle."

XLIX

Then Arjuna, whose flag bore the figure of an ape, looked at the Kauravas drawn up in battle array; as the fighting was about to begin, he took up his bow and said to Kṛṣṇa, "I wish to see my opponents who are eager for battle and whom I have to fight in the great struggle. Station my chariot, O Kṛṣṇa, between the two armies!" As requested by Arjuna, Kṛṣṇa drove the chariot to a position between the two armies.

Arjuna saw his closest kinsmen, related to him as father or grandfather, uncle or brother, son or grandson, preceptor as well as companion and friend, on both sides. Overcome by this sight, he said in sorrow and compassion, "O Kṛṣṇa, when I see my own people ready to fight and eager for battle, my limbs shudder, my mouth is dry, my body shivers, and my hair stands on end. Furthermore, I see evil portents, and I can see no good in killing my own kinsmen. It is not right and proper that we should kill our own kith and kin, the Kauravas. How can we be happy if we slay our own people?" Having said these words, Arjuna threw away his bow and arrows, and sat down sorrowfully on the seat of his car.

When he observed that Arjuna was overcome with compassion and that tears were welling up in his eyes, Kṛṣṇa said these words to him who was thus troubled and dejected: "O Arjuna, why have you become so depressed in this critical hour? Such dejection is unknown to noble men; it does not lead to the heavenly heights, and on earth it can only cause disgrace. Do not yield to cowardice, for it is not worthy of you. Cast away this faintness of heart and arise."

Arjuna said, "O Kṛṣṇa, how can I strike with my arrows people like the grandsire Bhīṣma and the preceptor Droṇa, who are worthy of my respect?" After such reflection, he finally told Kṛṣṇa, "I will not fight."

Kṛṣṇa smiled at Arjuna, so troubled in mind and dejected in spirit, and said, "You grieve for those for whom you should not grieve. The wise do not lament the dead or pine for the living. Anyone who believes that this kills, or thinks that this is killed, fails to understand that one neither kills nor is killed. The embodied soul merely casts off old bodies and enters new ones, just as a person discards used garments and puts on new clothes."

"The soul that lives in every human body is eternal and immortal," Kṛṣṇa went on to say. "Therefore do not grieve for any creature. As a Kṣatriya, your duty is to fight a righteous battle. This is the highest good for you, and you should not falter at this hour. Such a fight is an open door to heaven, and happy are they who engage in such a battle. Either you will win a victory and enjoy the earth, or be killed and go to heaven. Therefore arise, O Arjuna, and be determined to fight. Get ready for battle without thought of pleasure and pain, gain and loss, victory and defeat. In this way, you will not incur any sin. Remember that you have a right to action alone, but not to the fruits thereof. Be not motivated by the desire for the fruits of action. At the same time, do not pursue a policy of inaction."

"O Arjuna," he continued, "in this world I have taught a twofold way of life: the way of knowledge for men who engage in contemplation, and the way of works for men of action. One cannot maintain even one's physical life without action. Therefore, do your allotted work regardless of results, for men attain the highest good by doing work without attachment to its results. Resign yourself to me and fix your consciousness in the self, without desire or egoism, and then fight, freed from your fever."

Arjuna replied, "My confusion has been dispelled by this supreme discourse concerning the self, which you have given me out of your grace." Kṛṣṇa said, "I am Time itself, grown mature, capable of destroying the world, and now engaged in subduing it. Even without your effort, all the opposing warriors shall cease to exist. Therefore arise and win great glory, conquer your enemies, and enjoy a prosperous kingdom. They are already slain by me and you, O Arjuna, are merely the occasion. Kill Droṇa, Bhīṣma, Jayadratha, Karṇa, and all the other great warriors whom I have already doomed. Do not fear, but fight and conquer your enemies in battle."

"O Lord," said Arjuna, "I desire to know the true nature of 'renunciation' and of 'relinquishment;.' "Kṛṣṇa replied, "The wise understand 'renunciation' to mean the giving up of those works which are prompted by desire. 'Relinquishment' means the abandonment of the fruits of all works. It is not right to renounce one's duty, but when one performs a prescribed duty, with detachment and without thought of the fruit thereof, that is 'relinquishment.' Courage, vigour, resourcefulness, steadfastness in battle, generosity, and leadership are the natural duties of a Kṣatriya.

"The Lord dwells in the hearts of all men and causes them to turn round by his power as if they were mounted on a machine," Kṛṣṇa concluded. "Seek shelter in him with your whole being, and you shall attain supreme peace and the eternal station by his grace." "My bewilderment is gone," said Arjuna. "By your grace, O Kṛṣṇa, I have been made to realize my true duties. My doubts have been dispelled and I stand ready to do your bidding."

L

When the two armies, which resembled two oceans, were ready for battle and surging continuously, the brave King Yudhiṣṭhira doffed his armour and cast aside his excellent weapon. Quickly alighting from his chariot, he proceeded on foot, with joined hands and with restrained speech, in the direction of the hostile host, towards his grandfather, Bhīṣma, whom he addressed thus: "O invincible one, I salute you. We shall fight with you. Give us your permission and your blessings." Bhīṣma replied, "O son, I am pleased with you. Fight and triumph. Whatever else you may have desired, may you obtain it in this battle! O king, man is the slave of wealth, though wealth is no one's slave. And I am bound to the Kurus by wealth." To this, Yudhiṣṭhira answered, "O wise one, I pray that, desiring my welfare from day to day, you may keep my interests in mind, while you fight for the Kurus."

Then, in the midst of the army, Yudhiṣṭhira loudly proclaimed, "Whoever will choose us, him I shall accept as our ally." Thereupon Yuyutsu said with a cheerful heart to Yudhiṣṭhira, "I shall fight against the Kauravas in this battle, O king! I shall fight on your side, if you will accept me." So, abandoning the Kurus, Yuyutsu went over to the Pāṇḍava army to the accompaniment of kettledrums.

On the forenoon of that awful day the terrible battle began. The Kurus and the Sṛñjayas, both desirous of victory in battle, roared like lions and made both the sky and the earth resound with their war cries. In that general melee thousands of single combats took place between car-warriors, horsemen, and foot soldiers. Just for a short while that engagement was a beautiful sight. Soon, however, the fighting became confused and fierce in the extreme, with heroes rushing against each other in the melee.

In the afternoon Durmukha, Kṛtavarmā, Kṛpa, Śalya, and Vivirṃśati surrounded Bhīṣma and began to protect him. Thus sheltered by those five mighty car-warriors, Bhīṣma penetrated the Pāṇḍava host. With his bow stretched to a circle, he shot therefrom blazing arrows that resembled virulent poison. Creating continuous lines of arrows in all directions, that hero slew many Pāṇḍava car-warriors, naming each victim beforehand. When the troops of the Pāṇḍavas were routed and crushed all over the field, the sun set and nothing could be seen. Then, while Bhīṣma proudly stood surveying the battlefield, the Pāṇḍavas withdrew their forces for the night.

. . .

MAHĀPRASTHĀNIKA PARVA

XCIV

After hearing the details of the destruction of the Vṛṣṇis, Yudhiṣṭhira decided to leave the world. He said to Arjuna, "Time cooks every creature in its cauldron and binds us all with its cords. You can see that what has taken place is due to Fate." Thus addressed, Arjuna repeated the word—" Fate, Fate"—endorsing the view of his eldest brother, the wise Yudhiṣṭhira.

Bhīma and the twins fully supported Arjuna's views. Yudhiṣṭhira, determined to retire from the world and acquire merit, made over the kingdom to his regent Yuyutsu. Installing Parikṣit on the throne and anointing him as king, Yudhiṣṭhira sadly said to Subhadrā, "This son of your son will be the king of the Kurus. The survivor of the Yadus, Vajra, has also been made a king. Parikṣit will rule in Hāstinapura, while the Yādava prince, Vajra, will rule in Iṅdraprastha. You should protect him."

Renouncing his ornaments, Yudhiṣṭhira wore the bark of trees. Bhīma and Arjuna and the twins and the illustrious Draupadī clad themselves likewise. Seeing the princes in that guise the royal ladies wept aloud. Having performed the preliminary religious rites, they consigned their sacred fire to the water.

The five brothers, with Draupadī forming the sixth, and a dog forming the seventh member of the party, then started on their journey from the city to Hāstinapura followed for some distance by the citizens and the royal ladies. Setting their minds on yoga, and resolved to observe the vow of renunciation, those great souls passed through various countries and crossed many rivers and seas.

Then they beheld in the northern direction the great Himālayan mountain. Crossing the Himālayan range, they saw a vast sea of sand. Next appeared the towering mountain Meru, highest of peaks. As they were proceeding quickly, rapt in yoga, Draupadī fell from yoga, and dropped on the earth. Seeing her fall, Bhīma said to Yudhiṣṭhira, "O king, this princess never did anything sinful. Why did she fall by the wayside?" Yudhiṣṭhira replied, "She was partial to Arjuna."

The wise Sahadeva now dropped down. Thereupon Bhīma said to the king, "This son of Mādrī used to serve us all with great humility. Why has he fallen?" Yudhisthira replied, "He thought nobody was his equal in wisdom. That sin is the reason for the prince's fall."

Seeing both Draupadī and Sahadeva fall, the brave Nakula, whose love for his brothers was very great, fell next. Upon the fall of the heroic and handsome Nakula, Bhīma once more spoke to the king. "This brother of ours was righteous and always obeyed our commands. He was also of peerless beauty. Why has he fallen?" Yudhiṣṭhira replied, "He thought that there was nobody who equalled him in personal beauty. It is for this vanity that Nakula has fallen."

Seeing Nakula and the others fall, Arjuna, the hero of white horses, destroyer of hostile heroes, fell down in great grief. When that foremost of men, Arjuna, who was gifted with the energy of Indra, fell, Bhīma said to the king, "I do not recollect a single untruth uttered by the great Arjuna. Indeed, not even in jest did he say anything false. What is the sin whose evil consequence has made him fall?" Yudhiṣṭhira replied, "Proud of his heroism, Arjuna had said that he would conquer all our enemies in a single day. This, however, he did not do. Hence he has fallen down."

Having answered thus, the king went on. Then Bhīma fell. As he was falling, Bhīma said to King Yudhiṣṭhira the just, "O king! I who am dear to you have fallen! Why have I dropped down? Tell me." "You were a gluttonous eater," said Yudhiṣṭhira, "and you ate without regard to the wants of others. You also used to boast of your strength. It is for that, O Bhīma, that you have fallen." Having spoken these words Yudhiṣṭhira went on, without looking back. He had only one companion left, the dog, which continued to follow him.

XCV

Causing heaven and earth to reverberate, Indra came to Yudhiṣṭhira on a chariot and asked him to ascend it. Seeing his brothers fallen on the earth, and burning with grief, Yudhiṣṭhira said to Indra, "My brothers have all fallen here! They must go with me. Without them I do not wish to go to the celestial region, O lord! The delicate princess Draupadī, deserving of every comfort, should also go with us! Please permit this."

"You will behold your brothers in the celestial region." Iṅdra replied. "They have reached there before you. You will see them all there, along with Draupadī. Do not give way to grief, O chief of the Bhāratas! They renounced their human bodies before going there, O king! As for you, it has been ordained that you shall go there in this very body."

Yudhiṣṭhira said, "This dog, O lord, is highly devoted to me. He should go with me. My heart is full of compassion for him." "Today you have acquired immortality and a status equal to mine," replied Iṅdra. "Prosperity and high success attend you, and all the felicities of heaven are open to you. Cast off this dog. There will be no cruelty in doing so."

"O lord of a thousand eyes!" answered Yudhiṣṭhira. "It is extremely difficult for one of virtuous conduct to commit an unrighteous act. I do not wish for prosperity if I have to abandon a creature who is devoted to me." Hearing these words of King Yudhiṣṭhira the just, the dog was transformed into Dharma, the god of Virtue. Well pleased with Yudhiṣṭhira, the deity praised him in a sweet voice. He said, "You are well born, O king of kings, and endued with the intelligence and good conduct of your fathers! You have mercy for all creatures. Just now, out of consideration for the dog which was devoted to you, you renounced the very car of the celestials. Hence, O king, there is no one in heaven to equal you."

Then Dharma, Iṅdra, the maruts, the Aśvins, and other deities, as well as the celestial sages, made Yudhiṣṭhira ascend Iṅdra's car, bound for heaven. Amidst that concourse of celestials, Nārada, foremost of all speakers, and conversant with all the worlds, said these words, "Yudhiṣṭhira has transcended the achievements of all the royal sages who are here. Covering the universe by his fame and splendour and by the nobility of his conduct, he has reached heaven in his own human body! No one else has been known to achieve this."

Hearing these words of Nārada, the righteous King Yudhiṣṭhira saluted the celestials and all the royal sages present, and said, "Happy or miserable, whatever be the region where my brothers are now, I wish to go there. I do not wish to stay anywhere else."

Iṅdra addressed Yudhiṣṭhira, "O king of kings, live in this place, which you have earned by your meritorious deeds. Why do you still cherish human affections?" Yudhiṣṭhira replied, "O conquerer of Daityas, I do not wish to live anywhere, separated from my brothers. I wish to go where they have gone, and where that foremost of women, Draupadī, has gone!"

SVARGA-ĀROHANIKA PARVA

XCVI

Though he could not see Draupadī and his brothers anywhere in heaven, Yudhiṣṭhira saw Duryodhana radiant with prosperity and seated on an excellent seat. Thereupon he was suddenly overcome by anger and turned away from the sight. He said, "O you gods, I have no wish to see Duryodhana! I wish to go where my brothers are."

Nārada smilingly told him, "O king of kings! Meet Duryodhana politely now. This is heaven, O king! There can be no enmities here!" Despite Narada's words, Yudhiṣṭhira persisted in asking about his brothers, saying, "If these eternal regions are reserved for heroes like Duryodhana, that unrighteous and sinful wretch, that man who was the destroyer of friends and of the whole world, that man for whose sake the entire earth was devastated, then I wish to see what regions have been attained by those great heroes, my brothers of high vows, performers of promises, truthful in speech, and distinguished for courage, and by the great Karṇa, by Dhṛṣtadyumna, by Sātyaki, by the sons of Dhṛṣtadyumna and those other Kṣatriyas who met with death in the observance of their duties. Where are those kings, O Nārada? I do not see them here, nor Virāta nor Drupada nor the other great Kṣatriyas headed by Dhṛṣṭaketu. I wish to see them all, as well as Śikhandī, the Pāñcāla prince, the sons of Draupadī, and Abhimanyu, who was irresistible in battle."

Addressing the celestials, Yudhiṣṭhira continued, "O foremost of gods! What is heaven to me if I am separated from my brothers? To me, heaven is where those brothers of mine are. This, in my opinion, is not heaven." "If you wish to go there, O son," replied the gods, "go forthwith. If the king of the celestials permits, we are ready to do what you like." Then they told their messenger, "Show Yudhiṣṭhira his friends and kinsmen."

The royal son of Kuṅti and the celestial messenger went together to where the other Pāṇḍavas were. The heavenly messenger went first, followed by the king. The path was difficult, trodden by men of sinful deeds, and foetid with the stench of corpses. Along that inauspicious path the righteous king went, filled with various thoughts.

Seeing that foul region, Yudhiṣṭhira asked the celestial messenger, "How far must we go along a path like this?" When Yudhiṣṭhira the just spoke to him, the messenger of heaven stopped in his course and replied, "Thus far I have come with you. The dwellers of the celestial region ordered me to stop at this point. If you are tired, O king of kings, you may return with me!"

Yudhiṣṭhira was disconsolate and stupefied by the foul stench. Resolved to return, he retraced his steps. But as the righteous king turned back stricken with sorrow, he heard piteous cries all around: "O son of Dharma, O royal sage, O you of holy birth, O Pāṇḍava, stay a while as a favour to us! At your approach a delightful breeze has begun to blow, bearing the sweet smell of your body. We have been greatly refreshed by this. Remain here, O Bhārata, for some time! As long as you are here tortures cease to afflict us."

From all sides, the king heard these and many other piteous appeals, uttered by persons in distress. The voices of those woebegone and afflicted persons seemed to him to be familiar, although he could not place them. Unable to recognize the voices, Yudhiṣṭhira inquired, "Who are you? Why do you stay here?" In reply, they answered him from all sides, saying, "I am Karṇa!" "I am Bhīma!" "I am Arjuna!" "I am Nakula!" "I am Sahadeva!" "I am Dhṛṣṭadyumna!" "I am Draupadī!" "We are the sons of Draupadī!"

Hearing those painful cries, the royal Yudhiṣṭhira asked himself, "What perverse destiny is this? What are the sins which were committed by those great beings, Karṇa and the sons of Draupadī and the slender-waisted princess of Pāñcāla, that they have been compelled to live in this region of foul smell and great distress? I am not aware of any sin that can be attributed to these persons. By what act of merit has Dhṛtarāṣṭra's son, King Duryodhana, with all his wicked followers, acquired such prosperity?"

Musing thus, Yudhiṣṭhira was filled with righteous indignation, and censured the celestials as well as Dharma himself. Though almost overcome by the foul smell, he told the celestial messenger, "Go back to those whose messenger you are. Tell them that I shall not return to them, but shall stay here since my companionship has brought comfort to these suffering brothers of mine."

XCVII

King Yudhiṣṭhira had not waited for more than a moment when all the celestials, headed by Iṅdra, appeared. The God of Righteousness, in his embodied form, also came to see Yudhiṣṭhira.

Upon the arrival of those celestials of radiant bodies and noble deeds, the darkness that had enveloped that region immediately disappeared. The tortures afflicting those of sinful deeds were no longer to be seen. The river Vaitaranī, the thorny Śalmali, the iron jars, and the terrible boulders of rock also vanished from sight, as did the repulsive corpses which the Kuru king had seen. Then, because of the presence of the celestials, a gentle breeze, bringing with it a pleasant and fragrant odour, pure and delightfully cool, began to blow on that spot.

Iṅdra, the lord of the celestials, consoled Yudhiṣṭhira, saying, "O mighty Yudhiṣṭhira! Join the ranks of the celestials who are pleased with you. These illusions have ended. Hell, O son, should be seen by all kings. There is some good and bad in all things. You once deceived Droṇa concerning his son, and have therefore been shown hell by an act of deception. Like yourself, Bhīma, Arjuna, and Draupadī have reached hell by an act of deception. Your brothers and the other kings who fought on your side have all attained to their respective places. Let the fever of your heart be dispelled! Here is the celestial river, sacred and sanctifying the three worlds. It is called the celestial Gaṅgā. Plunging into it, you will attain your proper place."

Then Dharma the god of virtue said, "O king, your brothers were not such as to deserve hell. All this has been an illusion created by the king of the celestials. O son, all kings must see hell at least once. Hence you have for a little while been subjected to this great sorrow. Neither Arjuna, nor Bhīma, nor the twins, nor Karṇa, ever truthful in speech and endued with great courage, could be deserving of hell for a long time. Nor could the princess Draupadī be deserving of that place of sinners. Come, come, O Bhārata, and see Gaṅgā, who flows over the three worlds."

The royal sage then proceeded with Dharma and all the other celestials. Having bathed in the celestial river Gaṅgā, sacred and purifying, he renounced his human body. Assuming a celestial form, Yudhiṣṭhira the just, through that bath, became divested of all his enmities and his grief.

Surrounded by the celestials, he then went away from there, accompanied by Dharma, as the great sages praised him. Finally he reached the place where those heroes, the Pāṇḍavas and the Dhārtarāṣṭras, freed from human wrath, were enjoying each his respective position.

XCVIII

Thus honoured by the celestials, the maruts, and the sages, Yudhiṣṭhira joined his kinsmen. He saw Kṛṣṇa in his Brahmā-form, being worshipped by the heroic and radiant Arjuna. In another place, he saw Karṇa, foremost of warriors, resembling a dozen suns in splendour. Elsewhere he saw the mighty Bhīma sitting in the midst of the maruts.

In the place belonging to the Aśvins, Yudhiṣṭhira saw Nakula and Sahadeva blazing with splendour. He also saw Draupadī, the princess of Pāñcāla, decked in garlands of lotuses. Having reached the celestial region, she was sitting there, radiant as the Sun. King Yudhiṣṭhira suddenly wished to question her. The illustrious Indra, king of the celestials, anticipating this, said, "This one is the goddess of prosperity herself. It was for your sake that she took human form, without being born of any mother, O Yudhiṣṭhira! For your pleasure she was created by the wielder of the trident. She was born in the race of Drupada and was the wife of you all. These five blessed Gandharvas, bright like fire, are the sons of Draupadī and yourselves."

"Look at Dhṛtarāṣṭra, the king of the Gandharvas, who was the eldest brother of your father," continued Indra. 'This one, Karṇa, is the son of Kuntī and of the Sun-god. He is your eldest brother, though he was known as the son of Rādhā. Look at the son of Subhadrā, invincible in battle, now staying with the Moon-god. He is the powerful bowman Abhimanyu, now shining with the gentle effulgence of the Moon. Here is the mighty archer Pāṇḍu, now united with Kuntī and Mādrī. Look at the royal Bhīṣma, the son of Śantanu, now in the midst of the Vasus.[5] Know this one by the side of Bṛhaspati to be your preceptor Droṇa."

Indra concluded by saying, "These and other kings, O son of Pāṇḍu, who fought on your behalf, now walk with the Gandharvas or yakṣas or other superhuman beings. Some have attained to the dignity of guhyakas,

O king. Having renounced their bodies, they have conquered the celestial region by the merit they acquired through word, thought, and deed."

XCIX

Hearing this history from Vaiṣampāyana in the intervals of the sacrificial rites, King Janamejaya was filled with wonder. The sacrificial priests then completed the remaining rites. Having rescued the snakes from a fiery death, Āstīka was filled with joy. King Janamejaya pleased, with profuse gifts, all the Brāhmaṇas, who, thus honoured by the king, returned to their respective abodes. After the learned Brāhmaṇas had left, King Janamejaya returned from Takṣaśila to Hāstinapura.

Sauti[6] said to the sages assembled in the forest of Naimiśa, "I have now recounted everything that Vaiśampāyana narrated, at the command of Vyāsa, to King Janamejaya at his snake sacrifice. This great history, which is sacred and excellent, was composed by the sage Vyāsa of truthful speech, whose desire was to spread the fame of the great Pāṇḍavas and that of the other Kṣatriyas throughout the world. As the sacred ocean and the snow-clad mountain are both regarded as mines of precious gems, so is this *Mahābhārata.*"

END NOTES

1. Name of a mountain, meaning literally "a hundred peaks."
2. Guru-dakṣiṇā is the offering that pupils make to their preceptor on the successful conclusion of their studies.
3. To avoid confusion with the Lord Kṛṣṇa, she will be invariably referred to hereafter as Draupadī.
4. In other recensions, there is reference to a silent prayer by Draupadī addressed to Lord Kṛṣṇa to come to her rescue.
5. The Vasus, whose number is usually eight, were originally personifications of natural phenomena—Āpa (water), Dhruva (the Pole-Star), Soma (the moon), Dhava or Dhara, Anila (the wind), Anala (fire), Pratyuṣa (the dawn), and Prabhāsa (light). Bhīṣma, as explained on p. 7, above, was one of the eight Vasus.
6. He is called Sūta in the Poona edition.

QUESTIONS

1. What is dharma according to the *Mahabharata,* and how is it reflected in the actions of the characters of this story?
2. What does the *Mahabharata* reveal about ancient understandings of gender, class, and society?
3. Krishna speaks to Arjuna of the importance of "renunciation." What does he mean by this?
4. What does Yudhisthira's love for his family say about how to lead a morally upright life?

DOCUMENT

THE BURDENS OF EMPIRE

Thucydides

Thucydides' incomplete History of the Peloponnesian War *(431–404 B.C.E.), the greatest work of history surviving from the ancient western world, depicts the struggle between a federation of democratic city-states led by Athens and a federation of oligarchies headed by Sparta. Little is known of the author's life. He was an Athenian of the upper classes, born sometime between 460 and 455 B.C.E., who served as a general of the Athenian forces in 424 B.C.E., and was a devoted follower of the great Athenian politician Pericles. Thucydides tells his readers that he began to write his history soon after the beginning of the Peloponnesian war, so that it has much of the character of an eyewitness account, but internal evidence shows that he must have continued to revise his work down to the end of his life, around 400 B.C.E.*

After an introductory book, the work divides into four sections: an account of the Ten Years War (431–421 B.C.E., Books 2 to 5.24), the interwar period (421–415 B.C.E., Book 5.25–116), the Sicilian Expedition (415–413 B.C.E., Books 6 and 7), and the so-called Decelian War (413–411 B.C.E., Book 8). These twenty years, in Thucydides' telling, describe an arc of political and moral decline for Athens, ending with a disastrous defeat in Sicily and the temporary triumph of oligarchic forces inside Athens. Such a story would seem to offer numerous opportunities for moralistic comment and patriotic bluster, but Thucydides resisted these temptations. He was less interested in assigning blame than in understanding the workings of power and human nature. Such an understanding, he believed, was the true purpose of history, and its achievement in Thucydides' book was the basis of his claim that his work would be "a possession for all time."

In this famous passage from Book 2, Thucydides imaginatively reconstructed Pericles' last speech, in which the leader defends himself for a disastrous military decision, and tells the Athenians that their empire is like a tyranny which they must hold or be destroyed by the hatred of their subject cities and rivals.

After the second invasion of the Peloponnesians there had been a change in the spirit of the Athenians. Their land had been twice devastated, and they had to contend with the war and the plague at the same time. Now they began to blame Pericles for having persuaded them to go to war and to hold him responsible for all the misfortunes which had overtaken them; they became eager to make peace with Sparta and actually sent ambassadors there, who failed to achieve anything. They were then in a state of utter hopelessness, and all their angry feelings turned against Pericles.

Pericles himself saw well enough how bitterly they felt at the situation in which they found themselves; he saw, in fact, that they were behaving exactly as he had expected that they would. He therefore, since he was still general, summoned an assembly with the aim of putting fresh courage into them and of guiding their embittered spirits so as to leave them in a calmer and more confident frame of mind. Coming before them, he made the following speech:

'I expected this outbreak of anger on your part against me, since I understand the reasons for it; and I have called an assembly with this object in view, to remind you of your previous resolutions and to put forward my own case against you, if we find that there is anything unreasonable in your anger against me and in your giving way to your misfortunes. My own opinion is that when the whole state is on the right course it is a better thing for each separate individual than when private interests are satisfied but the state as a whole is going downhill. However well off a man may be in his private life, he will still be involved in the general ruin if his country is destroyed; whereas, so long as the state itself is secure, individuals have a much greater chance of recovering from their private misfortunes. Therefore, since a state can support individuals in their suffering, but no one person by himself can bear the load that rests upon the state, is it not right for us all to rally to her defence? Is it not wrong to act as you are doing now? For you have been so dismayed by disaster in your homes that you are losing your grip on the common safety; you are attacking me for having spoken in favour of war and yourselves for having voted for it.

'So far as I am concerned, if you are angry with me you are angry with one who has, I think, at least as much ability as anyone else to see what ought to be done and to explain what he sees, one who loves his city and one who is above being influenced by money. A man who has the knowledge but lacks the power clearly to express it is no better off than if he never had any ideas at all. A man who has both these qualities, but lacks patriotism, could scarcely speak for his own people as he should. And even if he is patriotic as well, but not able to resist a bribe, then this one fault will expose everything to the risk of being bought and sold. So that if at the time when you took my advice and went to war you considered that my record with regard to these qualities was even slightly better than that of others, then now surely it is quite unreasonable for me to be accused of having done wrong.

'If one has a free choice and can live undisturbed, it is sheer folly to go to war. But suppose the choice was forced upon one—submission and immediate slavery or danger with the hope of survival: then I prefer the man who stands up to danger rather than the one who runs away from it. As for me, I am the same as I was, and do not alter; it is you who have changed. What has happened is this: you took my advice when you were still untouched by misfortune, and repented of your action when things went badly with you; it is because your own resolution is weak that my policy appears to you to be mistaken. It is a policy which entails suffering, and each one of you already knows what this suffering is; but its ultimate benefits are still far away and not yet clear for all to see. So, now that a great and sudden disaster has fallen on you, you have weakened in carrying out to the end the resolves which you made. When things happen suddenly, unexpectedly, and against all calculation, it takes the heart out of a man; and this certainly has happened to you, with the plague coming on top of everything else. Yet you must remember that you are citizens of a great city and that you were brought up in a way of life suited to her greatness; you must therefore be willing to face the greatest disaster and be determined never to sacrifice the glory that is yours. We all look with distaste on people who arrogantly pretend to a reputation to which they are not entitled; but equally to be condemned are those who, through lack of moral fibre, fail to live up to the reputation which is theirs already. Each of you, therefore, must try to stifle his own particular sorrow as he joins with the rest in working for the safety of us all.

'And if you think that our war-time sufferings may grow greater and greater and still not bring us any nearer to victory, you ought to be satisfied with the arguments which I have often used on other occasions to show that there is no good reason for such fears. But there is this point also which I shall mention. In thinking of the greatness of your empire there is one advantage you have which, I think, you have never yet taken into consideration, nor have I mentioned it in my previous speeches. Indeed, since it sounds almost like boasting, I should not be making use of this argument now if it were not for the fact that I see that you are suffering from an unreasonable feeling of discouragement. Now, what you think is that your empire consists simply of your allies: but I have something else to tell you. The whole world before our eyes can be divided into two parts, the land and the sea, each of which is valuable and useful to man. Of the whole of one of these parts you are in control—not only of the area at present in your power, but elsewhere too, if you want to go further. With your navy as it is today there is no power on earth—not the King of Persia nor any people under the sun—which can stop you from sailing where you wish. This power of yours is something in an altogether different category from all the advantages of houses or of cultivated land. You may think that when you lose them you have suffered a great loss, but in fact you should not take things so hardly; you should weigh them in the balance with the real source of your power and see that, in comparison, they are no more to be valued than gardens and other elegances that go with wealth. Remember, too, that freedom, if we preserve our freedom by our own efforts, will easily restore us to our old position; but to submit to the will of others means to lose even what we still have. You must not fall below the standard of your fathers, who not only won an empire by their own toil and sweat, without receiving it from others, but went on to keep it safe so that they could hand it down to you. And, by the way, it is more of a disgrace to be robbed of what one has than to fail in some new undertaking. Not courage alone, therefore, but an actual sense of your superiority should animate you as you go forward against the enemy. Confidence, out of a mixture of ignorance and good luck, can be felt even by cowards; but this sense of superiority comes only to those who, like us, have real reasons for knowing that they are better placed than their opponents. And when the chances on both sides are equal, it is intelligence that confirms courage—the intelligence that makes one able to look down on one's opponent, and which proceeds not by hoping for the best (a method only valuable in desperate situations), but by estimating what the facts are, and thus obtaining a clearer vision of what to expect.

'Then it is right and proper for you to support the imperial dignity of Athens. This is something in which you all take pride, and you cannot continue to enjoy the privileges unless you also shoulder the burdens of empire. And do not imagine that what we are fighting for is simply the question of freedom or slavery: there is also involved the loss of our empire and the dangers arising from the hatred which we have incurred in administering it. Nor is it any longer possible for you to give up this empire, though there may be some people who in a mood of sudden panic and in a spirit of political apathy actually think that this would be a fine and noble thing to do. Your empire is now like a tyranny: it may have been wrong to take it; it is certainly dangerous to let it go. And the kind of people who talk of doing so and persuade others to adopt their point of view would very soon bring a state to ruin, and would still do so even if they lived by themselves in isolation. For those who are politically apathetic can only survive if they are supported by people who are capable of taking action. They are quite valueless in a city which controls an empire, though they would be safe slaves in a city that was controlled by others.

'But you should not be led astray by such citizens as these; nor should you be angry with me, you who came to the same conclusion as I did about the necessity for making war. Certainly the enemy have invaded our country and done as one might have expected they would do, once you refused to give in to them; and then the plague, something which we did not expect, fell upon us. In fact out of everything else this has been the only case of something happening which we did not anticipate. And I know that it is very largely because of this that I have become unpopular, quite unfairly, unless you are also going to put down to my credit every piece of unexpected good fortune that comes your way. But it is right to endure with resignation what the gods send, and to face one's enemies with courage. This was the old Athenian way: do not let any act of yours prevent it from still being so. Remember, too, that the reason why Athens has the greatest name in all the world is because she has never given in to adversity, but has spent more life and labour in warfare than any other state, thus winning the greatest power that has ever existed in history, such a power that will be remembered for ever by posterity, even if now (since all things are born to decay) there should come a time when we were forced to yield: yet still it will be remembered that of all Hellenic powers we held the widest sway over the Hellenes, that we stood firm in the greatest wars against their combined forces and against individual states, that we lived in a city which had been perfectly equipped in every direction and which was the greatest in Hellas.

'No doubt all this will be disparaged by people who are politically apathetic; but those who, like us, prefer a life of action will try to imitate us, and, if they fail to secure what we have secured, they will envy us. All who have taken it upon themselves to rule over others have incurred hatred and unpopularity for a time; but if one has a great aim to pursue, this burden of envy must be accepted, and it is wise to accept it. Hatred does not last for long; but the brilliance of the present is the glory of the future stored up for ever in the memory of man. It is for you to safeguard that future glory and to do nothing now that is dishonourable. Now, therefore, is the time to show your energy and to achieve both these objects. Do not send embassies to Sparta: do not give the impression that you are bowed down under your present sufferings! To face calamity with a mind as unclouded as may be, and quickly to react against it—that, in a city and in an individual, is real strength.'

. . .

QUESTIONS

1. What does Pericles believe is the proper relationship between the state and the individual? How does Pericles use these ideas about the relationship of the state to the individual to defend his own actions?
2. What does empire mean to Thucydides; how is an empire won an how is it lost?

3. What are the burdens of empire? How does empire create external danger and internal division for an imperial society?
4. Pericles calls Athenians to struggle and to endure sacrifice. He also says, "All things are born to decay." So why struggle; why make sacrifices?

DOCUMENT

TYPES OF POLITICAL CONSTITUTION

Aristotle

Aristotle (384–322 B.C.E.) ranks among the greatest philosophers of classical Antiquity, Although large parts of his philosophical system were no longer accepted after the seventeenth century, many of his writings (especially on ethics, politics, and psychology) continue to arouse interest today. Born at Stageira in Macedonia (and thus often called the Stagirite), at the age of seventeen Aristotle went to study in Athens, where he became a student of Plato and a member of the Platonic Academy until his master's death in 347 B.C.E. After an unsuccessful bid to lead the Academy, Aristotle spent several years teaching and doing research in Asia Minor, then became tutor to Alexander the Great, the son of King Philip of Macedonia. After Alexander's accession to the throne, Aristotle returned to Athens, where he stayed from around 334 B.C.E. until shortly before his death. There he established his own school and research center, the Lyceum, in competition with the Platonic Academy. This is symbolic of the divergences between Aristotle's and Plato's thought on a number of key philosophical issues.

Among the more significant differences between Plato and Aristotle are the Stagirite's rejection of the theory of ideas and his attempt to construct a systematic philosophy embracing not only moral philosophy, but also logic, natural philosophy, and metaphysics. Furthermore, the style of the works is significantly different. Many of Aristotle's works have been lost, so it is not possible to speak of his total production authoritatively; most of the surviving

"Types of Political Constitution," in *The Politics*, by Aristotle, translated by T. A. Sinclair, revised edition, copyright © 1981 by Trevor J. Saunders, 186–200. Reprinted by permission of Penguin Books Ltd.

works are either lecture notes or systematic treatises not designed for a broad public, and in some cases the history of these texts' transmission has done them a real disservice. The result is a rather dry, "scientific" style dictated by the systematic scope of the works and their procedure by proof and argumentation, although this is often enlivened by Aristotle's polemical stance toward other thinkers. The lecture notes often suffer from extreme conciseness and editorial interventions; these can make for slow reading and have given rise to a rich commentary literature. However, most readers agree that the works more than repay the effort involved in studying them.

The Politics, *written probably during Aristotle's second sojourn in Athens, is a powerful work of political theory and analysis that continues to challenge readers today. Apparently delivered originally as lectures to Aristotle's students, the work discusses fundamental points of political theory (what is the purpose of the state? who can be rightfully called a citizen?), studies and critiques the various kinds of constitutions, theoretical and real, and concludes with a description of Aristotle's ideal state. As in his* Ethics, *Aristotle was strongly moved by teleological considerations: In his discussion of the relative merits of the various constitutions, for example, he frequently urged his readers to guide their analysis by a consideration of the final purpose of government, namely, human flourishing. Throughout, he emphasized the importance of justice and virtue in politics.*

The present selection from Book III starts by asking how many political constitutions exist, and distinguishes the three good ones (monarchy, aristocracy, and polity) from their opposite corrupt forms (respectively, tyranny, oligarchy, and democracy). Aristotle first based these distinctions on the number and aims of those who rule; he then considered these classifications from the standpoint of the rulers' wealth and proceeded to ask what other criteria were relevant in the distribution of power. Finally, a consideration of the various possible ruling elements (the common people or the rich) gives occasion to comment on the intrinsic injustice of any of these specific arrangements.

III. vi

CORRECT AND DEVIATED CONSTITUTIONS DISTINGUISHED

1278b6 Having settled these questions, we must proceed to our next and ask whether we are to posit only one constitution or more than one; and if more than one, what they are and how many, and what the differences are between then. The 'constitution' of a state is the organization of the offices,[1] and in particular of the one that is sovereign over all the others. Now in every case the citizen-body of a state is sovereign; the citizen-body *is* the constitution. Thus in democracies the people are sovereign, in oligarchies the few. That, we say, is what make the one constitution differ from the other; and the same criterion can be applied to the others also.

1278b15 We ought at the outset to state the purpose for which the state has come to be, as well as the number of kinds of authority controlling men and their life as members of an association. At the beginning of this work, when we drew a distinction between household-management and mastership, we also stated that by nature man is a political animal.[2] Hence men have a desire for life together, even when they have no need to seek each other's help. Nevertheless, common interest too is a factor in bringing them together, in so far as it contributes to the good life of each. The *good* life is indeed their chief end, both communally and individually; but they form and continue to maintain a political association[3] for the sake of life itself. Perhaps we may say that there is an element of good even in mere living, provided that life is not excessively beset with troubles. Certainly most men, in their desire to keep alive, are prepared to face a great deal of suffering, as if finding in life itself a certain well-being and a natural sweetness.

1278b30 But to return to authority: it is not difficult to distinguish its recognized styles (I often speak about their definition in my public lectures).[4] First, although the natural slave and the natural master really have the same interest, rule of master over slave is exercised primarily for the benefit of the master and only incidentally for the benefit of the slave, because if the slave deteriorates the master's rule over him is inevitably impaired.

1278b37 Then there is the authority of a man over his wife, his children, and his whole household, to which we give the name 'household-management'.

This is exercised either for the benefit of those subject to the authority, or for some benefit common to both parties. In itself it is for the benefit of the subject, as we see by the analogy of the other skills, such as that of a doctor or of an athlete's trainer, who would only incidentally be concerned with their own interests. (For of course there is nothing to prevent a trainer on occasion being himself a member of the team in training, as the man who steers the ship is always one of the members of the ship's company. The trainer or pilot looks to the good of those under his authority, but when he himself is one of them he gets the same benefit out of it incidentally as they do, in that the pilot is a member of the ship's company, and the trainer becomes one of those in training, while yet remaining their trainer.)

1279a8 That is why,[5] whenever authority in the *state* is constituted on a basis of equality and similarly between citizens, they expect to take turns in exercising it. This principle is very old but in earlier times it was applied in a natural and proper manner: men expected each to take a turn at public service,[6] and during tenure of office to look after the interest of someone else, who then did the same for him. But nowadays there is more to be gained out of public affairs and offices, so men want to be in office continuously. They could hardly be more zealous in their place-hunting if they were ill and their recovery depended on securing office.

1279a16 It is clear then that those constitutions which aim at the common good are right, as being in accord with absolute justice; while those which aim only at the good of the rulers are wrong. They are all deviations from the right constitutions. They are like the rule of master over slave, whereas the state is an association of free men.

III. vii

CLASSIFICATION OF CORRECT AND DEVIATED CONSTITUTIONS

1279a22 Having drawn these distinctions we must next consider what constitutions there are and how many. We begin with those that are correct, since when these have been defined it will be easy to see the deviations. As we have seen, 'constitution' and 'citizen-body' mean the same thing, and the citizen-body is the sovereign power in states. Sovereignty necessarily resides either in one man, or in a few, or in the many.

Whenever the one, the few, or the many rule with a view to the common good, these constitutions must be correct; but if they look to the private advantage, be it of the one or the few or the mass, they are deviations. For either we must say that those who do not participate are not citizens, or they must share in the benefit.[7]

1279a32 The usual name for right constitutions are as follows: (a) Monarchy[8] aiming at the common interest: kingship. (b) Rule of more than one man but only a few: aristocracy (so called either because the *best* men rule or because it aims at what is *best* for the state and all its members).[9] (c) Political control exercised by the mass of the populace in the common interest: polity. This is the name common to all constitutions.[10] It is reasonable to use this term, because, while it is possible for one man or a few to be outstanding in point of virtue, it is difficult for a larger number to reach a high standard in all forms of virtue—with the conspicuous exception of military virtue, which is found in a great many people. And that is why in this constitution the defensive element is the most sovereign body, and those who share in the constitution are those who bear arms.

1279b4 The corresponding deviations are: from kingship, tyranny; from aristocracy, oligarchy; from polity, democracy. For tyranny is monarchy for the benefit of the monarch, oligarchy for the benefit of the men of means, democracy for the benefit of the men without means. None of the three aims to be of profit to the common interest.

III. viii
AN ECONOMIC CLASSIFICATION OF CONSTITUTIONS

1279b11 We must however go into a little more detail about what each of these constitutions is. Certain difficulties are involved, which one whose aim is strictly practical might be allowed to pass over; but a man who examines each subject from a philosophical standpoint cannot neglect them: he has to omit nothing, and state the truth about each topic.

1279b16 Tyranny, as has been said, is a monarchy which is exercised like a mastership[11] over the association which is the state; oligarchy occurs when the sovereign power of the constitution is in the hands of those with possession, democracy when it is in the hands of those who have no stock of possessions and are without means. The first difficulty concerns definitions. Suppose the majority to be well-off, and to be sovereign in the state; then we have a democracy, since the mass of the people is sovereign. So too, if it is somewhere the case that those who do not own property, while fewer in number than those who do, are more powerful and in sovereign control of the constitution, then that is called an oligarchy, since the few are sovereign. It looks therefore as if there were something wrong with our way of defining constitutions.[12]

1279b26 Even if we try to include both criteria of nomenclature, combining wealth with fewness of numbers in the one case (calling it oligarchy when those who are both wealthy and few hold office), lack of wealth with large numbers in the other (calling it democracy when those who are both poor and numerous hold office)—even then we are only raising a fresh difficulty. For if there is not in fact any other constitution than those with which we have been dealing,[13] what names can we give to the two just mentioned, one in which the wealthy are more numerous, and one in which the poor are less numerous, each category being in its own case in sovereign control of the constitution? The argument seems to show that it is a matter of accident whether those who are sovereign be few or many (few in oligarchies, many in democracies): it just happens that way because everywhere the rich are few and the poor are many. So in fact the grounds of difference have been given wrongly: what really differentiates oligarchy and democracy is wealth or the lack of it. It inevitably follows that where men rule because of the possession of wealth, whether their number be large or small, that is oligarchy, and when the poor rule, that is democracy. But, as we have said, in actual fact the former are few, the latter many. Few are wealthy, but all share freedom alike: and these are the grounds of their respective claims to the constitution.[14]

III. ix
THE JUST DISTRIBUTION OF POLITICAL POWER

1280a7 First we must grasp what definitions of oligarchy and democracy men put forward, and in particular what is the oligarchic and what is the democratic view of justice. For all adhere to a justice of some kind, but they do not proceed beyond a certain point, and are not referring to the whole of justice in the sovereign sense when they speak of it. Thus it is thought that justice is equality; and so it is, but not for all persons, only for those that are equal. Inequality also is thought to be just; and so it is, but not for all, only for the unequal. We make bad mistakes if we neglect this 'for whom' when we are deciding what is just. The reason is that we are making judgements about ourselves, and people are generally bad judges where their own interests are involved. So, as justice is relative to people, and applies in the same ratio to the things and to the persons (as pointed out in my *Ethics*),[15] these disputants, while agreeing as to equality of the thing, disagree about the persons for whom,[16] and this chiefly for the reason already stated, that they are judging their own case, and therefore badly.

1280a21 There is also this further reason, namely that both parties are talking about justice in a *limited* sense, and so imagine themselves to be talking about justice unqualifiedly. Thus it is an error when men unequal in one respect, e.g. money, suppose themselves unequal in all, just as it is an error when men equal in one respect, e.g. in being free, suppose themselves equal in every respect. To argue thus is to neglect the decisive point. If persons originally come together and form an association for the sake of property, then they share in the state[17] in proportion to their ownership of property. This is the apparent strength of the oligarchs' view that it is *not* just that out of a sum of a hundred minae he that contributed only one should receive equal shares with him who found the remaining ninety-nine; and that this applies equally to the original sum and to any profits subsequently made. But a state's purpose is not merely to provide a living but to make a life that is good. Otherwise it might be made up of slaves or animals other than man, and that is impossible, because slaves and animals do not participate in happiness,[18] nor in a life that involves choice.

1280a34 A state's purpose is also to provide something more than a military pact of protection against injustice, or to facilitate mutual acquaintance and the exchange of goods, for in that case Tyrrhenians and Carthaginians, and all others with commercial treaties with each other, would be taken as citizens of a single state. Certainly they have import agreements, treaties to prevent injustice, and written documents governing their military alliance. But in the first place each has its separate officials: there are none in common to which they are both equally subject for these purposes. Secondly, neither side is concerned with the *quality* of the other, or with preventing the behaviour of any person covered by the agreements from being unjust or wicked, but only with the prevention of injustice as between each other. But all who are anxious to ensure government under good laws make it their business to have an eye to the virtue and vice of the citizens. It thus becomes evident that that which is genuinely and not just nominally called a state must concern itself with virtue. Otherwise the association is a mere military alliance, differing only in location and restricted territorial extent from an alliance whose parties are at a distance from each other; and under such conditions law becomes a mere agreement, or, as Lycophron[19] the sophist put it, 'a mutual guarantor of justice',[20] but quite unable to make citizens good and just.

1280b12 That this is true will be clear from some further illustrations. Suppose you merge the territories into one, making the walls of Corinth and Megara contiguous: that still does not make a single state of them, nor would it even if they established rights of marriage between the two, though this is one of the ties peculiarly characteristic of states. Or again, suppose you had 10,000 people living apart from each other, but near enough not to become dissociated: carpenter, farmer, shoemakers and suchlike are there, and furthermore they have laws prohibiting injustice in their transactions with each other; yet, so long as their association does not go beyond such things as commercial exchange and military alliance, that is still not a state. And why not? you may ask. The reason is certainly not that the association is loosely knit. For even if they actually moved close together, and maintained an association such as I have described, with each man still treating his own household like a state, and if they mutually supported each other, as in a defensive alliance, against injustice only, even then that would not be considered a state, not at any rate in the strict sense, since the nature of their intercourse is the same whether they move close together or stay apart.

1280b29 It is clear therefore that the state is not an association of people dwelling in the same place, established to prevent its members from committing injustice against each other, and to promote transactions. Certainly all these features must be present if there is to be a state; but even the presence of every one of them does not make a state *ipso facto*. The state is an association intended to enable its members, in their households and the kinships,[21] to live *well;* its purpose is a perfect and self-sufficient life. However, this will not be attained unless they occupy one and the same territory and intermarry. It is indeed on that account that we find in states connections between relatives by marriage, brotherhoods, sacrifice to the gods, and the various civilized pursuits of a life lived together. All these activities are the product of affection, for it is our affection for others that causes us to choose to live together; thus they all contribute towards that good life which is the purpose of the state; and a state is an association of kinships and villages which aims at a perfect and self-sufficient life—and that, we hold, means living happily and nobly.[22]

1281a2 So we must lay it down that the association which is a state exists not for the purpose of living together but for the sake of noble actions. Those who contribute most to this kind of association are for that very reason entitled to a larger share in the state than those who, though they may be equal or even superior in free birth and in family, are inferior in the virtue that belongs to a citizen. Similarly they are entitled to a larger share than those who are superior in riches but inferior in virtue.

All this makes it clear that all those who dispute about constitutions are using the term 'justice' in a limited sense.

III. x

JUSTICE AND SOVEREIGNTY

1281a11 Another question is 'Where ought the sovereign power of the state to reside?' With the mass of the people? With the rich? With the respectable? With one man, the best of all? Or a tyrant? There are objections to all these. Thus suppose the poor use their numerical superiority to make a distribution of the property of the rich: is not that unjust? 'No, by Zeus,' it may be said, 'it has been done justly, by a decision of the sovereign power.' But what else can we call the very height of injustice? And if the majority, having laid their hands on everything, again distribute the possessions of the few, they are obviously destroying the state. But virtue does not destroy its possessor, nor is justice destructive of the state. So it is clear that this law too cannot be just. Or, secondly, if it *is* just, any actions taken by a tyrant also must be just: his superior strength enables him to use force, just as the mass of the people use force on the rich.

Thirdly, is it just for the few and the wealthy to rule? If so, and they too do this and plunder and help themselves to the goods of the mass, then that is just. And if *that* is so, then it is just in the former case also. The answer clearly is that all these three states of affairs are bad and not just.

1281a28 The fourth alternative, that the respectable should rule and have sovereign power over everything, means that all the rest must be without esteem, being debarred from the honour of holding office under the constitution. For offices, we say, are honours; and if the same persons hold office all the time, the rest must be without honour. Is then the fifth alternative better, that one man, the most worthy, should rule? But this is yet more oligarchical, because it leaves still larger numbers without honour. It might be objected that it is a bad thing for any human being, subject to the affections that enter the soul, to have sovereign power, which ought to be reserved for the law. But that will not make any difference to the problem-cases we have been discussing: there may be a law, but it may have a bias towards oligarchy or democracy, so that exactly the same results will ensue.

END NOTES

1. In this chapter both 'office' and 'authority' translate *archē*, literally 'rule'. 'Rule of a master' translates *despoteia*.
2. *Politikon zōon*, 'an animal whose nature is to live in a *polis* (state)'; cf. I ii, n. 14.
3. *Politikē koinōnia*, 'the association that takes the form of a *polis* (state)'; cf. I i.
4. Or, 'external ("extra-mural"?) or published treatises'.
5. I.e. since a ruler looks after the interests of the ruled, the former claims in due course reciprocal service from the latter.
6. *Leitourgein;* cf. IV iv, n. 11.
7. If, that is, they are to be called citizens.
8. 'Monarch' means literally 'the rule of one'.
9. *Aristos* means 'best'.
10. *Politeia* means 'constitution'.
11. I.e. over slaves; the reference is to the end of III vi.
12. Because we expect to find the ruling class in democracy to be *poor*, and in an oligarchy to be *rich*.
13. In III vii.
14. I.e. to control it, by being citizens and therefore entitled to hold office.
15. I.e. it is just to give more (property, privileges, etc) to the more deserving (persons), less to the less deserving. The reference is to *Nicomachean Ethics*, V iii.
16. I.e. to agree that two things are equal (in size, value, etc.) is easy; to agree that two *persons* are equal (in worth or merit) is difficult, because the criteria are highly disputable.
17. I.e. the association in question: see I i.

18. 'Happiness' is the customary but inadequate translation of *eudaimonia*, the state of well-being which consists in living in the exercise of all, especially the highest (i.e. rational and ethical), faculties of man.
19. Lycophron's date is uncertain. He was probably a pupil of Gorgias (*c*. 483–376), and had sceptical views about the merits of noble birth. Little else is known of him. On this passage, see R. G. Mulgan, *Journal of the History of Ideas*, 40 (1979), pp. 121–8, and W. K. C. Guthrie's reply (p. 128).
20. *Dikaia* (neuter plural), literally 'just things'; perhaps 'just claims'.
21. *Genē, 'kinship-groups', 'clans'*.
22. *Kalos*, 'fine', 'good'.

QUESTIONS

1. What is Aristotle's definition of "just"? What is the relationship of justice to injustice?
2. What is political justice?
3. What is the relationship of justice to law? Does justice require law? Is lawfulness the same as justness?
4. What is the connection between a person's intentions and the justice or injustice of his or her actions?

DOCUMENT

FEAR AND THE SPREAD OF ROMAN TYRANNY

Cicero

Marcus Tullius Cicero (106–43 B.C.E.), the greatest of Rome's public speakers as well as a leading philosopher and writer, also had an active political career. Although he was born in a provincial town and was not an aristocrat, he became a successful advocate and started to establish a reputation in his twenties. After studying philosophy in Greece, he returned to Rome and entered public life, serving in a series of high offices at the youngest statutory age. His attacks on a corrupt governor of Sicily in 70 brought him considerable fame. During his term as consul (chief magistrate) in 63, he suppressed an attempted revolution, gaining both popularity and a hostility that led to his exile from Rome for four years. Thereafter, though he remained a public figure, he was increasingly sidelined as generals like Pompey and Caesar seized power. He used these years to publish a great variety of works, including fifty-eight of his speeches, numerous treatises on philosophy and rhetoric, and hundreds of letters. He returned to the political stage in 44 when he launched a series of attacks on Marc Antony—the famous Philippics. *This act of political courage in defense of the old republican values of Rome led to his execution in the following year.*

In the present selection, from the second book of Cicero's popular moral treatise On Duties, *the Roman statesman argued that fear is ultimately not an effective tool of government, and traced the decline of Rome to its reliance on force rather than goodwill. Machiavelli had this passage in mind in his famous discussion of "Whether It Is Better to Be Feared than Loved" in* The Prince.

There are a number of reasons why people may, on occasion be willing not merely to help some individual, but actually to subordinate themselves to his authority and power. The motives which induce them to do this include, goodwill; gratitude for favours conferred; the other person's eminence; the calculation that submission may prove a source of profit; the fear that if they do not subject themselves voluntarily their subjection may in any case be imposed by force; the reliance on promises given by the other party; or finally—as we have so often seen in our own country—the actual receipt of a bribe, about which I said something just now.

However, the best of all means of looking after one's own interests is by winning affection. I mentioned fear: but to make people frightened is the way not to maintain one's position but to lose it. Ennius wrote: 'People hate the man they fear; and the man they hate they want to see dead.'[1] And he was perfectly right. Only recently we had occasion to learn, if we did not know it already, that no amount of power, however enormous, can stand up against widespread unpopularity. That tyrant of ours, when he was alive, had to be endured by the State, since he had suppressed its operations by brute force. Now that he is dead, it is true, Rome has become more his slave even than it was in his lifetime; all the same, his death is an excellent illustration of the disastrous results of getting oneself generally hated. And the same lesson is taught by the similar fates of all other despots, scarcely any of whom have ever escaped the same sort of end. For fear is a very poor guarantee that power will last. The only possible way to keep it is by mobilizing goodwill.

Rulers who keep the populations down by force will obviously have to employ brutal methods, like masters who feel compelled to treat their servants harshly because they cannot keep them in order in any other way. But to make oneself feared deliberately, in a free state, is a lunatic procedure. For however drastically a man may have suppressed the free operation of the law and intimidated the spirit of liberty, sooner or later these submerged blessings will be brought up to the surface again, either by inarticulate public feeling or through the secret ballots which elect officers of state. And freedom suppressed and then regained bites more sharply than if it had never been in peril. So here is a principle which has the widest possible application, a principle that ensures not only a man's safety but his prosperity and power: it is better to win affection than fear. That is the right recipe for getting what we want and achieving success, both in our private and our public lives.

Men who are eager to terrorize others will inevitably become frightened of the very people they are intimidating. Think of the excruciating anxieties of the elder Dionysius, who was so terrified by his barber's razor that he preferred to singe his own hair with burning coal. And what do you imagine was the state of mind of Alexander of Pherae? History tells us that he loved his wife Thebe very much. All the same, whenever he wanted to visit her bedroom after dinner we are told that he ordered a barbarian, some creature covered with Thracian tattoos, to walk in front of him brandishing a drawn sword. He also sent members of his bodyguard ahead with instructions to search the lady's jewel-cases and make sure no weapons were hidden among her clothes. What an unhappy man he must have been, if he believed a barbarous branded slave was more likely to be loyal than his own wife! However, he turned out to be perfectly right. For in the end Thebe, suspecting he had a mistress, did actually assassinate him.

No power on earth, if it labours beneath the burden of fear, can possibly be strong enough to survive. Witness Phalaris, who became notorious for his unequalled cruelty. He was not, it is true, the victim of domestic treachery, like Alexander of Pherae whose fate I was speaking of. Nor was he murdered by a small group of conspirators, like our man here in Rome. Phalaris's end was different: the whole population of Agrigentum rose up in revolt and went for him. And remember the case of Demetrius, whom the Macedonians abandoned in a body to go over to Pyrrhus. Consider what happened to the Spartans, too. When they exercised their supremacy oppressively, almost the entire body of their allies deserted them and stood as passive spectators watching the disastrous Spartan defeat at Leuctra.[2]

You will see that I prefer to prove my point by examples taken from foreign history rather than from our own. But I do also want to say this. As long as the Roman people governed its empire by goodwill and not injustice, our wars were fought either to protect our subject allies or to defend our own territory. When the wars were over, their after-effects were merciful—or at least no more severe than they had to be. In those days the Roman Senate was a haven of refuge for foreign kings, for whole peoples and nations. The one ambition of our officials and commanders was to gain glory by loyally and justly upholding the safety of our provinces and allies. And so it could truthfully be said that we were not so much the rulers of the world as its protectors.

Even before Sulla's time these traditional high standards were already on the wane. Since the time of his triumph, we have abandoned such ideals altogether. When we treated our own fellow-citizens with such brutality, it could no longer seem wrong to inflict even the most frightful oppressions on our allies. Sulla's cause, it is true, was a just one; but his victory proved appalling. Planting his spear in the Forum he proceeded to auction the possessions of men who were patriots and people of substance—or, at the very least, every one of them was a Roman citizen.[3] Yet he had the effrontery to declare that the objects he was selling were spoils he had won from an enemy in war. After him came a man whose cause was not right but evil; and his success was even more horrible than Sulla's.[4] Mere confiscations of the property of individual citizens were far from enough to satisfy him. Whole provinces and countries succumbed to his onslaught, in one comprehensive universal catastrophe. Entire foreign nations were given over to ruin and destruction.

Lately the world has been given a specific illustration of the sort of commonwealth that has vanished. For we have seen, with our own eyes, a model of the vanquished city of Massilia carried in a Roman triumphal procession.[5] And yet it was only by the staunch support of this community, now the victim of conquest and triumph, that our generals in the past were able to win their own Triumphs, returning victorious from Transalpine wars. That is by no means the only injury to our allies that I could mention. But I have singled it out, because there has never been a greater crime under the sun.

Surely, then, our present sufferings are all too well deserved. For had we not allowed outrages to go unpunished on all sides, it would never have been possible for a single individual to seize tyrannical power. As heirs of his personal estate only a few names were listed; but to take over his ambitions a whole host of vile characters was ready. The seeds and causes of civil wars will always be with us for as long as people remember that blood-soaked spear in the Forum—and as long as they hope to see it come again. Publius Sulla was the man who brandished it, when his kinsman was dictator, and it was the same Publius Sulla again, thirty-six years later, who had the effrontery to stand beside another spear, set up for an even more abominable auction.[6] And there was yet another Sulla too: a clerk under the first dictator, he was city treasurer under the second. Such are the proofs that, while there are such vastly lucrative rewards, civil war will never end.

Here in the city nothing is left—only the lifeless walls of houses. And even they look afraid that some further terrifying attack may be imminent. The real Rome has gone for ever.

END NOTES

1. Possibly from the *Thyestes* of Ennius.
2. Alexander of Pherae in Thessaly reigned from 3169 to 358. The army of Demetrius Poliorcetes (336–283 B.C.E.), son of Antigonus I of Macedonia, deserted in 288 to King Pyrrhus of Epirus. The Spartans were defeated by the Thebans at Leuctra in 371.
3. Sulla occupied Rome in 82 B.C.E. and became dictator in the following year. The Romans used to set up a spear as a sign of an auction-sale; the custom was derived from the sale of booty taken in war.
4. Caesar.
5. Massilia (Marseille), besieged and taken in 49 B.C.E. by Caesar. Cicero is referring to the multiple Triumph he celebrated in 46, and to the earlier alliance with Massilia which had enabled Rome to annex the province of Gallia Narbonensis (southern France) in 121 B.C.E.
6. Under Caesar. Publius Cornelius Sulla was the nephew of Lucius Cornelius Sulla the dictator. Nevertheless, Cicero spoke in Publius's defence in 62 B.C.E. (the *Pro Sulla*). The third Sulla mentioned was a freedman of the dictator.

QUESTIONS

1. What reasons, according to Cicero, might induce people to submit themselves to the government of others?
2. Why is "winning affection" the best way to convince people to obey the authority of a leader? Are Cicero's reasons for preferring affection as a means to this end moral, practical, or both?
3. How does Cicero reach this conclusion; how does he demonstrate it? How does he explain, "It is better to win affection than fear?"
4. What is "the real Rome" and what has happened to it? Why?

DOCUMENT

ROMAN LAW ON FUGITIVE SLAVES

The Digest of Roman Law

Around 530 C.E., the Emperor Justinian ordered legal experts to compile the corpus of Roman laws and jurisprudence as part of his program to restore and extend the Roman Empire. The most important book for historians of the Roman Empire in this collection was the so-called Digest, *edited by the jurist Tribonian. The* Digest *contained a collection of opinions, arranged by topics, by leading Roman jurists. All of the jurists included, the most important being Ulpian, Paulus and Callimachus, had lived before 300 C.E. The texts of the* Digest *thus reveal Roman thinking on legal issues from a period when the Empire still enjoyed great prestige, wealth, and stability. They are our best evidence of Roman legal practice and the principles underlying the enforcement of Roman law.*

In the two passages given in this selection, the Digest *cited opinions of Roman jurists and various other sources of law such as senatorial decrees to define what a fugitive slave was and summarize the laws relating to their recovery and punishment.*

Ofilius[1] defines what a fugitive slave is: A runaway is a slave who remains absent from the house of his master for the sake of flight, by which he seeks to hide himself from his master.

"Fugitive Slaves and Maroon Communities," by Ulpian, reprinted from *Spartacus and the Slave Wars: A Brief History with Documents*, translated and edited by Bernard D. Shaw.

But Caelius says that man also is a fugitive who flees with the intent of not returning to his master but who changes his mind and returns to him. For no one, he says, who is guilty of such a grave offense becomes innocent simply because of his remorse.

Cassius writes, simply, that man is a fugitive slave who leaves his master with purposeful intent.

Likewise, in Vivianus it is stated that being a fugitive is to be determined by the man's intent. . . so that he is not a runaway who has fled from a teacher to whom he has been given for training, if perhaps he fled because he had been maltreated by the man. . . and Vivianus states the same principle if he was savagely abused by the man.

. . . Nor can that man be said to be a runaway who has come to such a state of despair that he wishes to hurl himself off a height. . . . It is simply the case that he wishes to end his own life. . . .

Caelius also writes that if you purchase a slave who then hurls himself into the Tiber River, he will not be classified as a runaway as long as he escaped from his master with the intention of killing himself. But if he planned his flight first, and then later changed his mind and threw himself into the Tiber, then he is still classified as a fugitive. He holds the same view concerning a slave who throws himself off a bridge. . . .

Likewise, Caelius states that if a slave, while he is on the farm, leaves the farmhouse with the intention of escaping but is apprehended by someone before he has got beyond the lands [boundaries] of the farm, he would seem to be a fugitive, for it is his intent that makes him a runaway.

Likewise, he states that even the slave who takes even one or two steps in flight or who just begins to run, if he is not able to evade his master who is hunting him down, is a fugitive.

For he correctly states that flight is a type of liberty, in that the slave has gained freedom from his master's power, even if only for the moment.

ULPIAN

The Law Concerning Fugitive Slaves

Third Century A.D.

He who hides a runaway slave is himself a thief.

The Senate has decreed that fugitive slaves are not to be allowed onto rural domains, nor are they to be protected by the domain managers or by the agents of the landowners, and it has established a penalty for this crime. In the case of those persons who have either restored the runaway slaves to their owners or brought them before the municipal magistrates within twenty days, the Senate grants forgiveness for their earlier non-compliance. By the terms of the same decree of the Senate, immunity from punishment is granted to the person who, after discovering runaway slaves on his lands, returns them to their master or hands them over to the magistrates within the prescribed time.

Moreover, this same decree of the Senate has granted the right of entry to any soldier or ordinary civilian to the lands of senators or ordinary civilians for the purpose of making a search for fugitive slaves. The *Lex Fabia*[2] and a *senatus consultum* issued when Modestus was consul concerned this same matter. This measure [the Senate's decree] held that persons who propose to make a search for runaway slaves should present a letter to the local magistrates, and that a fine of one hundred gold pieces is to be levied against those magistrates who, when they have been presented with such a letter, fail to assist the persons making the search. Furthermore, the same penalty applies in the case of the man who does not allow such a search to be made of his property. There is also a general letter[3] issued by the emperors Marcus Aurelius and Commodus in which it is declared that governors, municipal magistrates, and local militia units of the army are to give assistance to owners who are searching for their runaway slaves. They are to assist with the return of the runaways who are discovered, and, further, they are to see that those persons with whom the slaves found refuge are to be punished if a crime has been committed.

Any person whosoever apprehends a runaway slave must produce him in public.

Magistrates are rightly warned that they are to guard runaway slaves carefully to keep them from escaping.

The term *fugitive* includes even the slave who "wanders off" without permission. The jurist Labeo, in his first book on the *Praetor's Edict,* however, writes that the term *fugitive* does not include a child born from a slave woman who is a runaway.

To be "produced in public" means to be handed over to municipal magistrates or to officials of the state. . . .

Fugitive slaves are to be kept under guard up to the time when they are taken before the prefect of the night watch (at Rome) or before the provincial governor.

The names of these slaves, as well as the marks on their bodies and the person to whom they belong, are to be reported to the magistrate, so that the fugitives can be more easily identified and apprehended. The word *marks* also includes scars. The law is the same if one posts the notice in writing in public or places it on a building.

Callistratus in his sixth book on judicial hearings: Simple runaways are to be returned to their owners, but if they have acted as if they were free men, they are usually punished more severely.

Ulpian in his seventh book on the duties of the proconsul: The emperor Antoninus Pius wrote a legal reply that if a man wishes to search for a runaway slave on another man's land, he can approach the governor of the province, who will then issue a letter to him. If the situation warrants, the governor will also assign an assistant to the man so that he will be permitted to enter the other man's property and conduct a search. The same governor shall exact a penalty from the man who does not allow his property to be searched. Likewise, the emperor Marcus Aurelius, in a speech that he read in the senate, granted the right of entry to imperial as well as senatorial and private lands to those who wish to search for fugitive slaves, and he permitted them to make a thorough search for the tracks and the hiding places of those who are concealing runaways.

END NOTES

1. This name and all the others cited in this document (e.g., Caelius, Cassius) are those of Roman jurists whose opinions are being cited.
2. A law dated to the first or second century B.C.E. that legislated against kidnapping, treating a free man as a slave, or persuading another person's slave to escape.
3. A decree issued by the emperor in the form of a letter to his officials that had general legal force for all the citizens of the empire.

QUESTIONS

1. What are the different definitions of "fugitive slave"? What explains these differences? Do these differences matter?
2. What ideas about the relationship between action and intention are at work in these varying definitions?
3. Do non-slaves, including those who do not own slaves, have an obligation to make the law of slavery work? What does this say about the place of slavery in Roman society?
4. What is the authority for these different definitions and for the other wrongs described here? Where does law come from and how is the law made known? Why would it be difficult to implement the law regarding fugitive slaves?

DOCUMENT

EXCERPT FROM SURA 4, "WOMEN"

The Qur'an

The Qur'an is believed by Muslims to be the eternal, uncreated Word of God revealed to Muhammad by the Angel Gabriel between the years 610 and 632 C. E. It was written down, collected, and arranged at some later point; Muslim tradition believes this took place during the rule of the Caliph 'Uthman (d. 656), but there is much scholarly contention on this point.

The Qur'an is the sacred text and fundamental document of Islam and Islamic civilization. Written in Arabic, it consists of 114 Suras, or chapters, arranged in order of descending length. There is great thematic and stylistic variation not only throughout the Qur'an, but often within each Sura. There is also very little narrative or explanation in it; as a result, it is a very opaque without outside reference to the tradition that has grown up around it. This tradition is particularly important to Muslims because they need to determine the chronological order of the chapters, as, according to religious doctrine, later verses are held to abrogate earlier ones whenever there is a contradiction between them.

This sura, 'al-Nisa' ("Women"), is held by Muslim tradition to have been revealed in Medina when Muhammad's favorite wife, 'Aisha, was brought into his house to live with him (she is said to have been nine years old when she commenced her marital duties). It deals largely with the status of women, outlining the rights and duties both of women and of Muslim men toward them.

AL-NISA'

In the Name of Allah, the Compassionate, the Merciful

1 O people, fear your Lord who created you from a single soul,[1] and from it 1
He created its mate,[2] and from both He scattered abroad many men and
women; and fear Allah in whose name you appeal to one another, and invoke family relationships. Surely Allah is a watcher over you.

Render unto the orphans their property and do not exchange worthless things for good ones, and do not devour their property together with your property. That indeed is a great sin!

If you fear that you cannot deal justly with the orphans, then marry such of the women as appeal to you, two, three or four; but if you fear that you cannot be equitable, then only one, or what your right hands own.[3] That is more likely to enable you to avoid unfairness.[4]

And give women their dowries as a free gift, but if they choose to give you anything of it, then consume it with enjoyment and pleasure.

5 But do not give the feeble-minded the property that Allah assigned to 5
you as a means of livelihood. Provide for them therefrom, clothe them and
speak kindly to them.

Test the orphans until they reach the age of marriage; then, if you discern in them sound judgement, deliver to them their property; and do not consume it extravagantly and hastily before they come of age. He who is rich should be abstinent, and he who is poor should consume fairly. And when you deliver to them their property, call in witnesses thereon. God suffices as a Reckoner!

Men should have a share of what parents and kinsmen leave behind; and women a share or what parents and kinsmen leave, whether small or large, as an obligatory portion.

And if the division is attended by kinsmen, orphans or poor men, then give them a share of it and speak to them kindly.

And let those who worry about the weak offspring they may leave behind them[5] be mindful [of the orphans]. Let them fear Allah and speak justly.

10 Those who devour the property of orphans unjustly, devour fire in their bellies, and they will burn in a blazing fire.

Allah commands you, with respect to your children, that the male shall inherit the equivalent of the share of two females. If there be more than two females, then they should receive two-thirds of what he[6] leaves; but if there is only one female, she is entitled to one-half. To each of his parents, one-sixth of what he leaves, if he has any children; but if he has no children, then his parents will inherit him, the mother receiving one-third. But if he has any brothers, then his mother receives one-sixth, after any will he had made or any debt he had incurred [is taken care of]. Your fathers and sons – you know not who of them is of greater advantage to you. This is a law from Allah; Allah surely is All-Knowing, Wise.

You are entitled to half of what your wives leave, if they have no children; but if they have any children, then you are entitled to one-quarter of what they leave, after any will they had made or any loan they had incurred [is taken care of]. And they are entitled to one-quarter of what you leave, if you have no children; but if you have any children, then they are entitled to one-eighth of what you leave, after any will you had made or loan you had incurred [is taken care of]. And if a man or a woman dies having no children or parents, but has a brother or a sister, then each shall have one-sixth; if they are more than that, then they shall share one-third, after any will made or debt incurred [is taken care of] without prejudice. This is a commandment from Allah, and Allah is All-Knowing, Wise.

These are the ordinances of Allah, and whoever obeys Allah and His Apostle, He will admit him into gardens beneath which rivers flow, abiding therein forever. That is the great victory!

But whoever disobeys Allah and His Apostle and transgresses His bounds, He will admit him into the Fire, wherein he shall abide forever, and his will be a demeaning punishment!

15 As for those of your women who commit adultery, call four witnesses from your own against them; and if they testify, then detain them in the houses till death overtakes them or Allah opens another way for them.[7]

If two [men] of you commit it, punish them both. If they repent and mend their ways, then leave them alone. Allah is truly All-Forgiving, Merciful.

Allah has taken upon Himself to accept the repentance of those who commit evil in ignorance and then repent immediately after that. Those, He will forgive and Allah is All-Knowing, Wise.

But not the repentance of those who commit evil deeds, and when one of them is faced with death, he says: "Now I repent"; nor the repentance of those who die as unbelievers. For these, we have prepared a very painful punishment!

O believers, it is not lawful for you to inherit the women [of deceased kinsmen] against their will;[8] nor restrain them in order to take away part of what you had given them, unless they commit flagrant adultery. Associate with them kindly; and if you feel aversion towards them, it may well be that you will he averse to something, from which Allah brings out a lot of good.

If you wish to have one wife in the place of another and you have given either of them a heap of gold, do not take any of it back. Would you take it by recourse to injustice and manifest sin?

For how can you take it back, when you have been intimate one with the other, and they had taken from you a solemn pledge?

And do not marry women that your fathers had married, unless it has already happened. Surely it is indecent and hateful, and it is an evil course!

Unlawful to you are your mothers, your daughters, your sister, your paternal and maternal aunts, your brother's daughters and sister's daughters, your foster-mothers who gave you suck, your foster-sisters, your wives' mothers, your step-daughters who are in your custody, born to your wives whom you have lain with. But if you have not lain with them, then you are not at fault. [It is also not lawful to marry] the wives of your sons who are of your own loins, or to take in two sisters together, unless this has already happened. Allah is truly All-Forgiving and Merciful!

Or married women, except those your right hands possess.[9] This is Allah's decree for you. Beyond these it is lawful for you to seek, by means of your wealth, any women, to marry and not to debauch. Those of them you have enjoyed, you should give them their dowries as a matter of obligation; but you are not liable to reproach for whatever you mutually agree upon, apart from the obligatory payment.[10] Allah is indeed All-Knowing, Wise!

Whoever of you cannot afford to marry a free, believing woman, let him choose from whatever your right hands possess[11] of believing girls.

Allah knows best your faith; you come one from the other. So marry them with their parents' leave and give them their dowry honourably, as chaste women, neither committing adultery nor taking lovers. If they are legally married and commit adultery, their punishment shall be half that of a free woman. Such is the law for those of you who fear committing sin; but to abstain is better for you. Allah is All-Forgiving and Merciful!

Allah wants to explain to you [His laws] and to guide you along the paths of those who preceded you, and to be Merciful to you. Allah is All-Knowing, Wise!

Allah also wants to be Merciful to you, but those who follow their lusts want you to deviate greatly from the right course.

Allah wishes to lighten your burden; for man was created weak.

O believers, do not consume your wealth illegally, unless there be trading by mutual agreement among you; and do not kill yourselves. Allah is indeed Merciful to you!

30 And whoever acts aggressively and wrongfully, We shall cast him in 30
the Fire; this being an easy matter for Allah.

If you avoid the grave sins you are forbidden, We will remit your evil deeds and let you enter into an honourable place.[12]

Do not covet that with which Allah has favoured some of you over the others. Men have a share of what they earned, and women a share of what they earned. And ask Allah to give you of His bounty. Allah indeed has knowledge of everything!

To every one We have appointed heirs to inherit part of what the parents or the kinsmen bequeath. Those with whom you made a compact, give them their share. Surely Allah is witness to everything.

Men are in charge of women, because Allah has made some of them excel the others, and because they spend some of their wealth. Hence righteous women are obedient, guarding the unseen which Allah has guarded. And those of them that you fear might rebel, admonish them and abandon them in their beds and beat them. Should they obey you, do not seek a way of harming them; for Allah is Sublime and Great!

35 And if you fear a breach between the two,[13] then send forth an arbiter 35
from his relatives and another arbiter from her relatives. If they both desire reconciliation, Allah will bring them together. Allah is indeed All-Knowing, Well-informed.

Worship Allah and do not associate with Him anything. Show kindness to the parents, to kinsmen, to orphans, the destitute, the close and distant neighbour, the companion by your side, the wayfarer and those whom your right hands possess. Allah does nor love the arrogant and boastful,

Those who are niggardly, and order people to be niggardly, and conceal what Allah has given them of His bounty, We have prepared for the unbelievers a demeaning punishment;

And for those who spend their wealth in order to show off, and do not believe in Allah and the Last Day. He who has the Devil as a companion, an evil companion has he!

And what would it cost them were they to believe in Allah and the Last Day and spend part of what Allah has provided for them? Allah knows them very well!

40 Surely Allah will not wrong anyone an atom's weight; and if it is a good 40
deed, He will multiply it and give from Himself in addition a great reward.

How then will it be, when We bring forward from each nation a witness[14] and We bring you[15] forth as a witness against them?

On that day, those who disbelieved and disobeyed the Apostle will wish that the earth were levelled upon them, and they will conceal nothing from Allah.

O believers, do not approach prayer while you are drunk, until you know what you are unclean – unless you are on a journey – until you have washed yourselves. And if you are sick or on a journey, or if any one of you has relieved himself, or you have touched women and could not find water, you might rub yourselves with clean earth, wiping your faces and hands with it. Allah indeed is Pardoning, All-Forgiving!

Have you not considered those who have received a portion of the Book, procuring error and wanting you to go astray?

45 Allah knows best your enemies; Allah suffices as Protector, Allah suf- 45
fices as Supporter!

Some of the Jews take words out of their context and say: "We have heard, but disobey; and hear as though you hear not." And [they] say; "*ra'ina*,[16] twisting their tongues and slandering religion. Had they said: "We have heard and we obey: hear and look at us", it would have been better for them and more upright; but Allah has cursed them on account of their disbelief, so they – except for a few – do not believe.

O People of the Book, believe in what We have revealed confirming what you already possess, before We obliterate faces, turning them on their backs, or curse them as We have cursed the Sabbath-breakers, and Allah's command was accomplished!

END NOTES

1. Adam
2. Eve.
3. Captives of war or slave-girls
4. It should be noted that this verse permits polygamy under special circumstances, but docs not enjoin it. No less important is the fact that this verse was revealed following the Battle of Uhud in which seventy Muslim fighters were killed, leaving many widows and other dependant without a provider for them. Hence most commentators regard the permission as an exception and not a rule.
5. That is, after their death.
6. The deceased father,
7. This verse was later abrogated and replaced by a hundred lashes for the unmarried and stoning for the married. See Sura 24. verse 2.
8. The women of deceased relatives. Among the pre-Islamic Arbas, it was the custom that when a man died, his elder son or other relatives had the right to "own" his widow or widows. Then they either married them, themselves, without giving a dowry, or married them to others, or prohibited them from marriage.
9. The captives of war or slave-girls.
10. The dowry.
11. The captives of war or slave-girls.
12. That is, into Paradise.
13. The husband and wife.
14. Its prophet.
15. Muhammad.
16. A word of abuse.

QUESTIONS

1. What is the relative share of inheritance of male and female children? Of husbands and wives?
2. What treatment does the text enjoin for women who might be disobedient?
3. What does verse 3 mean when it states, "If you fear that you cannot deal justly with the orphans, then marry such of the women as appeal to you, two, three or four"?
4. What is the attitude displayed in this chapter toward women?

DOCUMENT

EXCERPT FROM SURA 5, "THE TABLE"

The Qur'an

The Qur'an is believed by Muslims to be the eternal, uncreated Word of God revealed to Muhammad by the Angel Gabriel between the years 610 and 632 C.E. It was written down, collected, and arranged at some later point; Muslim tradition believes that this took place during the rule of the Caliph 'Uthman (d. 656), but there is much scholarly contention on this point.

The Qur'an is the sacred text and fundamental document of Islam and Islamic civilization. Written in Arabic, it consists of 114 Suras, or chapters, arranged in order of descending length. There is great thematic and stylistic variation not only throughout the Qur'an, but often within each Sura. There is also very little narrative or explanation in it; as a result, it is very opaque without outside reference to the tradition that has grown up around it. This tradition is particularly important to Muslims because they need to determine the chronological order of the chapters, as, according to religious doctrine, later verses are held to abrogate earlier ones whenever there is a contradiction between them.

Sura 5, al-Ma'ida ("the table") is held by Muslim religious tradition to have been revealed to Muhammad in Medina, after the Hijra. Although it contains many legal precepts, it, like the other longer Suras, deals mainly with clarifying the religious status of the old revealed religions (Judaism and Christianity) and their relationship to the new dispensation of the Qur'an.

AL-MÁIDA

In the Name of Allah, the Compassionate, the Merciful

1 O believers, fulfil your obligations. Lawful to you are the beasts of the 1
flock, except what is being recited to you now; "Game is unlawful to you
while you are on pilgrimage." Allah decrees whatever He pleases.

O believers, do not violate the rites of Allah, or the sacred month, or
the sacrificial offerings, or the animals with garlands, or those who repair
to the Sacred House, seeking the bounty and pleasure of their Lord. When
you are through with the rites of pilgrimage, you can go hunting. And let
not the hatred of those who debar you from the Sacred Mosque prompt
you to transgress. Fear Allah; Allah is severe in retribution.

You are forbidden the eating of carrion, blood, the flesh of swine as
well as whatever is slaughtered in the name of any one other than Allah.
[You are forbidden] also the animals strangled or beaten to death, those
that fall and die, those killed by goring with the horn or mangled by wild
beasts, except those which you slaughter and those sacrificed on stones set
up [for idols]. [You are forbidden] to use divining arrows;[1] it is an evil
practice. Today, those who disbelieve have despaired of your religion; so
do not fear them, but fear Me. Today, I have perfected your religion for
you, completed My grace on you and approved Islam as a religion for you.
Yet, whoever is compelled by reason of hunger,[2] but not intending to sin,
then surely Allah is All-Forgiving, Merciful.

They ask you: "What is lawful to them?" say: "The good things are
lawful; and such hunting birds or hounds that you have taught, as Allah
has taught you. You may eat whatever they catch for you, mentioning
Allah's name over it. Fear Allah, for Allah is, indeed, quick in reckoning!"

5 This day the good things have been made lawful to you; the food of 5
the People of the Book is lawful to you, and your food is lawful to them;
and so are the believing women who are chaste, and the chaste women of
those who were given the Book before you, provided you give them their
dowries and take them in marriage, not in fornication or as mistresses. If
any one denies the faith, his work shall be of no avail to him, and in the
Hereafter he will rank with the losers.

O believers, if you rise to pray, wash your faces and your hands up to
the elbows and wipe your heads and your feet up to the ankles. If you are

unclean, then cleanse yourselves; and if you are sick or on a journey, and if one of you has come from the restroom, or if you have touched women and cannot find any water, then take some clean earth and wipe your faces and hands with it. Allah does not wish to burden you, but to purify you and complete His grace upon you, that you may be thankful.

And remember Allah's grace upon you and His covenant with which he bound you, when you said: "We hear and we obey." Fear Allah; Allah indeed knows well the thoughts in the hearts!

O believers, be dutiful to Allah and bearers of witness with justice; and do not let the hatred of a certain group drive you to be unequitable. Be equitable; that is nearer to piety, and fear Allah. Allah indeed is fully aware of what you do!

Allah has promised those who believe and do the good deeds—they shall have forgiveness and a great reward.

10 But those who disbelieve and deny our revelations—those are the people of Hell.

O believers, remember Allah's grace upon you, when certain people intended to reach out to you with their hands but Allah restrained them. Fear Allah, and in Allah let the believers put their trust.

Allah made a covenant with the Children of Israel, and We raised among them twelve chieftains. And Allah said: "I am with you. Surely, if you perform the prayer, give the alms, believe in My apostles and support them and lend Allah a fair loan,[3] I will forgive you your sins and admit you into gardens, beneath which rivers flow. But if any one of you disbelieves afterwards, he certainly strays from the right path.

And on account of their violating their covenant, We cursed them and caused their hearts to harden; they take the words[4] out of their context and forget part of what they were enjoined, and you do not cease to find them treacherous, except for a few of them. Yet, pardon them and forgive; God surely loves those who do good to others.

And with some of those who say: "We are Christians", we made a covenant; but they forgot part of what they were reminded of; so we stirred up enmity and hatred among them till the Day of Resurrection. Allah will let them know what they did.

15 O People of the Book,[5] Our Apostle came to you to show you much of what you used to conceal of the Book[6] and to pardon a great deal. Indeed, a light and a clear Book[7] has come to you from Allah.

Allah guides with it those who seek His good pleasure to the paths of peace, brings them out of the shadows of darkness into the light, by His leave, and guides them to a straight path.

Unbelievers are those who say: "Allah is the Messiah, son of Mary." Say: "Who could prevent Allah, if He wished, from destroying the Messiah, son of Mary, and his mother too, together with all those on the face of the earth?" To Allah belongs the kingdom of the heavens and the earth and what lies between them. He creates whatever He pleases, and Allah has power over everything!

The Jews and the Christians have said: "We are Allah's children and His beloved." Say: "Why then does He punish you for your sins? You are rather human beings, part of those whom He has created. He forgives whom He pleases and punishes whom He pleases." And to Allah belongs the kingdom of the heavens and the earth and what is in between, and unto Him is the final return!

O People of the Book, Our Apostle has come to you to make clear to you [the religious tenets] after a cessation of apostles, lest you should say: "No bearer of good news or a warner has come to us." So now a bearer of good news and a warner has come to you; and Allah has power over everything!

20 And when Moses said to his people; "O my people, remember Allah's 20
grace upon you, how He raised up prophets among you, made you kings and gave you what He has not given any other nation.

"My people, enter the Holy Land which Allah ordained for you,[8] and do not turn back, lest you become the losers."

They said: "O Moses, there is in it a mighty people; we shall not enter it until they leave it. If they leave it, then we shall enter."

Two men of those who feared [Allah] and whom Allah favoured said: "Enter the gate and [fall] upon them; if you enter it, you will be victorious. In Allah put your trust, if you are true believers."

They said: "O Moses, we shall never enter it, so long as they are in it. So, go forth, you and your Lord, and fight; we are staying put here."

25 He said: "Lord, I have no power over anybody other than myself and 25
my brother; so separate us from the ungodly people."

Allah said: "It shall be forbidden them for forty years, during which they shall wander aimlessly in the land; so do not grieve for the ungodly people!"

And recite to them in all truth the tale of Adam's two sons, when they offered a sacrifice, which was accepted from one, but not accepted from the other. The latter said: "I will surely kill you", the other replied: "Allah accepts only from the God-fearing.

"Should you stretch your hand out to kill me, I will not stretch my hand out to kill you; for I fear Allah, Lord of the Worlds.

"I only wish that you be charged with my sin and yours and thus be one of the companions of the Fire; and that is the reward of the evil-doers."

Then, his soul prompted him to kill his brother; and so he killed him and became one of the losers.

30 Then, Allah sent forth a raven digging the earth to show him how to 30
bury his brother's corpse. He said: "Woe is me, am I unable to be like this raven and bury the corpse of my brother?" Thus he became one of the remourseful.

For that reason, we decreed for the Children of Israel that whoever kills a soul, not in retaliation for a soul or corruption in the land, is like one who has killed the whole of mankind; and whoever saves a life is like one who saves the lives of all mankind. Our apostles came to them with the clear proofs; but afterwards many of them continued to commit excesses in the land.

Indeed, the punishment of those who fight Allah and His Apostle and go around corrupting the land is to be killed, crucified, have their hands and feet cut off on opposite sides, or to be banished from the land. That is a disgrace for them in this life, and in the life to come theirs will be a terrible punishment.

Except for those who repent before you overpower them. Know, then, that Allah is All-Forgiving, Merciful.

35 O believers, fear Allah and seek the means to win His favour. Fight in 35
His way so that you may prosper.

As to the unbelievers, even if they had all there is on earth and the like of it too to redeem themselves from the punishment of the Day of Resurrection therewith, it will not be accepted from them, and a very painful punishment shall be in store for them.

They will then wish to come out of the Fire, but they will never come out, and theirs is an everlasting punishment!

As for the thieves, whether male or female, cut off their hands in punishment for what they did, as an exemplary punishment from Allah. Allah is Mighty and Wise.

But whoever repents after his wrongdoing and mends his ways, Allah will forgive him. Allah is indeed All-Forgiving, Merciful! . . .

END NOTES

1. Arrows used by pre-Islamic Arabs to cast lots.
2. That is, compelled to eat what is forbidden.
3. That is, if you spend in the way ordered by Allah.
4. The words in the Torah.
5. The Jews and the Christians.
6. The Scriptures.
7. The Qur'an.
8. That is, ordained that you should enter.

QUESTION

1. What kinds of animals are forbidden for eating?
2. What steps does the Sura prescribe before prayer?
3. Why, according to this Sura, was Muhammad sent by God?
4. In what ways is the attitude toward Jews and Christians displayed in this chapter similar to or different from displayed in Sura 3?

DOCUMENT

EXCERPT FROM SURA 47, "MUHAMMAD"

The Qur'an

The Qur'an is believed by Muslims to be the eternal, uncreated Word of God revealed to Muhammad by the Angel Gabriel between the years 610 and 632 C.E. It was written down, collected, and arranged at some later point; Muslim tradition believes that this took place during the rule of the Caliph 'Uthman (d. 656), but there is much scholarly contention on this point.

The Qur'an is the sacred text and fundamental document of Islam and Islamic civilization. Written in Arabic, it consists of 114 Suras, or chapters, arranged in order of descending length. There is great thematic and stylistic variation not only throughout the Qur'an, but often within each Sura. There is also very little narrative or explanation in it; as a result, it is very opaque without outside reference to the tradition that has grown up around it. This tradition is particularly important to Muslims because they need to determine the chronological order of the chapters since, according to religious doctrine, later verses are held to abrogate earlier ones whenever there is a contradiction between them.

This Sura, "Muhammad," is one of only two occasions in the Qur'an in which a seventh-century person is mentioned by name. The Sura is also known as "Qital" ("War") because of the amount of space devoted to that subject within it. Most Muslim commentators hold that it was revealed at Medina, after Muhammad had already become the political leader of a community.

MUHAMMAND (THE PROPHET)

In the Name of Allah, the Compassionate, the Merciful

1 Those who have disbelieved and barred others from the path of Allah, He 1
will render their works perverse;

But those who have believed and done the righteous deeds and believed in what was sent down upon Muhammad, which is the Truth from their Lord, He will remit their sins and set their minds aright.

That is because those who have disbelieved have followed falsehood, but those who have believed have followed the truth from their Lord. Thus does Allah frame their parables for mankind.

So, when you meet the unbelievers, strike their necks till you have bloodied them, then fasten the shackles. Thereupon, release them freely or for a ransom, till the war is over. So be it. Yet had Allah wished, He would have taken vengeance upon them, but He wanted to test you by one another. Those who die in the cause of Allah, He will not render their works perverse.

5 He shall guide them and set their minds aright; 5

And shall admit them into Paradise which He has made known to them.

O believers, if you support Allah, He will support you and steady your footsteps.

But as to the unbelievers, wretched are they and perverse are their works.

That is because they despised what Allah has sent down; so He foiled their actions.

10 Did they not travel in the land and see what was the fate of those who 10
preceded them? Allah brought utter destruction on them; and the like of this awaits the unbelievers.

That is because Allah is the Protector of the believers, but the unbelievers shall have no protector.

Allah shall admit those who believe and do the righteous deeds into gardens beneath which rivers flow; but the unbelievers shall take their pleasure and eat like cattle, and the Fire shall be their abode.

How many a city that was mightier than your city,[1] which cast you out, have We destroyed, and they had no supporter?

Is he who relies on a clear proof from his Lord like one whose evil action has been embellished for him? They have simply followed their fancies.

15 The likeness of the Garden which the God-fearing have been promised is this: rivers of water not stagnant, rivers of milk whose taste has not changed, rivers of wine delighting its drinkers and rivers of distilled honey. Therein they have every variety of fruit and forgiveness from their Lord too. Are they to be compared with those who dwell in the Fire forever and are given to drink boiling water which will rip up their bowels?

There are some of them who listen to you, but as soon as they leave you, they say to those who have been given the Knowledge: "What did he say just now?" Such are those upon whose hearts Allah has set a seal and who have followed their fancies.

But those who are rightly guided, He increases them in guidance and accords them their piety.

Do they, then, only expect that the Hour should come upon them suddenly? In fact, its signs have already come. How then, when it comes, will they regain their recollection?

So, know that there is no god but Allah, and ask forgiveness for your sins and for the believers, men and women. Allah knows your goings and comings, and your settling down.

20 The believers say: "If only a sura is sent down", but when a sound sura is sent down and fighting is mentioned therein, you will see those in whose hearts is a sickness look at you like one who has fainted in the throes of death. Far better for them,

Would have been obedience and a fair word! So when the matter is resolved, it would have been better for them to be true to Allah.

Would you, perhaps, if you were to rule, spread corruption in the land and sever the bonds of your kin?

Such are those whom Allah has cursed, and has made them deaf and blotted out their eyesight.

Will they not ponder the Qur'an, or are there locks upon their hearts?

25 Surely, those who have turned upon their heels after the Guidance was manifested to them, it was Satan who insinuated to them and deluded them.

That is because they said to those who disliked what Allah has sent down: "We shall obey you in part of the matter", but Allah knows their secretiveness.

How, then, will it be when the angels shall carry them off, beating their faces and their buttocks?

That is because they have followed what has angered Allah and were averse to His good pleasure. So He has foiled their works.

Or do those in whose hearts is a sickness think that Allah will not bring their rancours to light?

30 Had We wished, We would have shown them to you, so that you might 30
know them by their mark. And you shall surely know them by their distorted speech. Allah knows your works.

And We shall test you so as to know who are the fighters among you and who are the steadfast; and We shall test your news.

Indeed, those who have disbelieved and barred from Allah's path and were at odds with the Apostle, after the Guidance became manifest to them, will not cause Allah any harm, and He will foil their works.

O believers, obey Allah and obey the Apostle and do not render your actions vain.

Indeed, those who have disbelieved and barred from Allah's path, then died as unbelievers, Allah will not forgive them.

35 So do not weaken and call for peace, while you have the upper hand 35
and Allah is with you. He will not stint you your actions.

Indeed, this present life is but sport and amusement; and if you believe and are God-fearing, He will give you your wages and will not ask you for your possessions.

Were He to ask you for them and press you, you will surely be niggardly, and He will bring your rancours to light.

There you are; you are called upon to spend freely in Allah's cause, but some of you are niggardly. Yet he who is niggardly is only niggardly unto himself. Allah is the All-Sufficient and you are the destitute. If you turn back, He will replace you by a people other than you, and they will not be like you at all.

END NOTE

1. Mecca.

QUESTIONS

1. What is the behavior this Sura enjoins toward unbelievers?
2. What are the respective descriptions of Paradise and Hell given in this Sura?
3. What is the Sura referring to by the phrase "the Hour"? How imminent does it describe the Hour as being?
4. What does the exhortatory tone of this Sura, and its attitudes toward war and peace respectively, reveal about the political situation of the believers during that time?

DOCUMENT

PROPHETIC TRADITIONS ABOUT JIHAD

Abu Da'ud Sulayman ibn
Ash'ath al-Azadi al-Sijistani

Sunni Islam's fundamental texts are the Qur'an (the text believed to have been revealed to the Prophet Muhammad by the Angel Gabriel between 610 and 632 C.E.), and the hadith, *or transmitted reports about the Prophet Muhammad and his Companions, as compiled by Muslim theologians in collections more than two centuries after his death. In the Sunni Muslim view, the six canonical texts have the same authority in legal questions as does the Qur'an itself. One of the six authors of a canonical collection was Abu Da'ud al-Sijistani. Born in 817 C.E. in today's Afghanistan, he traveled widely collecting oral traditions reporting the Prophet Muhammad's alleged statements and actions, eventually settling in the southern Iraqi city of Basra. He died in 889.*

His main work is his hadith collection, Kitab al-Sunan *("Book of Traditions"), which is one of the most important foundational texts of Sunni Islam. It consists of 4,800 traditions chosen by Abu Da'ud from among the 500,000 he allegedly collected. One entire book of the work, from which these selections are taken, is devoted to* jihad.

Reprinted from *Sunan Abu Dawud*, translated by Ahmad Hasan, (1990), Nusrat Ali Nasri for Kitab Bhavan.

CHAPTER 855

Exellence of Fighting the Romans[1] Over Against Other Communities

(2482) 'Abd al-Khabīr reported on the authority of his grandfather Thābit b. Qais. A woman called Umm Khallād came to the Prophet (may peace be upon him) while she was veiled. She was searching for her son who had been killed (in the battle) Some of the Companions of the Prophet (may peace be upon him) said to her: You have come here asking for your son while veiling your face? She said: If I am afflicted with the loss of my Son, I shall not suffer the loss of my modesty. The Apostle of Allah (may peace be upon him) said: You will get the reward of two martyrs for your son. She asked : Why is that so, Apostle of Allah? He replied: Because the people of the Book have killed him.[2] . . .

CHAPTER 858

Excellence of Killing an Infidel

(2489) Abū Hurairah reported the Apostle of Allah (may peace be upon him) as saying: An infidel and the one who killed him will never be brought together in Hell.[3]

CHAPTER 859

Respect to be Shown by Those Who Stay at Home to Women of Those Who Are Engaged in *Jīhād*

(2490) Buraidah reported the Apostle of Allah (may peace be upon him) as saying Respect to be shown by those who stay at home to the women of those who are engaged in *jihād* is to be like that shown to their mothers. If any man among those who stay at home is entrusted with the oversight of one's family who is engaged in *jihād* and betrays him, he will be set up for him on the Day or Resurrection, and he (the *mujāhid*) will be told: This (man) was entrusted with the oversight of your family, so take what you want from his good deeds. The Apostle of Allah (may peace be upon him) turned towards us and said: So what do you think.[4]. . . .

CHAPTER 865

Abomination of Keeping Away from Fighting in Allah's Path

(2496) Abū Hurairah reported the Prophet (may peace be upon him) as saying: He who dies without having fought or having felt fighting (against the infidels) to be his duty will die guilty of a kind of hypocrisy.[5]

(2497) Abū Umāmah reported the Prophet (may peace be upon him) as saying: He who does not join the warlike expedition (*jihād*), or equip a warrior, or looks well after a warrior's family when he is away, will be smitten by Allah with a sudden calamity.[6]

Yazīd b 'Abd Rabbihī said in his tradition: "before the Day of Resurrection".

(2498) Anas reported the Prophet (may peace be upon him) as saying: Use your property, your persons any your tongues in striving against the polytheists.[7] . . .

CHAPTER 872

On a Person Who Fights So That Allah's Word May Have Preeminence

(2511) Abū Mūsā said: A bedouin came to the Apostle of Allah (may peace be upon him) and said: One man fights for reputation, one fights for being praised, one fights for booty, and one for his place to be seen.[8] (Which of them is in Allah's path?) The Apostle of Allah (may peace be upon him) replied: The one who fights that Allah's word may have preeminence is in Allah's path. [9]

(2512) 'Amr said: I heard from Abū Wā'il a tradition which surprised me; he then narrated the tradition to the same effect (as mentioned before).

(2513) 'Abd Allah b. 'Amr said: Apostle of Allah, tell me about *jihād* and fighting. He replied: 'Abd Allah b. 'Amr, if you fight with endurance seeking from Allah your reward, Allah will resurrect you showing endurance and seeking your reward from Him, but if you fight for vain show seeking to acquire much,[10] Allah will resurrect you making a vain show and seeking to acquire much. In whatever you fight or are killed, 'Abd Allah b. 'Amr, in that state Allah will resurrect you.

CHAPTER 873

On the Excellence of Martyrdom

(2514) 'Abd Allah b. 'Abbas reported the Apostle of Allah (may peace be upon him) as saying: When your brethren were smitten at the battle of Uhud, Allah put their spirits in the crops of green birds which go down to the rivers of Paradise, eat its fruit and nestle in lamps of gold in the shade of the Throne. Then when they experienced the sweetness of their food, drink and rest, they asked: Who will tell our brethren about us that we are alive in Paradise provided with provision, in order that they might not be disinterested in *jihād* and recoil in war?[11] Allah Most High said: I shall tell them about you ; so Allah sent down; "And do not consider those who have been killed in Allah's path," till the end of the verse.[12]

(2515) Hasanā', daughter of Mu'āwīyah, reported on the authority of her paternal uncle: I asked the Prophet (may peace be upon him): Who are in Paradise? He replied: Prophets are in Paradise, martyrs[13] are in Paradise, infants are in Paradise and children buried alive are in Paradise.

CHAPTER 874

Acceptance of the Intercession of a Martyr

(2516) Abū al-Dardā' reported the Apostle of Allah (may peace be upon him) as saying: The intercession of a martyr will be accepted for seventy members of his family.[14]

Abū Dāwūd said: The correct name of the narrator is Rabāh b.al-Walīd (and not al-Walīd b. Rabāh as occurred in the chain of narrators in the text of the tradition).

CHAPTER 875

On the Visibility of Light at the Martyr's Grave

(2517)'Ā'ishah[15] (may Allah be pleased with her) said: When Negus died, we were told that a light would be seen perpetually at his grave.[16]

END NOTES

1. Romans = Byzantines, or Christians generally, in Medieval Islamic Usage.
2. This shows that fighting with the people of the Book (i.e. Jews and Christians) carries more reward than fighting with others.
3. This means that a person who kills an infidel while fighting in Allah's path (i.e. *jihād*) will have his sins remitted and forgiven, and will, therefore, go to Paradise. The infidel will inevitably go to Hell. Thus the man who killed an infidel will not be brought together in Hell with him.
4. Those who cannot participate in *jihād* and stay at home are required to look after the families of those who are engaged in *jihād*. If anyone betrays them, his good deeds will be given to the *mujāhid* as a punishment.
5. A man who is a true Muslim covets the dominance of lslam. Hs will surely fight against the infidels. If he is unable to do so due to poverty or some valid reason, he will feel it a duty at heart. He will always have the-intention to participate in *jihād* whenever he finds an opportunity. But a man who neither fights in Allah's path nor has the intention to do so is like the hypocrites who do not want the promotion of Islam sincerely.
6. A Muslim is duty bound to take part in *jihād* either in person or by helping others who are going to fight. It a man has no share in *jihād*, he might be punished by Allah even in this world.
7. To struggle in the path of Allah with property (*amwāl*) means to spend one's property to promote the cause of Islam; to fight with one's life and person meaus to participate io *jihūd* in person; and to struggle with one's tongue means to argue against the contentions of the infidels and to establish the teachings of Islam by delivering lectures. This might also mean cursing on the enemy of Islam.
8. Meaning that the degree of his bravery and his eminent position should be manifest to others.
9. This shows that a Muslim should fight in Allah's path sincerely, and not for achieving selfish ends. The goal of a warrior should be to promote the cause of Allah and to exalt His word,
10. Meaning that he takes prides in himself and show the people that he excels others in bravery, property and the number of people fighting along with him. Such a man will get no reward on the Day of Judgment.
11. This tradition indicates the excellence at martyrdom and the highest reward which a martyr achieves after his death in the next world.
12. Qur'ān, iii. 169,
13. Martyrs shall be admitted to Paradise after their death in battle.
14. Since a martyr sacrifices his life in Allah's path, he will be given the right of intercession on the Day of Judgment in favour of seventy persons of his family who are destined to go to Hall-fire. His intercession shall be accepted, and these person will be saved from Hell-firs and sent to Paradise.
15. The favorite wife of the Prophet Muhammad.
16. This shows that Nagua, Emperor of Ethiopia, who embraced Islam in the lifetime of the Prophet (may peace be upon him) must have died a martyr. That is why a light would be seen at his grave.

QUESTIONS

1. What are some of the rewards promised to those who die while fighting "in the path of God" (traditions no.s 873–875)?
2. What does tradition no. 872 declare to be the only proper motive for fighting the jihad?
3. Why does the Prophet say (tradition no. 865) that those who die without having fought against infidels are guilty of hypocrisy?
4. Why does the Prophet declare (tradition no. 855) that fighting Jews and Christians carries more religious merit than fighting other non-Muslims (e.g., Turkish Shamanists or Hindus)?

DOCUMENT

THE PHILOSOPHY OF ZHUANGZI

Zhuangzi

It is no coincidence that the ideologies of Confucianism, Daoism (Taoism), and Legalism all emerged at a time of great chaos in China, when warring states battled each other for territory and dominance. The great philosophers, among them Confucius (c. 551 to c. 479 B.C.E.), Laozi (Lao Tzu), Zhuangzi (Chuang-tzu, c. 369 to 286 B.C.E.), and Han Feizi (Han Fei-tzu, d. 233 B.C.E.), struggled to develop and articulate philosophies that might restore harmony to their fractured world. Confucians believed that benevolence, virtue, ritual, and veneration for one's parents and king would lead to an orderly society. They had deep faith in ethics and the positive role that good government could play in improving people's lives. Han Feizi and the Legalist School had a more pessimistic view of human nature; they believed that only an authoritarian government and a strict, comprehensive legal code could restore social control. And the Daoists believed that individual and societal harmony could only be achieved by following the Dao or the Way.

But what was the Way and how did one go about finding it? One man who seemed to know was Zhuangzi, the Daoist philosopher whose name is also the title of the book from which these selections were excerpted. (The author or authors of the Zhuangzi *are unknown.) He rejected Confucian attitudes about death and scoffed at the notion that the only things worth learning came from books written by ancient sages. He believed that anyone could find the Way, and even a king could learn from a lowly butcher. Zhuangzi loved to joust with Confucian scholars like Huizi (Hui Tzu), whom he viewed as inflexible and overly concerned with ceremony, ritual, and governing. Zhuangzi was said to have spurned offers to serve in courts of various rulers, preferring to follow the Way.*

When Chuang Tzu's wife died, Hui Tzu came to the house to join in the rites of mourning. To his surprise he found Chuang Tzu sitting with an inverted bowl on his knees, drumming upon it and singing a song.[1] 'After all,' said Hui Tzu, 'she lived with you, brought up your children, grew old along with you. That you should not mourn for her is bad enough; but to let your friends find you drumming and singing—that is going too far!' 'You misjudge me,' said Chuang Tzu. 'When she died, I was in despair, as any man well might be. But soon, pondering on what had happened, I told myself that in death no strange new fate befalls us. In the beginning we lack not life only, but form. Not form only, but spirit. We are blended in the one great featureless indistinguishable mass. Then a time came when the mass evolved spirit, spirit evolved form, form evolved life. And now life in its turn has evolved death. For not nature only but man's being has its seasons, its sequence of spring and autumn, summer and winter. If some one is tired and has gone to lie down, we do not pursue him with shouting and bawling. She whom I have lost has lain down to sleep for a while in the Great Inner Room. To break in upon her rest with the noise of lamentation would but show that I knew nothing of nature's Sovereign Law. That is why I ceased to mourn.'

Chuang Tzu and Hui Tzu were strolling one day on the bridge over the river Hao. Chuang Tzu said, 'Look how the minnows dart hither and thither where they will. Such is the pleasure that fish enjoy.' Hui Tzu said, 'You are not a fish. How do you know what gives pleasure to fish?' Chuang Tzu said, 'You are not I. How do you know that I do not know what gives pleasure to fish?' Hui Tzu said, 'If because I am not you, I cannot know whether you know, then equally because you are not a fish, you cannot know what gives pleasure to fish. My argument still holds.' Chuang Tzu said, 'Let us go back to where we started. You asked me how I knew what gives pleasure to fish. But you already knew how I knew it when you asked me. You knew that I knew it by standing here on the bridge at Hao.' . . .

When Confucius was about to travel westward to the land of Wei, his disciple Yen Hui asked the music-master Chin, 'What do you think about the Master's journey?' 'I am sorry to say,' replied Chin, 'that your Master will certainly fail.' 'Why do you think so?' said Yen Hui. . . .

'The "former kings" that your Master applauds, what are they but straw dogs that have had their day? Yet he takes his disciples to lodge and sleep in their presence. Small wonder that the tree under which he taught in Sung was cut down, that his footprints were erased in Wei, that he failed alike in Chou and Shang.[2] What were all these afflictions but the bad dreams that haunt those who meddle with the dead and done? . . . If, because a boat has taken well to the water, one tries to travel in it by land, one may push till the end of one's life and get no further than a couple of yards. Our time and that of the Former Kings are as different as land from water; the Empire of Chou over which they ruled and this land of Lu are as different as boat from chariot. Your Master tries to treat the Lu of today as though it were the Chou of long ago. This is like pushing a boat over dry land. Not only is he labouring in vain; he is bound to bring himself to disaster. . . . Take a monkey and dress it up in the robes of our ancestor duke Tan. It would certainly not be happy till it had bitten and clawed every scrap of clothing from its back; and surely the days of old are no less different from today than a monkey is different from duke Tan?

'Once when Hsi Shih, the most beautiful of women, was frowning and beating her breast, an ugly woman saw her and thought, "Now I have found out how to become beautiful!" So she went home to her village and did nothing but frown and beat her breast. When the rich men of the village saw her, they bolted themselves into their houses and dared not come out; when the poor people of the village saw her they took wife and child by the hand and ran at top speed. This woman had seen that someone frowning was beautiful and thought that she had only to frown in order to become beautiful.

'No, I am sorry to say I do not think your Master will be a success.'

Once Chuang Chou[3] dreamt that he was a butterfly. He did not know that he had ever been anything but a butterfly and was content to hover from flower to flower. Suddenly he woke and found to his astonishment that he was Chuang Chou. But it was hard to be sure whether he really was Chou and had only dreamt that he was a butterfly, or was really a butterfly, and was only dreaming that he was Chou.

King Hui of Wei had a carver named Ting. When this carver Ting was carving a bull for the king, every touch of the hand, every inclination of the shoulder, every step he trod, every pressure of the knee, while swiftly and lightly he wielded his carving-knife, was as carefully timed as the movements of a dancer in the *Mulberry Wood*. . . . 'Wonderful,' said the king. 'I could never have believed that the art of carving could reach such a point as this.' 'I am a lover of Tao,' replied Ting, putting away his knife, 'and have succeeded in applying it to the art of carving. When I first began to carve I fixed my gaze on the animal in front of me. After three years I no longer saw it as a whole bull, but as a thing already divided into parts. Nowadays I no longer see it with the eye; I merely apprehend it with the soul. My sense-organs are in abeyance, but my soul still works. Unerringly my knife follows the natural markings, slips into the natural cleavages, finds its way into the natural cavities. And so by conforming my work to the structure with which I am dealing, I have arrived at a point at which my knife never touches even the smallest ligament or tendon, let alone the main gristle.

'A good carver changes his knife once a year; by which time the blade is dented. An ordinary carver changes it once a month; by which time it is broken. I have used my present knife for nineteen years, and during that time have carved several thousand bulls. But the blade still looks as though it had just come out of the mould. Where part meets part there is always space, and a knife-blade has no thickness. Insert an instrument that has no thickness into a structure that is amply spaced, and surely it cannot fail to have plenty of room. That is why I can use a blade for nineteen years, and yet it still looks as though it were fresh from the forger's mould.

'However, one has only to look at an ordinary carver to see what a difficult business he finds it. One sees how nervous he is while making his preparations, how long he looks, how slowly he moves. Then after some small, niggling strokes of the knife, when he has done no more than detach a few stray fragments from the whole, and even that by dint of continually twisting and turning like a worm burrowing through the earth, he stands back, with his knife in his hand, helplessly gazing this way and that, and after hovering for a long time finally curses a perfectly good knife and puts it back in its case.'

'Excellent,' said the king of Wei. 'This interview with the carver Ting has taught me how man's vital forces can be conserved.[4]. . .

When Chuang Tzu was angling in the river P'u, the king of Ch'u sent two high officers of state, who accosting Chuang Tzu announced that the king wished to entrust him with the management of all his domains. Rod in hand and eyes still fixed upon his line, Chuang Tzu replied, 'I have been told that in Ch'u there is a holy tortoise that died three thousand years ago. The king keeps it in the great hall of his ancestral shrine, in a casket covered with a cloth. Suppose that when this tortoise was caught, it had been allowed to choose between dying and having its bones venerated for centuries to come or going on living with its tail dragging in the mud, which would it have preferred?' 'No doubt,' said the two officers, 'it would have preferred to go on living with its tail dragging in the mud.' 'Well then, be off with you,' said Chuang Tzu, 'and leave me to drag my tail in the mud.'

END NOTES

1. Both his attitude and his occupation were the reverse of what the rites of mourning demand.
2. I.e. Sung.
3. I.e. Chuang Tzu.
4. The text of this story is very corrupt; but the general sense is clear. I have followed the renderings of Chu Kuei-yao and Kao Hêng.

QUESTIONS

1. Judging from the selections here, what kind of a man do you think Zhuangzi was? How would you describe him?
2. Why did Zhuangzi believe that it was futile to study the wisdom of ancient rulers as Confucians recommended?
3. The brief story of Zhuangzi's "butterfly dream" is among the most famous stories about the philosopher. What do you think it means?
4. The early Chinese philosophers sought to create a harmonious society. Do you think the philosophy of Zhuangzi might be used to achieve that goal? Explain your answer.

DOCUMENT

ON KUBILAI KHAN

Marco Polo

Marco Polo (1254–1324), born in Venice to a merchant family, followed in his father's footsteps in terms of both occupation and geography. In 1271 Marco Polo became a merchant and with his father, he traveled to China, where Marco, his father Niccolo, and Marco's uncle Maffeo served Khubilai Khan for twenty years. Marco sailed back to Venice in 1295, At that time Venice was at war with Genoa. The ship he traveled on was captured and Marco was taken prisoner. He probably wrote his famous manuscript, The Travels, *with another prisoner, a romance writer named Rusticello from Pisa, at the end of the thirteenth century while in prison. The veracity of Marco Polo's account has been questioned in recent years, and some scholars even suggest that he did not reach China at all. However, Marco Polo's writings were very popular in Europe and had a strong impact on European attitudes toward China.*

Khubilai (Kubilai) Khan (1215–1294), grandson of the legendary Genghis (Chinggis) Khan, was the founder and first emperor of China's Yuan Dynasty (1279–1368). Khubilai faced the daunting task of ruling the vast empire of China and his own Mongol people. Most scholars agree that he did far better at the former than the latter. Although Mongol rule was condemned by many Confucian Chinese scholars, who considered the nomadic Mongols barbaric, the Yuan Dynasty ushered in a period of cosmopolitanism that brought traders and other visitors to China from all over the world. Khubilai ruled first from the city of Khan-balik (the Mongol term for Beijing or Peking), then in his new capital of Taidu (Tadu), just northeast of Khan-balik. Taidu was a city laid out in the classic Chinese style, and Khubilai also incorporated a number of Chinese rituals designed to appeal to his subjects.

This excerpt includes Marco Polo's description of the great Khan and his family, and some of the rituals observed when Khubilai convened his court and hosted banquets in one of his luxurious palaces. Polo also paints a vivid picture of the grandeur of Tadu.

I have come to the point in our book at which I will tell you of the great achievements of the Great Khan now reigning. The title Khan means in our language 'Great Lord of Lords'. And certainly he has every right to this title; for everyone should know that this Great Khan is the mightiest man, whether in respect of subjects or of territory or of treasure, who is in the world today or who ever has been, from Adam our first parent down to the present moment. And I will make it quite clear to you in our book that this is the plain truth, so that everyone will be convinced that he is indeed the greatest lord the world has ever known. Here, then, is my proof.

First, you should know that he is undoubtedly descended in the direct imperial line from Chinghiz Khan; for only one of that lineage may be Lord of all the Tartars. He is sixth in succession of the Great Khans of all the Tartars, having received the lordship and begun his reign in the year of Christ's nativity 1256. He won the lordship by his own valour and prowess and good sense; his kinsfolk and brothers tried to debar him from it, but by his great prowess he won it. And you must know that it was properly his by right. From the beginning of his reign down to the present year 1298 is a period of forty-two years. His age today may well be as much as eighty-five years. Before he became Khan, he used to go out regularly on military expeditions and he showed himself a valiant soldier and a good commander. . . .

. . . Let me tell you next of the personal appearance of the Great Lord of Lords whose name is Kubilai Khan. He is a man of good stature, neither short nor tall but of moderate height. His limbs are well fleshed out and modelled in due proportion. His complexion is fair and ruddy like a rose, the eyes black and handsome, the nose shapely and set squarely in place.

He has four consorts who are all accounted his lawful wives; and his eldest son by any of these four has a rightful claim to be emperor on the death of the present Khan. They are called empresses, each by her own name. Each of these ladies holds her own court. None of them has less than 300 ladies in waiting, all of great beauty and charm. They have many eunuchs and many other men and women in attendance, so that each one of these ladies has in her court 10,000 persons. When he wishes to lie with one of his four wives, he invites her to his chamber; or sometimes he goes to his wife's chamber. . . .

. . . When the Great Khan is holding court, the seating at banquets is arranged as follows. He himself sits at a much higher table than the rest at the northern end of the hall, so that he faces south. His principal wife sits next to him on the left. On the right, at a somewhat lower level, sit his sons in order of age, Chinghiz the eldest being placed rather higher than the rest, and his grandsons and his kinsmen of the imperial lineage. They are so placed that their heads are on a level with the Great Khan's feet. Next to them are seated the other noblemen at other tables lower down again. And the ladies are seated on the same plan. All the wives of the Khan's sons and grandsons and kinsmen are seated on his left at a lower level, and next to them the wives of his nobles and knights lower down still. And they all know their appointed place in the lord's plan. The tables are so arranged that the Great Khan can see everything, and there are a great many of them. But you must not imagine that all the guests sit at table; for most of the knights and nobles in the hall take their meal seated on carpets for want of tables. Outside the hall the guests at the banquet number more than 40,000. For they include many visitors with costly gifts, men who come from strange countries bringing strange things, and some who have held high office and aspire to further advancement. Such are the guests who attend on such occasions, when the Great Khan is holding court or celebrating a wedding. . . .

. . . I can assure you that the Great Khan has such a store of vessels of gold and silver that no one who did not see it with his own eyes could well believe it. And the waiters who serve his food and drink are certain of his barons. They have their mouths and noses swathed in fine napkins of silk and gold, so that the food and drink are not contaminated by their breath or effluence. . . .

. . . There are many instruments in the hall, of every sort, and when the Great Khan is about to drink they all strike up. As soon as the cup-bearer has handed him the cup, he retires three paces and kneels down; and all the barons and all the people present go down on their knees and make a show of great humility. Then the Great Khan drinks. And every time he drinks the same performance is repeated. Of the food I say nothing, because everyone will readily believe that there is no lack of it. . . .

. . . Now let me tell you something of the bounties that the Great Khan confers upon his subjects. For all his thoughts are directed towards helping the people who are subject to him, so that they may live and labour and increase their wealth. You may take it for a fact that he sends emissaries and inspectors throughout all his dominions and kingdoms and provinces to learn whether any of his people have suffered a failure of their crops either through weather or through locusts or other pests. And if he finds that any have lost their harvest, he exempts them for that year from their tribute and even gives them some of his own grain to sow and to eat—a magnificent act of royal bounty. This he does in the summer. And in winter he does likewise in the matter of cattle. If he finds any man whose cattle have been killed by an outbreak of plague, he gives him some of his own, derived from the tithes of other provinces, and to help him further he relieves him of tribute for the year. . . .

. . . On the banks of a great river in the province of Cathay there stood an ancient city of great size and splendour which was named Khan-balik, that is to say in our language 'the Lord's City'. Now the Great Khan discovered through his astrologers that this city would rebel and put up a stubborn resistance against the Empire. For this reason he had this new city built next to the old one, with only the river between. And he removed the inhabitants of the old city and settled them in the new one, which is called Taidu, leaving only those whom he did not suspect of any rebellious designs; for the new city was not big enough to house all those who lived in the old.

Taidu is built in the form of a square with all its sides of equal length and a total circumference of twenty-four miles. It is enclosed by earthern ramparts, twenty paces high and ten paces thick at the base; the sides slope inwards from base to summit, so that at the top the width is only about three paces. They are all battlemented and white-washed. They have twelve gates, each surmounted by a fine, large palace. So on each of the four sides there are three gates and five palaces, because there is an additional palace at each corner. In these palaces there are immense halls, which house the weapons of the city guards.

I assure you that the streets are so broad and straight that from the top of the wall above one gate you can see along the whole length of the road to the gate opposite. The city is full of fine mansions, inns, and dwelling-houses. All the way down the sides of every main street there are booths and shops of every sort. All the building sites throughout the city are square and measured by the rule; and on every site stand large and spacious mansions with ample courtyards and gardens. These sites are allotted to heads of households, so that one belongs to such-and-such a person, representing such-and-such a family, the next to a representative of another family, and so all the way along. Every site or block is surrounded by good public roads; and in this way the whole interior of the city is laid out in squares like a chess-board with such masterly precision that no description can do justice to it.

In this city there is such a multitude of houses and of people, both within the walls and without, that no one could count their number. Actually there are more people outside the walls in the suburbs than in the city itself. There is a suburb outside every gate, such that each one touches the neighbouring suburbs on either side. They extend in length for three or four miles. And in every suburb or ward, at about a mile's distance from the city, there are many fine hostels which provide lodging for merchants coming from different parts: a particular hostel is assigned to every nation, as we might say one for the Lombards, another for the Germans, another for the French. Merchants and others come here on business in great numbers, both because it is the Khan's residence and because it affords a profitable market. And the suburbs have as fine houses and mansions as the city, except of course for the Khan's palace.

You must know that no one who dies is buried in the city. If an idolater dies there, his body is taken to the place of cremation, which lies outside all the suburbs. And so with the others also; when they die they are taken right outside the suburbs for burial. Similarly, no act of violence is performed inside the city, but only outside the suburbs.

Let me tell you also that no sinful woman dares live within the city, unless it be in secret no woman of the world, that is, who prostitutes her body for money. But they all live in the suburbs, and there are so many of them that no one could believe it. For I assure you that there are fully 20,000 of them, all serving the needs of men for money. They have a captain general, and there are chiefs of hundreds and of thousands responsible to the captain. This is because, whenever ambassadors come to the Great Khan on his business and are maintained at his expense, which is done on a lavish scale, the captain is called upon to provide one of these women every night for the ambassador and one for each of his attendants. They are changed every night and receive no payment; for this is the tax they pay to the Great Khan. From the number of these prostitutes you may infer the number of traders and other visitors who are daily coining and going here about their business.

You may take it for a fact that more precious and costly wares are imported into Khan-balik than into any other city in the world. Let me give you particulars. All the treasures that come from India—precious stones, pearls, and other rarities—are brought here. So too are the choicest and costliest products of Cathay itself and every other province. This is on account of the Great Khan himself, who lives here, and of the lords and ladies and the enormous multitude of hotel-keepers and other residents and of visitors who attend the courts held here by the Khan. That is why the volume and value of the imports and of the internal trade exceed those of any other city in the world. It is a fact that every day more than 1,000 cart-loads of silk enter the city; for much cloth of gold and silk is woven here. Furthermore, Khan-balik is surrounded by more than 200 other cities, near and far, from which traders come to it to sell and to buy. So it is not surprising that it is the centre of such a traffic as I have described.

In the centre of the city stands a huge palace in which is a great bell; in the evening this peals three times as a signal that no one may go about the town. Once this bell has sounded the due number of peals, no one ventures abroad in the city except in case of childbirth or illness; and those who are called out by such emergencies are obliged to carry lights. Every night there are guards riding about the city in troops of thirty or forty, to discover whether anyone is going about at an abnormal hour, that is after the third peal of the bell. If anyone is found, he is promptly arrested and clapped into prison. Next morning he is examined by the officials appointed for the purpose, and if he is found guilty of any offence, he is punished according to its gravity with a proportionate number of strokes of a rod, which sometimes cause death. They employ this mode of punishment in order to avoid bloodshed, because their *Bakhshi,* that is, the adepts in astrology, declare that it is wrong to shed human blood.

It is ordered that every gateway must be guarded by 1,000 men. You must not suppose that this guard is maintained out of mistrust of the inhabitants. It is there, in fact, partly as a mark of respect to the Great Khan who lives in the city, partly as a check upon evil-doers—although, because of the prophecy of his astrologers, the Khan does harbour certain suspicions of the people of Cathay.

QUESTIONS

1. Which of Khubilai Khan's qualities does Marco Polo admire most? Why?
2. What impressions might Europeans gather about Chinese civilization from this description of Khubilai and his surroundings?
3. Confucians in China disdained merchants as unproductive and consumed by the vulgar pursuit of profit. Why might the Mongols have been more open to outside traders than the Chinese?
4. Most Chinese considered the Mongols barbarians. Why do you think Marco Polo had such a different impression?

DOCUMENT

ODA NOBUNAGA AND MT. HIEI

St. Luis Frois

The Japan into which Oda Nobunaga (1534–1582) was born was divided into many warring feudal domains, each with its own armies commanded by a daimyo *or lord, and the* shogun *(military ruler) ruled in name only. Nobunaga was a brilliant military strategist who laid the groundwork for the unification of Japan by Toyotomi Hideyoshi (1536–1598) and Tokugawa Ieyasu (1542–1616), with the latter eventually becoming* shogun. *Nobunaga took advantage of Portuguese weaponry to gain enough power to influence the shogunal succession before the Tokugawa era (1603–1868). However, Nobunaga has gone down in history less for his skills than for his ruthlessness. Not surprisingly, these heavy-handed techniques had some unintended and unwanted consequences, and Nobunaga was murdered in 1582 by one of his own generals.*

Nobunaga's most infamous act was his torching of the large Mt. Hiei monastic/academic complex in 1571 and the massacre of all of those within, allegedly as revenge for the monks' support for one of his military rivals. The monks on Mt. Hiei belonged to the Tendai Buddhist sect, and although their slaughter was by any account an atrocity, it must be understood that during this violent time, Buddhist temples had their own armies and the soldier monks of Mt. Hiei had long threatened the capital city of Kyoto. At Mt. Hiei and in subsequent battles, Oda Nobunaga eliminated the threat of the monastic armies, one important step on the road to unification.

Oda Nobunaga was quite tolerant toward foreign missionaries, in part because they were not Buddhist and also because foreign trade brought new weaponry and wealth. This eyewitness account of the destruction of Mt. Hiei was written by Luis Frois (1532–1597), a Portuguese Jesuit who landed in Japan in 1563. He is remembered for his published history of Japan and the detailed, insightful observations about Japanese society he included in his many letters to family and fellow missionaries. This particular description testified to Frois's closeness to Nobunaga and is surprisingly objective, given the violence of the attack.

THE DESTRUCTION OF HIEIZAN

On his arrival at Sakamoto he realised that as he was accompanied by an army of 30,000 men he was in a good position to take revenge on the bonzes of the universities of Hieizan, and so he assembled his whole army to overcome the monks. When the bonzes learnt of his intention and saw that there was no other expedient, they sent word offering him 300 bars of gold (each one worth 45 silver *taels*) and 200 bars were sent from the town of Katata. But not one of them would Nobunaga accept, declaring that he had not come there to enrich himself with gold but to punish their crimes with all severity and rigour. When the satraps of the universities heard this reply, although they knew that Nobunaga had but scant respect for the *kami* and *hotoke*, they still did not believe that he would destroy the idol of Sannō, for it was greatly venerated and its punishments were no less feared. And so for this reason they all decided to gather in the temple (which is on the top of the mountain) and to abandon all the other monasteries and their treasures. At the same time the bonzes persuaded the people of the town of Sakamoto to go up as well with their womenfolk and children.

Knowing that he had them all on the top of the mountain, Nobunaga immediately gave orders to set fire to Sakamoto and to put to the sword all those found within the town. This was on September 29th of this year, 1571, the Feast of the Dedication of the glorious St. Michael. And in order to show the bonzes who were up the mountain the little regard he paid to the chimeras (which they had described to him) of the punishments of Sannō, the second thing that he did was to burn all the temples of this idol which were below the foot of the mountain; he also destroyed by fire the seven universities so that nothing at all was left of them. Then deploying his army of 30,000 men in the form of a ring around the mountain, he gave the order to advance to the top. The bonzes began to resist with their weapons and wounded about 150 soldiers. But they were unable to withstand such a furious assault and were all put to the sword, together with the men, women and children of Sakamoto, which is near the foot of the mountain.

The next day, the last in September and the Feast of the glorious St. Jerome, they burnt down the large temple of Sannō, which, as I have said, was on the top of the mountain. Then Nobunaga ordered a large number of musketeers to go out into the hills and woods as if on a hunt; should they find any bonzes hiding there, they were not to spare the life of a single one of them. And this they duly did. But Nobunaga was not satisfied with this victory and desired to slake his thirst for vengeance even more and to increase his fame. So he commanded his whole army to go and plunder the remaining houses of the bonzes and to burn down all the four hundred odd temples of those famous universities of Hieizan. And on that same day all of them were destroyed, burnt down and reduced to ashes. Then he ordered the army to the town of Katata, which was unable to offer resistance and was also laid waste by fire. They told me that there had perished about 1,500 bonzes and the same number of layfolk, men, women and children.

QUESTIONS

1. How did Oda Nobunaga destroy the mighty monastery at Mt. Hiei?
2. How did the monks attempt to prevent the attack?
3. Why do you think Nobunaga destroyed the monastery complex so brutally, and even extended the slaughter to nearby villagers?
4. What does the account indicate about Oda Nobunaga's religious beliefs?

DOCUMENT

EARLY ENCOUNTERS WITH THE JAPANESE

Anonymous

When Commodore Matthew Perry sailed into Uraga Bay near the Japanese capital city of Edo (later renamed Tokyo) in 1853, he set in motion a series of changes within Japan that soon forced the government of the Tokugawa shoguns *(military rulers) to abandon its isolationist policies and open a number of Japanese ports to foreign trade. By 1868, domestic dissatisfaction among many in the ruling* samurai *class erupted in open rebellion against the* shogun, *in theory to restore power to the emperor. The Meiji Restoration ushered in a new era of rapid Japanese modernization and industrialization that eventually led to Japanese nationalism, imperialism, and domination in East Asia.*

But before it was deposed, the government of the shogun *recognized that open ports and commercial relations with the United States did not automatically bring mutual understanding, respect, or profit. In order to learn more about American society, government, and the economy—with the goal of establishing a more equal relationship and improving Japan's status in the world—the Tokugawa government sent a group of officials to the United States in 1860 to meet with President James Buchanan and tour the country. The mission generated considerable interest among the American public and was extensively covered by the U.S. media.*

The first selection excerpted here appeared in the New York Times *in June 1860, and expresses great relief at their departure and considerable*

Reprinted from *Harpers Weekly*, May 26, 1860.

apprehension about the one-sided nature of the current relationship between Japan and the United States. The second selection, printed about a month earlier in Harpers Weekly, *took a more positive tone, lauding the Japanese as far more "civilized" than the Russians or Chinese, and predicting a profitable trade between Japan and the Pacific Northwest.*

OUR PARTING GUESTS

Our Japanese visitors take their departure for home to-day. It may seem discourteous, but we cannot help saying we are glad they have gone. Their visit has not been without a certain interest to us, but we have had enough of it. They may be, and doubtless are, very respectable persons at home,—but their social intercourse with us has not been expecially fascinating. When persons can neither speak nor understand a syllable of each other's language, and are compelled to converse through the medium of a double interpretation, their intercourse must lack something of the ease and grace essential to cordial and protracted delight in each other's society. The pantomime of the Japanese is expressive enough, but pantomime at the best is a very unsatisfactory style of conversation. One tires of it after a while, even on the stage. In the affairs of daily life, a very little of it will suffice for a long time.

The Japanese, moreover, have very little of that personal beauty,—that majesty of demeanor, graceful dignity of manners or even elegance of outward appearance, which sometimes answer in place of social qualities, and render their possessors favorites in the best social circles. They are small of stature, tawney in complexion, sleepy and feeble in their physical appearance and habits, and with only those characteristics calculated to excite a momentary curiosity. They may be very wise at home, but they have been quite as prudent here in their displays of wisdom as in their expenditures of money. We doubt whether any of our citizens, or any of the corporations which have paid them visits more or less formal, have learned from them anything whatever concerning their country, its government, its people, their habits, commerce, and future policy towards other nations, than they knew before. . . .

The truth is, the Japanese came to acquire knowledge,—not to impart it. An enlightened curiosity,—a desire to explore the secret of the strength and power of that formidable civilization of the West, which has so startled the apathy of the slumbering East by its cannon and its conquests, had quite as much to do with their visit as any liberal wish to cultivate closer relations with other Powers and throw open the gates of Niphon [Nippon] to the commerce of the world. We have done our utmost to gratify and instruct them. We have shown them the wonders of our mechanics, the power of our machinery, and have taught them how to make and use it for themselves. We have given them models of our inventions, have instructed them in the processes of all the useful arts, and have even put into their hands the most formidable engines known to modern warfare. It will not be our fault if, with their quick ingenuity, they do not very speedily become able to fabricate for themselves all the great staples with which we have been hoping to supply them. The blame will not rest upon our shoulders, if they are not able to build and arm their forts with weapons of war as deadly as any known to us, and to resist successfully every attempt of American or English ships to force an entrance into their harbors. It is only a few years ago that the Japanese authorities applied to our Government, through Mr. Townsend Harris, for models of some of our cannon, and instruction as to their use. Our Government declined, from prudential motives, to accede to their request. But we have since grown more liberal, if they have not; and the [Japanese] Embassy takes back complete models of our best howitzers and Dahlgren guns, with full instruction as to the manufacture and use of everything required, both in offensive and defensive warfare. That they will profit by this excessive liberality on our part, we may rest assured. We can only hope that we may not find ourselves among the earliest victims of our over-zealous and mistaken benevolence.

What may be the ultimate results of this extraordinary Embassy, it is, of course, impossible to predict. Thus far the most remarkable fact about it is, that it should ever have been sent. We have received its members with marked and munificent hospitality. Our general Government has incurred an expense of some hundreds of thousands of dollars for its transport and maintenance. Our City has spent at least $100,000 in professed attempts at its entertainment. We have done everything in our power to make their visit agreeable and profitable to them. What we are to receive in return for all this we shall know in due time. At the latest advices the house of our Minister in Japan was guarded by troops to protect him from assassination. Whether our late visitors will be inclined or able to deal with us in a different spirit, after their return, remains to be seen. Our expectations, we confess, are not particularly sanguine.

OUR JAPANESE VISITORS

We devote several of our illustrated pages to the Japanese, who—at the time we write—are in Washington, enjoying the hospitalities of that thriving little town. A large sum of money was voted by Congress to defray the expenses of their reception. . . .

One or two members of Congress have alluded to this "fuss" as a "piece of nonsense." They are the lineal descendants of the people who said that the "fuss" in Boston, eighty odd years ago, about the Tea-duty was "all nonsense," and of the people who shouted aloud that the resistance to the Stamp-act, which ushered in the Revolution, was mere gammon. The fact is, that this Japanese embassy is a matter of the highest national and commercial importance.

The Japanese are the British of Asia. Like our ancestors of the British Isles, they are of insular origin, and full of insular virtues and insular prejudices. They despise foreigners; but they know how to take care of themselves. Many of their customs seem absurd to us; but they are honest in their adoption, and thorough in their observance. Their country produces a number of commodities which would find a sale here, and they consume many articles which we produce. Satisfy them that commercial intercourse with us would be beneficial to them, and a valuable trade will be created. Thus far, their only commercial correspondents have been the Dutch, who have driven hard bargains with them, and impressed them unfavorably with regard to Christian nations. We can undo the mischief that has been done if we produce a favorable impression on our visitors, and commence a trade under proper auspices.

Independently, however, of immediate commercial benefits, the establishment of friendly relations with the Japanese can not fail to be of marked advantage to our Pacific States. The State of Oregon and the future

State of Washington will necessarily become intimately connected with their nearest neighbors over the water. Of those neighbors Japan is the one best worth cultivating. The Russians of Northern Asia are hardly more than semi-barbarous, and the Chinese are such a peculiar race, and so entirely foreign to us in every sense of the word, that neither can compare, in respect of neighborly value, to the Japanese. By-and-by there will necessarily grow up an interchange not only of commodities but of men between our Pacific States and the empire of Japan. Our people will go to Japan . . . [and] will endeavor to show the Japanese the best side of the American character. On the other hand, the Japanese—if good relations be established between the two countries—will send out some of their people to plant Japanese colonies in our territory. On this interchange the benefit will be obvious and mutual. Civilized as we boast of being, we can learn much of the Japanese—if nothing more, we can learn the duty of obeying the laws.

QUESTIONS

1. Why does the first article about the departure of the Japanese mission begin with the rather impolite comment, "We are glad they have gone"?
2. What consequences did the American media see as likely to emerge from the newly established commercial and diplomatic relationship between the United States and Japan?
3. What did the American media see as the most negative and positive characteristics of the Japanese people? Why?
4. What do you think was meant by one author's comment, "The Japanese are the British of Asia"?

DOCUMENT

THE SALIC LAW

Anonymous

*The Salic Law (*Lex Salica*) was a set of laws codified under King Clovis (481–511) for the Salian Franks. The laws were drawn up by Gallo-Romans or Gauls trained in the Roman legal tradition and may include elements as old as the fourth century* C.E. Lex Salica *is written in Latin with a mixture of Germanic words. It deals mainly with monetary compensations (*wergeld*) for wrongs and with civil law concerning men and land. Title 59, clause 6, dealing with inheritance rules for allodial lands (i.e., family lands not held in benefice), states that in "concerning salic lands (*terra Salica*) no portion or inheritance is for a woman but all the land belongs to members of the male sex who are brothers." A capitulary of King Chilperic from around 575 expands this by admitting inheritance by a daughter in the absence of sons. The monarchy is nowhere mentioned. The Salic Law was reformulated under Charlemagne and still applied in the ninth century, but it slowly disappeared as it became incorporated into local common laws. By the fourteenth century it was completely forgotten and was first cited in medieval French legal literature in 1410. However, the insistence on male primogeniture was transmitted to later French legal sources, and the prejudice against female inheritance was an element in the rejection of female candidates for succession to the French monarchy. From the time of the Capetians forward, no woman ever reigned in France.*

Codified by the French King Volvis (481–511).

TITLE I. CONCERNING SUMMONSES.

1. If any one be summoned before the "Thing" by the king's law, and do not come, he shall be sentenced to 600 denars, which make 15 shillings (solidi).

2. But he who summons another, and does not come himself, shall, if a lawful impediment have not delayed him, be sentenced to 15 shillings, to be paid to him whom he summoned.

3. And he who summons another shall walk with witnesses to the home of that man, and, if he be not at home, shall bid the wife or any one of the family to make known to him that he has been summoned to court.

4. But if he be occupied in the king's service he can not summon him.

5. But if he shall be inside the hundred seeing about his own affairs, he can summon him in the manner explained above.

TITLE II. CONCERNING THEFTS OF PIGS, ETC.

1. If any one steal a sucking pig, and it be proved against him, he shall be sentenced to 120 denars, which make three shillings.

2. If any one steal a pig that can live without its mother, and it be proved on him, he shall be sentenced to 40 denars—that is, 1 shilling.

14. If any one steal 25 sheep where there were no more in that flock, and it be proved on him, he shall be sentenced to 2500 denars—that is, 62 shillings.

TITLE III. CONCERNING THEFTS OF CATTLE.

4. If any one steal that bull which rules the herd and never has been yoked, he shall be sentenced to 1800 denars, which make 45 shillings.

5. But if that bull is used for the cows of three villages in common, he who stole him shall be sentenced to three times 45 shillings.

6. If any one steal a bull belonging to the king he shall be sentenced to 3600 denars, which make 90 shillings.

TITLE IV. CONCERNING DAMAGE DONE AMONG CROPS OR IN ANY ENCLOSURE.

1. If any one finds cattle, or a horse, or flocks of any kind in his crops, he shall not at all mutilate them.

2. If he do this and confess it, he shall restore the worth of the animal in place of it, and shall himself keep the mutilated one.

3. But if he have not confessed it, and it have been proved on him, he shall be sentenced, besides the value of the animal and the fines for delay, to 600 denars, which make 15 shillings.

TITLE XI. CONCERNING THEFTS OR HOUSEBREAKINGS OF FREEMEN.

1. If any freeman steal, outside of the house, something worth 2 denars, he shall be sentenced to 600 denars, which make 15 shillings.

2. But if he steal, outside of the house, something worth 40 denars, and it be proved on him, he shall be sentenced, besides the amount and the fines for delay, to 1400 denars, which make 35 shillings.

3. If a freeman break into a house and steal something worth 2 denars, and it be proved on him, he shall be sentenced to 15 shillings.

4. But if he shall have stolen something worth more than 5 denars, and it have been proved on him, he shall be sentenced, besides the worth of the object and the fines for delay, to 1400 denars, which make 35 shillings.

5. But if he have broken, or tampered with, the lock, and thus have entered the house and stolen anything from it, he shall be sentenced, besides the worth of the object and the fines for delay, to 1800 denars, which make 45 shillings.

6. And if he have taken nothing, or have escaped by flight, he shall, for the housebreaking alone, be sentenced to 1200 denars, which make 30 shillings.

TITLE XII. CONCERNING THEFTS OR HOUSEBREAKINGS ON THE PART OF SLAVES.

1. If a slave steal, outside of the house, something worth two denars, he shall, besides paying the worth of the object and the fines for delay, be stretched out and receive 120 blows.

2. But if he steal something worth 40 denars, he shall either be castrated or pay 6 shillings. But the lord of the slave who committed the theft shall restore to the plaintiff the worth of the object and the fines for delay.

TITLE XIII. CONCERNING RAPE COMMITTED BY FREEMEN.

1. If three men carry off a free born girl, they shall be compelled to pay 30 shillings.

2. If there are more than three, each one shall pay 5 shillings.

3. Those who shall have been present with boats shall be sentenced to three shillings.

4. But those who commit rape shall be compelled to pay 2500 denars, which make 63 shillings.

5. But if they have carried off that girl from behind lock and key, or from the spinning room, they shall be sentenced to the above price and penalty.

6. But if the girl who is carried off be under the king's protection, then the "frith" (peace-money) shall be 2500 denars, which make 63 shillings.

7. But if a bondsman of the king, or a leet, should carry off a free woman, he shall be sentenced to death.

8. But if a free woman have followed a slave of her own will, she shall lose her freedom.

9. If a freeborn man shall have taken an alien bondswoman, he shall suffer similarly.

10. If any body take an alien spouse and join her to himself in matrimony, he shall be sentenced to 2500 denars, which make 63 shillings.

TITLE XIV. CONCERNING ASSAULT AND ROBBERY.

1. If any one have assaulted and plundered a free man, and it be proved on him, he shall be sentenced to 2500 denars, which make 63 shillings.

2. If a Roman have plundered a Salian Frank, the above law shall be observed.

3. But if a Frank have plundered a Roman, he shall be sentenced to 35 shillings.

4. If any man should wish to migrate, and has permission from the king, and shall have shown this in the public "Thing:" whoever, contrary to the decree of the king, shall presume to oppose him, shall be sentenced to 8000 denars, which make 200 shillings.

TITLE XV. CONCERNING ARSON.

1. If any one shall set fire to a house in which men were sleeping, as many freemen as were in it can make complaint before the "Thing;" and if any one shall have been burned in it, the incendiary shall be sentenced to 2500 denars, which make 63 shillings.

TITLE XVII. CONCERNING WOUNDS.

1. If any one have wished to kill another person, and the blow have missed, he on whom it was proved shall be sentenced to 2500 denars, which make 63 shillings.

2. If any person have wished to strike another with a poisoned arrow, and the arrow have glanced aside and it shall be proved on him: he shall be sentenced to 2500 denars, which make 63 shillings.

3. If any person strike another on the head so that the brain appears, and the three bones which lie above the brain shall project, he shall be sentenced to 1200 denars, which make 30 shillings.

4. But if it shall have been between the ribs or in the stomach, so that the wound appears and reaches to the entrails, he shall be sentenced to 1200 denars—which make 30 shillings—besides five shillings for the physician's pay.

5. If any one shall have struck a man so that blood falls to the floor, and it be proved on him, he shall be sentenced to 600 denars, which make 15 shillings.

6. But if a freeman strike a freeman with his fist so that blood does not flow, be shall be sentenced for each blow—up to 3 blows—to 120 denars, which make 3 shillings.

TITLE XVIII. CONCERNING HIM WHO, BEFORE THE KING, ACCUSES AN INNOCENT MAN.

If any one, before the king, accuse an innocent man who is absent, he shall be sentenced to 2500 denars, which make 63 shillings.

TITLE XIX. CONCERNING MAGICIANS.

1. If any one have given herbs to another so that he die, he shall be sentenced to 200 shillings (or shall surely be given over to fire).

2. If any person have bewitched another, and he who was thus treated shall escape, the author of the crime, who is proved to have committed it, shall be sentenced to 2500 denars, which make 63 shillings.

TITLE XXIV. CONCERNING THE KILLING OF LITTLE CHILDREN AND WOMEN.

1. If any one have slain a boy under 10 years—up to the end of the tenth—and it shall have been proved on him, he shall be sentenced to 24000 denars, which make 600 shillings.

3. If any one have hit a free woman who is pregnant, and she dies, he shall be sentenced to 28000 denars, which make 700 shillings.

6. If any one have killed a free woman after she has begun bearing children, he shall be sentenced to 24000 denars, which make 600 shillings.

7. After she can have no more children, he who kills her shall be sentenced to 8000 denars, which make 200 shillings.

TITLE XXX. CONCERNING INSULTS.

3. If any one, man or woman, shall have called a woman harlot, and shall not have been able to prove it, he shall be sentenced to 1800 denars, which make 45 shillings.

4. If any person shall have called another "fox," he shall be sentenced to 3 shillings.

5. If any man shall have called another "hare," he shall be sentenced to 3 shillings.

6. If any man shall have brought it up against another that he have thrown away his shield, and shall not have been able to prove it, he shall be sentenced to 120 denars, which make 3 shillings.

7. If any man shall have called another "spy" or "perjurer," and shall not have been able to prove it, he shall be sentenced to 600 denars, which make 15 shillings.

TITLE XXXIII. CONCERNING THE THEFT OF HUNTING ANIMALS.

2. If any one have stolen a tame marked stag (-hound?), trained to hunting, and it shall have been proved through witnesses that his master had him for hunting, or had killed with him two or three beasts, he shall be sentenced to 1800 denars, which make 45 shillings.

TITLE XXXIV. CONCERNING THE STEALING OF FENCES.

1. If any man shall have cut 3 staves by which a fence is bound or held together, or have stolen or cut the heads of 3 stakes, he shall be sentenced to 600 denars, which make 15 shillings.

2. If any one shall have drawn a harrow through another's harvest after it has sprouted, or shall have gone through it with a waggon where there was no road, he shall be sentenced to 120 denars, which make 3 shillings.

3. If any one shall have gone, where there is no way or path, through another's harvest which has already become thick, he shall be sentenced to 600 denars, which make 15 shillings.

TITLE XLI. CONCERNING THE MURDER OF FREE MEN.

1. If any one shall have killed a free Frank, or a barbarian living under the Salic law, and it have been proved on him, he shall be sentenced to 8000 denars.

2. But if he shall have thrown him into a well or into the water, or shall have covered him with branches or anything else, to conceal him, he shall be sentenced to 24000 denars, which make 600 shillings.

3. But if any one has slain a man who is in the service of the king, he shall be sentenced to 24000 denars, which make 600 shillings.

4. But if he have put him in the water or in a well, and covered him with anything to conceal him, he shall be sentenced to 72000 denars, which make 1800 shillings.

5. If any one have slain a Roman who eats in the king's palace, and it have been proved on him, he shall be sentenced to 12000 denars, which make 300 shillings.

6. But if the Roman shall not have been a landed proprietor and table companion of the king, he who killed him shall be sentenced to 4000 denars, which make 100 shillings.

7. But if he shall have killed a Roman who was to pay tribute, he shall be sentenced to 63 shillings.

9. If any one have thrown a free man into a well, and he have escaped alive, he (the criminal) shall be sentenced to 4000 denars, which make 100 shillings.

TITLE XLV. CONCERNING MIGRATORS.

1. If any one wish to migrate to another village and if one or more who live in that village do not wish to receive him,—if there be only one who objects, he shall not have leave to move there.

2. But if he shall have presumed to settle in that village in spite of his rejection by one or two men, then some one shall give him warning. And if he be unwilling to go away, he who gives him warning shall give him warning, with witnesses, as follows: I warn thee that thou may'st remain here this next night as the Salic law demands, and I warn thee that within 10 nights thou shalt go forth from this village. After another 10 nights he shall again come to him and warn him again within 10 nights to go away. If he still refuse to go, again 10 nights shall be added to the command, that the number of 30 nights may be full. If he will not go away even then, then he shall summon him to the "Thing," and present his witnesses as to the separate commands to leave. If he who has been warned will not then

move away, and no valid reason detains him, and all the above warnings which we have mentioned have been given according to law: then he who gave him warning shall take the matter into his own hands and request the "comes" to go to that place and expel him. And because he would not listen to the law, that man shall relinquish all that he has earned there, and, besides, shall be sentenced to 1200 denars, which make 30 shillings.

3. But if anyone have moved there, and within 12 months no one have given him warning, he shall remain as secure as the other neighbours.

TITLE XLVI. CONCERNING TRANSFERS OF PROPERTY.

1. The observance shall be that the Thunginus or Centenarius shall call together a "Thing," and shall have his shield in the "Thing," and shall demand three men as witnesses for each of the three transactions. He (the owner of the land to be transferred) shall seek a man who has no connection with himself, and shall throw a stalk into his lap. And to him into whose lap he has thrown the stalk, he shall tell, concerning his property, how much of it—or whether the whole or a half—he wishes to give. He in whose lap he threw the stalk shall remain in his (the owner's) house, and shall collect three or more guests, and shall have the property—as much as is given him—in his power. And, afterwards, he to whom that property is entrusted shall discuss all these things with the witnesses collected afterwards, either before the king or in the regular "Thing," he shall give the property up to him for whom it was intended. He shall take the stalk in the "Thing," and, before 12 months are over, shall throw it into the lap of him whom the owner has named heir; and he shall restore not more nor less, but exactly as much as was entrusted to him.

2. And if any one shall wish to say anything against this, three sworn witnesses shall say that they were in the "Thing" which the "Thunginus" or "Centenarius" called together, and that they saw that man who wished to give his property throw a stalk into the lap of him whom he had selected. They shall name by name him who threw his property into the lap of the other, and, likewise, shall name him whom be named his heir. And three other sworn witnesses shall say that he in whose lap the stalk was thrown had remained in the house of him who gave his property, and had there collected three or more guests, and that they had eaten porridge

at table, and that he had collected those who were bearing witness, and that those guests had thanked him for their entertainment. All this those other sworn witnesses shall say, and that he who received that property in his lap in the "Thing" held before the king, or in the regular public "Thing," did publicly, before the people, either in the presence of the king or in public "Thing"—namely on the Mallberg, before the "Thunginus"—throw the stalk into the lap of him whom the owner had named as heir. And thus 9 witnesses shall confirm all this.

TITLE L. CONCERNING PROMISES TO PAY.

1. If any freeman or leet have made to another a promise to pay, then he to whom the promise was made shall, within 40 days or within such term as was agreed when he made the promise, go to the house of that man with witnesses, or with appraisers. And if he (the debtor) be unwilling to make the promised payment, he shall be sentenced to 15 shillings above the debt which he had promised.

2. If he then be unwilling to pay, he (the creditor) shall summon him before the "Thing" and thus accuse him: I ask thee, 'Thunginus,' to bann my opponent who made me a promise to pay and owes me a debt." And he shall state how much he owes and promised to pay. Then the "Thunginus" shall say: "I bann thy opponent to what the law decrees." Then he to whom the promise was made shall warn him (the debtor) to make no payment or pledge of payment to any body else until he have fulfilled his promise to him (the creditor). And straightway on that same day, before the sun sets, he shall go to the house of that man with witnesses, and shall ask if he will pay that debt. If he will not, he (the creditor) shall wait until after sunset; then, if he have waited until after sunset, 120 denars, which make 3 shillings shall be added on to the debt. And this shall be done up to 3 times in 3 weeks. And if at the third time he will not pay all this, it (the sum) shall increase to 360 denars, or 9 shillings: so, namely, that, after each admonition or waiting until after sunset, 3 shillings shall be added to the debt.

3. If any one be unwilling to fulfil his promise in the regular assembly,—then he to whom the promise was made shall go the count of that place, in whose district he lives, and shall take the stalk and shall say: oh

count, that man made me a promise to pay, and I have lawfully summoned him before the court according to the Salic law on this matter; I pledge thee myself and my fortune that thou may'st safely seize his property. And he shall state the case to him, and shall tell how much he (the debtor) had agreed to pay. Then the count shall collect 7 suitable bailiffs, and shall go with them to the house of him who made the promise and shall say: thou who art here present pay voluntarily to that man what thou didst promise, and choose any two of those bailiffs who shall appraise that from which thou shalt pay; and make good what thou dost owe, according to a just appraisal. But if he will not hear, or be absent, then the bailiffs shall take from his property the value of the debt which he owes. And, according to the law, the accuser shall take two thirds of that which the debtor owes, and the count shall collect for himself the other third as peace money; unless the peace money shall have been paid to him before in this same matter.

4. If the count have been appealed to, and no sufficient reason, and no duty of the king, have detained him—and if he have put off going, and have sent no substitute to demand law and justice: he shall answer for it with his life, or shall redeem himself with his "wergeld."

TITLE LIV. CONCERNING THE SLAYING OF A COUNT.

1. If any one slay a count, he shall be sentenced to 2400 denars, which make 600 shillings.

TITLE LV. CONCERNING THE PLUNDERING OF CORPSES.

2. If any one shall have dug up and plundered a corpse already buried, and it shall have been proved on him, he shall be outlawed until the day when he comes to agreement with the relatives of the dead man, and they ask for him that he be allowed to come among men. And whoever, before he come to an arrangement with the relative, shall give him bread or shelter—even if they are his relations or his own wife—shall be sentenced to 600 denars which make xv shillings.

3. But he who is proved to have committed the crime shall be sentenced to 8000 denars, which make 200 shillings.

TITLE LVI. CONCERNING HIM WHO SHALL HAVE SCORNED TO COME TO COURT.

1. If any man shall have scorned to come to court, and shall have put off fulfilling the injunction of the bailiffs, and shall not have been willing to consent to undergo the fine, or the kettle ordeal, or anything prescribed by law: then he (the plaintiff) shall summon him to the presence of the king. And there shall be 12 witnesses who—3 at a time being sworn—shall testify that they were present when the bailiff enjoined him (the accused) either to go to the kettle ordeal, or to agree concerning the fine; and that he had scorned the injunction. Then 3 others shall swear that they were there on the day when the bailiffs enjoined that he should free himself by the kettle ordeal or by composition; and that 40 days after that, in the "mallberg," he (the accuser) had again waited until after sunset, and that he (the accused) would not obey the law. Then he (the accuser) shall summon him before the king for a fortnight thence; and three witnesses shall swear that they were there when he summoned him and when he waited for sunset. If he does not then come, those 9, being sworn, shall give testimony as we have above explained. On that day likewise, if he do not come, he (the accuser) shall let the sun go down on him, and shall have 3 witnesses who shall be there when he waits till sunset. But if the accuser shall have fulfilled all this, and the accused shall not have been willing to come to any court, then the king, before whom he has been summoned, shall withdraw his protection from him. Then he shall be guilty, and all his goods shall belong to the fisc, or to him to whom the fisc may wish to give them. And whoever shall have fed or housed him—even if it were his own wife—shall be sentenced to 600 denars, which make 15 shillings; until he (the debtor) shall have made good all that has been laid to his charge.

TITLE LVII. CONCERNING THE "CHRENECRUDA."

1. If any one have killed a man, and, having given up all his property, has not enough to comply with the full terms of the law, he shall present 12 sworn witnesses to the effect that, neither above the earth nor under it, has he any more property than he has already given. And he shall afterwards go into his house, and shall collect in his hand dust from the four corners

of it, and shall afterwards stand upon the threshold, looking inwards into the house. And then, with his left hand, he shall throw over his shoulder some of that dust on the nearest relative that he has. But if his father and (his father's) brothers have already paid, he shall then throw that dust on their (the brothers') children—that is, over three (relatives) who are nearest on the father's and three on the mother's side. And after that, in his shirt, without girdle and without shoes, a staff in his hand, he shall spring over the hedge. And then those three shall pay half of what is lacking of the compounding money or the legal fine; that is, those others who are descended in the paternal line shall do this.

2. But if there be one of those relatives who has not enough to pay his whole indebtedness, he, the poorer one, shall in turn throw the "chrenecruda" on him of them who has the most, so that he shall pay the whole fine.

3. But if he also have not enough to pay the whole, then he who has charge of the murderer shall bring him before the "Thing," and afterwards to 4 Things, in order that they (his friends) may take him under their protection. And if no one have taken him under his protection—that is, so as to redeem him for what he can not pay—then he shall have to atone with his life.

TITLE LIX. CONCERNING PRIVATE PROPERTY.

1. If any man die and leave no sons, if the father and mother survive, they shall inherit.

2. If the father and mother do not survive, and he leave brothers or sisters, they shall inherit.

3. But if there are none, the sisters of the father shall inherit.

4. But if there are no sisters of the father, the sisters of the mother shall claim that inheritance.

5. If there are none of these, the nearest relatives on the father's side shall succeed to that inheritance.

6. But of Salic land no portion of the inheritance shall come to a woman: but the whole inheritance of the land shall come to the male sex.

TITLE LXII. CONCERNING WERGELD.

1. If any one's father have been killed, the sons shall have half the compounding money (wergeld); and the other half the nearest relatives, as well on the mother's as on the father's side, shall divide among themselves.

2. But if there are no relatives, paternal or maternal, that portion shall go to the fisc.

QUESTIONS

1. Why does the Salic Law open with a list of subpoenas? What are the logistics of issuing a summons?
2. Dissect one of the longer Titles (e.g., Titles XLV; XLVI; or L) and speculate on the archaic practices required by that law.
3. What problems involve the swearing of oaths? How and why are oaths used?
4. What do the contents of this code, especially the different values put on different wrongs, suggest about economic practices and cultural norms in Salian society?

DOCUMENT

THE PAPACY LAYS CLAIM TO UNIVERSAL EMPIRE

Pope Gregory VII

The Investiture Controversy converted the bishop of Rome from a respected spiritual authority to a temporal power, the papacy, that rivaled the Holy Roman Empire and competed with kings and princes to exercise authority in Western Europe. The Roman Church became the center of a vast bureaucracy that aimed to control ecclesiastical and monastic property throughout Europe and claimed universal jurisdiction in a wide variety of legal cases. The Church's greatest leader in this epoch-making transformation was Pope Gregory VII, whose contest with Emperor Henry IV was perhaps the most dramatic struggle for power in the High Middle Ages.

The mysterious document known as the Dictatus Papae *or* Papal Formulae *is found in the registers of papal documents under the third year of Gregory VII. Its precise purpose is not known, but the most plausible hypothesis is that the twenty-seven formulae were meant to be the headings of a canon law collection, under which authorities could be marshalled supporting the papacy's various claims to temporal power. It is perhaps the single document most revealing of Gregory's ambitions for the papacy.*

1. That the Roman Church was founded by God alone.
2. That the Roman Pontiff alone is rightly to be called universal.
3. That he alone can depose or reinstate bishops.

Reprinted from *The Dictatus Papae, or Papal Formulae.*

4. That his legate, even if of lower grade, takes precedence, in a council, of all bishops and may render a sentence of deposition against them.
5. That the Pope may depose the absent.
6. That, among other things, we also ought not to stay in the same house with those excommunicated by him.
7. That for him alone it is lawful to enact new laws according to the needs of the time, to assemble together new congregations, to make an abbey of a canonry; and, on the other hand, to divide a rich bishopric and unite the poor ones.
8. That he alone may use the imperial insignia.
9. That the Pope is the only one whose feet are to be kissed by all princes.
10. That his name alone is to be recited in churches.
11. That his title is unique in the world.
12. That he may depose Emperors.
13. That he may transfer bishops, if necessary, from one See to another.
14. That he has power to ordain a cleric of any church he may wish.
15. That he who has been ordained by him may rule over another church, but not be under the command of others; and that such a one may not receive a higher grade from any bishop.
16. That no synod may be called a general one without his order.
17. That no chapter or book may be regarded as canonical without his authority.
18. That no sentence of his may be retracted by any one; and that he, alone of all, can retract it.
19. That he himself may be judged by no one.
20. That no one shall dare to condemn a person who appeals to the Apostolic See.
21. That to this See the more important cases of every church should be submitted.
22. That the Roman Church has never erred, nor ever, by the witness of Scripture, shall err to all eternity.
23. That the Roman Pontiff, if canonically ordained, is undoubtedly sanctified by the merits of St. Peter; of this St. Ennodius, Bishop of Pavia, is witness, many Holy Fathers are agreeable and it is contained in the decrees of Pope Symmachus the Saint.

24. That, by his order and with his permission, subordinate persons may bring accusations.
25. That without convening a synod he can depose and reinstate bishops.
26. That he should not be considered as Catholic who is not in conformity with the Roman Church.
27. That the Pope may absolve subjects of unjust men from their fealty.

QUESTIONS

1. What are some of the specific powers claimed by the Pope? How are these privileges or powers intended to support his authority?
2. Why is it significant that the Pope, "may absolve unjust men from their fealty"?
3. What is the ideological basis for the Pope's claims to authority? Why, according to Gregory's views, should the kings and princes of Europe accept these claims? What evidence is used by Gregory to demonstrate the legitimacy of his claims?
4. Can this document be thought of as a kind of European constitution? How was this constitution meant to work?

DOCUMENT

THE BLESSED SACRAMENT

Thomas à Kempis

Thomas à Kempis was born in 1380. His humble family lived in Kempen, near Düsseldorf. Thomas first attended the grammar school at Kempen, and then joined his brother at Deventer, where both became members of a Catholic brotherhood called the Congregation of the Common Life. This brotherhood, founded by the priest Gerard de Groote, was dedicated to revitalizing Christian devotion during a time of perceived corruption in the Church. The Congregation of the Common Life was recognized by Pope Gregory XI in 1376, and Thomas spent the rest of his life as a member of the brotherhood. He lived at Deventer for seven years, and then was admitted to the monastery of Mount St. Agnes in 1399. Thomas entered the priesthood in 1413. In 1425 he was elected sub-prior of the monastery of Mount St. Agnes, where his brother John served as prior. Thomas à Kempis died in 1471.

Thomas à Kempis lived a life not of action but of reflection and solitude. His fame rests on his authorship of deeply influential books of spirituality. Thomas wrote copiously, composing sermons, spiritual exercises, and biographies. But the most influential of his works was The Imitation of Christ. *The work was composed in Latin and has exerted a powerful influence for nearly six centuries. Stylistically simple, the work is based almost entirely on the Scriptures. Parts of* The Imitation *are composed as a dialogue between Jesus Christ and a disciple. The work explains the value of a life modeled on that of Christ, and how one can live such a life. The work's emphasis on renouncing worldly cares (and rewards) was consistent with the teachings of the*

Congregation of the Common Life. The Imitation of Christ *continued to have a powerful influence among Protestants and Catholic reformers after the Reformation.*

ON THE BLESSED SACRAMENT

The Voice of Christ

'COME TO ME, ALL WHO LABOUR AND ARE HEAVY LADEN, AND I WILL REFRESH YOU,' says the Lord.[1]
'THE BREAD THAT I WILL GIVE IS MY FLESH, FOR THE LIFE OF THE WORLD.'[2]
'TAKE AND EAT; THIS IS MY BODY WHICH SHALL BE OFFERED FOR YOU; DO THIS IN COMMEMORATION OF ME.'[3]
'WHOSOEVER EATS MY FLESH AND DRINKS MY BLOOD, DWELLS IN ME, AND I IN HIM.'[4] 'THESE THINGS THAT I HAVE TOLD YOU ARE SPIRIT AND LIFE.'[5]

Chapter 1
On the Deep Reverence with which Christ should be Received

THE DISCIPLE. O Christ, Eternal Truth, these are Your own words, although not spoken all at one time or in one place. And since they are Your words, and are true, I must accept them with gratitude and trust. They are Your words, and You have spoken them; they are also mine, since You have given them to me for my salvation. Gladly do I receive them from Your lips, that they may be the more deeply imprinted in my heart. Your words, so tender, so full of sweetness and love, give me courage; but my own sins appal me, and a stricken conscience restrains me from receiving so high a Sacrament.

You command me to approach You in faith if I wish to have part in You, and to receive the food of immortality if I desire life and glory. 'Come to Me,' You say, 'all who labour and are heavy laden, and I will refresh you.' O Lord my God! How sweet and loving in the ears of a sinner are these words, with which You invite the poor and needy to the Communion of Your most holy Body! But who am I, O Lord, that I should presume to approach You? The very Heaven of Heavens cannot contain You;[6] and yet You say, 'Come you all to Me.'

What is the meaning of this kindly invitation? Unaware of any good in me on which I may presume, how shall I dare to come? How shall I invite You into my house, who have so often done evil in Your sight? The Angels and Archangels do You reverence; Saints and holy men stand in awe of You; yet You say, 'Come you all to Me'! Unless You Yourself had said it, who would believe it true? And who would dare approach, unless it were Your command?

. . .

O my God, how earnestly did all these strive to please You! And how little, alas, can I do! How short is the time that I employ in preparing myself for Communion! Seldom am I entirely recollected, and very seldom free from all distraction. Yet in Your saving presence, O God, no unbecoming thought should enter my mind, for it is not an Angel, but the Lord of Angels who comes to be my guest.

How great a difference there is between the Ark of the Covenant and its relics, and Your most holy Body with its ineffable powers: between those sacrifices of the old Law which foreshadowed the Sacrifice to come, and the true Victim of Your Body, which fulfils all the ancient rites!

. . .

Many make pilgrimages to various places to visit the relics of the Saints, wondering at the story of their lives and the splendour of their shrines; they view and venerate their bones, covered with silks and gold. But here on the Altar are You Yourself, my God, the Holy of Holies, Creator of men and Lord of Angels! When visiting such places, men are often moved by curiosity and the urge for sight-seeing, and one seldom hears that any amendment of life results, especially as their conversation is trivial and lacks true contrition. But here, in the Sacrament of the Altar, You are wholly present, my God, the Man Christ Jesus; here we freely partake the fruit of eternal salvation, as often as we receive You worthily and devoutly. No levity, curiosity, or sentimentality must draw us, but firm faith, devout hope, and sincere love.

O God, invisible Creator of the world, how wonderful are Your dealings with us! How sweetly and graciously You welcome Your chosen, to whom

You give Yourself in this Sacrament! It passes all understanding; it kindles the love and draws the hearts of the faithful to Yourself. For Your faithful ones, who strive to amend their whole lives, receive in this most exalted Sacrament the grace of devotion and the love of virtue.

O wonderful and hidden grace of this Sacrament, known so well to Christ's faithful, but hidden from unbelievers and servants of sin! In this Sacrament, spiritual grace is conveyed, lost virtue restored to the soul, and its sin-ravaged beauty renewed. Such is the grace of this Sacrament, that from the fullness of devotion You afford greater powers not only to the mind, but to the frail body.

We cannot but regret and deplore our own carelessness and tepidity, which hinders us from receiving Christ with greater love, for in Him rests all our merit and hope of salvation. He is our Sanctification[7] and Redemption: He is the comfort of pilgrims, and the everlasting joy of the Saints. How sad it is that so many have small regard for this saving Mystery, which is the delight of Heaven and preservative of the whole world. Alas, man is so blind, and his heart so hard, that he does not appreciate more fully this wonderful gift, and, from frequent use of it, grows even less reverent towards it!

If this most holy Sacrament were celebrated in one place only, and were offered by one priest only in the whole world, men would rush to this place and to the priest of God, to be present at the divine mysteries. But there are now many priests, and in many places Christ is offered, that the grace and love of God may be better known to men, the more widely Holy Communion is diffused through the world. O good Jesus, eternal Shepherd, we thank You that You deign to refresh us poor exiles with Your precious Body and Blood, and invite us to receive these Mysteries, saying, 'Come to Me, all who labour and are heavy laden, and I will refresh you.'

Chapter 2
On the Great Goodness and Love of God in this Sacrament

THE DISCIPLE. Trusting wholly in Your goodness and great mercy, Lord, I come sick to my Saviour, hungry and thirsty to the Fount of Life,[8] needy to the King of Heaven, a creature to its Creator, desolate to my loving Comforter. Yet whence is this favour, that You should come to me?[9] What am I, that You should give me Your very Self? How dare a sinner appear before You? And how is it that You deign to visit a sinner? You know Your servant, and see that he possesses no good in himself that could merit this blessing. Thus do I confess my worthlessness; I acknowledge Your goodness, I praise Your kindness, and I offer my gratitude for Your boundless love.[10] You do this of Your own will; not on account of my merits, but solely that Your goodness may be more evident to me, Your love more richly imparted to me, and that You may more perfectly commend humility to me. Therefore, since it is Your pleasure and You have thus commanded it, Your will is my delight; may no wickedness in me obstruct it.

. . .

Lord, You are the Holy of Holies: I am the worst of sinners. Yet, O Lord, You stoop to me, who am not worthy even to raise my eyes towards You. Lord, You come to me, and desire to be with me; You invite me to Your Table; You wish to feed me with the Heavenly Food, the Bread of Angels. This Food is none other than Yourself, The Living Bread who came down from Heaven to give life to the world.[11]

See, from whom this love proceeds! See the Source whence this high glory shines! How deep a gratitude, how high a praise are Your due for all these blessings! How greatly to our profit and salvation was Your counsel when You instituted this Sacrament! How sweet and delightful the Feast in which You give Yourself to be our food! How wonderful are Your ways, O Lord; how mighty Your power, how infallible Your truth! You spoke the word, and all things were made;[12] You commanded, and it was done.

It is indeed wonderful to consider, worthy of faith, and transcending the mind of man, how You, my Lord and God, true God and true man, are wholly present under the simple forms of bread and wine, and are eaten without being consumed by whoso receives You. O Lord of all things, who stand in need of none, and who yet are pleased to dwell[13] in us by means of this Sacrament; keep my heart and body spotless, that with a glad and pure conscience I may be enabled to celebrate Your holy Mysteries, and receive to my eternal salvation those things that You have hallowed and ordained to Your own especial honour and for Your perpetual memorial.

Chapter 3
On the Value of Frequent Communion

. . .

Man's senses are prone to evil from his youth up,[14] and without the aid of this divine remedy he soon lapses into yet greater wickedness. Holy Communion both restrains a man from evil, and establishes him in goodness. For if I am so often careless and lukewarm now when I celebrate or communicate, what would become of me were I to neglect this remedy, or fail to seek this most powerful aid? And although I am neither fit nor rightly disposed to celebrate daily, yet I will endeavour at proper times to receive Your divine Mysteries, and present myself to receive this great grace. For this is the chief comfort of the faithful soul, as long as she dwells afar from You in this mortal body, that ever mindful of her God, she may often devoutly receive her Beloved.

O Lord God, Creator and Giver of life to all souls, how wonderful is Your kindness and mercy to us, that You should stoop to visit the poor and humble soul, and to satisfy her hunger with Your whole Divinity and Humanity! Happy the mind and blessed the soul that deserves to receive You with devotion, and in receiving You, to be filled with spiritual joy! How great a Lord does the soul receive! How beloved the Guest she welcomes! How delightful the Companion she invites to enter! How faithful the Friend she makes! How gracious and noble the Spouse she embraces—one to be loved and desired above all others! O dear and most beloved Lord, let Heaven and earth in all their beauty keep silence before You; for whatever of praise and beauty they possess comes from Your generous goodness. They cannot approach the beauty of Your Name, and Your Wisdom is infinite.[15]

Chapter 4
On the Many Blessings Granted to the Devout Communicant

THE DISCIPLE. O Lord my God, so direct Your servant with the blessings of Your goodness,[16] that I may worthily and devoutly approach Your glorious Sacrament. Stir up my heart to seek You, and rouse me from sleep and sloth. Visit me with Your salvation,[17] that my spirit may taste Your sweetness, which in this Sacrament lies richly concealed, as in a fountain. Give me light to reverence this great Mystery: give me strength, to believe with unshakeable faith. For this is Your work, and it is not within the power of man; it is by Your sacred institution, and not an invention of men. No one of himself is capable of grasping and understanding these things, which are beyond even the high knowledge of the Angels. How then shall I, an unworthy sinner, mere dust and ashes, search out and understand so deep and sacred a mystery?

Lord, in simplicity of heart,[18] in firm good faith, and at Your bidding, I approach You with hope and reverence. I firmly believe that You are truly present in this Sacrament, both God and Man. It is Your desire that I should receive You, and be united to You in love. Therefore, I implore Your mercy, and beg You to give me an especial grace, that I may wholly melt and overflow with love for You, and that henceforward I may seek no consolation but Yourself. For this most high and venerable Sacrament is the health of soul and body, the cure of every spiritual malady. By it, our vices are cured, our passions restrained, temptations are lessened, grace is given in fuller measure, and virtue once established is fostered; faith is confirmed, hope is strengthened, and love kindled and deepened.

. . .

Chapter 5
On the Dignity of the Sacrament, and of the Priestly Office

CHRIST. Had you the purity of the Angels, and the holiness of Saint John the Baptist, you would still be unworthy to receive or touch this Sacrament. For it is not due to any merit of his own that a man is allowed to consecrate and handle the Sacrament of Christ, and receive the Bread of Angels[19] as his food. High the office, and great the dignity of a priest, to whom is granted what is not granted to Angels; for only a rightly ordained priest has power to celebrate the Eucharist and to hallow the Body of Christ. The priest is the minister of God, using the words of God by His own command and appointment: but God Himself is the principal agent and unseen worker, to whose will all things are subject,[20] and whose command all creatures obey.

In all that relates to this sublime Sacrament, you should have regard to God's word, rather than your own senses or any visible sign. Therefore, when you approach the Altar, let it be with awe and reverence. Consider from whom this ministry proceeds, that has been delivered to you by the imposition of the Bishop's hands.[21] You have been made a priest, and ordained to celebrate the Sacrament: see, then, that you offer this sacrifice to God faithfully, regularly, and devoutly, and that your life is blameless.[22] Your obligations are now greater; you are bound to exercise stricter self-discipline, and to aim at a higher degree of holiness. A priest should be adorned with all virtues, and show an example of holy life to others.[23] His life should not be like that of worldly men, but like that of the Angels,[24] or of perfect men on earth.

A priest clothed in sacred vestments occupies the place of Christ, that he may humbly intercede with God for himself and for all men.[25] He wears the sign of the Cross both before and behind him, that he may be ever mindful of His Lord's Passion. He wears the Cross before him on his chasuble, that he may diligently observe the footsteps of Christ, and earnestly study to follow them.[26] His shoulders also are signed with the Cross, that he may in mercy and for the love of God bear every injury done him by others. He wears the Cross before him, that he may grieve for his own sins; behind him, that he may compassionately lament the sins of others, ever mindful that he is appointed a mediator between God and the sinner, and that he may not cease from prayer and the Holy Sacrifice until he deserve to win grace and mercy. And when a priest celebrates the Eucharist, he honours God, and gives joy to the Angels; he edifies the Church, helps the living, obtains rest for the departed, and makes himself a sharer in all good things.

. . .

Chapter 8
On the Offering of Christ on the Cross

CHRIST. Naked I hung on the Cross with arms outstretched, offering Myself freely to God the Father for your sins,[27] My whole Person a sacrifice of divine propitiation: you, too, must willingly offer yourself daily to Me in the Eucharist with all your powers and affections as a pure and holy offering. I require nothing less of you than that you should strive to yield yourself wholly to Me. Whatever you offer to Me besides yourself, I account as nothing; I seek not your gift, but yourself.[28]

Were you to possess everything in the world except Me, it could not satisfy you; so neither can anything you give Me be acceptable without the gift of yourself. Offer yourself to Me, and give yourself wholly to God; so shall your offering be acceptable.[29] I offered Myself wholly to the Father for you: I have given My very Body and Blood to be your food, that I may be all yours, and that you may be mine for ever. But if you trust in yourself, and do not offer yourself freely to My will, your offering is not complete, nor can our union be perfect. A free offering of yourself into the hands of God must therefore precede all your doings if you desire to obtain freedom and grace. The reason why so few receive inward light and freedom is that they cannot wholly renounce self. My words remain unalterable: whoever does not renounce everything cannot be My disciple.[30] Therefore if you wish to be My disciple, offer yourself to Me with all your heart.

Chapter 9
How we must Offer Ourselves wholly to God and Pray for all Men

THE DISCIPLE. Lord, all things in Heaven and earth are Yours.[31] I desire to give myself to You as a free offering, and to be Yours for ever. O Lord, in simplicity of heart I offer myself to You this day, to be Your servant for ever:[32] I do this as an act of homage to You, and as an act of perpetual praise. Accept me, together with the Holy Sacrifice of Your precious Body which I plead before You this day in the unseen presence of adoring Angels, that it may avail to my salvation and that of all Your people.

Lord, I offer on Your altar of reconciliation all the sins and offences that I have ever committed before You and Your holy Angels, from the day of my first sin until now, praying You to burn and consume them all in the fire of Your love. Blot out the stains of my sins, and cleanse my conscience[33] from all offences: restore the grace lost by my sin: grant me full forgiveness, and of Your mercy receive me with the kiss of peace.

What can I do to atone for my sins, but humbly confess and lament them, and constantly implore Your propitiation? Hear me, I beg, in Your mercy, as I stand before You, O my God. All my sins are utterly hateful to me, and I resolve never to commit them again . . .

. . .

Chapter 18
How we should Approach Christ's Sacrament Humbly, Submitting Reason to Holy Faith

CHRIST. Beware of curious and unprofitable inquiry into the Myseries of this most holy Sacrament, if you would avoid being plunged into the depths of doubt; for those who attempt to search into the majesty of God will be overwhelmed with its glory.[34] God can do more than man is able to comprehend; yet we may humbly and reverently search for truth, so long as the seeker is always willing to be taught, and to follow the sound teachings of the Fathers.

Blessed is that simplicity which rejects obscure inquiry and advances along the sure and open road of God's Commandments.[35] Many have lost their devotion by attempting to pry into matters too high for them. It is faith and a holy life that are required of you, not a lofty intellect or knowledge of the profound mysteries of God. For if you cannot understand or grasp things that are beneath you, how will you comprehend those that are above you? Therefore submit yourself to God, and humble your reason to faith, and the fight of knowledge shall be granted you in so far as it be profitable and necessary.

Some are sorely tempted about faith and the Sacraments, but this is due to the Devil rather than to themselves. Do not be anxious; do not fight your thoughts, or attempt to answer any doubts that the Devil suggests: trust in God's word, believe His Saints and Prophets, and the wicked enemy will flee from you.[36] Often it is very profitable that the servant of God should experience such doubts, since the Devil does not tempt unbelievers and sinners who are already his own; but he tempts and vexes the faithful and devout in every way he can.

Go forward, then, with simple, undoubting faith, and come to this Sacrament with humble reverence, confidently committing to almighty

God whatever you are not able to understand. God never deceives; but man is deceived whenever he puts too much trust in himself. God walks with the simple,[37] reveals Himself to the humble, gives understanding to little ones, discloses His secrets to pure minds, and conceals His grace from the curious and conceited.[38]

All reason and natural research must follow faith, but not precede or encroach on it. For in this most holy and excellent Sacrament faith and love precede all else, working in ways unknowable to man. The eternal God, transcendent and infinite in power, works mightily and unsearchably[39] both in heaven and earth,[40] nor can there be any searching out of His wonders.[41] For were the works of God readily understandable by human reason, they would be neither wonderful nor unspeakable.

END NOTES

1. Matt. xi, 28.
2. John vi, 51.
3. Luke xxii, 19; 1 Cor. xi, 24.
4. John vi, 56.
5. John vi, 63.
6. 1 Kings viii, 27.
7. 1 Cor. i, 30.
8. Ps. xxxvi, 9.
9. Luke i, 43.
10. Eph. ii, 4.
11. Ps. lxxviii, 25.
12. Ps. cxlviii, 5.
13. 2 Macc. xiv, 35.
14. Gen. viii, 21.
15. Ps. cxlvii, 5.
16. Ps. xxi, 3.
17. Ps. cvi, 4.
18. 1 Chron. xxix, 17.
19. Ps. lxxviii, 26.
20. Wisd. xii, 18.
21. 1 Tim. iv, 14.
22. 1 Tim. iii, 2; 2 Pet. iii, 14.
23. Titus ii, 7.
24. Phil. iii, 20.
25. Heb. v, 3; vii, 27.
26. 1 Pet. ii, 21.
27. Isa. liii, 7; Heb. ix, 28.
28. Phil. iv, 17.
29. Ecclus. xxxv, 7.

30. Luke xiv, 33.
31. 1 Chron. xxix, 11.
32. 1 Chron. xxix, 17.
33. Heb. ix. 14; 1 John i, 7.
34. Prov. xxv, 27.
35. Ps. cxix, 35.
36. James iv, 7.
37. Ps. cxix, 130.
38. Matt. xi, 25.
39. Job v, 9.
40. Ps. cxxxv, 6.
41. Isa. xl, 28.

QUESTIONS

1. What does the Disciple mean when he says that Christ is "wholly present" on the altar?
2. As he addresses Jesus in this dialogue, what does the Disciple think of himself? What kinds of language does Thomas use to describe the Disciple's relationship to Jesus?
3. How must one behave, what must one think, and what should one do while receiving communion? What effects will be produced by the proper receipt of the sacrament?
4. Why is it that only "a rightly ordained priest" should be allowed to celebrate the Eucharist? What powers does the priest possess; what obligations does he have? What do you think are the consequences of this exclusive privilege to preside over the sacrament?

DOCUMENT

THE VALUE OF MARRIAGE AND FAMILY

Leon Battista Alberti

Long considered by historians a prime example of the "universal man" of the Renaissance, Leon Battista Alberti (1404–1472) was a humanist author, architect, surveyer, art theorist, poet, painter, engineer, and mathematician. He was a member of a prominent and wealthy family of merchant-bankers who had been exiled from Florence in the 1390s but were restored in 1434 with the coming of the Medici to power. Leon Battista went to the universities of Padua and Bologna with the intention of studying law, but instead developed a passionate love of the Greek and Latin classics. In 1432, while in Rome, he was appointed an abbreviator (a type of bureaucrat) in the chancery of Pope Eugene IV, a position he held until 1464. There, among the ruins of Rome's ancient architectural splendor, he elaborated the principles of his chief work, the De re architectura *(*On Architecture, *begun 1449, printed 1485). While moving with the papal court between Rome and Florence, Alberti also composed his two major treatises on the arts, the* De pictura *(*On Painting, *1436) and* De statua *(*On Statuary, *undated), as well as numerous other works of fiction, poetry, and applied science. In 1441, he organized a poetical contest in Florence, known as the* Certame Coronario, *for the best work of poetry in Italian.*

While Alberti is perhaps best known for his writings on the fine arts, his Book of the Family *(1433–1439) represents an important expression of the ideals of the merchants and businessmen who created and supported the Renaissance in fifteenth-century Italy. A dialogue in four books, it treats the problem of paternal responsibility and conjugal love (Book I), marriage (Book II), the economic basis of the family and estate management (Book III), and friendship (Book IV). Against some ascetic ideals of the Middle Ages, Alberti argued that wealth and marriage were not things to be despised, but were part of good citizenship. The prologue to the work presents a famously optimistic argument for the power of reason and virtue to overcome Fortune, a theme that would later be taken up and transformed by Machiavelli.*

PROLOGUE

Remembering how much ancient history and the recollection of our ancestors together can teach us, how much we are able to see in our own times both in Italy and elsewhere, and how not a few families used to be most happy and glorious but have now disappeared and died out, I often marveled to myself and was saddened over how much power Fortune's unfairness and malignity wielded over men; and how Fortune was permitted with her will and temerity to seize families well provided with the most virtuous of men, abounding in everything precious, expensive, and most desired by men, and endowed with many honors, fame, great praise, authority, and public favor; and how she would deprive them of every happiness, place them in a state of poverty, loneliness, and misery, reduce them from a great number of wealthy ancestors to only a few descendants and from countless riches to the direst straits, and, from the most glorious splendor, subject them to so many calamities, casting them down into abject, dark, and tempestuous adversity. Ah! How many families we see today which are fallen and ruined! It would not be possible to count or to describe all of the noblest families among the ancients, such as the Fabii, the Decii, the Drusii, the Grachii, and the Marcelli, or others, who existed for a long time in our land, supporting the public good and the maintenance of liberty, and who conserved the authority and the dignity of their homeland both in peacetime and in wartime—very modest, prudent, and strong families, such that they were feared by their enemies and loved and revered by their friends. Of all these families, not only their magnificence and their grandeur but the very men themselves, and not only the men but their very names and their memories, have shrunk and faded away, and every trace of them has been completely blotted out and obliterated.

Thus it is not without good reason that I have always thought it well worth knowing whether or not Fortune possesses such power over human affairs and whether this supreme license is really hers that with her instability and inconstancy she may destroy the grandest and most respectable of families. I think about this question without much emotion, detached and free of every passion, and I think to myself, O, young Albertis, how our own Alberti family has been subject to so many adversities for such a long time now and how with the strongest of spirits it has persevered and with what complete reason and good counsel our Albertis have been able to cast off and with firm determination endure our own bitter misfortunes and the furious blows of our unjust fates, and I note that many blame Fortune without just cause as being most often the reason, and I observe that many who through their own stupidity have fallen upon bad times have blamed Fortune and have complained of being buffeted by her stormy waves when they themselves in their foolishness brought about their problems. And in this way, many inept people claim that some other force was the cause of their own errors.

But if anyone who would investigate with care what it is that exalts and increases the family and what it is which also maintains the family in the highest ranks of honor and happiness, that person would soon discover how men usually are the cause of their every good or their every evil, nor will they ever attribute the reasons for their acquisition of praise, greatness, or fame more to Fortune than to their own ability. This is true, and if we examine republics or recall all the past principalities, we will discover that in acquiring and increasing as well as in maintaining and conserving the majesty and the glory already achieved, Fortune was never more influential than the good and holy disciplines of living. Who can doubt this? Just laws and virtuous principles, prudent counsel, and strong and constant actions, love of country, faith, diligence, the impeccable and most laudable customs of the citizens—these have always been able, even without Fortune's favor, to earn and to acquire fame, or with Fortune's assistance, to expand and to increase one's country gloriously and to commend themselves to posterity, achieving immortality. . . .

So then, it can be said that Fortune is incapable and most weak in taking from us even the least part of our character, and we must judge ability as itself sufficient to attain and maintain every sublime and most excellent thing—the grandest of principalities, the most supreme praise, eternal fame, and immortal glory. And you can be sure that whatever you seek or hold dear, no matter what it may be, there is nothing easier for you to acquire or obtain than this nobility. Only the man who does not desire it is without it. And there, if we admit that character, discipline, and manly behavior are man's possessions insofar as they desire them, good counsel, prudence, strong, constant, and persevering spirits, reason, order and method, good arts and discipline, equity, justice, diligence are within reach and embrace so much dominion that they ultimately climb to the highest degree and heights of glory. Oh, young Albertis, who among you would think it an easy task to persuade me that, given the often observed changeability and inconstancy of weak and mortal things, ability—which cannot be denied to men insofar as their free will and willpower seize it and make it part of them—can easily be taken away from its most diligent and vigilant possessors or its many strong defenders? We shall always be of the opinion, just as I believe you also are, since you are all prudent and wise, than in political affairs and in the lives of men, reason is more important than Fortune, and prudence more powerful than blind chance. Nor would any man ever seem wise or prudent to me who placed his hope less in his own ability than in fortuitous events. Anyone will recognize that hard work, good skills, constant enterprises, mature counsel, honest endeavor, just will, and reasonable expectations have increased and enlarged, adorned, maintained, and defended both republics and principalities, and with these qualities any dominion may arise to glory, while without them, it may remain deprived of all its majesty and honor; if we recognize that desire, inertia, lasciviousness, perfidy, cupidity, inequity, libido, and the raw and unbridled passions of human spirits contaminate, divert, and undermine every grandiose, solid, and stable human accomplishment, we shall also recognize that the same rules apply to families as they do to principalities, and we must confess that families rarely fall into unhappy times for any other cause except their lack of prudence and diligence.

And thus, since I know this to be the case, Fortune with its most cruel of floods may overcome and submerge the families which, throwing themselves upon the mercies of such waves, have either not known how to control or contain themselves in times of prosperity or have not been prudent and strong in sustaining and regulating themselves when they were buffeted by adversities; and because I do not doubt in the least that solicitous and diligent fathers of families may render their families most grand and extremely happy by their careful management, good practices, honest customs, humanity, openness, and civility, it has therefore seemed worthwhile to me to investigate with every care and concern what useful precepts are appropriate for instructing fathers and the entire family on how they may finally reach the heights of supreme happiness and not be forced in time to succumb to inequitable and unforeseen Fortune. And as much free time as I have permitted to take from my other affairs, I have been delighted to have spent in searching among the ancient writers as many precepts as they have left us which are apt and useful for the good, honor, and growth of families; and since I discovered many perfect lessons there, I felt it my duty to collect them together and set them in some order so that, gathered together in one place, you might come to know them with less effort, and in coming to know them, you might follow them. I also think, after you have reviewed with me the sayings and authority of these good ancient writers on the one hand, and have considered, on the other, the excellent customs of our Alberti ancestors, you will come to this same conclusion and will conclude for yourselves that ability determines all your fortune. Nor will it delight you any the less in reading me to discover the good ancient manners of our Alberti house, for when you recognize that the counsel and the remembered customs of our older Albertis are completely applicable and most perfect, you will believe their precepts and embrace them. You will learn from them in what manner the family is increased, with what skills it becomes both fortunate and blessed, and with which type of procedure it acquires grace, good will, and friendship, and by means of what discipline it grows and spreads honor, fame, and glory, and in what ways it commends the family's name to eternal praise and immortality. . . .

[After Alberti's prologue, Book I opens during a single afternoon and evening in May 1421 as a number of the Alberti family gathers at a home in Padua, where they are visiting the dying Lorenzo Alberti (Leon Battista's father). The first book contains a discourse by Lorenzo on the role of the father in the family, the relative responsibilities of the old and the young, and the importance of education for the children.]

BOOK II

[Book II discusses the important question of taking a wife, an act which was usually more concerned with economic questions than with romantic love. For the middle-class family man, the choice of a wife involved complicated issues—gaining alliances with the family and relatives of the bride, receiving the all-important dowry along with the bride, and—most important—fathering the legitimate children who would guarantee the continuity of the all-important family line. In this book, the dying Lionardo offers advice to the young Leon Battista, who would have been seventeen years of age when the fictitious dialogue was supposed to have taken place—thus, a young man of marriageable age.]

. . . Let a man take a wife for two reasons: the first is to perpetuate himself with children, and the second is to have a steady and constant companion for his entire life. Therefore, you must seek to have a woman capable of bearing children and pleasing enough to serve as your perpetual companion.

It is said that in taking a wife, you must look for beauty, relatives, and wealth. . . . I think beauty in a woman may be judged not only in her charms and in the gentleness of her face but even more in her person, which should be shaped and adapted for carrying and giving birth to a great number of beautiful children. And among the beauties of a woman, above all, are her good manners; for while an unkempt, wasteful, greasy, and drunken woman may have a beautiful body, who would call her a beautiful wife? And the most important manners worthy of praise in a woman are modesty and purity. Thus Marius, that most illustrious Roman citizen, in his first speech to the Roman people declared: "Purity in women and work from men." And it certainly seems so to me as well. There is nothing more repulsive than an untidy, filthy woman. Who is so stupid as not to realize that a woman who does not take pleasure in appearing clean and neat not only in her clothes and her body but in her every act and word is not to be considered well mannered? And who cannot see that a badly mannered woman is only very rarely a virtuous one? How damaging women without virtue are to families will be considered and discussed elsewhere, but I would not know which would be the greatest misfortune for families—complete sterility or a woman without virtue. Thus, in a bride one must first look for beauty of spirit—that is, good behavior and virtue—and then one should seek in her physical appearance loveliness, grace, and charm, but also try to find someone well suited for bearing children with the kind of body that guarantees healthy and tall ones. There is an ancient proverb which says: "When you want children, pick your wife accordingly," and every virtue of hers will show forth greater in her beautiful children. This saying is very common among the poets: "A beautiful character comes from a beautiful body." Doctors urge that a wife not be too thin nor too overloaded with fat, for the latter are full of chills, menstrual occlusions, and are slow to conceive. They also prefer that a woman be by nature happy, fresh, and lively in her blood and in her whole being. Nor are they displeased if the girl is dark-complexioned. However, they do not accept girls who are too black, nor do they like small ones or praise those who are too large or too slender. They consider it most useful for the woman to have well-balanced and well-developed limbs if she is to give birth to many children. And they always prefer a young woman, for reasons which need not be explained here, but especially because they have a more adaptable character. Young girls are pure because of their age, they are not malicious by habit, and they are by nature bashful and free of all maliciousness; they are well disposed to learning quickly and they follow the habits and wishes of their husbands without stubbornness. These things, therefore, are what follows from our discussion and are the concerns that should be most usefully kept in mind when selecting the proper, prolific wife. To these considerations should be added that it would be an excellent sign if the young girl has a great number of brothers, since you can hope that when she is yours, she will be like her mother in bearing male children.

Now we have spoken about beauty. The wife's lineage is the next problem, and here we shall consider what things are proper and to be preferred. I believe that in choosing relatives, the first thing to do is to examine the lives and the customs of all one's prospective relatives. Many marriages have brought about the utter ruin of numerous families, according to what we hear or read about every day, because they involved relatives who were quarrelsome, picky, arrogant, and full of ill will. . . . Therefore, to sum up this issue in a few words, since I wish to be brief on this question, it is important to acquire new relatives who are not of vulgar birth, who can boast a patrimony which is not insignificant, who exercise a profession which is not vile, and who are modest and respectable in all their affairs, people who are not too superior to you, so that their greatness will not eclipse your own honor and dignity, or disturb your peace and tranquillity and that of your family, and also because if one of your new relatives fail, you will be able to give him your support and sustain him without too much difficulty and without sweating too much under the weight of the burden you are carrying. Nor would I wish for these same new relatives to be inferior to you, for while the first condition of superiority places you in a state of servitude to them, this second condition of inferiority will cause you expense. Let them be, therefore, your equals, and as we have already said, modest and respectable. Next is the problem of the dowry, which, it seems to me, should be not excessive but certain and prompt rather than enormous, doubtful, and remote. . . .

[With some reluctance and obvious embarrassment, the writer then turns to the actual engendering of children, the primary function of a proper bourgeois union.]

But let us consider our first topic of discussion. I have noted what kind of woman is most suitable for bearing children; now I believe we should next treat the question of how best children may be conceived, a subject which might well be avoided on account of certain considerations of modesty. But in this nevertheless vital matter, I shall be so circumspect and so very brief that anyone expecting to find this matter dealt with at this point will not be disappointed. Husbands should not couple with their wives in an agitated state of mind or when they are perturbed by fears or other like preoccupations, for such emotions as these that afflict the spirit deaden and weaken our vital spirits, and the other passions which inflame the spirit disturb and effect those vital seeds which then must produce the human image. Thus, one may observe how a father who is impetuous and strong and knowledgeable has engendered a son who is timid, weak, and foolish, on the one hand, while another father who is moderate and reasonable has given birth to a son who is crazy and brutish. In addition, it is necessary not to couple if the body and all its members are not well disposed and healthy. Doctors declare, with good reason, and offer examples to prove that if fathers and mothers are either sluggish, deadened by debauchery, or weakened by bad blood, as well as made feeble or devoid of vigor and pulse, it is reasonable to expect that their children, as is often the case, will turn out leprous, epileptic, disgusting, and misshapen or lacking in their bodily parts—all qualities which are not desirable in one's children. As a result, doctors recommend that such couplings be undertaken in a sober, tranquil, and as happy a state of mind as possible, and they believe that the best hour of the night occurs right after the first digestion is completed, at which time you are neither empty nor filled with bad foods but, rather, well along in your digestion and refreshed with sleep. They also recommend during this coupling to make youself intensely desired by the woman. They have yet many other recommendations, such as when it is excessively hot or when seeds and roots are hidden in the soil and frozen there; then one must wait for more temperate weather. But it would take too long a time to recite all their prescriptions, and perhaps I should keep better in mind to whom I am speaking. You are only young men, after all; perhaps this argument, which can be excused by the fact that I was drawn into it accidentally by the course of my discussion, is something I should examine explicitly. But even if I am to be blamed and should excuse myself for it, I am delighted that my error may nevertheless have served some useful purpose, and because of this, I consider what I have done less offensive than if I had delved more deeply into the question. . . .

BOOK III

[Book III celebrates the crucial middle-class values of Alberti's era, thrift and good management. Alberti uses a distant relative of Lorenzo, a man named Giannozzo, as the spokesman for his economic vision of the family.]

GIANNOZZO: . . . In those days I was young and spent and threw around my money.

LIONARDO: And now?

GIANNOZZO: Now, my dear Lionardo, I am prudent, and I realize that anyone who throws away his possessions is crazy. The man who has never experienced how miserable and fruitless it is to go about seeking the charity of others in times of need will never know just how useful money is. And the man who has not experienced the great difficulty with which money is acquired will spend it too easily. And the man who is not measured in his spending is usually quickly impoverished. And anyone in this world who lives in poverty, my children, will suffer many hardships and many deprivations, and he would perhaps be better off dying than living in misery and in want. Therefore, my dear Lionardo, believe me as a person who knows by experience and could not be any surer of the truth of this proverb of our peasants: "He who finds no money in his own purse will find even less in another's." My children, if you wish to be thrifty, you should protect yourself against superfluous expenses as if from a mortal enemy.

LIONARDO: Nevertheless, Giannozzo, I do not think that in your desire to avoid expenses, you would like to be or appear to be avaricious.

GIANNOZZO: God preserve me from that! Let our enemies be avaricious. There is nothing so contrary to fame or grace in men than avarice. What virtue could be so clear and noble as not to be obscured and rendered unrecognizable under the cloak of avarice? And as for the continuous anxiety which characterizes men who are too tight and stingy, it is a most odious thing; for they first expend a great deal of trouble in accumulating their wealth and are then made unhappy by spending it, the worst thing which inevitably occurs to the stingy. I never see them happy, they never enjoy any part of their fortune.

LIONARDO: But to avoid seeming cheap, people think it is necessary to spend extravagantly?

GIANNOZZO: And to avoid appearing mad, one must be thrifty. But why, God help us, should anyone not prefer to appear thrifty rather than extravagant? Believe me, as I have had experience and knowledge of these matters, such expenditures as these which are not very necessary are not praised by wise men, and I have never witnessed (nor do I believe you will ever witness) a great, lavish, and magnificent expenditure that has not been criticized for countless shortcomings by countless people: there is always too much of this, or not enough of that. See for yourself. If a person plans a banquet, although a banquet is a most civilized expense and a kind of tax or a tribute we pay to preserve the goodwill and the bonds among friends, yet aside from the confusion, the worry, and the other anxieties—this is required, that is needed, and this too is necessary—the bother and the worry wear you out before you have even begun your preparations; and besides all this, there is the throwing away of things, the damaging effects of sweeping and washing the entire house: nothing can stay locked up, one thing is lost, another is needed, you seek here, borrow from others, buy, spend, spend some more, and waste. And then, you add the regrets and the many second thoughts that trouble you during the banquet itself and afterward, which are worrisome and inestimable inconveniences, as well as too expensive, and yet, by the time the smoke in the kitchen has disappeared, all the favor you have gained from the banquet is gone, Lionardo—every bit of it—and you'll hardly be noticed for what you've done! If things were done moderately, few people will praise you for its avoidance of ostentation, but many will criticize you for your lack of extravagance. And these many are certainly right. For any expenditure which is not absolutely necessary, in my opinion, can come from nothing but madness. And if a man goes mad in any respect, he should go completely mad in that regard, since to seek to be reasonably mad has always been a double and completely incredible insanity. But let us ignore all these things, since they are minor compared to these other matters, which I shall now discuss. These expenditures for the entertainment and honoring of your friends can come only one or two times a year, and they bear with them an excellent cure for anyone who has tried them once, and if that person is not entirely out of his mind, I believe he will avoid a second try. Lionardo, consider the matter yourself and think about it a moment. Consider whether there is anything more likely to destroy not only a family but a community or a country than those—what do they call them in those books of yours, those people who spend without reason?

LIONARDO: Prodigals.

GIANNOZZO: Call them what you wish. If I were to invent a name for them, what could I call them but completely misguided souls? They are completely misguided themselves, and they lead others astray as well. Since it is the unhappy inclination of the young to frequent dens of iniquity rather than the workshops and to spend their time more willingly among lavish young spenders than among thrifty older people, other young people see these "prodigals" of yours abounding in every sort of delight, and they immediately run to join them, giving themselves over to lasciviousness, to overly refined pleasures, and to idleness while they avoid praiseworthy enterprises, placing their glory and happiness in the wasting away of their resources, no longer seeking praise for being virtuous and holding every principle of good management in low esteem. To tell the truth, who among them could ever become virtuous, living as they do, in the midst of so many flattering gluttons and liars, and besieged by the most vile and dishonest men, musicians, players, dancers, buffoons, pimps, and beribboned dressers in livery and frills? Perhaps this entire crowd does not run to sit on the doorstep of anyone who is "prodigal," as if at school or in a factory for vices, so that as a result young men used to such a life cannot leave? Oh, good God! To continue, what evil do such people not do? They steal from their fathers, parents, and friends, they pawn and they sell. Who could even tell the half of the perversities they commit? Every day you hear new complaints, every hour some fresh infamy springs up, and they continuously spread about greater hatred, envy, enmity, and disgrace. Finally, my Lionardo, these "prodigals" find themselves impoverished in their old age, without honor, and with very few friends—actually none at all; for those flattering hangers-on, whom they considered their friends when they gave themselves over to lavish expenditures and who called spending (that is, becoming poor) "virtue," those who with their glass in hand swore and promised to lay down their lives for them—all of these people act like fishes: as long as the bait swims on the water and stays afloat, a great school of fish will swarm around, but when the bait disappears, everything is empty and deserted. I don't want to go on and on with these arguments, nor to give you examples of such people, nor to recount to you how many people I have seen with my very eyes who have at first been very wealthy and who have then become impoverished because of their poor management; Lionardo, that story would be too long to tell, and even the entire day would not suffice. In order to be brief, let me say this: just as prodigality is evil, thrift is good, useful, and praiseworthy. Thrift causes harm to no one, and it is useful, to the family. And let me tell you, I know that thrift alone is sufficient to maintain you in such a way that you will never need anyone else. Thrift is a holy thing, and how many lascivious desires, how many dishonest appetites does thrift put behind us! Prodigal and lascivious youth, my dear Lionardo, has always been the cause of the ruin of every family. Older thrifty and modest men are the salvation of the family. One must be thrifty if only because in this fashion, you gain the peace of mind of knowing that you live very well with what Fortune has given you. For whoever lives contented with whatever he possesses, in my opinion, does not deserve to be called avaricious. These spendthrifts, instead, are the avaricious, for they do not know how to satisfy themselves with their spending, and thus, they are never content with their acquisitions and seek to prey upon others. However, do not think that I admire any excessive stinginess. Let me say only this: I cannot criticize too harshly a father of a family who lives more like a thrifty person than a lavish spender.

LIONARDO: If you dislike spendthrifts, Giannozzo, people who do not spend money should please you. But avarice, which according to what wise writers say, consists in desiring too much wealth, also consists in not spending.

GIANNOZZO: You speak the truth.

LIONARDO: Yet you do not like avarice?

GIANNOZZO: I certainly do not.

LIONARDO: Well, then, what would this thrift of yours consist of?

GIANNOZZO: You know, Lionardo, I am not a man of letters. I have tried all my life to understand things more by experience than by what others have said, and what I know I have learned more from the truth of experience than from the arguments of others. And when one of those people who spend all day reading books tells me "that's the way things are," I do not believe him unless I see an obvious reason for doing so, a reason which moves me to accept the argument rather than one which forces me to do so. And if another person, one who is uneducated, cites the same reason for the same things to me, I will believe him without his citing written authorities, just as much as I would a man who uses the testimony from a book, since I consider anybody who writes a book a man like myself. But perhaps I would not be able to reply to you in the organized fashion you would, since you always spend the day with a book in your hands. But look here, Lionardo, these spendthrifts about whom I was speaking a moment ago displease me because they spend without reason, and the avaricious also annoy me because they do not use things when they have need of them and also because they desire wealth too much. Do you know the kind of man I like? The kind of man who employs his possessions as much as he needs to and not a bit more; such a man saves the surplus; and such men I call thrifty.

LIONARDO: I understand you perfectly—you mean those men who know how to hold the mean between two little and too much.

GIANNOZZO: Yes, that's it.

LIONARDO: But how can we know what is too much and what is too little?

GIANNOZZO: Easily—by the ruler in our hand.

LIONARDO: I am waiting and anxious to see this ruler.

GIANNOZZO: Lionardo, this is very easily and usefully explained. With every expenditure, you must only make sure that the cost is no greater nor more burdensome nor larger than necessity demands, nor should it be less than honesty requires.

LIONARDO: Oh, Giannozzo, how much more useful in the affairs of this world is an experienced and practical man such as yourself than an unexperienced man of letters!

GIANNOZZO: What are you saying? Haven't you read these things in your books? And yet, people say that they find everything in books.

LIONARDO: That may be true, but I don't ever remember finding them. And if you knew, Giannozzo, how useful and to the point you have been, you would be amazed.

GIANNOZZO: Is that so? I am delighted if I have been of some help to you.

QUESTIONS

1. What does Fortune do? What limits or controls Fortune?
2. Why should a man marry? What qualities should he look for in a wife? Why does Alberti not discuss a woman's choices?
3. Why does Alberti discuss a person's mental and physical condition, and even the weather, when he or she is having sex? What are his ideas about procreation?
4. When and how is it appropriate to spend money and when is it not? What becomes of those who are prodigal?

DOCUMENT

A TRAVELER'S ACCOUNT OF THE MAQDASHAW AND KULWA SULTANATES

Ibn Battuta

Ibn Battuta was born in Morocco in 1304 into a wealthy family of Muslim merchants. He left home at age twenty-one, initially for the purpose of making the hajj *(or pilgrimage) to Mecca, and spent the next thirty years travellng throughout the Islamic world. He visited West Africa and South Asia as well as the East African coast. In total, his travels have been estimated at nearly 75,000 miles.*

Battuta's account of his travels is one of the most extensive sources on the medieval Islamic world. Although it appears that he kept notes during the course of his adventures, Battuta dictated the general narrative after his return to Morocco. It touches on a wide variety of trade networks, ethnographic information and religious practices.

I took ship at 'Aden, and after four days at sea reached Zayla' [Zeila], the town of the Berberah, who are a negro people. Their land is a desert extending for two months' journey from Zayla' to Maqdashaw. Zayla' is a large city with a great bazaar, but it is the dirtiest, most abominable, and most stinking town in the world. The reason for the stench is the quantity of its fish and the blood fo the camels that they slaughter in the streets.

Reprinted from *Ibn Battuta: Travels in Asia and Africa 1325-1354,* translated by H.A.R. Gibb, by permission of Kegan Paul.

When we got there, we chose to spend the night at sea, in spite of its extreme roughness, rather than in the town, because of its filth.

On leaving Zayla' we sailed for fifteen days and came to Maqdashaw [Mogdishu], which is an enormous town. Its inhabitants are merchants and have many camels, of which they slaughter hundreds every day [for food]. When a vessel reaches the port, it is met by *sumbugs*, which are small boats, in each of which are a number of young men, each carrying a covered dish containing food. He presents this to one of the merchants on the ship saying "This is my guest," and all the others do the same. Each merchant on disembarking goes only to the house of the young man who is his host, except those who have made frequent journeys to the town and know its people well; these live where they please. The host then sells his goods for him and buys for him, and if anyone buys anything from him at too low a price or sells to him in the absence of his host, the sale is regarded by them as invalid. This practice is of great advantage to them. When these young men came on board our vessel, one of them approached me. My companions said "This man is not a merchant, but a theologian," whereupon the young man called out to his friends "This is the qádí's guest." Amongst them was one of the qádí's men, who went to tell him of this, so he came down to the beach with a number of students, and sent one of them to me. When I disembarked with my party, I saluted him and his party, and he said, "In the name of God, let us go and salute the Shaykh." Thereupon I said "And who is this Shaykh?" he answered "The sultan," for they call the sultan 'the Shaykh." I said to him "When I have settled down I shall go to him," and he replied "It is the custom that whenever a theologian, or sharif, or man of religion comes here, he must see the sultan before taking his lodging." So I went to him as they asked. The sultan, whose name is Abú Bakr, is of Berberah origin, and he talks in the Maqdishí language, though he knows Arabic. When we reached the palace and news of my arrival was sent in, a eunuch came out with a plate containing betel leaves and areca nuts. He gave me ten leaves and a few nuts, the same to the qádí, and the rest to my companions and the qádí's students, and then said "Our master commands that he be lodged in the students' house." Later on the same eunuch brought food from the 'Shaykh's' palace. With him came one of wazírs, whose duty it was to look after the guests, and who said "Our master greets you and bids you welcome." We stayed there three days, food being brought to us three times a day, and on the fourth, a Friday, the qádí and one of the wazírs brought me a set of garments. We then went to the mosque and prayed behind the [sultan's] screen. When the 'Shaykh' came out I greeted him and he bade me welcome. He put on his sandals, ordering the qádí and myself to do the same, and set out for his palace on foot. All the other people walked barefooted. Over his head were carried four canopies of coloured silk, each surmounted by a golden bird. After the palace ceremonies were over, all those present saluted and retired.

I embarked at Maqdashaw for the Sawáhil country, with the object of visiting the town of Kulwá [Kilwa, Quiloa] in the land of the Zanj. We came to Mambasá [Mombasa], a large island two days' journey by sea from the Sawáhil country. It possesses no territory on the mainland. They have fruit trees on the island, but no cereals, which have to be brought to them from the Sawáhil. Their food consists chiefly of bananas and fish. The inhabitants are pious, honourable, and upright, and they have well-built wooden mosques. We stayed one night in this island, and then pursued our journey to Kulwá, which is a large town on the coast. The majority of its inhabitants are Zanj, jet-black in colour, and with tattoo-marks on their faces. I was told by a merchant that the town of Sufála lies a fortnight's journey [south] from Kulwá, and that gold dust is brought to Sufála from Yúfí in the country of the Límís, which is a month's journey distant from it. Kulwá is a very fine and substantially built town, and all its buildings are of wood. Its inhabitants are constantly engaged in military expeditions, for their country is contiguous to the heathen Zanj. The sultan at the time of my visit was Abu'l-Muzaffar Hasan, who was noted for his gifts and generosity. He used to devote the fifth part of the booty made on his expeditions to pious and charitable purposes, as ts prescribed in the Koran, and I have seen him give the clothes off his back to a mendicant who asked him for them. When this liberal and virtuous sultan died, he was succeeded by his brother Dáwúd, who was at the opposite pole from him in this respect. Whenever a petitioner came to him, he would say "He who gave is dead, and left nothing behind him to be given." Visitors would stay at his court for months on end, and finally he would make them some small gift, so that at last people gave up going to his gate.

QUESTIONS

1. According to Battuta, how do the people of Mombasa obtain food?
2. What is Battuta's general impression of the Swahili (the people of the Sawahil)?
3. Why is the system of assigning hosts to merchants "of great advantage" to the people of Mogdishu?
4. How is Battuta's experience of travel impacted by his identity as a Muslim?

DOCUMENT

THE ORIGINS OF MAYA CIVILIZATION

The Popul Vuh

The territory of the ancient Maya included the Yucatán peninsula, Belize, much of Guatemala, western Honduras and western El Salvador. The first humans inhabited the region around 11,000 B.C.E. The flourishing of the Maya, however, occurred between 250 and 900 C.E., known by archaeologists as the Classic Period. During this era, dozens of city-states contested with each other. The population of the area might have reached as high as ten million. Most of the large cities and ceremonial sites disappeared after 900 C.E. for reasons that are not fully understood. Maya people continued to live in the region, however. The first Europeans arrived in 1523.

The Maya built an extraordinary civilization. Their knowledge of mathematics, hydraulic engineering, astronomy, and construction were in many instances far beyond that of the Europeans who invaded their lands in the sixteenth century.

The Popol Vuh, *that in the Quiche Maya language means* Counsel Book *or* The Maya Book of the Dawn of Life and the Glories of the Gods and Kings, *is the Maya description of the creation of the world.*

And here is the beginning of the conception of humans, and of the search for the ingredients of the human body. So they spoke, the Bearer, Begetter, the Makers, Modelers named Sovereign Plumed Serpent:

"The dawn has approached, preparations have been made, and morning has come for the provider, nurturer, born in the light, begotten in the light. Morning has come for humankind, for the people of the face of the earth," they said. It all came together as they went on thinking in the darkness, in the night, as they searched and they sifted, they thought and they wondered.

And here their thoughts came out in clear light. They sought and discovered what was needed for human flesh. It was only a short while before the sun, moon, and stars were to appear above the Makers and Modelers. Broken Place, Bitter Water Place is the name: the yellow corn, white corn came from there.

And these are the names of the animals who brought the food: fox, coyote, parrot, crow. There were four animals who brought the news of the ears of yellow corn and white corn. They were coming from over there at Broken Place, they showed the way to the break.

And this was when they found the staple foods.

And these were the ingredients for the flesh of the human work, the human design, and the water was for the blood. It became human blood, and corn was also used by the Bearer, Begetter.

And so they were happy over the provisions of the good mountain, filled with sweet things, thick with yellow corn, white corn, and thick with pataxte and cacao, countless zapotes, anonas, jocotes, nances, matasanos, sweets—the rich foods filling up the citadel named Broken Place, Bitter Water Place. All the edible fruits were there: small staples, great staples, small plants, great plants. The way was shown by the animals.

And then the yellow corn and white corn were ground, and Xmucane did the grinding nine times. Corn was used, along with the water she rinsed her hands with, for the creation of grease; it became human fat when it was worked by the Bearer, Begetter, Sovereign Plumed Serpent, as they are called.

After that, they put it into words:

the making, the modeling of our first mother-father,
with yellow corn, white corn alone for the flesh,
food alone for the human legs and arms
for our first fathers, the four human works.

It was staples alone the made up their flesh.

These are the names of the first people who were made and modeled.

This is the first person: Jaguar Quitze.

And now the second: Jaguar Night.

And now the third: Mahucutah.

And the fourth: True Jaguar.

And these are the names of our first mother-fathers. They were simply made and modeled, it is said; they had no mother and no father. We have named the men by themselves. No woman gave birth to them, nor were they begotten by the builder, sculptor, Bearer, Begetter. By sacrifice alone, by genius alone they were made, they were modeled by the Maker, Modeler, Bearer, Begetter, Sovereign Plumed Serpent. And when they came to fruition, they came out human:

They talked and they made words.

They looked and they listened.

They walked, they worked.

They were good people, handsome, with looks of the male kind. Thoughts came into existence and they gazed; their vision came all at once. Perfectly they saw, perfectly they knew everything under the sky, whenever they looked. The moment they turned around and looked around in the sky, on the earth, everything was seen without any obstruction. They didn't have to walk around before they could see what was under the sky; they just stayed where they were.

As they looked, their knowledge became intense. Their sight passed through trees, through rocks, through lakes, through seas, through mountains, through plains. Jaguar Quitze, Jaguar Night, Mahucutah, and True Jaguar were truly gifted people.

And then they were asked by the builder and mason:

"What do you know about your being? Don't you look, don't you listen? Isn't your speech good, and your walk? So you must look, to see out under the sky. Don't you see the mountain-plain clearly? So try it," they were told.

And then they saw everything under the sky perfectly. After that, they thanked the Maker, Modeler:

"Truly now,
double thanks, triple thanks
that we've been formed, we've been given

our mouths, our faces,
we speak, we listen,
we wonder, we move,
our knowledge is good, we've understood
what is far and near,
and we've seen what is great and small
under the sky, on the earth.
Thanks to you we've been formed,
we've come to be made and modeled,
our grandmother, our grandfather,"

they said when they gave thanks for having been made and modeled. They understood everything perfectly, they sighted the four sides, the four corners in the sky, on the earth, and this didn't sound good to the builder and sculptor:

"What our works and designs have said is no good:

'We have understood everything, great and small,' they say." And so the Bearer, Begetter took back their knowledge:

"What should we do with them now? Their vision should at least reach nearby, they should see at least a small part of the face of the earth, but what they're saying isn't good. Aren't they merely 'works' and 'designs' in their very names? Yet they'll become as great as gods, unless they procreate, proliferate at the sowing, the dawning, unless they increase."

"Let it be this way: now we'll take them apart just a little, that's what we need. What we've found out isn't good. Their deeds would become equal to ours, just because their knowledge reaches so far. They see everything," so said

the Heart of Sky, Hurricane,
Newborn Thunderbolt, Raw Thunderbolt,
Sovereign Plumed Serpent,
Bearer, Begetter,
Xpiyacoc, Xmucane,
Maker, Modeler,

as they are called. And when they changed the nature of their works, their designs, it was enough that the eyes be marred by the Heart of Sky. They were blinded as the face of a mirror is breathed upon. Their eyes were weakened. Now it was only when they looked nearby that things were clear.

And such was the loss of the means of understanding along with the means of knowing everything, by the four humans. The root was implanted.

And such was the making, modeling of our first grandfather, our father, by the Heart of Sky, Heart of Earth.

And then their wives and women came into being Again, the same gods thought of it. It was as if they were asleep when they received them, truly beautiful women were there with Jaguar Quitze, Jaguar Night, Mahucutah, and True Jaguar. With their women there they became wider awake. Right away they were happy at heart again, because of their wives.

Celebrated Seahouse is the name of the wife of Jaguar Quitze.

Prawn House is the name of the wife of Jaguar Night.

Hummingbird House is the name of the wife of Mahucutah.

Macaw House is the name of the wife of True Jaguar.

So these are the names of their wives, who became ladies of rank, giving birth to the people of the tribes, small and great.

And this is our root, we who are the Quiché people. And there came to be a crowd of penitents and sacrificers. It wasn't only four who came into being then, but there were four mothers for us, the Quiché people. There were different names for each of the peoples when they multiplied, there in the east. Their names became numerous: Sovereign Oloman, Cohah, Quenech Ahau, as the names of the people who were there in the east are spoken. They multiplied, and it is known that the Tams and Ilocs began then. They came from the same place, there in the east.

Jaguar Quitze was the grandfather and father of the nine great houses of the Cauecs.

Jaguar Night was the grandfather and father of the nine great houses of the Greathouses.

Mahucutah was the grandfather and father of the four great houses of the Lord Quichés.

There were three separate lineages. The names of the grandfathers and fathers are not forgotten. These multiplied and flowered there in the east, but the Tams and Ilocs also came forth, along with thirteen allied tribes, thirteen principalities, including:

The Rabinals, Cakchiquels, those of the Bird House.

And the White Cornmeals.

And also the Lamacs, Serpents, Sweatbath House, Talk House, those of the Star House.

And those of the Quiba House, those of the Yokes House, Acul people, Jaguar House, Guardians of the Spoils, Jaguar Ropes.

It is sufficient that we speak only of the largest tribes from among the allied tribes; we have only noted the largest. Many more came out afterward, each one a division of that citadel. We haven't written their names, but they multiplied there, from out of the east. There came to be many peoples in the blackness; they began to abound even before the birth of the sun and the light. When they began to abound they were all there together; they stood and walked in crowds, there in the east.

There was nothing they could offer for sustenance, but even so they lifted their faces to the sky. They didn't know where they were going. They did this for a long time, when they were there in the grasslands: black people, white people, people of many faces, people of many languages, uncertain, there at the edge of the sky.

And there were mountain people. They didn't show their faces, they had no homes. They just traveled the mountains, small and great. "It's as if they were crazy," they used to say. They derided the mountain people, it was said. There they watched for the sunrise, and for all the mountain people there was just one language. They did not yet pray to wood and stone.

These are the words with which they remembered the Maker, Modeler, Heart of Sky, Heart of Earth. It was said that these were enough to keep them mindful of what was in shadow and what was dawning. All they did was ask; they had reverent words. They were reverent, they were givers of praise, givers of respect, lifting their faces to the sky when they made requests for their daughters and sons:

"Wait!
thou Maker, thou Modeler,
look at us, listen to us,
don't let us fall, don't leave us aside,
thou god in the sky, on the earth,
Heart of Sky, Heart of Earth,
give us our sign, our word,

as long as there is day, as long as there is light.
When it comes to the sowing, the dawning,
will it be a greening road, a greening path?
Give us a steady light, a level place,
a good light, a good place,
a good life and beginning.
Give us all of this, thou Hurricane,
Newborn Thunderbolt, Raw Thunderbolt,
Newborn Nanahuac, Raw Nanahuac,
Falcon, Hunahpu,
Sovereign Plumed Serpent,
Bearer, Begetter,
Xpiyacoc, Xmucane,
Grandmother of Day, Grandmother of Light,
when it comes to the sowing, the dawning,"

they said when they made their fasts and prayers, just watching intently for the dawn. There, too, they looked toward the east, watching closely for the daybringer, the great star at the birth of the sun, of the heat for what is under the sky, on the earth, the guide for the human work, the human design.

They spoke, those who are Jaguar Quitze, Jaguar Night, Mahucutah, and True Jaguar:

"We're still waiting for the dawning," they said, these great knowers, great thinkers, penitents, praisers, as they are called. And there was nothing of wood and stone in the keeping of our first mother-fathers, and they were weary at heart there, waiting for the sun. Already there were many of them, all the tribes, including the Yaqui people, all penitents and sacrificers.

"Let's just go. We'll look and see whether there is something to keep as our sign. We'll find out what we should burn in front of it. The way we are right now, we have nothing to keep as our own," said Jaguar Quitze, Jaguar Night, Mahucutah, and True Jaguar. They got word of a citadel. They went there.

And this is the name of the mountain where they went, Jaguar Quitze, Jaguar Night, Mahucutah, True Jaguar, and the Tams and Ilocs: Tulan Zuyua, Seven Caves, Seven Canyons is the name of the citadel. Those who were to receive the gods arrived there.

And they arrived there at Tulan, all of them, countless people arrived, walking in crowds, and their gods were given out in order, the first being those of Jaguar Quitze, Jaguar Night, Mahucutah, and True Jaguar. They were happy:

"We have found what we were looking for," they said. And this one was the first to come out:

Tohil is the name of the god loaded in the backpack borne by Jaguar Quitze. And the others came out in turn:

Auilix is the name of the god that Jaguar Night carried.

Hacauitz, in turn, is the name of the god received by Mahucutah.

Middle of the Plain is the name of the god received by True Jaguar.

And there were still other Quiché people, since the Tams also received theirs, but it was the same Tohil for the Tams, that's the name received by the grandfather and father of the Tam lords, as they are known today.

And third were the Ilocs: again, Tohil is the name of the god received by the grandfather and father of those lords, the same ones known today.

And such was the naming of the three Quichés. They have never let go of each other because the god has just one name: Tohil for the Quiché proper, and Tohil for the Tams and Ilocs. There is just one name for their god, and so the Quiché threesome has not come apart, those three. Tohil, Auilix, and Hacauitz are truly great in their very being.

And then all the tribes came in: Rabinals, Cakchiquels, those of the Bird House, along with the Yaqui people, as the names are today. And the languages of the tribes changed there; their languages became differentiated. They could no longer understand one another clearly when they came away from Tulan.

QUESTIONS

1. Why did the gods limit the sight of men?
2. What is the significance of the corn in these stories?
3. Why do you think that civilizations have constructed myths about their origins?
4. How does the Maya creation story compare and contrast with that of the Judeo-Christian or Muslim stories of creation?

INTRODUCTION

AZTEC HUMAN SACRIFICE

There are four questions about the practice of human sacrifice among the Aztecs. First, did the Aztecs sacrifice humans? Second, to what extent did the Aztecs sacrifice humans? Third, did the Aztecs cannibalize sacrifice subjects? And fourth, why did the Aztecs sacrifice humans?

Unquestionably, the Aztecs sacrificed humans. They were neither the first to practice human sacrifice, nor were they the only group in Mesoamerica to sacrifice humans. Their predecessors the Toltecs sacrificed humans, as did the Maya of Yucatán. Both of these were highly advanced peoples with enormous achievements in art and science. The evidence for the Aztecs is extensive in both their own sources and the records of the European invaders of the sixteenth century. Bernal Díaz del Castillo, who accompanied Hernán Cortés on his conquests, chronicled a number of examples in his The Discovery and Conquest of Mexico.

The controversies, however, grow more heated over the extent and reasons for human sacrifice. Robert C. Padden in his Hummingbird and the Hawk *maintains that the Aztecs killed tens of thousands in commemoration of their temple to their god Huitzilopochtli in 1487. Jacques Soustelle in* The Daily Life of the Aztecs *argues for a far more modest scale.*

Three theories emerge as to why the Aztecs sacrificed humans. First, and most generally accepted, is that Aztec religion required it. The Aztecs' gloomy view perceived the world was on its Fifth Sun. Four previous worlds had been destroyed. In the current world the sun was born from the sacrifice to the gods. It therefore required that the sun must be fed blood and water to keep it on its course in the sky. Blood was necessary to save the world and the people in it. The victim of human sacrifice was, consequently, not an enemy, but an almost divine being sent to the gods.

A second theory, widely disdained, maintains that human sacrifice was a means to sustain population in a region badly short of water for agriculture. This theory argues that the Aztecs needed the protein from human flesh and, as the population grew substantially after 1450, so did the practice of human sacrifice. Finally, and perhaps more reasonably, some historians argue that human sacrifice was a crucial instrument of the Aztec state. The cult of Huitzilopochtli was a brilliant invention by which to terrorize the other peoples of the Valley of Mexico and beyond. The religious justification for sacrifice was made up by the evil genius Tlacaellel to further the imperial ambitions of Tenochtitlan (the city of the Aztecs).

QUESTIONS

1. What reason for the Aztec practice of human sacrifice is most persuasive, and why?
2. The argument that the Aztecs practiced cannibalism on a wide scale is enormously offensive to Mexicans. Can you explain why?
3. The juxtaposition of human sacrifice with great achievement in art and science seems a contradiction. Do you agree or disagree and why?
4. Whatever explanation you accept concerning the practice of human sacrifice, how do you characterize the use of religion?

READING

THE WORLD, MAN, AND TIME

Jacques Soustelle

Unquestionably the Aztecs sacrificed humans. The evidence is extensive in both indigenous sources and the records of the European invaders of the sixteenth century. The controversies, however, grow more heated over the extent and reasons for human sacrifice. Robert C. Padden in his Hummingbird and the Hawk *maintains that the Aztecs killed tens of thousands in commemoration of their temple to their god Huitzilopochtli in 1487. Others like Jacques Soustelle in* The Daily Life of the Aztecs *argue for a far more modest scale.*

Three theories emerge as to why the Aztecs sacrificed humans. First, and most generally accepted, is that Aztec religion required it. The Aztecs' gloomy view perceived that the world was on its Fifth Sun. Four previous suns had been destroyed. In the current world the sun was born from the sacrifice to the gods. It therefore required that the sun must be fed blood and water to keep it on its course in the sky. Blood was necessary to save the world and the people in it. A second theory, widely disdained, argues that the Aztecs needed the protein from human flesh. Because the population grew substantially after 1450, so did the practice of human sacrifice. The Valley of Mexico had few domesticated animals for consumption. Finally, and perhaps more reasonably, some historians argue that human sacrifice was a crucial instrument of the Aztec state. The cult of Huitzilopochtli was a brilliant invention by which to terrorize the other peoples of the Valley of Mexico and beyond in order to induce them to succumb to Aztec rule.

Jacques Soustelle is the clearest proponent of explaining Aztec human sacrifice through their religion. In the selection here he explores the Aztec's grim world view, the rites and ceremonies surrounding human sacrifice, and the extraordinary relationship that developed between the sacrifice victims and the Aztec priests.

A SHIFTING, THREATENED WORLD

The Mexicans, like some other Central-American peoples, believed that several successive worlds had existed before ours and that each of them had fallen in ruins amid cataclysms in which mankind had been wiped out. These were the 'four suns'; and the age in which we live is the fifth. Each of these 'suns' is shown on monuments such as the Aztec calendar or the stone of the suns by a date, a date which is that of its end and which evokes the nature of the catastrophe which ended it: in this way the fourth epoch, for example, the 'sun of the water', which was drowned in a kind of Flood, has the date *naui atl,* 'four—water'.

Our world will have the same fate: its destiny is fixed by the date which has, as one might say, branded it at birth the date *naui ollin,* at which our sun first began to move. The glyph *ollin,* shaped like a Saint Andrew's cross, which shares the centre of the Aztec calendar with the sun-god's visage, has the double sense of 'movement' and of 'earthquake'. It symbolises both the first motion of the heavenly body when our age began and the cataclysms that will destroy our earth. At that moment the appearance of reality will be ripped open like a veil and the *Tzitzimime,* the monsters of the twilight who await the fatal hour beneath the western sky, will swarm out and hurl themselves upon the last survivors.

The ancient Mexicans believed in two primordial beings who were at the origin of all others, even of the gods: they were Ometecuhtli, 'the Lord of the Duality', and Omeciuatl, 'the Lady of the Duality'; and they lived at the summit of the world, in the thirteenth heaven, 'there where the air was very cold, delicate and iced.' Their unending fruitfulness produced all the gods, and from it all mankind is born. At the time with which this book is concerned these two great divinities had come in some degree to resemble those kings who reign but do not govern: they had been pushed into the background by the vigorous crowd of younger and more active gods. But it was still they who were held to have the privilege of fixing the birth-date of each living being, and thus its fate.

The gods, the descendants of the supreme Duality, in their turn were the creators of the earth: the most important act in this creation was clearly the birth of the sun; and this sun was born from sacrifice and blood. It is said that the gods gathered in the twilight at Teotihuacán, and one of them, a little leprous god, covered with boils, threw himself into a huge brazier as a sacrifice. He rose from the blazing coals changed into a sun: but this new sun was motionless; it needed blood to move. So the gods immolated themselves, and the sun, drawing life from their death, began its course across the sky.

This was the beginning of the cosmic drama in which humanity took on the rôle of the gods. To keep the sun moving in its course, so that the darkness should not overwhelm the world for ever, it was necessary to feed it every day with its food, 'the precious water' (*chalchiuatl*)—that is, with human blood. Sacrifice was a sacred duty towards the sun and a necessity for the welfare of men: without it the very life of the world would stop. Every time that a priest on the top of a pyramid held up the bleeding heart of a man and then placed it in the *quauhxicalli* the disaster that perpetually threatened to fall upon the world was postponed once more. Human sacrifice was an alchemy by which life was made out of death; and the gods themselves had given the example on the first day of creation.

As for man, his very first duty was to provide nourishment *intonan intota tlaltecuhtli tonatiuh,* 'for our mother and our father, the earth and the sun'; and to shirk this was to betray the gods and at the same time all mankind, for what was true of the sun was also true of the earth, the rain, growth and all the forces of nature. Nothing was born, nothing would endure, except by the blood of sacrifice.

The great god-king of the Toltecs, Quetzalcoatl, 'never would (offer up human victims) because he so loved his subjects, the Toltecs, and he presented only snakes in sacrifice, and birds and butterflies.' But Quetzalcoatl was expelled from Tula by the black magic of Tezcatlipoca; and so Mexico was delivered over to the blood-thirsty gods. In the most usual form of the rite, the victim was stretched out on his back on a slightly convex stone with his arms and legs held by four priests, while a fifth ripped him open with a flint knife and tore out his heart. The sacrifice also often took place in the manner which the Spaniards described as *gladiatorio:* the captive was tied to a huge disk of stone, the *temalacatl,* by a rope that left him free to move; he was armed with wooden weapons, and he had to fight several normally-armed Aztec warriors in turn. If, by any extraordinary chance, he did not succumb to their attacks, he was spared; but nearly always the 'gladiator' fell, gravely wounded, and a few moments later he died on the stone, with his body opened by the black-robed, long-haired priests. The warriors who were set apart for this kind of death wore ornaments and clothes of a special nature, and they were crowned with white down, as a symbol of the first light of the dawn, of the still uncertain hour when the soul of the resuscitated warrior takes its flight in the greyness towards our father the sun.

But these were not the only forms of sacrifice. Women were dedicated to the goddesses of the earth, and while they danced, pretending to be unaware of their fate, their heads were struck off; children were drowned as an offering to the rain-god Tlaloc; the fire-god's victims, anæsthetised by *yauhtli* (hashish), were thrown into the blaze; and those who personified the god Xipe Totec were fastened to a kind of frame, shot with arrows and then flayed—the priests dressed themselves in the skin. In most cases, the victim was dressed, painted and ornamented so as to represent the god who was being worshipped; and thus it was the god himself who died before his own image and in his own temple, just as all the gods had accepted death in the first days for the salvation of the world. And when ritual cannibalism was practiced on certain occasions, it was the god's own flesh that the faithful ate in their bloody communion.

There is no aspect of the Mexican civilisation that shocks our feelings as much as this. From the first contact between the Indians and the Europeans the horror and disgust that the newcomers felt for the human sacrifices helped them to convince themselves that the native religion came from hell and that its gods were no more than devils: from then onwards they were certain that Uitzilopochtli, Tlaloc, Tezcatlipoca and all the other gods of Mexico were in fact demons, and that everything that concerned them either directly or remotely should be rooted out for ever. The Aztec practice of human sacrifice was a great factor in making the two religions which confronted one another totally irreconcilable, and when the war broke out between the Spaniards and the Mexicans, in giving it a bitter and remorseless character from the moment the helpless conquistadores saw from afar the death of their comrades, whose grinning skulls they later found exposed on the *tzompantli.*

Clearly, it is difficult for us to come to a true understanding of what human sacrifice meant to the sixteenth century Aztec: but it may be observed that every culture possesses its own idea of what is and what is not cruel. At the height of their career the Romans shed more blood in their circuses and for their amusement than ever the Aztecs did before their idols. The Spaniards, so sincerely moved by the cruelty of the native priests, nevertheless massacred, burnt, mutilated and tortured with a perfectly clear conscience. We, who shudder at the tale of the bloody rites of ancient Mexico, have seen with our own eyes and in our own days civilised nations proceed systematically to the extermination of millions of human beings and to the perfection of weapons capable of annihilating in one second a hundred times more victims than the Aztecs ever sacrificed.

Human sacrifice among the Mexicans was inspired neither by cruelty nor by hatred. It was their response, and the only response that they could conceive, to the instability of a continually threatened world. Blood was necessary to save this world and the men in it: the victim was no longer an enemy who was to be killed but a messenger, arrayed in a dignity that was almost divine, who was sent to the gods. All the relevant descriptions, such as those that Sahagún took down from his Aztec informants, for example, convey the impression not of a dislike between the sacrificer and the victim nor of anything resembling a lust for blood, but of a strange fellow-feeling or rather—and this is vouched for by the texts—of a kind of *mystical kinship.*

'When a man took a prisoner he said, "Here is my well-beloved son." And the captive said, "Here is my revered father.' " The warrior who had made a prisoner and who watched him die before the altar knew that sooner or later he would follow him into the hereafter by the same kind of death. 'You are welcome: you know what the fortune of war is—today for you, tomorrow for me,' said the emperor to a captured chief. As for the prisoner himself, he was perfectly aware of his fate and he had been prepared from his childhood to accept it: he agreed, stoically. More than that, he would refuse a clemency that crossed his destiny or the divine will, even if it were offered him.

Tlacahuepan, the Mexican leader, who was a prisoner of the *Chalca* in the reign of Motecuhzoma I, had distinguished himself so much by his bravery that when he was captured his enemies offered him a part of their territory for himself and the other Aztecs they had taken. He would not only have his life, but he would be lord of that section: they even asked him to command the troops of Chalco. Tlacahuepan's only reply was to kill himself, shouting to his fellow-prisoners, 'Mexicans, I am going, and I shall wait for you.'

The story of Tlahuicole, a lord of Tlaxcala, who was taken by the Mexicans, was no less famous. They admired him so much that instead of sacrificing him they entrusted him with the command of a body of soldiers in the war against Michoacán: but on his return, covered with honours, from this expedition, the Tlaxcaltec refused to withhold himself any longer from his fate. He insisted upon his death, and died upon the sacrificial stone.

To a less extent this was also the attitude of all the other victims. It was the attitude of the young man who, having lived for a year in princely luxury, was to die at the end of it in front of the image of Tezcatlipoca; and it was that of the women who calmly danced and sang while the dark-robed priests behind them waited for the moment to make their heads fall like ears of maize when they are plucked from the stem. The sensitivity of the Indians, moulded by a powerful and very ancient tradition, was not the same as that of the Europeans of their epoch: the Aztecs were unmoved by the scenes in their blood-soaked temples, but they were horror-struck by the tortures that the Spaniards brought with them from the land of the Inquisition.

It is only these foregoing considerations that allow one to understand the meaning of war for the ancient Mexicans, the meaning of the continual war towards which all the energies of the city were directed. Certainly it is not incorrect to interpret the history of Tenochtitlan between 1325 and 1519 as that of an imperialist state which steadily pursues its aim of expansion by conquest. But that is not all. As the Mexican dominion spread, so their very victories created a pacified zone all round them, a zone which grew wider and wider until it reached the edges of their known world. Where then were the victims to come from? For they were essential to provide the gods with their nourishment, *tlaxcaltiliztli.* Where could one find the precious blood without which the sun and the whole frame of the universe was condemned to annihilation? It was essential to remain in a state of war, and from this need arose the strange institution of the war of flowers, *xochiyaoyotl,* which seems to have come into being after the terrible famines which ravaged central Mexico in 1450.

The sovereigns of Mexico, Texcoco and Tlacopan and the lords of Tlaxcala, Uexotzinco and Cholula mutually agreed that, there being no war, they would arrange combats, so that the captives might be sacrificed to the gods: for it was thought, indeed, that the calamities of 1450 were caused by too few victims having been offered, so that the gods had grown angry. Fighting was primarily a means of taking prisoners; on the battlefield the warriors did their utmost to kill as few men as possible. War was not merely a political instrument: it was above all a religious rite, a war of holiness.

At bottom the ancient Mexicans had no real confidence in the future: their fragile world was perpetually at the mercy of some disaster—there were not only the natural cataclysms and the famines, but more than that, on certain nights the monstrous divinities of the west appeared at the cross-roads; and there were the wizards, those dark envoys from a mysterious world; and every fifty-two years there was the great fear that fell upon all the nations of the empire when the sun set on the last day of the 'century' and no man could tell whether it would ever rise again.

In all the cities and throughout the countryside the fires were put out: the close-packed crowds, filled with intense anxiety, gathered on the slopes of Uixachtecatl, while on the mountain-top the priests watched the Pleiades. The constellation mounted towards the zenith: but would it go on? Or would it stop, and would the hideous monsters of the end of the world come swarming out? The astronomer priest made a sign: a prisoner was stretched out on the stone. With a dull sound the flint knife opened his chest and in the gaping wound they spun the fire-stick, the *tlequauitl.* The miracle took place and the flame sprang up, born from this shattered breast; and amid shouts of joy messengers lit their torches at it and ran to carry the sacred fire to the four corners of the central valley. And so the world had escaped its end once more. But how heavy and blood-drenched a task it was for the priests and the warriors and the emperors, century after century to repel the unceasing onslaughts of the void.

QUESTIONS

1. In the Aztec's religion, who created the world?
2. What kept the sun in the heavens?
3. What is mystical kinship?
4. What was the relationship between Aztec religion and the construction of their vast political empire?

READING

THE ECOLOGICAL BASIS FOR AZTEC SACRIFICE

Michael J. Harner

Unquestionably the Aztecs sacrificed humans. The evidence is extensive in both their own sources and the records of the European invaders of the sixteenth century. The controversies, however, grow more heated over the extent and reasons for human sacrifice. Robert C. Padden in his Hummingbird and the Hawk *maintains that the Aztecs killed tens of thousands in commemoration of their temple to their god Huitzilopochtli in 1487. Jacques Soustelle in* The Daily Life of the Aztecs *argues for a far more modest scale.*

Three theories emerge as to why the Aztecs sacrificed humans. First, and most generally accepted, is that Aztec religion required it. The Aztecs' gloomy view perceived that the world was on its Fifth Sun. Four previous suns had been destroyed. In the current world the sun was born from the sacrifice to the gods. It therefore required that the sun must be fed blood and water to keep it on its course in the sky. Blood was necessary to save the world and the people in it. A second theory, widely disdained, argues that the Aztecs needed the protein from human flesh. As the population grew substantially after 1450, so did the practice of human sacrifice. The Valley of Mexico had few domesticated animals for consumption. Finally, and perhaps more reasonably, some historians argue that human sacrifice was a crucial instrument of the Aztec state. The cult of Huitzilopochtli was a brilliant invention by which to terrorize the other peoples of the Valley of Mexico and beyond in order to induce them to succumb to Aztec rule.

Michael J. Harner, an anthropologist, reading through the Spanish sources about the conquests of the Aztecs and exploring the ecological and environmental limitations of the Valley of Mexico, concluded that neither politics nor religion were the reasons for the Aztec practice of human sacrifice. In this selection he discusses the biological basis for his conclusions. He ingeniously picks out references by the chroniclers of the Spanish conquest that refer to the consumption of human flesh by the Aztecs. Not surprisingly, his determination that the Aztecs practiced widespread cannibalism created a firestorm of negative reactions, particularly in Mexico.

For this paper I have chosen to focus on the cultural distinctiveness of Mesoamerica especially as exemplified by the human sacrificial complex of the Aztecs. Anthropologists such as Kroeber (1959:199) have long pointed to pre-Conquest Mexican human sacrifice as representing an extreme in known cultural behavior. Among state societies in the ethnological record, the Aztecs sacrificed unparalleled numbers of human victims, 20,000 a year being a commonly cited figure. . . .

. . . I will offer an explanation as to why the peculiar development of the Aztec sacrificial complex occurred at that time and place and how it was a natural result of distinctive ecological problems.

Before further focusing on the particularities of the Aztec situation, it may be useful to review some of the basic ecological assumptions that are involved in the population pressure theory of social evolution. . . . Human population growth is as much an unmistakable prehistoric and historic trend as the evolution of technology. The long-term increase of human population has led to increasing degradation of wild flora and fauna used for food. The extinction of many big-game mammals by the end of the European Paleolithic and by Paleo-Indians in the New World is the first outstanding evidence of this human-caused environmental degradation. The evolution into the Old World Mesolithic with its shift to marine resources and small-game hunting, and the development of a New World cultural analogue, can be seen as continuing and necessary responses to such environmental degradation. The increasing scarcity of wild game and food plants soon made the innovation of plant and animal domestication desirable and competitively efficient in several regions of the planet. With the passage of time and the further growth of human populations, more areas became similarly degraded, and plant and animal domestication necessarily became ever more widely adopted, providing an increasing proportion of the diet.

The need for intensified domesticated food production was especially felt early in such fertile, but environmentally circumscribed localities as the riverine valleys surrounded by less desirable terrain. Under such circumstances, climate and environment permitting, plants always became domesticated; but herbivorous mammals apparently could not be unless appropriate species existed. The Valley of Mexico, with its fertile and well-watered bottom lands surrounded by mountains, fits well the environmental circumscription model. Population growth increased relatively steadily in this circumscribed area up to the Conquest.

In the Old World the domestication of herbivorous mammals proceeded apace with the domestication of food plants. In the New World, however; the ancient hunters completely eliminated potential herbivorous mammalian domesticates from the Mesoamerican area. It was only in the Andean region and in southern South America that some *Camelops* species, especially the llama and alpaca, managed to survive the ancient onslaught and thus were available in later times for domestication along with another important local herbivore, the guinea pig (*Cavia porcellus*). In the Mesoamerican area the *Camelops* species became extinct at least several thousand years before domesticated food production had to be undertaken seriously. Nor was the guinea pig available. In Mesoamerica, emphasis was on the domestication of wild fowl, such as the turkey, as well as of the dog for food. . . .

As population pressure increased in the Valley of Mexico, wild game supplies were decreasingly available to provide protein for the diet. The seriousness of population pressure in general in the Valley during the time of the Aztecs has been discussed by many researchers.

THE EXTENT OF AZTEC SACRIFICE AND CANNIBALISM

The contrast between Mesoamerica and the Andes in terms of the existence of domesticated herbivores was matched by the contrast between the Inca and Aztec emphasis on human sacrifice. In the Inca Empire, the other major political entity in the New World at the time of the Conquest, annual human sacrifices could, at most, apparently be measured only in the hundreds. Among the Aztecs, the figures were incomparably greater. The annual figure of "20,000" so commonly mentioned is of uncertain significance. . . .

The most famous single sacrifice was at the dedication of the main pyramid in Tenochtitlan, in 1487. . . .

A thorough analysis of the early reports on numbers of Aztec sacrificial victims . . . estimates an overall annual mean of 15,000 victims in a Central Mexican population estimated at 2,000,000 [a number] radically scale[d] down [from] the originally reported figures without really presenting adequate evidence to support his reductions. . . .

Furthermore, *Woodrow Borah,* who is now possibly the leading authority on the demography of Central Mexico around the time of the Conquest, has given me permission to cite his new unpublished estimate of the number of persons sacrificed in Central Mexico in the fifteenth century; *250,000 per year*, or equivalent to one percent of the total population (Borah, personal communication). This quarter of a million annual figure, according to Borah (personal communication), is consistent with the existence of thousands of temples throughout the Triple Alliance alone and with the sacrifice of an estimated one thousand to three thousand persons at each temple per year.

Beyond those numbers is the question of what was done with the bodies after the sacrifices. The evidence of Aztec cannibalism has largely been ignored and consciously or unconsciously covered up. One must go back to Conquest and immediately post-Conquest sources to gain an awareness of its importance in Aztec life. Bernal Díaz, other conquistadores such as Cortés, and Sahagún are among the most reliable. Less reliable but basically in accord with the others is Durán (1971).

While some sacrificial victims, such as children sacrificed to Tlaloc by drowning or persons suffering skin diseases, were not eaten, the overwhelming majority of the sacrificed captives appear to have been consumed. A major objective, and sometimes the only objective, of Aztec war expeditions was to capture prisoners for sacrifice. While some might be sacrificed and eaten on the field of battle, most were taken to home communities or to the capital, where they were kept in wooden cages until they were sacrificed by the priests at the temple-pyramids. Most of the sacrifices involved tearing out the heart, offering it to the sun and, with some blood, also to the idols. The corpse then was tumbled down the steps of the pyramid, where elderly attendants cut off the arms, legs, and head. While the head went onto the local skull rack, at least three of the limbs were normally property of the captor, who formally retained ownership of the victim. He then hosted a feast at his quarters, of which the central dish was a stew of tomatoes, peppers, and the limbs of the victim. The torso of the victim, in Tenochtitlan at least, went to the royal zoo to feed carnivorous mammals, birds, and snakes. Where towns lacked zoos, the fate of the torsos is not certain. . . .

Besides the firsthand accounts from the Conquest, the works of Father Bernardino de Sahagún are probably the single most thorough and reliable source on the subject under consideration. Arriving in Mexico less than a decade after the Conquest, and using Aztec nobles as informants, he transcribed their written or dictated information in Nahuatl as a series of books. These volumes have the strength of presenting the upper-class insiders' view of Aztec culture; but this is also a limitation. For example, certain aspects of their behavior which might seem remarkable and significant to a European or to an anthropologist, such as cannibalism, probably were too routine an aftermath of sacrifice normally to deserve comment. Nevertheless, some very interesting details on such practices are provided. For example, Sahagún, in describing the ceremonies of the month of Tlacaxipeualiztli, states:

> And so they [the war captives] were brought up [the pyramid temple steps] before [the sanctuary of] Uitzilopochtli.
> Thereupon they stretched them, one at a time, down on the sacrificial stone; then they delivered them into the hands of six priests, who threw them upon their backs, and cut open their breasts with a wide-bladed flint knife.

> And they named the hearts of the captives "precious eagle-cactus fruit." They lifted them up to the sun, the turquoise prince, the soaring eagle. They offered it to him; they nourished him with it. And when it had been offered, they placed it in the eagle-vessel. And these captives who had died they called "eagle men."
>
> Afterwards they rolled them over; they bounced them down; they came tumbling down head over heels, and end over end, rolling over and over; thus they reached the terrace at the base of pyramid. And here they took them up.
>
> And the old men, the *quaquacuilti,* the old men of the tribal temples, carried them there to their tribal temples, where the captor had promised, undertaken, and vowed [to take a captive].
>
> There they took [the slain captive] up, in order to carry him to the house [of the captor], so that they might eat him. There they portioned him out, cutting him to pieces and dividing him up. First of all they reserved for Moctezuma a thigh, and set forth to take it to him.
>
> And [as for] the captor, they there applied the down of birds to his head and gave him gifts. And he summoned his blood relations, he assembled them, that they might go to eat at the house of him who had taken the captive.
>
> And here they cooked each one a bowl of stew of dried maize, called *tlacatlaolli,* which they set before each, and in each was a piece of the flesh of the captive. . . .

Given the long-standing written documentation of significant Aztec cannibalism in connection with the sacrificial complex, one cannot help but wonder why the evidence has been so ignored. Both Vaillant and Soustelle, for example, in their classic synthetic works on Aztec culture each only allow one sentence in their texts on the subject of Aztec cannibalism. Specifically, Vaillant states, "Ceremonial cannibalism was sometimes practised, in the belief that the eater could absorb the virtues of the eaten, but this rite cannot be considered a vice."

The apparent defensiveness of Vaillant's statement may be a key to the neglect of this subject. Modern Mexicans and anthropologists probably have tended to be embarrassed by the topic, the former partly for nationalistic reasons, and the latter in part because of the desire to portray native peoples in the best possible light in order to combat ethnocentrism. Ironically, both these attitudes may ultimately represent European ethnocentrism regarding cannibalism, a natural product of a continent that had relatively abundant livestock for meat and milk.

NUTRITIONAL ASPECTS

The question naturally arises as to the nutritional role the consumption of human flesh might have played in the Aztec diet. Soustelle volunteers that the diet of the commoners included only "rarely any meat, such as game, venison, or poultry (turkey)." He similarly states, "The poorer people ate turkey only on great occasions" and also notes. "Poor people and the lakeside peasants skimmed a floating substance from the surface which was called *tecuitlatl,* 'stone dung'; it was something like cheese, and they squeezed it into cakes; they also ate the spongy nests of water-fly larvae". . .

Despite the apparent scarcity of meat in the diet of the commoners, they theoretically could get the necessary eight essential amino acids from their maize and bean crops, the two foods complementing each other in their essential amino acid components. One of the problems with relying on beans and maize was that they would have to be ingested in large enough quantities simultaneously or nearly simultaneously in order to provide the body with the eight essential amino acids in combination in order for them to be used to rebuild body tissues: otherwise the dietary protein would simply be converted to energy.

Thus, in order for the Aztecs to obtain their essential amino acids from the maize-bean combination it would have been necessary for them to be able to consume large quantities of both plants together on a year-round basis. But seasonal crop failures and famines were common among the Aztecs. . . . Under these conditions it is clear that the necessary maize-bean combination could not be relied upon as a source of the essential amino acids. To the reader who may wonder how the Aztecs might have known they needed the essential amino acids, it should be parenthetically pointed out that the human body, like that of other organisms perfected under natural selection, is a homeostatic entity that under conditions of nutritional stress naturally seeks out the dietary elements in which it is deficient. If living organisms did not have this innate capacity, they would not survive.

Another dietary problem for the Aztecs was the scarcity of fats. While the exact amount of fatty acids required by the human body remains a subject of uncertainty among nutritionists, there is agreement that fats provide a longer-lasting energy source than carbohydrates, due to the slower rate of metabolism. It is noteworthy that fatty meat, by providing both fat and the essential proteins, assures the utilization of the essential amino acids for tissue building, since the fat will provide the necessary source of energy that must also be supplied if the dietary protein is not to be siphoned off as a purely caloric contribution.

If Aztec cannibalism was a response to growing population pressure, one would expect it to increase in frequency through time. There is indeed a numerical rise in the capture and sacrifice of human victims during the three-quarters of a century preceding the Conquest. . . .

Turning to the Aztec case, let us propose that 15,000 victims were eaten annually in Tenochtitlan, a conservative figure in light of Borah's new estimate of a quarter of a million sacrificial victims per year in Central Mexico. . . .

If we were to use an estimate of 300,000 inhabitants and postulate 15,000 sacrificial victims annually consumed in the city, the ratio of victims to the consuming population would be five to one hundred as being a significant annual contribution to dietary protein. But there are additional special factors in the Aztec case.

First, the famines and seasonal food scarcities so characteristic of the Aztec economy make it necessary to take into account that the consumption of human flesh was probably not evenly distributed throughout the year or years, but made its most significant contribution precisely at those times when the protein resources were otherwise at their lowest ebb. Thus it seems highly likely that even if only one percent of the population in Central Mexico was eaten in an average year, the timing of such consumption to coincide with periods of hunger would have more than made up for the overall low average annual percentage involved. Furthermore, it must be kept in mind that the members of the Aztec Triple Alliance were the general winners in warfare and thus undoubtedly consumed a higher proportion of victims than their enemies.

Secondly, a minority of the Aztec population seems to have been entitled to eat human flesh. . . .

The "right to eat human flesh" may possibly have been really the privilege to eat it at one's own volition, i.e., to host a banquet or to buy a slave in the marketplace for that purpose; thus a large segment of the supposedly unqualified population may have had at least occasional access, by invitation, to cannibalistic banquets. At the same time, it is clear from Sahagún's statement above that there were ritual anthropophagic feasts from which the commoners were excluded. But the point of this paper is not to prove that cannibalism made a contribution to the diet of the total population; rather, it is to explain the extremity of the Aztec sacrificial complex. It is not essential for this argument that a majority of the Aztec population had to take part in human flesh banquets. What is essential is to demonstrate that the sacrificed captives typically were eaten; . . .

SOME IMPLICATIONS

Superficially, it might appear that the Aztec prohibition against human flesh-eating by ordinary or lower class persons would cast doubt upon the potentiality of cannibalism to motivate the masses of Aztec society to engage in wars for prisoners. Actually, however, the prohibition was, if anything, a goad to the lower class to participate in the wars, since the right to eat human flesh could normally only be achieved by single-handedly taking captives in battle . . .

With an understanding of the importance of cannibalism in Aztec culture, and of the ecological reasons for its existence, some of the more distinctive institutions of the Aztecs begin to make sense anthropologically. For example, the long-standing question of whether the political structure of the Aztecs is or is not definable as an empire can be reexamined. A problem here has been that the Aztecs frequently withdrew from conquered territory without establishing administrative centers or garrisons. This Aztec "failure" to consolidate in the Old World fashion even puzzled Cortés, who asked Moctezuma for an explanation of why he allowed Tlaxcala to maintain its independence. Reportedly Moctezuma replied that it was done, so that his people could obtain captives for sacrifice. In other words, since the Aztecs did not normally eat persons of their own polity, which would have been socially and politically disruptive, they viewed it essential to have conveniently nearby "enemy" populations on whom they could prey for captives. This kind of behavior makes perfect sense in terms of Aztec cannibalism. The Aztecs were unique among the world's states in having a cannibal empire. For this reason, they often did not conform to models of imperial colonization which were based upon empires possessing domesticated herbivores to provide meat or milk. . . .

Beyond this, upon reflection, one should perhaps explicitly mention what is implicit in this paper: that the materialist or ecological research strategy employed here, and the results achieved, make it unnecessary to attribute to the Aztecs, as Lévi-Strauss has done, "a maniacal obsession with blood and torture" or to call upon psychoanalytic theory, as Wolf seems to suggest, to explain "this fanatic obsession with blood and death." Lévi-Strauss refers, with some justification, to the Aztecs as "that open wound in the flank of Americanism." But why have they been an "open wound?" Because given mentalist or idealist research strategies, there can be no explanation of the basic causality involved in the evolution of such a distinctive culture. The causes of the differences between cultures cannot be found in the universal characteristics of the human mind, nor in a theory that they are pathological excrescences of that mind.

QUESTIONS

1. What was the source of protein for the vast majority of Aztecs?
2. According to Harner, what was the extent of Aztec human sacrifice?
3. What is Harner's view of the political ramifications of the practice of cannibalism?
4. What are the crucial flaws in Harner's argument that cannibalism resulted from a shortage of protein?

READING

AZTECS: AN INTERPRETATION

Inga Clendinnen

Unquestionably the Aztecs sacrificed humans. The evidence is extensive in both the indigenous sources and the European Invades of the sixteenth century. The controversies, however, grow more heated over the extent and reasons for human sacrifice. Robert C. Padden in his Hummingbird and the Hawk *maintains that the Aztecs killed tens of thousands in commemoration of their temple to their god Huitzilopochtli in 1487. Jacques Soustelle in* The Daily Life of the Aztecs *argues for a far more modest scale. Three theories emerge as to why the Aztecs sacrificed humans. First, and most generally accepted, is that Aztec religion required it. The Aztecs' gloomy view perceived that the world was on its Fifth Sun. Four previous suns had been destroyed. In the current world the sun was born from the sacrifice to the gods. It therefore required that the sun must be fed blood and water to keep it on its course in the sky. Blood was necessary to save the world and the people in it. A second theory, widely disdained, argues that the Aztecs needed the protein from human flesh. As the population grew substantially after 1450, so did the practice of human sacrifice. The Valley of Mexico had few domesticated animals for consumption. Finally, and perhaps more reasonably, some historians argue that human sacrifice was a crucial instrument of the Aztec state. The cult of Huitzilopochtli was a brilliant invention by which to terrorize the other peoples of the Valley of Mexico and beyond in order to induce them to succumb to Aztec rule.*

Inga Clendinnen is one of the most innovative and controversial historians of the Spanish conquest in the Valley of Mexico and in Yucatán. She concentrates on reading the Spanish chroniclers, analyzing not only what the chroniclers wrote, but what they left out of their version of events, as well. In the selection here, she is particularly concerned with the discrepancy between . . . "the high decorum and fastidious social and aesthetic sensibility of the Mexica [another name for Aztecs], and the massive carnality of the killings." She also discusses the rites and ceremonies of the sacrifices, as well as the relationship between the Aztecs and their sacrifice victims. Clendinnen argues that the cooperation of the victims was a result of the structure of Aztec warfare and religion.

There is one activity for which the 'Aztecs' were notorious: the large-scale killing of humans in ritual sacrifices. The killings were not remote top-of-the pyramid affairs. If only high priests and rulers killed, they carried out most of their butchers' work *en plein air*, and not only in the main temple precinct, but in the neighbourhood temples and on the streets. The people were implicated in the care and preparation of the victims, their delivery to the place of death, and then in the elaborate processing of the bodies: the dismemberment and distribution of heads and limbs, flesh and blood and flayed skins. On high occasions warriors carrying gourds of human blood or wearing the dripping skins of their captives ran through the streets, to be ceremoniously welcomed into the dwellings; the flesh of their victims seethed in domestic cooking pots; human thighbones, scraped and dried, were set up in the courtyards of the households—and all this among a people notable for a precisely ordered polity, a grave formality of manner, and a developed regard for beauty.

Europeans, from the first Spanish conquerors who saw Mexica society in action to those of us who wistfully strive to, have been baffled by that unnerving discrepancy between the high decorum and fastidious social and aesthetic sensibility of the Mexica world, and the massive carnality of the killings and dismemberings: between social grace and monstrous ritual. . . . a few grandly simple explanations for the mass killings were aired: human sacrifice as a device to enrich a protein-poor diet; human sacrifice as the invention of a sinister and cynical élite, a sort of amphetamines-for-the-people account; human sacrifice as technology, the Mexica response to the second law of thermodynamics, with the taking of the hot and pulsing human heart their despairing effort to replace energy lost by entropic waste. Over the last decade scholarly interest has spiralled back to the meanings of the activity which consumed so much Mexica time and energy, but recent studies have remained pitched at an ideological or a theological level of abstraction, which in my view too often assumes that which most needs to be demonstrated. . . .

. . . [T]he Mexica attached no shame to such matters. It is Mexica picturings which dwell on the slow tides of blood down the steps of the pyramids, on skull-faced deities chewing on human limbs, on human hearts pulped into stone mouths. Three and four decades after the Spanish conquest old men were still ready to talk in lingering detail about the old festivals to scribes trained under the new order. They told of the great warrior festivals with the lines of victims dragged or driven up the wide steps of the pyramids to meet the waiting priests. At other festivals few died, but those few most ceremoniously. Some selected individuals were transformed into ambulant images of the Sacred Ones. They were fêted through the streets, to dance and die before the deities they represented—and then sometimes danced again, their flayed skins stretched over the living bodies of priest or warrior celebrants. The killings, whether large or small, were frequent: part of the pulse of living.

The Mexica laity were not physically involved in the acts of killing: at that point they were watchers only. But their engagement was nonetheless close, and all were complicit in it, either by way of the customary rotation through the calpullis of duties at a particular major temple, or more directly by personal involvement in a group festivity, as when the salt-workers or the fisher people purchased, prepared, and presented a special victim, or through the excitements in the household of a local warrior who had taken a prisoner for sacrifice. All participated in the care of victims in life, and in their dismemberment and processing in death. Warrior captives who were to die in major ceremonies were kept close by the local temples, probably in the cages the Spaniards insisted on seeing as fattening coops, and their care was a charge on the local people. They were a source of pride and diversion, being fed, paraded, probably taunted, over the weeks and possibly months of their captivity. As the time of death drew near they were ritually prepared: forced to keep vigil; decked in appropriate regalia; processed through the streets, often to the place where they were to die. Finally they were prodded through the elaborate routines which were a prelude to their ascent of Huizilopochtli's pyramid. There they would be seized, forced back over the killing stone, a priest pressing down each limb to keep the chest tautly arched, while a fifth drove the wide flint blade of the sacrificial knife into the chest and dragged out the still-pulsing heart. The heart was raised to the Sun and the plundered body let to fall aside. It was then sent soddenly rolling down the pyramid steps, to be collected at the base by old men from the appropriate calpulli temple, who would carry it away through the streets for dismemberment and distribution. So we have a careful, calculated shepherding of men, women, and children to their deaths. . . .

Mexica victims were purely victims. . . . It is the combination of violence with apparent impersonality, the bureaucratic calculation of these elaborated Mexica brutalities, together with their habituated and apparently casual incorporation into the world of the everyday, which chills. . . .

. . . [I]t is necessary to establish the external circumstances of the practice: who the victims were, and how they were variously managed through to their deaths; what distinctions and categorizations the Mexica made within that large category of 'victim', and how they understood each group in terms of its relationship to themselves, to humankind, and to the gods.

The killing performances which most distinguished the Mexica from their neighbours were the great ceremonies which celebrated major moments in Mexica imperial rule: the installation of a new ruler, the dedication of a great temple or work of engineering. The victims who died in such ceremonies were foreigners, probably distant ones, and marked by garment, custom, and language as exotics: victims of a major war, or captives taken by subject or allied peoples, delivered as tribute to be consumed in a Mexica triumph. Although allocated between the wards for maintenance, they probably developed few connections with the local people throughout their period of captivity. Given the daunting size and unfamiliarity of the Mexica city, their social and physical isolation, and the high visibility of their own tribal affiliations in speech and dress, escape was not a plausible notion. . . .

Those massive killings marked particular and rare occasions, but the four seasonal festivals which marked the four periods for major tribute payments—Tlacaxipeualiztli, Etzalqualiztli, Ochpaniztli, and Panquetzaliztli—were also distinguished by numbers of killings, although opinions vary as to how many died. Surprisingly, the mode of the disposal of the bodies remains mysterious. We are usually told that skulls were spitted on the skull racks, limbs apportioned for ritual cannibalism, and the trunks fed to the flesh-eating birds and beasts in Moctezoma's menagerie, but such disposal techniques would clearly be inadequate. The bodies were perhaps burnt, although during their stay in the city Cortés and his men make no mention of any pyres or corpse-laden canoes, the detritus of human killings being confined, in their accounts, to the temple precincts. The land-locked lakes, precious sources of water and aquatic foods, offered no solution, so this large empirical matter remains unresolved. The provenance of the festival victims is less mysterious. They were probably drawn from tribute paid in slaves, and from the 'bank' of warriors captured during the season of war, . . . The Mexica seasonal killings of captives and warriors spoke most urgently in words and actions about feeding the earth powers and the sun. . . .

There is a strange docility in the behaviour of the non-warrior victims of the mass killings which suggests the depth of their social and psychological dislocation. If some faltered on the long climb, most apparently trudged up the pyramid steps with minimal prodding. While the acquiescence of these doomed creatures was possibly induced by demoralization, bewilderment, and fear—we have no reason to think their guardians were tender—their resignation might well have been assisted by drugs. . . .

The nomination of so few drugs used in rituals and the silence of the sources on the administering of powerful sedatives does not preclude the possibility of their extensive use. Mind-altering drugs were important to the Mexica, as to all Amerindians, who out of a relatively unpromising flora have developed an incomparably rich pharmacopoeia, especially in hallucinogens: a pharmacopoeia which could have been developed only through the most determined and intrepid experimentation. The final preparation of the victims was a matter for the priests, who were presumably close-mouthed about how they achieved their effects. . . .

. . . In Tenochtitlan notable captives, or those taken in a major campaign, were presented before the idol of Huitzilopochtli and then displayed at the royal palace before Moctezoma, while speeches were made on the death they would die. The warrior from a Nahua city participant in Mexica understandings of war was particularly cherished, being tended by stewards in the local temple and constantly visited, adorned, and admired by his captor and the captor's devoted entourage of local youths. Such a man presented for death before Huitzilopochtli's shrine crowning the great temple pyramid ideally leapt up the steps shouting the praises of his city. (That act of courage might have been made easier by the great bulk of the pyramid, which loomed so huge that a man at the base or on the long climb upwards could not see what awaited him.) Some, we are told, faltered on the stairs, and wept or fainted. They were dragged up by the priests. But, for most, pulque, anger, pride, or the narrowing existential focus of their days somehow got them through.

Mexica combat at its best was a one-to-one contest of preferably close-matched combatants, with one predestined to triumph, one to die. Given the fated outcome, and given the warrior obligation to seek and embrace the 'flowery death' on the field of battle or the killing stone, no shame need attach to defeat. The captive was in a deep sense the reflex of his captor, who accordingly took a tense and proprietary interest in that final performance. The quality of his own courage would be on public trial there.

QUESTIONS

1. What were the occasions for Aztec human sacrifice?
2. What explains the docility of the victims on their way to death?
3. What were to the Aztecs the best deaths?
4. Who were the victims of sacrifice?

READING

Introduction to MECCAN TRADE AND THE RISE OF ISLAM

Patricia Crone

Scholarship on the early Islamic period is made difficult by the lack of extant primary sources. The earliest surviving sources describing Arabian on the eve of Islam were written about two-hundred years after the events they describe—after the Islamic religion had already undergone several centuries of development, and had already established an official version of its own history.

Patricia Crone, professor of Islamic History at the Institute for Advanced Study in Princeton, has been a controversial researcher in the field of early Islam. In this article, the Introduction to her book Meccan Trade and the Rise of Islam, *she argues that the classical accounts of Mecca as a large and important trading emporium are inaccurate, and that it probably took place on a much smaller scale than is claimed by early Arabic sources.*

INTRODUCTION

Every first-year student knows that Mecca at the time of the Prophet was the centre of a far-flung trading empire, which plays a role of some importance in all orthodox accounts of the rise of Islam. Indeed, the international trade of the Meccans has achieved such fame that not only first-year students, but also professional Islamicists have come to consider documentation to be quite superfluous. Thus Montgomery Watt, whose well-known interpretation of Muhammad's life centres on the impact of commercial wealth on the social and moral order in Mecca, devotes less than a page of his two-volume work to a discussion of the commerce from which the wealth in question supposedly derived; and with references he dispenses altogether.[1] But what do we actually know about Meccan trade? The groundwork on the subject was done by Lammens, a notoriously unreliable scholar whose name is rarely mentioned in the secondary literature without some expression of caution or disapproval, but whose conclusions would nonetheless appear to have been accepted by Watt.[2] More recently, various aspects of the question have been taken up and richly documented by Kister.[3] Kister's work is apparently held to corroborate the picture drawn up by Lammens; there is, at least, no appreciable difference between the portraits of Meccan trade presented by Watt on the basis of Lammens, by Shaban on the basis of Kister, and by Donner on the basis of both.[4] But, in fact, neither Lammens nor Kister provides support for the conventional account, the former because his work collapses on inspection of his footnotes, the latter because his impeccable footnotes undermine our basic assumptions concerning the nature of the trade. What follows is evidence to the effect that Meccan trade is nothing if not a problem.

The conventional account of Meccan trade begs one simple question: what commodity or commodities enabled the inhabitants of so unpromising a site to engage in commerce on so large scale? That the trading empire grew up in an unexpected place is clear, if not always clearly brought out. There have, of course, been commercial centres in Arabia that developed in areas of comparable barrenness, notably Aden. But Aden and other coastal cities of south Arabia all owed their existence to the sea, as Muqaddasī noted, whereas Mecca was an inland town.[5] It did have a little port, Shu'ayba,[6] and the Koran speaks at length about the miraculous navigability of the sea.[7] The sources are agreed that the Meccans traded with Ethiopia, and there is even an isolated tradition which asserts that they used to engage in maritime trade with Rūm.[8] But the Meccans had no timber[9] and no ships;[10] they made no use of their port when blockaded by

Muḥammad,[11] and neither Shu'ayba nor the sea receives much attention in the tradition.

Centres of caravan trade, on the other hand, have usually been located in less hostile environments and within closer proximity to their customers than was Mecca; witness Minaean Dedan, Roman Palmyra, and Ibn Rashīd's Ḥā'il. By way of compensation, Mecca is frequently credited with the advantage of having been located at the crossroads of all the major trade routes in Arabia,[12] or at least with having been a natural halt on the so-called incense route from south Arabia to Syria.[13] But as Bulliet points out, these claims are quite wrong. Mecca is tucked away at the edge of the peninsula: "only by the most tortured map reading can it be described as a natural crossroads between a north-south route and an east-west one."[14] And the fact that it is more or less equidistant from south Arabia and Syria does not suffice to make it a natural halt on the incense route. In the first place, the caravans which travelled along this route stopped at least sixty-five times on the way; they were under no constraint to stop at Mecca merely because it happened to be located roughly midway. "On a journey of some two months duration the concept of a halfway point as a natural resting place is rather strained."[15] In the second place, barren places do not make natural halts wherever they may be located, and least of all when they are found at a short distance from famously green environments. Why should caravans have made a steep descent to the barren valley of Mecca when they could have stopped at Ṭā'if? Mecca did, of course, have both a well and a sanctuary, but so did Ṭā'if, which had food supplies, too. In the third place, it would appear that Mecca was not located on the incense route at all. Going from south Arabia to Syria via Mecca would have meant a detour from the natural route, as both Müller and Groom have pointed out; and Groom estimates that the incense route must have bypassed Mecca by some one-hundred miles.[16] Mecca, in other words, was not just distant and barren; it was off the beaten track, as well. "The only reason for Mecca to grow into a great trading center," according to Bulliet, "was that it was able somehow to force the trade under its control."[17] It is certainly hard to think of any other. But what trade? What commodity was available in Arabia that could be transported at such a distance, through such an inhospitable environment, and still be sold at a profit large enough to support the growth of a city in a peripheral site bereft of natural resources? In Diocletian's Rome it was cheaper to ship wheat from Alexandria to Rome at a distance of some 1,250 miles than to transport it fifty miles by land.[18] The distance from Najrān to Gaza was roughly 1,250 miles, not counting the detour to Mecca. "A caravan takes a month to go to Syria and a month to return," as the Meccans objected when Muhammad claimed to have visited Jerusalem by night. Whatever the Meccans sold, their goods must have been rare, much coveted, reasonably light, and exceedingly expensive.

One can read a great many accounts of Meccan trade without being initiated into the secret of what the Meccans traded in, but most Islamicists clearly envisage them as selling incense, spices, and other exotic goods, "By the end of the sixth century A.D. they had gained control of most of the trade from the Yemen to Syria—an important route by which the West got Indian luxury goods as well as South Arabian frankincense," as Watt informs us, Mecca was "a transfer-point in the long distance trade network between India, Africa and the Mediterranean," as we are told in the more recent statement by Donner. Similar statements are commonplace in the secondary literature.[22] Incense, spices, slaves, silk, and so forth would indeed fit the bill. The source for all this, however, is Lammens, and on turning to Kister one finds the Meccans engaged in a trade of a considerably humbler kind. The international trade of the Meccans here rests on articles such as leather and clothing, which the Meccans, moreover, advertise as being *cheap*. There is no incense, nor any other spices, in the work of Kister, and the same is true of that of Sprenger, who likewise identified the chief article of export as leather.[23] Clearly, something is amiss. Did the Meccans really trade in incense, spices, and other luxury goods? If not, could they have founded a commercial empire of international dimensions on the basis of leather goods and clothing? The answer to both questions would appear to be no, and it is for this reason that Meccan trade is a problem.

Why do Islamicists find it so easy to believe that the Meccans traded in incense, spices, and the like? Presumably because Arabia is indelibly associated with this kind of goods in the mind of every educated person. Besides, what other significant articles were available in Arabia for the Meccans to export? Because the classical spice trade of Arabia is so famous, practically every account of Meccan trade tends to be cast in its image; or in other words, Meccan trade tends to be described on the basis of stereotypes. The sterotypes in question may be summarized as follows.

Already in the third millennium B.C. the south Arabians traded in incense, later also in foreign goods; indeed, the very earliest commercial and cultural contacts between the Mediterranean and the lands around the Indian ocean were established via the overland incense route.[24] In any case, there is no doubt that the trade was fully developed by about 900 B.C., when the Queen of Sheba visited Solomon and when the Arabs assuredly controlled the sea route to India;[25] and they certainly supplied Egypt with Indian spices, fabrics, and precious stones about this time.[26] They also supplied ancient Iraq for Assyrian policy vis-à-vis Arabia was dictated by concern for the security of the incense route, though some are of the opinion that the trade between Babylonia and India only fell into Arab hands on the Achaemenid conquest of Iraq.[28] At all events, they soon offered their customers all the products of India, the Far East, and tropical Africa from Abyssinia to Madagascar.[29] They were a curious people in that they sailed to Africa and India, but transported their goods by caravan on reaching their native shores: this was because their boats, though adequate for long-distance journeys, were too primitive for navigation in the Red Sea and, apparently, also the Persian Gulf.[30] But they were perfectly capable of keeping the Indians out of the Red Sea, and it is because they guarded their commercial monopoly with such jealousy that we are so ill-informed about this early trade.[31] We can, however, rest assured that all the bustling commerce described by Pliny (d. 79 A.D.) and the *Periplus* (probably about 50 A.D.) was part of the normal scene in ancient Saba some nine hundred years before.[32] We can also rest assured that it was part of the normal scene some five hundred years later. The south Arabian hold on the India trade somehow survived the establishment of direct commercial contact between India and the Greco Roman world, so that when in due course south Arabia declined, the Meccans took over the task of satisfying the enormous Roman demand for luxury goods.[33] The Meccans used the same overland route; indeed, it was on their control of the old incense route that their commercial predominance in Arabia rested.[34] And they exported the same goods: Arabian frankincense, East African ivory and gold, Indian spices, Chinese silk, and the like.[35] It was only on the Arab conquest of the Middle East that this venerable trade came to an end, after a lifespan of some fifteen hundred or twenty-five hundred years.

All this, of course, is somewhat incredible; in what follows I shall devote myself to a demonstration that it is also quite untrue. The south Arabian trade in incense and spices is not nearly as old as is commonly assumed, and the goods in question were not invariably sent north by caravan: the last allusion to the overland route dates from the first (or, as some would have it, early second) century A.D., and the transit trade would appear to have been maritime from the start. Neither the incense trade nor the transit trade survived long enough for the Meccans to inherit them, and there was no such thing as a Meccan trade in incense, spices, and foreign luxury goods. At least, the Islamic tradition is quite unaware that the Meccans are supposed to have handled this type of goods, and the Greeks to whom they are supposed to have sold them had never even heard of Mecca. Meccan trade there was, if we trust the Islamic tradition. But the trade described in this tradition bears little resemblance to that known from Lammens, Watt, or their various followers.

END NOTES

1. W. M. Watt, *Muhammad at Mecca*, p. 3.
2. H. Lammens, *La Mecque à la veille de l'hégire; id.*, "La république marchande de la Mecque vers l'an 600 de notre ére"; cf. also *id., La cité arabe de Tāif à la veille de l'hégire.* That Lammens is the source behind Watt's presentation is clear both from considerations of content and from the fact that he is the only authority mentioned there. Lammens is reproved for having been too sure about the details of financial operations in Mecca, but his conclusion that the operations in question were of considerable complexity is accepted (Watt, *Muhammad at Mecca*, p. 3).
3. See in particular M. J. Kister, "Mecca and Tamīm (Aspects of Their Relations)"; and *id.*, "Some Reports Concerning Mecca from Jāhiliyya to Islam."
4. M. A. Shaban, *Islamic History, A New Interpretation*, pp. 2 ff; that this presentation is based on the work of Kister is stated at p. 2n. F. M. Donner, "Mecca's Food Supplies and Muhammad's Boycott"; the reader is referred to the works of Lammens and Kister at p. 25n.
5. Muḥammad b. Aḥmad al-Muqaddasī. *Descriptio imperii moslemici*, pp. 85 (Aden), 95 (coastal cities in general). There is something of a parallel to Mecca in pre-Islamic Shabwa, an inland city in a barren environment, which was also a cult centre and a centre of trade (cf. EI^2; *s.v.* Ḥaḍramawt [Beeston]). But the rulers of Shabwa had the good fortune to control the frankincense-producing areas of Arabia so that they could decree more or less at will where they wished the frankincense to be collected (a point to which I shall return). There was nothing comparable in the vicinity of, or under the control of, Mecca.

6. Not Jār, as Donnor says ("Mecca's Food Supplies," p. 254). Jār was the port of Medina, Shu'ayba being that of Mecca until it was replaced by Jedda in the caliphate of 'Uthmān (cf. *EI²* *s.vv.* Djār, Djudda; cf. also G. R. Hawting, "The Origin of Jedda and the Problem of al-Shu'ayba."
7. Forty times, according to S. Fraenkel, *Die aramäischen Fremdwörter im arabischen,* p. 211. This is odd, as Barthold points out, for there is no record of Muḥammad having travelled by sea, or even of having gone close to it, and the descriptions are very vivid (W. W. Barthold, "Der Koran und das Meer").
8. Aḥmad Ibn Ḥanbal, *al-'Ilal,* I, 244, no. 1,410 (first noted by Kister, "Some Reports," p. 93). Compare the tradition in Sulaymān b. Aḥmad al-Ṭabarānī, *al-Mu'jam al-ṣaghīr,* I, 113, according to which the Companions of the Prophet used to enagage in maritime trade with Syria (also first noted by Kister).
9. When Quraysh rebuilt the Ka'ba shortly berfore the *hijra,* the timber for its roof came from a Greek ship which had been wrecked at Shu'ayba (thus Muḥammad b. 'Abdullāh al-Azraqī, *Kitāb akhbār Makka,* pp. 104 f., 107; Muḥammad Ibn Sa'd, *al-Ṭabaqāt al-kubrā, I,* 145; Yāqūt b. 'Abdallāh, *Kitāb Mu'jam al-buldān,* III, 301, *s.v.* Shu'ayba; Aḥmad b. 'Alī Ibn Ḥajar al-'Asqalānī, *Kitāb al-iṣāba fī tamyīz al-ṣaḥāba,* I, 141, no. 580, *s.v.* Bāqūm. The parallel version anachronistically has the ship stranded at Jedda ('Abd al-Malik Ibn Hishām. *Das Leben Muhammed's nach Mohammed Ibn Ishâk,* p. 122; Muḥammad b. Jarīr al-Ṭabarī, *Ta'rīkh al-rusul wa'l-mulūk,* ser. I, p. 1,135). A more elaborate version has it that the ship was carrying building material such as wood, marble, and iron for the rebuilding of an Ethiopian church destroyed by the Persians (Ismā'īl b. 'Umar Ibn Kathīr, *al-Bidāya wa'l-nihāya,* II, 301, citing the *Maghāzī* of Sa'īd b. Yaḥyā al-Umawī; similarly 'Alī b. al-Ḥusayn al-Mas'ūdī, *Kitāb murūj al-dhahab,* IV, 126 f.) Cf. also [M.] Gaudefroy-Demombynes, *Le pèlerinage à la Mekke,* pp. 33 f.
10. The *muhājirūn* who went to Ethiopia travelled in ships belonging to some obviously foreign merchants; Quraysh pursued them, but had to stop on reaching the coast (Ṭabarī, *Ta'rīkh,* ser, 1, pp. 1,181 f.; Ibn Sa'd, *Ṭabaqāt,* 1, 204).
11. "Avoid the coast and take the Iraq route," as a Qurashī advised when the route to Syria was blocked (Muḥammad b. 'Umar al-Wāqidī, *Kitāb al-maghāzī,* 1, 197). This point has been made several times before, first probably by Lammens (*Mecque,* p. 381).
12. This idea goes back to Lammens (*Mecque,* p. 118; "République," pp. 26, 51), and has since been repeated by Watt, *Muhammad at Mecca,* p. 3; Shaban, *Islamic History,* 1, 6; M. Rodinson, *Mohammed,* p. 39; P. K. Hitti, *Capital Cities of Arab Islam,* p. 7; I. Shahid (Kawar), "The Arabs in the Peace Treaty of A.D. 561," p. 192.
13. This idea also goes back to Lammens (cf. "République," p. 51, where it is one of the most important halts on this route, *Mecque,* p. 118, where it is probably such a halt). It was cautiously accepted by B. Lewis, *The Arabs in History,* p. 34, and wholeheartedly by Hitti, *Capital Cities,* p. 5.
14. R. W. Bulliet, *The Camel and the Wheel,* p. 105 and n40 thereto. Lammens adduced Balādhurī's version of the Ḥudaybiyya agreement in favour of his view. In this agreement, safety is granted to people travelling (from Medina) to Mecca on *ḥajj* or *'umra,* or on their way to Ṭā'if or the Yemen, as well as to people travelling (from Mecca) to Medina on their way to Syria and the east (Aḥmad b. Yaḥyā al-Balādhurī, *Kitāb futūḥ al-buldān,* p. 36; *id., Ansāb al-ashrāf,* 1, 351. Other versions of the treaty lack such a clause, cf. *EI²*, *s.v.* al-Ḥudaybiya and the references given there). This certainly suggests that people might go via Mecca to the Yemen; but it is from Medina, not Mecca, that they are envisaged as going to Syria and Iraq. (Lammens frequently adduced information about Medina as valid for Mecca, as well.)

15. Bulliet, *Camel and the Wheel,* p. 105.
16. W. W. Müller, *Weihrauch,* col. 723; N. Groom, *Frankincense and Myrrh,* p. 193. In W. C. Brice, ed., *An Historical Atlas of Islam,* pp. 14 f., 19, the incense route still goes via Mecca.
17. Bulliet, *Camel and the Wheel,* p. 105.
18. A.H.M. Jones, "The Economic Life of the Towns of the Roman Empire," p. 164; compare N. Steensgaard, *Carracks, Caravans and Companies,* p. 40.
19. See the helpful list of distances, in both miles and days' journey, in Groom, *Frankincense,* p. 213.
20. Ibn Hishām, *Leben,* p. 264.
21. Watt, *Muhammad at Mecca,* p. 3; similarly *id., Muhammad, Prophet and Statesman,* p. 1; *id.,* "Ḳuraysh" in *EI*².
22. Donner, "Mecca's Food Supplies," p. 250. See, for example, H.A.R. Gibb, *Islam,* pp. 17, 26; B. Aswad, "Social and Ecological Aspects in the Origin of the Islamic State," p. 426; Hitti, *Capital Cities,* p. 7; Shahid, "Arabs in the Peace Treaty," pp. 190 ff.; cf. *id.,* "Two Qur'ānic Sūras: *al-Fīl* and *Qurayš,*" p. 436 (I am grateful to Dr. G. M. Hinds for drawing my attention to this article); I. M. Lapidus, "The Arab Conquests and the Formation of Islamic Society," p. 60; Groom, *Frankincense,* p. 162.
23. Kister, "Mecca and Tamīm," p. 116. A. Sprenger, *Das Leben und die Lehre des Moḥammad,* III, 94 f.
24. C. Rathjens, "Die alten Welthandelstrassen und die Offenbarungsreligionen," pp. 115, 122.
25. H. von Wissmann, *Die Mauer der Sabäerhauptstadt Maryab,* p. 1; R. Le Baron Bowen, "Ancient Trade Routes in South Arabia," p. 35. A similar view seems to be implied in G. L. Harding, *Archaeology in the Aden Protectorates,* p. 5. It is not clear whether the spices which the Queen of Sheba throws at the feet of Solomon in Rathjens, "Welthandelstrassen," p. 122, are envisaged as both Arabian and Indian. Müller certainly does not commit himself to such a view, though he cautiously accepts her as evidence of the existence of the south Arabian incense trade (*Weihrauch,* col. 745).
26. W. H. Schoff, tr., *The Periplus of the Erythraean Sea,* p. 3. (References by translator and page are to Schoff's comments, those by title and paragraph to the translation.)
27. T. W. Rosmarin, "Aribi und Arabien in den babylonisch-assyrischen Quellen.", pp. 2, 7, 22; A. van den Branden, *Histoire de Thamoud,* p. 6.
28. Thus J. Kennedy, "The Early Commerce of Babylon with India," p. 271.
29. Rathjens, "Welthandelstrassen," p. 122.
30. Thus B. Doe, *Southern Arabia,* p. 50; Rathjens, "Welthandelstrassen," p. 115, both with reference to the Red Sea only. Kennedy, "Early Commerce," pp. 248 f., implies that they were equally incapable of navigation in the Persian Gulf. But Doe assumes that the primitive boats of the Gerrheans were good enough for navigation in the Persian Gulf (*Southern Arabia,* p. 50), and Schoff assumes that those of the south Arabians were good enough for navigation in the Red Sea, too (Schoff, *Periplus,* p. 3), which makes the use of the overland route even odder.
31. Schoff, *Periplus,* pp 88 f.; E. H. Warmington, *The Commerce between the Roman Empire and India,* pp. 11, 13. Cf. below, Ch. 2 n105.
32. On the date of the *Periplus,* see now M. G. Raschke, "New Studies in Roman Commerce with the East," pp. 663 ff. with full references to the huge literature on the question. For Saba, See G. W. van Beek. "The Land of Sheba," p. 48; cf. also *id.,* "Frankincense and Myrrh in Ancient South Arabia," p. 146.
33. Schoff, *Periplus,* p. 6; H. Hasan, *A History of Persian Navigation,* p. 48; Donner, "Mecca's Food Supplies," p. 250.

34. Watt, *Muhammad at Mecca,* p. 3; Shahid, "Two Qur'ānic Sūras," p. 436. Similarly R. Paret, "Les villes de Syrie du sud et les routes commerciales d'Arabie à la fin du vi[e] siècle," pp. 441 f.; R. Simon, "Ḥums et īlāf, ou commerce sans guerre," p. 222 (though Simon's work is in other respects a refreshing attempt to go beyond hackneyed truths).
35. Detailed documentation will be given in chapter 3; but compare for example Doe, *Southern Arabia*, p. 52 (with reference to the sixth and fifth centuries B.C.) and Donner, "Mecca's Food Supplies," pp. 250, 254 (with reference to the sixth and early seventh centuries A.D.).

QUESTIONS

1. What is the basic question Crone raises about Meccan trade?
2. What problems does Crone raise regarding Shu'ayba, the port of Mecca?
3. What, according to Crone, are the problems raised by Mecca's location?
4. What is the dilemma posed by the respective assumptions of a trade in luxury goods on the one hand, and of cheap leather good and clothing on the other?
5. What are the "stereotypes" Crone enumerates?
6. What are the historical assumptions one must make in order to maintain that either the incense trade or the transit trade were the source of Meccan mercantile strength?

DOCUMENT

A MISSION TO THE GREAT KHAN

William of Rubruck

Not much is known about the life of William of Rubruck, a Franciscan friar and author of one of the most important reports on the Mongol Empire by a European of the Middle Ages. It seems likely that he was born between 1215 and 1230, probably in a village in French Flanders. Among the first things known with certainty is that Friar William was in Palestine in 1253, when King Louis IX of France sent him on a mission to the Mongols. Stopping first in Constantinople, William and his companions set out on the long journey that would eventually take them to Karakorum in central Mongolia. The exact purpose of his mission remains a matter of debate; while it is certain that evangelism played a role, William also mentions the goal of freeing Christian prisoners, although he was careful to play down any official diplomatic purpose for his trip. In any case, Friar William seems not to have met with much success on any front, beyond the completion of the journey itself and the production of a written report soon after his return to Europe in 1255. It was perhaps in 1257 that William met with the English scientist philosopher Roger Bacon, who was greatly taken with William's report and cited him often in his own work. The date of William's death remains as obscure as his birth.

The report William made for King Louis often reads like a memoir, filled with the author's own reactions to events and people. But if personal opinions appear frequently throughout the work, it also contains facts and observations of a quantity and quality hitherto unknown in Western accounts of the Mongol

"A Mission to the Great Khan," by William of Rubruck, reprinted from *The Portable Medieval Reader*, from *Journey of William of Rubruck*; edited by William Woodville Rockhill, pp. 446–476. Reproduced with permission of David Higham Associates Limited.

Empire. The present selection includes passages from the opening and closing of the work, as well as selections about the author's encounters with Nestorian Christians and an inebriated interpreter.

To the most excellent lord and most Christian Louis, by the grace of God illustrious king of the French [Louis IX], from Friar William of Rubruck, the meanest in the order of Minor Friars, greetings, and may he always triumph in Christ. It is written in Ecclesiasticus of the wise man: "He shall go through the land of foreign peoples, and shall try the good and evil in all things." This, my lord King, have I done, and may it have been as a wise man and not as a fool; for many do what the wise man doth, though not wisely, but most foolishly; of this number I fear I may be. Nevertheless in whatever way I may have done, since you commanded me when I took my leave of you that I should write you whatever I should see among the Tartars, and you did also admonish me not to fear writing a long letter, so I do what you enjoined on me, with fear, however, and diffidence, for the proper words that I should write to so great a monarch do not suggest themselves to me.

Be it known then to your Sacred Majesty that in the year of our Lord one thousand CCLIII, on the nones of May (7th May), I entered the Sea of Pontus, which is commonly called Mare Majus, or the Greater Sea. . . .

On the Octave of the Innocents (3rd January, 1254) we were taken to court; and there came certain Nestorian priests, whom I did not know to be Christians, and they asked me in what direction I prayed. I said, "To the east." And they asked that because we had shaved our beards, at the suggestion of our guide, so as to appear before the chan according to the fashion of our country. 'Twas for this that they took us for Tuins, that is idolaters. They also made us explain the Bible. Then they asked us what kind of reverence we wanted to make the chan, according to our fashion, or according to theirs. I replied to them, "We are priests given to the service of God. Noblemen in our country do not, for the glory of God, allow priests to bend the knee before them. Nevertheless, we want to humble ourselves to every man for the love of God. We come from afar: so in the first place then, if it please you, we will sing praises to God who has brought us here in safety from so far, and after that we will do as it shall please your lord, this only excepted, that nothing be required of us contrary to the worship and glory of God." Then they went into the house, and repeated what I had said. It pleased the lord, and so they placed us before the door of the dwelling, holding up the felt which hung before it; and, as it was the Nativity, we began to sing:

"A solis ortus cardine
Et usque terre limitem
Christum canamus principem
Natum Maria virgine."

When we had sung this hymn, they searched our legs and breasts and arms to see if we had knives upon us. They had the interpreter examined, and made him leave his belt and knife in the custody of a door-keeper. Then we entered, and there was a bench in the entry with *cosmos,* and near by it they made the interpreter stand. They made us, however, sit down on a bench near the ladies. The house was all covered inside with cloth of gold, and there was a fire of briars and wormwood roots—which grow here to great size—and of cattle dung, in a grate in the centre of the dwelling. He (Mangu) was seated on a couch, and was dressed in a skin spotted and glossy, like a seal's skin. He is a little man, of medium height, aged forty-five years, and a young wife sat beside him; and a very ugly, full-grown girl called Cirina, with other children sat on a couch after them. This dwelling had belonged to certain Christian lady, whom he had much loved, and of whom he had had this girl. Afterwards he had taken this young wife, but the girl was the mistress of all this *ordu,* which had been her mother's.

He had us asked what we wanted to drink, wine or *terracina,* which is rice wine *(cervisia),* or *caracosmos,* which is clarified mare's milk, or *bal,* which is honey mead. For in winter they make use of these four kinds of drinks. I replied: "My lord, we are not men who seek to satisfy our fancies about drinks; whatever pleases you will suit us." So he had us given of the rice drink, which was clear and flavoured like white wine, and of which I tasted a little out of respect for him, but for our misfortune our interpreter was standing by the butlers, who gave him so much to drink, that he was drunk in a short time. After this the chan had brought some falcons and other birds, which he took on his hand and looked at, and after a long while he bade us speak. Then we had to bend our knees. He had his interpreter, a certain Nestorian, who I did not know was a Christian, and we had our interpreter, such as he was, and already drunk. Then I said: "In the first place we render thanks and praise to God, who has brought us from so far to see Mangu Chan, to whom God has given so much power on earth. And we pray Christ, by whose will we all live and die, to grant him a happy and long life." For it is their desire, that one shall pray for their lives. Then I told him: "My lord, we have heard of Sartach that he was a Christian, and the Christians who heard it rejoiced greatly, and principally my lord the king of the French. So we came to him, and my lord the king sent him letters by us in which were words of peace, and among other things he bore witness to him as to the kind of men we were, and he begged him to allow us to remain in his country, for it is our office to teach men to live according to the law of God. He sent us, however, to his father Baatu, and Baatu sent us to you. You it is to whom God has given great power in the world. We pray then your mightiness to give us permission to remain in your dominion, to perform the service of God for you, for your wives and your children. We have neither gold, nor silver, nor precious stones to present to you, but only ourselves to offer to you to serve God, and to pray to God for you. At all events give us leave to remain here till this cold has passed away, for my companion is so feeble that he cannot with safety to his life stand any more the fatigue of travelling on horseback."

My companion had told me of his infirm condition, and had adjured me to ask for permission to stay, for we supposed that we would have to go back to Baatu, unless by special grace he gave us permission to stay. Then he began his reply: "As the sun sends its rays everywhere, likewise my sway and that of Baatu reach everywhere, so we do not want your gold or silver." So far I understood my interpreter, but after that I could not understand the whole of any one sentence: 'twas by this that I found out he was drunk, and Mangu himself appeared to me tipsy. His speech, it seemed to me, however, showed that he was not pleased that we had come to Sartach in the first place rather than to him. Then I, seeing that I was without interpreter, said nothing, save to beg him not to be displeased with what I had said of gold and silver, for I had not said that he needed or wanted such things, but only that we would gladly honour him with things temporal as well as spiritual. Then he made us arise and sit down again, and after awhile we saluted him and went out, and with us his secretaries and his interpreter, who was bringing up one of his daughters. And they began to question us greatly about the kingdom of France, whether there were many sheep and cattle and horses there, and whether they had not better go there at once and take it all. And I had to use all my strength to conceal my indignation and anger; but I answered, "There are many good things there, which you would see if it befell you to go there."

Then they appointed someone to take care of us, and we went to the monk. And as we were coming out of there to go to our lodgings, the interpreter I have mentioned came to me and said: "Mangu Chan takes compassion on you and allows you to stay here for the space of two months: then the great cold will be over. And he informs you that ten days hence there is a goodly city called Caracarum. If you wish to go there, he will have you given all you may require; if, however, you wish to remain here, you may do so, and you shall have what you need. It will, however, be fatiguing for you to ride with the court." I answered: "May the Lord keep Mangu Chan and give him a happy and long life! We have found this monk here, whom we believe to be a holy man and come here by the will of God. So we would willingly remain here with him, for we are monks, and we would say our prayers with him for the life of the chan." Then he left us without a word. And we went to a big house, which we found cold and without a supply of fuel, and we were still without food, and it was night. Then he to whom we had been entrusted gave us fuel and a little food. . . .

A certain woman from Metz in Lorraine, Paquette by name, and who had been made a prisoner in Hungary, found us out, and she gave us the best food she could. She belonged to the *ordu* of the Christian lady of whom I have spoken, and she told me of the unheard-of misery she had endured before coming to the *ordu.* But now she was fairly well off. She had a young Ruthenian husband, of whom she had had three right fine-looking boys, and he knew how to make houses, a very good trade among them. Furthermore, she told us that there was in Caracarum a certain master goldsmith, William by name, a native of Paris: and his family name was Buchier, and the name of his father was Laurent Buchier.

She believed that he had still a brother living on the Grand Pont, called Roger Buchier. She also told me that he supported a young man whom he considered as his son, and who was a most excellent interpreter. But as Mangu Chan had given this said master three hundred iascot, that is three thousand marks, and L workmen to do a certain work, she feared he would not be able to send his son to me. She had heard people in the *ordu* saying, "The men who have come from your country are good men, and Mangu Chan would be pleased to speak with them, but their interpreter is worth nothing." 'Twas for this that she was solicitous about an interpreter. So I wrote to this master of my coming, asking him if he could send me his son; and he replied that in that month he could not, but the following he would have finished his task and then he would send him to me. . . .

Toward the middle of Lent, the son of Master William arrived bringing a beautiful crucifix, made in French style, with a silver image of the Christ fixed on it. Seeing it, the monks and priests stole it, though he was to have presented it from his master to Bulgai, the grand secretary of the court; when I heard of this I was greatly scandalized.

This young man also informed Mangu Chan that the work he had ordered to be done was finished; and this work I shall here describe to you. Mangu had at Caracarum a great palace, situated next to the city walls, enclosed within a high wall like those which enclose monks' priories among us. Here is a great palace, where he has his drinkings twice a year: once about Easter, when he passes there, and once in summer, when he goes back (westward). And the latter is the greater (feast), for then come to his court all the nobles, even though distant two months' journey; and then he makes them largess of robes and presents, and shows his great glory. There are there many buildings as long as barns, in which are stored his provisions and his treasures. In the entry of this great palace, it being unseemly to bring in there skins of milk and other drinks, Master William the Parisian had made for him a great silver tree, and at its roots are four lions of silver, each with a conduit through it, and all belching forth white milk of mares. And four conduits are led inside the tree to its tops, which are bent downward, and on each of these is also a gilded serpent, whose tail twines round the tree. And from one of these pipes flows wine, from another *caracosmos,* or clarified mare's milk, from another *bal,* a drink made with honey, and from another rice mead, which is called *terracina;* and for each liquor there is a special silver bowl at the foot of the tree to receive it. Between these four conduits in the top, he made an angel holding a trumpet, and underneath the tree he made a vault in which a man can be hid. And pipes go up through the heart of the tree to the angel. In the first place he made bellows, but they did not give enough wind. Outside the palace is a cellar in which the liquors are stored, and there are servants all ready to pour them out when they hear the angel trumpeting. And there are branches of silver on the tree, and leaves and fruit. When then drink is wanted, the head butler cries to te angel to blow his trumpet. Then he who is concealed in the vault, hearing this, blows with all his might in the pipe leading to the angel, and the angel places the trumpet to his mouth, and blows the trumpet right loudly. Then the servants who are in the cellar, hearing this, pour the different liquors into the proper conduits, and the conduits lead them down into the bowls prepared for that, and then the butlers draw it and carry it to the palace to the men and women. . . .

Finally, the letters he [Mangu Chan] sends you being finished, they called me and interpreted them to me. I wrote down their tenor, as well as I could understand through an interpreter, and it is as follows:

"The commandment of the eternal God is, in Heaven there is only one eternal God, and on Earth there is only one lord, Chingis Chan, the Son of God, Demugin, (or) Chingis, 'sound of iron.'" (For they call him Chingis, "sound of iron," because he was a blacksmith; and puffed up in their pride they even say that he is the son of God.) "This is what is told you. Wherever there be a Moal [Mongol], or a Naiman, or a Merkit or a Musteleman, wherever ears can hear, wherever horses can travel, there let it be heard and known; those who shall have heard my commandments and understood them, and who shall not believe and shall make war against us, shall hear and see that they have eyes and see not; and when they shall want to hold anything they shall be without hands, and when they shall want to walk they shall be without feet: this is the eternal command of God. . . .

"This, through the virtue of the eternal God, through the great world of the Moal, is the word of Mangu Chan to the lord of the French, King Louis, and to all the other lords and priests and to all the great realm of the French, that they may understand our words. For the word of the eternal

God to Chingis Chan has not reached unto you, either through Chingis Chan or others who have come after him." . . .

Master William, once your subject, sends you a girdle ornamented with a precious stone, such as they wear against lightning and thunder; and he sends you endless salutations, praying always for you; and I cannot sufficiently express to God or to you the thanks I owe him. In all I baptized VI persons there.

So we separated with tears, my companion remaining with Master William, and I alone with my interpreter going back with my guide and one servant, who had an order by which we were to receive every four days one sheep for the IIII of us.

In two months and ten days we came to Baatu, and (on the way there) we never saw a town, nor the trace of any building save tombs, with the exception of one little village, in which we did not eat bread; neither did we ever take a rest in those two months and X days except for one day only, when we could not get horses. We came back for the most part of the way through the same peoples, though generally through different districts; for we went in winter and came back in summer by parts farther to the north, fifteen days excepted, when both in going and in coming back we had to keep along a river between mountains, where there is no grass except close to the river. We had to go for two days—sometimes for three days—without taking any other nourishment than *cosmos.* Sometimes we were in great danger, not being able to find any people, at moments when we were short of food, and with worn-out horses.

It seems to me inexpedient to send another friar to the Tartars, as I went, or as the preaching friars go; but if the lord pope, who is the head of all Christians, wishes to send with proper state a bishop, and reply to the foolishness they have already written three times to the Franks (once to Pope Innocent the Fourth of blessed memory, and twice to you: once by David, who deceived you, and now by me), he would be able to tell them whatever he pleased, and also make them reply in writing. They listen to whatever an ambassador has to say, and always ask if he has more to say; but he must have a good interpreter—nay, several interpreters—abundant travelling funds, etc.

QUESTIONS

1. What is the purpose of William of Rubruck's travels? What does he hope to gain?
2. William translates a letter from Mangu Chan. How does the Chan describe himself? How does this description compare to the ways William addresses or describes the French king? How does it differ?
3. Differences of language are a problem throughout William's encounter with the Tartars. How does William address this problem? What confusions does it create?
4. Why does William think it would be useless to send another friar to the Tartars? Would it be useful to send a bishop?

DOCUMENT

THE FIRST CRUSADE REACHES BYZANTIUM

Anna Comnena

Anna Comnena (1083–1153) was the highly educated and ambitious daughter of a successful Byzantine emperor, Alexius Comnenus (who ruled from 1081–1118). Raised at the court, she studied literature and philosophy and developed a real understanding of military matters. When she was very young, she was engaged to the son of a former emperor who was next in line for the throne. When Alexius had a son, however, Anna's hopes were replaced by bitterness. After her husband's early death, Anna married an aristocrat, Nicephorus Bryennius, who wrote a history of his own times. When Nicephorus was also named Caesar, second only to the emperor, it seemed that Anna might after all become an empress, but her hated brother John Comnenus (who ruled from 1118–1143) succeeded. After Anna was involved in two plots to murder him, she was exiled to a monastery, where she spent the last decades of her life, much of it devoted to writing a history in praise of her father. Her work stresses the campaigns of Alexius and reveals the highly negative Byzantine view of the Crusaders who passed through his empire.

This selection explains the origin of the Crusade and the character of its participants, from the hostile Byzantine viewpoint.

He had no time to relax before he heard a rumour that countless Frankish armies were approaching. He dreaded their arrival, knowing as he did their

"The First Crusade Reaches Byzantium," from *The Alexiad of Anna Comnena*, translated by E. R. A. Sewter, copyright © 1969 by E. R. A. Sewter, 308–313. Reprinted by permission of Penguin Books Ltd.

uncontrollable passion, their erratic character and their irresolution, not to mention the other peculiar traits of the Kelt, with their inevitable consequences: their greed for money, for example, which always led them, it seemed, to break their own agreements without scruple for any chance reason. He had consistently heard this said of them and it was abundantly justified. So far from despairing, however, he made every effort to prepare for war if need arose. What actually happened was more far-reaching and terrible than rumour suggested, for the whole of the west and all the barbarians who lived between the Adriatic and the Straits of Gibraltar migrated in a body to Asia, marching across Europe country by country with all their households. The reason for this mass-movement is to be found more or less in the following events. A certain Kelt, called Peter, with the surname Koukoupetros,[1] left to worship at the Holy Sepulchre and after suffering much ill-treatment at the hands of the Turks and Saracens who were plundering the whole of Asia, he returned home with difficulty. Unable to admit defeat, he wanted to make a second attempt by the same route, but realizing the folly of trying to do this alone (worse things might happen to him) he worked out a clever scheme. He decided to preach in all the Latin countries. A divine voice, he said, commanded him to proclaim to all the counts in France that all should depart from their homes, set out to worship at the Holy Shrine and with all their soul and might strive to liberate Jerusalem from the Agarenes.[2] Surprisingly, he was successful. It was as if he had inspired every heart with some divine oracle. Kelts assembled from all parts, one after another, with arms and horses and all the other equipment for war. Full of enthusiasm and ardour they thronged every highway, and with these warriors came a host of civilians, outnumbering the sand of the sea shore or the stars of heaven, carrying palms and bearing crosses on their shoulders. There were women and children, too, who had left their own countries. Like tributaries joining a river from all directions they streamed towards us in full force, mostly through Dacia. The arrival of this mighty host was preceded by locusts, which abstained from the wheat but made frightful inroads on the vines. The prophets of those days interpreted this as a sign that the Keltic army would refrain from interfering in the affairs of Christians but bring dreadful affliction on the barbarian Ishmaelites, who were the slaves of drunkenness and wine and Dionysos. The Ishmaelites are indeed dominated by

Dionysos and Eros; they indulge readily in every kind of sexual licence, and if they are circumcised in the flesh they are certainly not so in their passions. In fact, the Ishmaelites are nothing more than slaves—trebly slaves—of the vices of Aphrodite.[3] Hence they reverence and worship Astarte and Ashtaroth, and in their land the figure of the moon and the golden image of Chobar[4] are considered of major importance. Corn, because it is not heady and at the same time is most nourishing, has been accepted as the symbol of Christianity. In the light of this the diviners interpreted the references to vines and wheat. So much for the prophecies. The incidents of the barbarians' advance followed in the order I have given and there was something strange about it, which intelligent people at least would notice. The multitudes did not arrive at the same moment, nor even by the same route—how could they cross the Adriatic *en masse* after setting out from different countries in such great numbers?—but they made the voyage in separate groups, some first, some in a second party and others after them in order, until all had arrived, and then they began their march across Epirus. Each army as I have said, was preceded by a plague of locusts, so that everyone, having observed the phenomenon several times, came to recognize locusts as the forerunners of Frankish battalions. They had already begun to cross the Straits of Lombardy in small groups when the emperor summoned certain leaders of the Roman forces and sent them to the area round Dyrrachium and Avlona, with instructions to receive the voyagers kindly and export from all countries abundant supplies for them along their route; then to watch them carefully and follow, so that if they saw them making raids or running off to plunder the neighbouring districts, they could check them by light skirmishes. These officers were accompanied by interpreters who understood the Latin language; their duty was to quell any incipient trouble between natives and pilgrims. I would like here to give a clearer and more detailed account of the matter.

The report of Peter's preaching spread everywhere, and the first to sell his land and set out on the road to Jerusalem was Godfrey.[5] He was a very rich man, extremely proud of his noble birth, his own courage and the glory of his family. (Every Kelt desired to surpass his fellows.) The upheaval that ensued as men *and* women took to the road was unprecedented within living memory. The simpler folk were in very truth led on by a desire to worship at Our Lord's tomb and visit the holy places, but the more villainous characters (in particular Bohemond and his like) had an ulterior purpose, for they hoped on their journey to seize the capital itself, looking upon its capture as a natural consequence of the expedition. Bohemond disturbed the morale of many nobler men because he still cherished his old grudge against the emperor. Peter, after his preaching campaign, was the first to cross the Lombardy Straits, with 80,000 infantry and 100,000 horsemen. He reached the capital via Hungary.[6] The Kelts, as one might guess, are in any case an exceptionally hotheaded race and passionate, but let them once find an inducement and they become irresistible.

The emperor knew what Peter had suffered before from the Turks and advised him to wait for the other counts to arrive, but he refused, confident in the number of his followers. He crossed the Sea of Marmora and pitched camp near a small place called Helenopolis. Later some Normans, 10,000 in all, joined him but detached themselves from the rest of the army and ravaged the outskirts of Nicaea, acting with horrible cruelty to the whole population; they cut in pieces some of the babies, impaled others on wooden spits and roasted them over a fire; old people were subjected to every kind of torture. The inhabitants of the city, when they learnt what was happening, threw open their gates and charged out against them. A fierce battle ensued, in which the Normans fought with such spirit that the Nicaeans had to retire inside their citadel. The enemy therefore returned to Helenopolis with all the booty. There an argument started between them and the rest (who had not gone on the raid)—the usual quarrel in such cases—for the latter were green with envy. That led to brawling, whereupon the daredevil Normans broke away for a second time and took Xerigordos by assault. The sultan's reaction was to send Elkhanes with a strong force to deal with them. He arrived at Xerigordos and captured it; of the Normans some were put to the sword and others taken prisoner. At the same time Elkhanes made plans to deal with the remainder, still with Koukoupetros. He laid ambushes in suitable places, hoping that the enemy on their way to Nicaea would fall into the trap unawares and be killed. Knowing the Keltic love of money he also enlisted the services of two determined men who were to go to Peter's camp and there announce that the Normans, having seized Nicaea, were sharing out all the spoils of the city. This story had an amazing effect on Peter's men;

they were thrown into confusion at the words 'share' and 'money'; without a moment's hesitation they set out on the Nicaea road in complete disorder, practically heedless of military discipline and the proper arrangement which should mark men going off to war. As I have said before, the Latin race at all times is unusually greedy for wealth, but when it plans to invade a country, neither reason nor force can restrain it. They set out helter-skelter, regardless of their individual companies. Near the Drakon they fell into the Turkish ambuscade and were miserably slaughtered. So great a multitude of Kelts and Normans died by the Ishmaelite sword that when they gathered the remains of the fallen, lying on every side, they heaped up, I will not say a mighty rides or hill or peak, but a mountain of considerable height and depth and width, so huge was the mass of bones. Some men of the same race as the slaughtered barbarians later, when they were building a wall like those of a city, used the bones of the dead as pebbles to fill up the cracks. In a way the city became their tomb. To this very day it stands with its encircling wall built of mixed stones and bones. When the killing was over, only Peter with a handful of men returned to Helenopolis. The Turks, wishing to capture him, again laid an ambush, but the emperor, who had heard of this and indeed of the terrible massacre, thought it would be an awful thing if Peter also became a prisoner. Constantine Euphorbenus Catacalon (already mentioned often in this history) was accordingly sent with powerful contingents in warships across the straits to help him. At his approach the Turks took to their heels. Without delay Catacalon picked up Peter and his companions (there were only a few) and brought them in safety to Alexius, who reminded Peter of his foolishness in the beginning and added that these great misfortunes had come upon him through not listening to his advice. With the usual Latin arrogance Peter disclaimed responsibility and blamed his men for them, because (said he) they had been disobedient and followed their own whims. He called them brigands and robbers, considered unworthy therefore by the Saviour to worship at His Holy Spulchre. Some Latins, after the pattern of Bohemond and his cronies, because they had long coveted the Roman Empire and wished to acquire it for themselves, found in the preaching of Peter an excuse and cause of this great upheaval by deceiving more innocent people. They sold their lands on the pretence that they were leaving to fight the Turks and liberate the Holy Sepulchre.

END NOTES

1. Steven Runciman suggests that *chtou* or *kiokio* (Picard words) meaning 'little' may be the origin of this name. He was known to his contemporaries as Peter the Little but we know him as Peter the Hermit.
2. Another name (like Ishmaelites) for the Turks, i.e. descendants of Hagar.
3. Anna is unfair to the Mohammedans, but other authors accuse them of excessive wine-bibbing. She seems to be unaware that Aphrodite, Astarte and Ashtaroth are identical goddesses of love.
4. Chobar (or Chabar), meaning 'The Great', was the name given by the Saracens to the goddesses of love. 'Moon' should perhaps be supplanted by 'star' (the Greek *astron* may refer to Lucifer). . . .
5. Godfrey of Bouillon, Duke of Lower Lorraine.
6. The Crusaders arrived at Constantinople on 1 August 1096. They crossed the Bosphorus on 6 August. The attack on Nicaea, which was the headquarters of the Seljuq sultan (Kilij Arslan), took place in September.

QUESTIONS

1. What does Anna think of the invading Christians from the West? What different images does she use to describe them?
2. How does Anna's description of the Western invaders differ from the reasoning for invasion given by Peter and the others who come from the West?
3. What orders does the emperor give for receiving the foreigners? Why?
4. What qualities lead to the failure of Peter and his followers? How does Peter explain this failure?

DOCUMENT

WHY THE CRUSADERS FAILED

William of Tyre

William of Tyre (c. 1130–c. 1186) was a politician and archbishop whose first-hand knowledge of the Middle East led him to write a history of medieval Palestine. The nationality of his family is uncertain, although it seems likely that they were merchants of Italian or French extraction. Before his ordination as Archdeacon of Tyre (in modern Lebanon) in 1167, William studied at both Paris and Bologna. He became an important figure in the kingdom of Jerusalem, serving King Amaury as a diplomat to Constantinople and as tutor to the king's son in the early 1170s. William's influential role in secular and ecclesiastical government continued after he was appointed Archbishop of Tyre in 1175, and he was sent by Pope Alexander III on another diplomatic mission to Constantinople in 1179. It was during these years that William's History of Deeds beyond the Sea *was brought to completion, a history of crusading activities in the East that was probably finished in 1184. William also wrote at least one other historical work that has not survived.*

William made careful use of a substantial number of sources in the composition of his History, *and the result is an extremely valuable account of the twelfth century crusader kingdom of Jerusalem. For the years 1144 forward, he wrote on the basis of direct experience as well as documentary evidence. The work's descriptions and character sketches benefit from William's intelligent and lucid style, and he was careful throughout to enumerate and categorize his account into clear analytical categories. The present selection demonstrates this flair for analysis as well as William's concern that his narrative "not wander about aimlessly," leading him to discuss the religious, military, and political causes for crusading failures in the Holy Land.*

At this point I must digress somewhat from the course of my story, not to wander about aimlessly, but to bring out something of value. The question is often asked, and quite justly, why it was that our fathers, though less in number, so often bravely withstood in battle the far larger forces of the enemy and that often by divine grace a small force destroyed the multitudes of the enemy, with the result that the very name of Christian became a terror to nations ignorant of God, and thus the Lord was glorified in the works of our fathers. In contrast to this, the men of our times too often have been conquered by inferior forces; in fact, when with superior numbers they have attempted some exploit against adversaries less strong, their efforts have been fruitless and they have usually been forced to succumb.

The first reason that presents itself, as we carefully and thoughtfully study this condition of our times, looking for aid to God, the Author of all things, is that our forefathers were religious men and feared God. Now in their places a wicked generation has grown up, sinful sons, falsifiers of the Christian faith, who run the course of all unlawful things without discrimination. . . .

A second reason occurs to us in passing. In earlier times, those first revered men who came to the lands of the East led by divine zeal and aflame with spiritual enthusiasm for the faith were accustomed to military discipline; they were trained in battle and familiar with the use of weapons. The people of the East, on the contrary, through long-continued peace, had become enervated; they were unused to the art of war, unfamiliar with the rules of battle, and gloried in their state of inactivity. Therefore it is not strange that men of war, even though few in number, easily held their own even against larger numbers and could boast of their superiority in carrying off the palm of victory. For in such matters (as those who have had more experience in war know better than I), facility in arms due to long and continual practice, when opposed to untrained strength and lack of persistence, generally wins.

A third reason, no less important and effective, forces itself upon my attention. In former times almost every city had its own ruler. To speak after the manner of Aristotle, they were not dependent on one another; they were rarely actuated by the same motives, but, in fact, very often by those directly opposite. To contend in battle against adversaries of widely differing and frequently conflicting ideas, adversaries who distrusted each other, involved less peril. Those who feared their own allies not less than the Christians could not or would not readily unite to repulse the common danger or arm themselves for our destruction. But now, since God has so willed it, all the kingdoms adjacent to us have been brought under the power of one man. Within quite recent times, Zangi, a monster who abhorred the name of Christian as he would a pestilence, the father of this Nureddin who has lately died, first conquered many other kingdoms by force and then laid violent hands on Rages, also called Edessa, which even within our memory was the splendid and notable metropolis of the Medes. He took this city with all its territories and put to death all faithful believers found within its borders.

Then his son, Nureddin, drove the king of Damascus from his own land, more through the treachery of the latter's subjects than by any real valour, seized that realm for himself, and added it to his paternal heritage. Still more recently, the same Nureddin, with the assiduous aid of Shirkuh, seized the ancient and wealthy kingdom of Egypt as his own, in the manner already related more fully when the reign of King Amaury was under discussion.

Thus, as has been said, all the kingdoms round about us obey one ruler, they do the will of one man, and at his command alone, however reluctantly, they are ready, as a unit, to take up arms for our injury. Not one among them is free to indulge any inclination of his own or may with impunity disregard the commands of his overlord. This Saladin, whom we have had occasion to mention so frequently, a man of humble antecedents and lowly station, now holds under his control all these kingdoms, for fortune has smiled too graciously upon him. From Egypt and the countries adjacent to it, he draws an inestimable supply of the purest gold of the first quality known as *obryzum.* Other provinces furnish him numberless companies of horsemen and fighters, men thirsty for gold, since it is an easy matter for those possessing a plenteous supply of this commodity to draw men to them. . . .

QUESTIONS

1. What does William think of his own era compared to earlier ones? What explains the differences between his era and earlier ones?
2. What, in William's mind, is the relationship between spiritual purity and military valor?
3. Why was it possible for the first Crusaders to succeed against their foes? Did their enemies' circumstances make it easier to defeat them?
4. What political and military circumstances have changed among non-Christians since that time? Why should these developments make Christians nervous, according to William?

DOCUMENT

HENRY THE NAVIGATOR'S SEARCH FOR NEW LANDS

Gomes de Azurara

Gomes Eannes de Azurara was a fifteenth-century Portuguese chronicler and historian. His exact date and place of birth are unknown, although he was most likely born in the town of Azurara, in the Portuguese province of Minho, around the beginning of the fifteenth century. He is first documented in 1450, when he wrote his Chronicle of the Siege and Capture of Ceuta. *Azurara's most important work was completed in 1453, an account of the life and career of Prince Henry the Navigator, known as the* Chronicle of Guinea. *The success of this work earned him an important post in the Royal Archives in 1454, and he appears to have enjoyed as well several lucrative benefices associated with the Order of Christ. While the date of his death is unknown, it seems that he lived until after 1472, having written at least one other chronicle.*

Prince Henry the Navigator (1394–1460), fifth son of King John I of Portugal, was Europe's greatest patron of naval exploration and the most important precursor of Ferdinand and Isabella of Spain, who sponsored the voyages of Christopher Columbus. From his residence on the Sagres peninsula near Cape St. Vincent, Prince Henry organized a series of voyages that explored the islands of the Atlantic and the coast of Africa as far south as Sierra Leone. Between 1420 and 1460 the Azores, the Canary Islands, and Madeira were discovered and settled by Portuguese fishermen and sailors. Prince Henry replaced the casual fishing and trading voyages typical of the

"Henry the Navigator's Search for New Lands," by Gomes de Azurara, reprinted from *The Portable Medieval Reader*, from *Chronicle of the Discovery and Conquest of Guinea*; translated by C. R. Beazley and E. Prestage, pp. 491–494. Reproduced with permission of David Higham Associates Limited.

early fifteenth century with a systematic program of progressive exploration much further south. He has sometimes been described as a Renaissance humanistic prince, seeking to exploit the knowledge of the ancients and modern sciences to increase his power, but there is little to support this interpretation, and modern historians tend to place his mental outlook firmly within that of the late-Medieval world.

And you should note well that the noble spirit of this prince, by a sort of natural constraint, was ever urging him both to begin and to carry out very great deeds. For which reason, after the taking of Ceuta he always kept ships well armed against the Infidel, both for war, and because he had also a wish to know the land that lay beyond the isles of Canary and that cape called Bojador, for that up to his time, neither by writings, nor by the memory of man, was known with any certainty the nature of the land beyond that cape. Some said indeed that Saint Brandan had passed that way; and there was another tale of two galleys rounding the cape, which never returned. But this doth not appear at all likely to be true, for it is not to be presumed that if the said galleys went there, some other ships would not have endeavoured to learn what voyage they had made. And because the said Lord Infant wished to know the truth of this—since it seemed to him that if he or some other lord did not endeavour to gain that knowledge, no mariners or merchants would ever dare to attempt it (for it is clear that none of them ever trouble themselves to sail to a place where there is not a sure and certain hope of profit)—and seeing also that no other prince took any pains in this matter, he sent out his own ships against those parts, to have manifest certainty of them all. And to this he was stirred up by his zeal for the service of God and of the king Edward his lord and brother, who then reigned. And this was the first reason of his action.

The second reason was that if there chanced to be in those lands some population of Christians, or some havens, into which it would be possible to sail without peril, many kinds of merchandise might be brought to this realm, which would find a ready market, and reasonably so, because no other people of these parts traded with them, nor yet people of any other that were known; and also the products of this realm might be taken there, which traffic would bring great profit to our countrymen.

The third reason was that, as it was said that the power of the Moors in that land of Africa was very much greater than was commonly supposed, and that there were no Christians among them, nor any other race of men; and because every wise man is obliged by natural prudence to wish for a knowledge of the power of his enemy; therefore the said Lord Infant exerted himself to cause this to be fully discovered, and to make it known determinately how far the power of those infidels extended.

The fourth reason was because during the one and thirty years that he had warred against the Moors, he had never found a Christian king, nor a lord outside this land, who for the love of our Lord Jesus Christ would aid him in the said war. Therefore he sought to know if there were in those parts any Christian princes, in whom the charity and the love of Christ was so ingrained that they would aid him against those enemies of the faith.

The fifth reason was his great desire to make increase in the faith of our Lord Jesus Christ and to bring to him all the souls that should be saved—understanding that all the mystery of the Incarnation, Death, and Passion of our Lord Jesus Christ was for this sole end—namely the salvation of lost souls—whom the said Lord Infant by his travail and spending would fain bring into the true path. . . .

Now the Infant always received home again with great patience those whom he had sent out, as captains of his ships, in search of that land, never upbraiding them with their failure, but with gracious countenance listening to the story of the events of their voyage, giving them such rewards as he was wont to give to those who served him well, and then either sending them back to search again or despatching other picked men of his household, with their ships well furnished, making more urgent his charge to them, with promise of greater guerdons, if they added anything to the voyage that those before them had made, all to the intent that he might arrive at some comprehension of that difficulty. And at last, after twelve years, the Infant armed a "barcha" and gave it to Gil Eannes, one of his squires, whom he afterwards knighted and cared for right nobly. And he followed the course that others had taken; but touched by the selfsame terror, he only went as far as the Canary Islands, where he took some captives and returned to the kingdom. Now this was in the year of Jesus Christ 1433, and in the next year the Infant made ready the same vessel, and calling Gil Eannes apart, charged him earnestly to strain every nerve to pass that cape, and even if he could do nothing else on that voyage, yet he should consider that to be enough. "You cannot find," said the Infant, "a peril so great that the hope of reward will not be greater, and in truth I wonder much at the notion you have all taken on so uncertain a matter—for even if these things that are reported had any authority, however small, I would not blame you, but you tell me only the opinions of four mariners, who come but from the Flanders trade or from some other ports that are very commonly sailed to, and know nothing of the needle or sailing-chart. Go forth, then, and heed none of their words, but make your voyage straightway, inasmuch as with the grace of God you cannot but gain from this journey honour and profit." The Infant was a man of very great authority, so that his admonitions, mild though they were, had much effect on the serious-minded. And so it appeared by the deed of this man, for he, after these words, resolved not to return to the presence of his lord without assured tidings of that for which he was sent. And as he purposed, so he performed—for in that voyage he doubled the cape, despising all danger, and found the lands beyond quite contrary to what he, like others, had expected.

QUESTIONS

1. What motivates Henry's interest in exploration?
2. What is the state of European knowledge about the African coast? Why does Henry doubt its validity?
3. How does Henry compare to other princes?
4. What kind of leader is Henry? What does he do to encourage the captains of his ships?

DOCUMENT

A VENETIAN DESCRIBES THE PORTUGUESE WEST AFRICAN TRADE

Alvise da Cadamosto

Prince Henry the Navigator (1394–1460), fifth son of King John I of Portugal, was Europe's greatest patron of naval exploration and the most important precursor of Ferdinand and Isabella of Spain, who sponsored the voyages of Christopher Columbus. From his residence on the Sagres peninsula near Cape St. Vincent, Prince Henry organized a series of voyages that explored the islands of the Atlantic and the coast of Africa as far south as Sierra Leone. Between 1420 and 1460 the Azores, the Canary Islands, and Madeira were discovered and settled by Portuguese fishermen and sailors. Prince Henry replaced the casual fishing and trading voyages typical of the early fifteenth century with a systematic program of progressive exploration much further south. He has sometimes been described as a Renaissance humanistic prince, seeking to exploit the knowledge of the ancients and modern sciences to increase his power, but there is little to support this interpretation, and modern historians tend to place his mental outlook firmly within that of the late-Medieval world.

The selection given here is from an account of the Portuguese West African trade by Alvise da Ca'da Mosto or Cadamosto (c. 1426–1483), a Venetian merchant who was licensed by Prince Henry to trade in Guinea. He made two voyages, probably in 1455–56, as commander of a Portuguese expedition down the coast of Africa, and is credited with the discovery of Cape Verde. His account of his expeditions, published posthumously in 1507, describes the native populations and discusses how Africans responded to their encounters with Europeans. His account is strictly that of a businessman, and lacks the fantastical details usually found in late-Medieval travel literature.

THE VOYAGES OF CADAMOSTA

Chapter IX
The Description of Capo Bianco and the Islands Nearest to It

We set sail from this island[1] making due south towards Ethiopia; and in a few days reached Capo Blanco about 770 miles from the Canaries. It is to be noted that, leaving these islands to sail towards this cape, one goes along the coast of Africa which is constantly on the left hand; you sail well offshore, however, and do not sight land, because the Isole di Canaria are very far out to sea to the west, each one further than its neighbour. Thus you keep a course far out from land, until you have covered at least two-thirds of the passage from the islands to Capo Bianco and then draw near on the left hand to the coast until land is sighted, in order not to run past the said Cape without recognising it, because beyond it no land is seen for a considerable distance. The coast runs back at this cape, forming a gulf which is called the "Forna dargin."[2] This name Dargin is derived from an islet in the gulf called Argin by the people of the country. This gulf runs in more than fifty miles, and there are three more islands, to which the Portuguese have given these names: Isola Bianca, from its sands: Isola da le Garze,[3] because the first Portuguese found on it so many eggs of these sea birds that they loaded two boats from the caravels with them: the third Isola de Cuori. All are small, sandy, and uninhabited. On this Dargin there is a supply of fresh water, but not on the others.

Note that when you set out beyond the Strecto de Zibelterra [keeping this coast on the left hand, that is, of Barbary] towards Ethiopia, you do not find it inhabited by these Barbari except as far as the Cauo de Chantin.[4] From this cape along the coast to Capo Blanco commences the sandy country which is the desert that ranges on its northern confines with the mountains, which cut off our Barbary from Tunis, and from all these places of the coast. This desert the Berbers call Sarra:[5] on the south it marches with the Blacks of lower Ethiopia: it is a very great desert, which takes well-mounted men fifty to sixty days to cross—in some places more, and some less. The boundary of this desert is on the Ocean Sea at the coast, which is everywhere sandy, white, arid, and all equally low-lying: it does not appear to be higher in one place than another, as far as the said Capo Bianco, which is so called because the Portuguese who discovered it saw it to be sandy and white, without signs of grass or trees whatsoever. It is a very fine cape, like a triangle, that is, on its face; it has three points, distant the one from the other about a mile.

On this coast there are very large fisheries[6] of various and most excellent large fish without number, like those of our Venetian fisheries, and other kinds. Throughout this Forna Dargin there is little water, and there are many shoals, some of sand, others of rock. There are strong currents in the sea, on account of which one navigates only by day, with the lead in hand, and according to the state of the tide. Two ships have already been wrecked upon these banks. The aforesaid Cauo de Chantin stands approximately north-east of Capo Bianco.

You should also know that behind this Cauo Bianco on the land, is a place called Hoden,[7] which is about six days inland by camel. This place is not walled, but is frequented by Arabs, and is a market where the caravans arrive from Tanbutu,[8] and from other places in the land of the Blacks, on their way to our nearer Barbary. The food of the peoples of this place is dates, and barley, of which there is sufficient, for they grow in some of these places, but not abundantly. They drink the milk of camels and other animals, for they have no wine. They also have cows and goats, but not many, for the land is dry. Their oxen and cows, compared with ours, are small.

They are Muhammadans, and very hostile to Christians. They never remain settled, but are always wandering over these deserts. These are the men who go to the land of the Blacks, and also to our nearer Barbary. They are very numerous, and have many camels on which they carry brass and silver from Barbary and other things to Tanbuto and to the land of the Blacks. Thence they carry away gold and pepper,[9] which they bring hither. They are brown complexioned, and wear white cloaks edged with a red stripe: their women also dress thus, without shifts. On their heads the men wear turbans in the Moorish fashion, and they always go barefooted. In these sandy districts there are many lions, leopards, and ostriches, the eggs of which I have often eaten and found good.

You should know that the said Lord Infante of Portugal has leased this island of Argin to Christians [for ten years], so that no one can enter the bay to trade with the Arabs save those who hold the license. These have dwellings on the island and factories where they buy and sell with the said Arabs who come to the coast to trade for merchandise of various kinds, such as woollen cloths, cotton, silver, and "alchezeli,"[10] that is, cloaks, carpets, and similar articles and above all, corn, for they are always short of food. They give in exchange slaves whom the Arabs bring from the land of the Blacks,[11] and gold *tiber*.[12] The Lord Infante therefore caused a castle[13] to be built on the island to protect this trade for ever. For this reason, Portuguese caravels are coming and going all the year to this island.

These Arabs also have many Berber horses,[14] which they trade, and take to the Land of the Blacks, exchanging them with the rulers for slaves. Ten or fifteen slaves are given for one of these horses, according to their quality. The Arabs likewise take articles of Moorish silk, made in Granata and in Tunis of Barbary, silver, and other goods, obtaining in exchange any number of these slaves, and some gold. These slaves are brought to the market and town of Hoden; there they are divided: some go to the mountains of Barcha,[15] and thence to Sicily, [others to the said town of Tunis and to all the coasts of Barbary], and others again are taken to this place, Argin, and sold to the Portuguese leaseholders. As a result every year the Portuguese carry away from Argin a thousand slaves.[16] Note that before this traffic was organized, the Portuguese caravels, sometimes four, sometimes more, were wont to come armed to the Golfo d'Argin, and descending on the land by night, would assail the fisher villages, and so ravage the land. Thus they took of these Arabs both men and women, and carried them to Portugal for sale: behaving in a like manner along all the rest of the coast, which stretches from Cauo Bianco to the Rio di Senega and even beyond. This is a great river, dividing a race which is called Azanaghi[17] from the first Kingdom of the Blacks. These Azanaghi are brownish, rather dark brown than light, and live in places along this coast beyond Cauo Bianco, and many of them are spread over this desert inland. They are neighbours of the above mentioned Arabs of Hoden.

They live on dates, barley, and camel's milk: but as they are very near the first land of the Blacks, they trade with them, obtaining from this land of the Blacks millet and certain vegetables, such as beans, upon which they support themselves. They are men who require little food and can withstand hunger, so that they sustain themselves throughout the day upon a mess of barley porridge. They are obliged to do this because of the want of victuals they experience. These, as I have said, are taken by the Portuguese as before mentioned and are the best slaves of all the Blacks. But, however, for some time all have been at peace and engaged in trade. The said Lord Infante will not permit further hurt to be done to any, because he hopes that, mixing with Christians, they may without difficulty be converted to our faith, not yet being firmly attached to the tenets of Muhammad, save from what they know by hearsay.

These same Azanaghi have a strange custom: they always wear a handkerchief on the head with a flap[18] which they bring across the face, covering the mouth and part of the nose. For they say that the mouth is a brutish thing, that is always uttering wind and bad odours so that it should be kept covered, and not displayed, likening it almost to the posterior, and that these two portions should be kept covered. It is true that they never uncover it, except when they eat, and not otherwise for I have seen many of them.

There are no lords among them, save those who are richer: these are honoured and obeyed to some degree by the others. They are a very poor people, liars, the biggest thieves in the world, and exceedingly treacherous. They are men of average height, and spare. They wear their hair in locks down to their shoulders, almost in the German fashion—but their hair is black, and anointed every day with fish oil, so that it smells strongly, the which they consider a great refinement.

Chapter XI[19]

The Exchange of Salt for Gold: and the Distance It Travels

That woman who has the largest breasts is considered more beautiful than the others: with the result that each woman, to increase their size, at the age of seventeen or eighteen when the breasts are already formed, places across her chest a cord, which she binds around the breasts, and draws tight with much force; in this way the breasts are distended, and frequent pulling every day causes them to grow and lengthen so much that many reach the navel. Those that have the biggest prize them as a rare thing.

You should know that these people have no knowledge of any Christians except the Portuguese, against whom they have waged war for [thirteen or] fourteen years, many of them having been taken prisoners, as I have already said, and sold into slavery. It is asserted that when for the first time they saw sails, that is, ships, on the sea (which neither they nor their forefathers had ever seen before), they believed that they were great sea-birds with white wings, which were flying, and had come from some strange place: when the sails were lowered for the landing, some of them, watching from far off, thought that the ships were fishes. Others again said that they were phantoms that went by night, at which they were greatly terrified. The reason for this belief was because these caravels within a short space of time appeared at many places, where attacks were delivered, especially at night, by their crews. Thus one such assault might be separated from the next by a hundred or more miles, according to the plans of the sailors, or as the winds, blowing hither and thither, served them. Perceiving this, they said amongst themselves, "If these be human creatures, how can they travel so great a distance in one night, a distance which we could not go in three days?" Thus, as they did not understand the art of navigation, they all thought that the ships were phantoms. This I know is testified to by many Portuguese who at that time were trading in caravels on this coast, and also by those who were captured on these raids. And from this it may be judged how strange many of our ways appeared to them, if such an opinion could prevail.

Beyond the said mart of Edon [Oden], six days journey further inland, there is a place called Tagaza, that is to say in our tongue "cargador,"[20] where a very great quantity of rock-salt is mined. Every year large caravans of camels belonging to the above mentioned Arabs and Azanaghi, leaving in many parties, carry it to Tanbutu,[21] thence they go to Melli,[22] the empire of the Blacks, where, so rapidly is it sold, within eight days of its arrival all is disposed of at a price of two to three hundred *mitigalli*[23] a load, according to the quantity: [a *mitigallo* is worth about a ducat:] then with the gold they return to their homes.

In this empire of Melli it is very hot, and the pasturage is very unsuitable for four footed animals: so that of the majority which come with the caravans no more than twenty-five out of a hundred return. There are no quadrupeds in this country, because they all die, and many also of the Arabs and Azanaghi sicken in this place and die, on account of the great heat. It is said that on horseback it is about forty days from Tagaza to Tanbutu, and thirty from Tanbutu to Melli.

I enquired of them what the merchants of Melli did with this salt, and was told that a small quantity is consumed in their country. Since it is below the meridional and on the equinoctial, where the day is constantly about as long as the night, it is extremely hot at certain seasons of the year: this causes the blood to putrefy, so that were it not for this salt, they would die. The remedy they employ is as follows: they take a small piece of the salt, mix it in a jar with a little water, and drink it every day. They say that this saves them. The remainder of this salt they carry away on a long journey in pieces as large as a man can, with a certain knack, bear on his head.

You must know that when this salt is carried to Melli by camel it goes in large pieces [as it is dug out from the mines], of a size most easily carried on camels, two pieces on each animal. Then at Melli, these blacks break it in smaller pieces, in order to carry it on their heads, so that each man carries one piece, and thus they form a great army of men on foot, who transport it a great distance. Those who carry it have two forked sticks, one in each hand: when they are tired, they plant them in the ground, and rest their load upon them. In this way they carry it until they reach certain waters: I could not learn from them whether it is fresh or sea water, so that I do not know if it is a river or the sea, though they consider it to be the sea. [I think however it must be a river, for if it were the sea, in such a hot country there would be no lack of salt.] These Blacks are obliged to carry it in this way, because they have no camels or other beasts of burden, as these cannot live in the great heat. It may be imagined how many men are required to carry it on foot, and how many are those who consume it every year. Having reached these waters with the salt, they proceed in this fashion: all those who have the salt pile it in rows, each marking his own. Having made these piles, the whole caravan retires half a day's journey. Then there come another race of blacks who do not wish to be seen or to speak. They arrive in large boats, from which it appears that they come from islands, and disembark. Seeing the salt, they place a quantity of gold opposite each pile, and then turn back, leaving salt and gold.

When they have gone, the negroes who own the salt return: if they are satisfied with the quantity of gold, they leave the salt and retire with the gold. Then the blacks of the gold return, and remove those piles which are without gold. By other piles of salt they place more gold, if it pleases them, or else they leave the salt. In this way, by long and ancient custom, they carry on their trade without seeing or speaking to each other. Although it is difficult to believe this, I can testify that I have had this information from many merchants, Arab as well as Azanaghi, and also from persons in whom faith can be placed.

Chapter XIV
The Rio de Senega, Which Divides the Desert from the Fertile Land

When we had passed in sight of this Cauo Bianco, we sailed on our journey to the river called the Rio de Senega, the first river of the Land of the Blacks, which debouches on this coast. This river separates the Blacks from the brown people called Azanaghi, and also the dry and arid land, that is, the above mentioned desert, from the fertile country of the Blacks. The river is large; its mouth being over a mile wide, and quite deep. There is another mouth a little distance beyond, with an island between. Thus it enters the sea by two mouths, and before each of them about a mile out to sea are shoals and broad sand-banks. In this place the water increases and decreases every six hours, that is, with the rise and fall of the tide. The tide ascends the river more than sixty miles, according to the information I have had from Portuguese who have been [many miles] up it [in caravels]. He who wishes to enter this river must go in with the tide, on account of the shoals and banks at the mouth. From Cauo Bianco it is 380 miles to the river: all the coast is sandy within about twenty miles of the mouth. It is called Costa de Antte rotte, and is of the Azanaghi, or brown men.

It appears to me a very marvellous thing that beyond the river all men are very black, tall and big, their bodies well formed; and the whole country green, full of trees, and fertile: while on this side, the men are brownish, small, lean, ill-nourished, and small in stature: the country sterile and arid. This river is said to be a branch of the river Nile, of the four royal rivers: it flows through all Ethiopia, watering the country as in Egypt: passing through "lo caiero," it waters all the land of Egypt.

Chapter XXXIX
The Elevation of Our North Star; and the Six Stars Opposite

During the days we spent at the mouth of this river,[24] we saw the pole star once only; it appeared very low down over the sea, therefore we could see it only when the weather was very clear. It appeared about a third of a lance above the horizon. We also had sight of six stars low down over the sea, clear, bright, and large. By the compass, they stood due south, in the following fashion.[25]

```
     *
*        *   *   *
     *
```

This we took to be the southern wain, though we did not see the principal star, for it would not have been possible to sight it unless we had lost the north star. In this place we found the night to be 13 [eleven and a half] hours, and the day 11 [twelve and a half] hours, that is, in the first days of July, or more accurately on the second of the month.

This country is hot at all seasons of the year. It is true that there is some variation, and what they call a winter: thus beginning in the aforesaid month [of July] until the end of October it rains continuously almost every day from noon, in the following way: clouds rise continually over the land from the E.N.E., or from the E.S.E., with very heavy thunder, lightning and thunderbolts. Thus an excessive quantity of rain falls, and at this season the negroes begin to sow in the same manner as those of the kingdom of Senega. Their sustenance is entirely millet and vegetables, flesh and milk.

I understand that in the interior of this country, [on account of the great heat of the air] the rain which falls is warm. In the morning, when day breaks, there is no dawn at the rising of the sun, as in our parts, where between dawn and sunrise there is a short interval before the shadows of night disperse: the sun appears suddenly, though it is not light for the space of half an hour, as the sun is dull and, as it were, smoky on first rising. The cause of this appearance of the sun early in the morning, contrary to what happens in our country, cannot, I think, arise from any other circumstance than the extreme lowness of the land, devoid of mountains, and all my companions were of this opinion.

END NOTES

1. Palma. The distance is about 570 nautical miles.
2. Arguim, discovered in 1443 by Nuno Tristão, where a fort was erected by Prince Henry in 1448 for the protection of merchants. Its good water and safe anchorage quickly made it a valuable *entrepôt,* and it became an important trading centre. The Arab name was "Ghir," and Azurara calls it "Gete."
3. Island of Herons (Azurara: I, p. 63, and II, pp. 320–1), one of the Arguim Islands. The big expedition of 1444 rested here and refreshed themselves on the multitude of young birds.
4. Cape Cantin, 32° 36′ N., 9° 14′ W.
5. Sahara. The mountains are the Atlas range.
6. The fishing fields were already being exploited under Prince Henry's license.
7. Wadan, an important desert market about 350 miles east of Arguim. Later, in 1487, when the Portuguese were endeavouring to penetrate the interior they attempted to establish a trading factory at Wadan which acted as a feeder to Arguim, tapping the north-bound caravan traffic and diverting some of it to the west coast.
8. Timbuktu
9. Malaguetta pepper
10. Probably the coarse cloth called by El Bekri in the eleventh century "chigguiza," which was doubtless the "shigge" purchased by Barth in Timbuktu in the nineteenth century (Barth: *Travels,* iv, p. 443).
11. The Portuguese had now established in West Africa the insidious practice of inciting the coast tribes to raid their neighbours for slaves.
12. The Arabic *thibr* or *tibar,* meaning gold dust.
13. Built by Prince Henry in 1448.
14. Leo Africanus, writing in the sixteenth century, makes several references to the trade in Barbary horses for which there was an excellent market in the Sudan. Later the Portuguese regularly shipped out horses to barter for slaves.
15. Barca in Cyrenaica
16. According to Azurara (II, p. 288), up to the year 1448 the total number of Africans who had been carried captive to Portugal during Prince Henry's time was only 927. This passage indicates how rapidly the slave trade was increasing.
17. The Azanaghi or Azaneguys, as Azurara calls them, were the Sanhaja, historically the most important of the Tuareg tribes, and widely distributed over the western Sahara.
18. The *litham,* still worn by the Tuareg; hence their name Mulenththemin, meaning the Veiled People. In Roman and Byzantine times they appear not to have worn the veil, and when or why they took to it remains a problem to which no acceptable solution has been found. Its use appears always to have been restricted to the men.
19. This and subsequent chapters are misnumbered in the original version.
20. "A load, or charge"; other texts have "bisaccia d'oro", i.e. wallet of gold, the gold not being obtained locally, but in exchange for salt.
21. Timbuktu
22. Mali
23. One *mithgal* or *mitkal* equalled about ⅛ oz. of gold.
24. The Gambia
25. The first recorded notice of the Southern Cross.

QUESTIONS

1. What features does Cadamosto focus on as he describes the islands and waters along the African coast? Why does he concentrate on these features?
2. What commodities are traded between the Arabs and the Portuguese? Where do the Arabs get the goods they exchange with the Portuguese?
3. Who are the Azanaghi? How does Cadamosto describe them and why does he want to provide so much detail about them?
4. How is salt used? How is the salt trade conducted?

DOCUMENT

VASCO DA GAMA EXPLORES THE INDIAN OCEAN

Anonymous

After the death of Prince Henry the Navigator in 1460, there is comparatively little information about the Portuguese exploration of the African route to India. Only in the 1490s does the documentation improve. From that period, there is an anonymous eyewitness account of the famous voyage of Vasco da Gama (c. 1468–1524), the first Portuguese navigator to round the Cape of Good Hope, explore East Africa, cross the Indian Ocean, and reach the Malibar coast of India. Da Gama's first voyage (1497–99) was an official naval expedition sent out by King Manuel I; its aim was to conduct an armed reconnaissance of the Western Indian Ocean with a view to establishing trade relations with India, which at that time dominated the richest trading system in the world. As a result of da Gama's discoveries it became evident that the Portuguese would not be welcome in a trading system controlled by Arabic and Muslim traders, and that the only way the Portuguese were likely to enjoy commercial success in that part of the world was through military dominance. The next Portuguese expedition of 1502–03, also commanded by da Gama, was therefore a military expedition of twenty ships, including warships, which conducted military operations against the Hindu and Arab traders of the Malibar coast and the northwest Indian Ocean.

The document excerpted here, written by a member of da Gama's first expedition, possibly a soldier, describes vividly the hostility da Gama's four

Reprinted from A Journal of the *First Voyage of Vasco da Gama*, written 1497–1499 and published in 1898.

ships met in the Western Indian Ocean. The writer labors under the misapprehension, characteristic of a number of early Portuguese sources, that Hinduism was a variety of Christianity.

MOMBAÇA

On Saturday [April 7] we cast anchor off Mombaça, but did not enter the port. No sooner had we been perceived than a *zavra*[1] manned by Moors came out to us; in front of the city there lay numerous vessels all dressed in flags.[2] And we, anxious not to be outdone, also dressed our ships, and we actually surpassed their show, for we wanted in nothing but men, even the few whom we had being very ill. We anchored here with much pleasure, for we confidently hoped that on the following day we might go on land and hear mass jointly with the Christians reported to live there under their own *alcaide*[3] in a quarter separate from that of the Moors.

The pilots who had come with us told us there resided both Moors and Christians in this city; that these latter lived apart under their own lords, and that on our arrival they would receive us with much honour and take us to their houses. But they said this for a purpose of their own, for it was not true. At midnight there approached us a *zavra* with about a hundred men, all armed with cutlasses [tarçados] and bucklers. When they came to the vessel of the captain-major they attempted to board her, armed as they were, but this was not permitted, only four or five of the most distinguished men among them being allowed on board. They remained about a couple of hours, and it seemed to us that they paid us this visit merely to find out whether they might not capture one or the other of our vessels.

On Palm Sunday [April 8] the King of Mombaça sent the captain-major a sheep and large quantities of oranges, lemons and sugar-cane, together with a ring, as a pledge of safety, letting him know that in case of his entering the port he would be supplied with all he stood in need of. This present was conveyed to us by two men, almost white, who said they were Christians, which appeared to be the fact. The captain-major sent the king a string of coral-beads as a return present, and let him know that he purposed entering the port on the following day. On the same day the captain-major's vessel was visited by four Moors of distinction.

Two men were sent by the captain-major to the king, still further to confirm these peaceful assurances. When these landed they were followed by a crowd as far as the gates of the palace. Before reaching the king they passed through four doors, each guarded by a doorkeeper with a drawn cutlass. The king received them hospitably, and ordered that they should be shown over the city. They stopped on their way at the house of two Christian merchants, who showed them a paper [carta], an object of their adoration, on which was a sketch of the Holy Ghost.[4] When they had seen all, the king sent them back with samples of cloves, pepper and corn,[5] with which articles he would allow us to load our ships.

On Tuesday [April 10], when weighing anchor to enter the port, the captain-major's vessel would not pay off, and struck the vessel which followed astern. We therefore again cast anchor. When the Moors who were in our ship saw that we did not go on, they scrambled into a *zavra* attached to our stern; whilst the two pilots whom we had brought from Moçambique jumped into the water, and were picked up by the men in the *zavra.* At night the captain-major "questioned" two Moors [from Moçambique] whom we had on board, by dropping boiling oil upon their skin, so that they might confess any treachery intended against us. They said that orders had been given to capture us as soon as we entered the port, and thus to avenge what we had done at Moçambique. And when this torture was being applied a second time, one of the Moors, although his hands were tied, threw himself into the sea, whilst the other did so during the morning watch.

About midnight two *almadias,* with many men in them, approached. The *almadias* stood off whilst the men entered the water, some swimming in the direction of the *Berrio,* others in that of the *Raphael.* Those who swam to the *Berrio* began to cut the cable. The men on watch thought at first that they were tunny fish, but when they perceived their mistake they shouted to the other vessels. The other swimmers had already got hold of the rigging of the mizzen-mast. Seeing themselves discovered, they silently slipped down and fled. These and other wicked tricks were practised upon us by these dogs, but our Lord did not allow them to succeed, because they were unbelievers.

Mombaça is a large city seated upon an eminence washed by the sea. Its port is entered daily by numerous vessels. At its entrance stands a pillar, and by the sea a low-lying fortress. Those who had gone on shore told us that in the town they had seen many men in irons; and it seemed to us that these must be Christians, as the Christians in that country are at war with the Moors.

The Christian merchants in the town are only temporary residents, and are held in much subjection, they not being allowed to do anything except by the order of the Moorish King.

It pleased God in his mercy that on arriving at this city all our sick recovered their health, for the climate ["air"] of this place is very good.

After the malice and treachery planned by these dogs had been discovered, we still remained on Wednesday and Thursday [April 11 and 12].

MOMBAÇA TO MALINDI

We left in the morning [April 13], the wind being light, and anchored about eight leagues from Mombaça, close to the shore. At break of day [April 14] we saw two boats [*barcas*] about three leagues to the leeward, in the open sea, and at once gave chase, with the intention of capturing them, for we wanted to secure a pilot who would guide us to where we wanted to go. At vesper-time we came up with one of them, and captured it, the other escaping towards the land. In the one we took we found seventeen men, besides gold, silver, and an abundance of maize and other provisions; as also a young woman, who was the wife of an old Moor of distinction, who was a passenger. When we came up with the boat they all threw themselves into the water, but we picked them up from our boats.

That same day [April 14] at sunset, we cast anchor off a place called Milinde [Malindi], which is thirty leagues from Mombaça. The following places are between Mombaça and Milinde, viz., Benapa, Toça and Nuguoquioniete.

MALINDI[6]

On Easter Sunday [April 15] the Moors whom we had taken in the boat told us that there were at this city of Melinde four vessels belonging to Christians from India, and that if it pleased us to take them there, they would provide us, instead of them, Christian pilots and all we stood in need of, including water, wood and other things. The captain-major much desired to have pilots from the country, and having discussed the matter with his Moorish prisoners, he cast anchor off the town, at a distance of about half a league from the mainland. The inhabitants of the town did not venture to come aboard our ships, for they had already learnt that we had captured a vessel and made her occupants prisoners.

On Monday morning [April 16] the captain-major had the old Moor taken to a sandbank in front of the town, where he was picked up by an *almadia.* The Moor explained to the king the wishes of the captain-major, and how much he desired to make peace with him. After dinner the Moor came back in a *zavra*, accompanied by one of the king's cavaliers and a sharif: he also brought three sheep. These messengers told the captain-general that the king would rejoice to make peace with him, and to enter into friendly relations; that he would willingly grant to the captain-major all his country afforded, whether pilots or anything else. The captain-major upon this sent word that he proposed to enter the port on the following day, and forwarded by the king's messengers a present consisting of a *balandrau,*[7] two strings of coral, three wash-hand basins, a hat, little bells and two pieces of *lambel.*[8]

Consequently, on Tuesday [April 17] we approached nearer to the town. The king sent the captain-major six sheep, besides quantities of cloves, cumin, ginger, nutmeg and pepper, as also a message, telling him that if he desired to have an interview with him he (the king) would come out in his *zavra,* when the captain-major could meet him in a boat.

On Wednesday [April 18], after dinner, when the king came up close to the ships in a *zavra,* the captain-major at once entered one of his boats, which had been well furnished, and many friendly words were exchanged when they lay side by side. The king having invited the captain-major to come to his house to rest, after which he (the king) would visit him on board his ship, the captain-major said that he was not permitted by his master to go on land, and if he were to do so a bad report would be given of him. The king wanted to know what would be said of himself by his people if he were to visit the ships, and what account could he render them? He then asked for the name of our king, which was written down for him, and said that on our return he would send an ambassador with us, or a letter.

When both had said all they desired, the captain-major sent for the Moors whom he had taken prisoner, and surrendered them all. This gave much satisfaction to the king, who said that he valued this act more highly than if he had been presented with a town. And the king, much pleased, made the circuit of our ships, the bombards of which fired a salute. About three hours were spent in this way. When the king went away he left in the ship one of his sons and a sharif, and took two of us away with him, to whom he desired to show his palace. He, moreover, told the captain that as he would not go ashore he would himself return on the following day to the beach, and would order his horsemen to go through some exercises.

The king wore a robe [royal cloak] of damask trimmed with green satin, and a rich *touca*. He was seated on two cushioned chairs of bronze, beneath a round sunshade of crimson satin attached to a pole. An old man, who attended him as page, carried a short sword in a silver sheath. There were many players on *anafils,* and two trumpets of ivory, richly carved, and of the size of a man, which were blown from a hole in the side, and made sweet harmony with the *anafils*.

On Thursday [April 19] the captain-major and Nicolau Coelho rowed along the front of the town, bombards having been placed in the poops of their long-boats. Many people were along the shore, and among them two horsemen, who appeared to take much delight in a sham-fight. The king was carried in a palanquin from the stone steps of his palace to the side of the captain-major's boats. He again begged the captain to come ashore, as he had a helpless father who wanted to see him, and that he and his sons would go on board the ships as hostages. The captain, however, excused himself.

We found here four vessels belonging to Indian Christians. When they came for the first time on board Paulo da Gama's ship, the captain-major being there at the time, they were shown an altar-piece representing Our Lady at the foot of the cross, with Jesus Christ in her arms and the apostles around her. When the Indians saw this picture they prostrated themselves, and as long as we were there they came to say their prayers in front of it, bringing offerings of cloves, pepper, and other things.

These Indians are tawny men; they wear but little clothing and have long beards and long hair, which they braid. They told us that they ate no beef. Their language differs from that of the Arabs, but some of them know a little of it, as they hold much intercourse with them.

On the day on which the captain-major went up to the town in the boats, these Christian Indians fired off many bombards from their vessel, and when they saw him pass they raised their hands and shouted lustily *Christ! Christ!*[9]

That same night they asked the king's permission to give us a night-fête. And when night came they fired off many bombards, sent up rockets, and raised loud shouts.

These Indians warned the captain-major against going on shore, and told him not to trust to their "fanfares," as they neither came from their hearts nor from their good will.

On the following Sunday, the 22nd of April, the king's *zavra* brought on board one of his confidential servants, and as two days had passed without any visitors, the captain-major had this man seized, and sent word to the king that he required the pilots whom he had promised. The king, when he received this message, sent a Christian pilot,[10] and the captain-major allowed the gentleman, whom he had retained in his vessel, to go away.

We were much pleased with the Christian pilot whom the king had sent us. We learnt from him that the island of which we heard at Moçambique as being inhabited by Christians was in reality an island subject to this same King of Moçambique; that half of it belonged to the Moors and the other half to the Christians; that many pearls were to be found there, and that it was called Quyluee.[11] This is the island the Moorish pilots wanted to take us to, and we also wished to go there, for we believed that what they said was true.

The town of Malindi lies in a bay and, extends along the shore. It may be likened to Alcouchette.[12] Its houses are lofty and well white-washed, and have many windows; on the landside are palmgroves, and all around it maize and vegetables are being cultivated.

We remained in front of this town during nine days, and all this time we had fêtes, sham-fights, and musical performances ["fanfares"].

ACROSS THE GULF—THE ARABIAN SEA

We left Malindi on Tuesday, the 24th of the month [of April] for a city called Qualecut [Calecut], with the pilot whom the king had given us. The coast there runs north and south, and the land encloses a huge bay with a strait. In this bay,[13] we were told, were to be found many large cities of Christians and Moors, including one called Quambay [Cambay], as also six-hundred known islands, and within it the Red Sea and the "house" [Kaabah] of Mecca.

On the following Sunday [April 29] we once more saw the North Star, which we had not seen for a long time.

On Friday, the 18th of May, after having seen no land for twenty-three days, we sighted lofty mountains, and having all this time sailed before the wind we could not have made less than 600 leagues. The land, when first sighted,[14] was at a distance of eight leagues, and our lead reached bottom at forty-five fathoms. That same night we took a course to the S.S.W., so as to get away from the coast. On the following day [May 19] we again approached the land, but owing to the heavy rain and a thunderstorm,[15] which prevailed whilst we were sailing along the coast, our pilot was unable to identify the exact locality. On Sunday [May 20] we found ourselves close to some mountains,[16] and when we were near enough for the pilot to recognise them he told us that they were above Calecut, and that this was the country we desired to go to.

CALECUT

[*Arrival*] That night [May 20] we anchored two leagues from the city of Calecut, and we did so because our pilot mistook *Capua,*[17] a town at that place, for Calecut. Still further there is another town called *Pandarani.*[18] We anchored about a league and a half from the shore. After we were at anchor, four boats [*almadias*] approached us from the land, who asked of what nation we were. We told them, and they then pointed out Calecut to us.

On the following day [May 21] these same boats came again alongside, when the captain-major sent one of the convicts to Calecut, and those with whom he went took him to two Moors from Tunis, who could speak Castilian and Genoese. The first greeting that he received was in these words: "May the Devil take thee! What brought you hither?" They asked what he sought so far away from home, and he told them that we came in search of Christians and of spices. They said: "Why does not the King of Castile, the King of France, or the Signoria of Venice send hither?" He said that the King of Portugal would not consent to their doing so, and they said he did the right thing. After this conversation they took him to their lodgings and gave him wheaten bread and honey. When he had eaten he returned to the ships, accompanied by one of the Moors, who was no sooner on board, than he said these words: "A lucky venture, a lucky venture! Plenty of rubies, plenty of emeralds! You owe great thanks to God, for having brought you to a country holding such riches!" We were greatly astonished to hear his talk, for we never expected to hear our language spoken so far away from Portugal.

[*A description of Calecut*] The city of Calecut is inhabited by Christians. They are of a tawny complexion. Some of them have big beards and long hair, whilst others clip their hair short or shave the head, merely allowing a tuft to remain on the crown as a sign that they are Christians. They also wear moustaches. They pierce the ears and wear much gold in them. They go naked down to the waist, covering their lower extremities with very fine cotton stuffs. But it is only the most respectable who do this, for the others manage as best they are able.[19]

The women of this country, as a rule, are ugly and of small stature. They wear many jewels of gold round the neck, numerous bracelets on their arms, and rings set with precious stones on their toes. All these people are well-disposed and apparently of mild temper. At first sight they seem covetous and ignorant.

[*A message sent to the King*] When we arrived at Calecut the king was fifteen leagues away. The captain-major sent two men to him with a message, informing him that an ambassador had arrived from the King of Portugal with letters, and that if he desired it he would take them to where the king then was.

The king presented the bearers of this message with much fine cloth. He sent word to the captain bidding him welcome, saying that he was about to proceed to Qualecut [Calecut]. As a matter of fact, he started at once with a large retinue.

[*At anchor at Pandarani,* May 27] A pilot accompanied our two men, with orders to take us to a place called Pandarani, below the place [Capua] where we anchored at first. At this time we were actually in front of the city of Calecut. We were told that the anchorage at the place to which we were to go was good, whilst at the place we were then it was bad, with a stony bottom, which was quite true; and, moreover, that it was customary for the ships which came to this country to anchor there for the sake of safety. We ourselves did not feel comfortable, and the captain-major had no sooner received this royal message than he ordered the sails to be set, and we departed. We did not, however, anchor as near the shore as the king's pilot desired.

When we were at anchor, a message arrived informing the captain-major that the king was already in the city. At the same time the king sent a *bale,*[20] with other men of distinction, to Pandarani, to conduct the captain-major to where the king awaited him. This *bale* is like an *alcaide*, and is always attended by two hundred men armed with swords and bucklers. As it was late when this message arrived, the captain-major deferred going.

[*Gama goes to Calecut*] On the following morning, which was Monday, May 28th, the captain-major set out to speak to the king, and took with him thirteen men, of whom I was one. We put on our best attire, placed bombards in our boats, and took with us trumpets and many flags. On landing, the captain-major was received by the *alcaide,* with whom were many men, armed and unarmed. The reception was friendly, as if the people were pleased to see us, though at first appearances looked threatening, for they carried naked swords in their hands. A palanquin was provided for the captain-major, such as is used by men of distinction in that country, as also by some of the merchants, who pay something to the king for this privilege. The captain-major entered the palanquin, which was carried by six men by turns. Attended by all these people we took the road of Qualecut, and came first to another town, called Capua. The captain-major was there deposited at the house of a man of rank, whilst we others were provided with food, consisting of rice, with much butter, and excellent boiled fish. The captain-major did not wish to eat, and when we had done so, we embarked on a river close by, which flows between the sea and the mainland, close to the coast.[21] The two boats in which we embarked were lashed together, so that we were not separated. There were numerous other boats, all crowded with people. As to those who were on the banks I say nothing; their number was infinite, and they had all come to see us. We went up that river for about a league, and saw many large ships drawn up high and dry on its banks, for there is no port here.

When we disembarked, the captain-major once more entered his palanquin. The road was crowded with a countless multitude anxious to see us. Even the women came out of their houses with children in their arms and followed us.

[*A Christian Church*][22] When we arrived [at Calecut] they took us to a large church, and this is what we saw:—

The body of the church is as large as a monastery, all built of hewn stone and covered with tiles. At the main entrance rises a pillar of bronze as high as a mast, on the top of which was perched a bird, apparently a cock. In addition to this, there was another pillar as high as a man, and very stout. In the centre of the body of the church rose a chapel,[23] all built of hewn stone, with a bronze door sufficiently wide for a man to pass, and stone steps leading up to it. Within this sanctuary stood a small image which they said represented Our Lady. Along the walls, by the main entrance, hung seven small bells.[24] In this church the captain-major said his prayers, and we with him.

We did not go within the chapel, for it is the custom that only certain servants of the church, called *quafees,*[25] should enter. The *quafees* wore some threads passing over the left shoulder and under the right arm, in the same manner as our deacons wear the stole. They threw holy water over us, and gave us some white earth,[26] which the Christians of this country are in the habit of putting on their foreheads, breasts, around the neck, and on the forearms. They threw holy water upon the captain-major and gave him some of the earth, which he gave in charge of someone, giving them to understand that he would put it on later.

Many other saints were painted on the walls of the church, wearing crowns. They were painted variously, with teeth protruding an inch from the mouth, and four or five arms.[27]

Below this church there was a large masonry tank, similar to many others which we had seen along the road.

[*Progress through the Town*] After we had left that place, and had arrived at the entrance to the city [of Calecut] we were shown another church, where we saw things like those described above. Here the crowd grew so dense that progress along the street became next to impossible, and for this reason they put the captain into a house, and us with him.

The king sent a brother of the *bale,* who was a lord of this country, to accompany the captain, and he was attended by men beating drums, blowing *anafils* and bagpipes, and firing off matchlocks. In conducting the captain they showed us much respect, more than is shown in Spain to a king. The number of people was countless, for in addition to those who surrounded us, and among whom there were two thousand armed men, they crowded the roofs and houses.

[*The King's Palace*] The further we advanced in the direction of the king's palace, the more did they increase in number. And when we arrived there, men of much distinction and great lords came out to meet the captain, and joined those who were already in attendance upon him. It was then an hour before sunset. When we reached the palace we passed through a gate into a courtyard of great size, and before we arrived at where the king was, we passed four doors, through which we had to force our way, giving many blows to the people. When, at last, we reached the door where the king was, there came forth from it a little old man, who holds a position resembling that of a bishop, and whose advice the king acts upon in all affairs of the church. This man embraced the captain when he entered the door. Several men were wounded at this door, and we only got in by the use of much force.

[*A Royal Audience, May 28*] The king was in a small court, reclining upon a couch covered with a cloth of green velvet, above which was a good mattress, and upon this again a sheet of cotton stuff, very white and fine, more so than any linen. The cushions were after the same fashion. In his left hand the king held a very large golden cup [spittoon], having a capacity of half an almude [8 pints]. At its mouth this cup was two palmas [16 inches] wide, and apparently it was massive. Into this cup the king threw the husks of a certain herb which is chewed by the people of this country because of its soothing effects, and which they call *atambor.*[28] On the right side of the the king stood a basin of gold, so large that a man might just encircle it with his arms: this contained the herbs. There were likewise many silver jugs. The canopy above the couch was all gilt.

The captain, on entering, saluted in the manner of the country: by putting the hands together, then raising them toward Heaven, as is done by Christians when addressing God, and immediately afterwards opening them and shutting the fists quickly. The king beckoned to the captain with his right hand to come nearer, but the captain did not approach him, for it is the custom of the country for no man to approach the king except only the servant who hands him the herbs, and when anyone addresses the king he holds his hand before the mouth, and remains at a distance. When the king beckoned to the captain he looked at us others, and ordered us to be seated on a stone bench near him, where he could see us. He ordered that water for our hands should be given us, as also some fruit, one kind of which resembled a melon, except that its outside was rough and the inside sweet, whilst another kind of fruit resembled a fig, and tasted very nice.[29] There were men who prepared these fruits for us; and the king looked at us eating, and smiled; and talked to the servant who stood near him supplying him with the herbs referred to.

Then, throwing his eyes on the captain, who sat facing him, he invited him to address himself to the courtiers present, saying they were men of much distinction, that he could tell them whatever he desired to say, and they would repeat it to him (the king). The captain-major replied that he was the ambassador of the King of Portugal, and the bearer of a message which he could only deliver to him personally. The king said this was good, and immediately asked him to be conducted to a chamber. When the captain-major had entered, the king, too, rose and joined him, whilst we remained where we were. All this happened about sunset. An old man who was in the court took away the couch as soon as the king rose, but allowed the plate to remain. The king, when he joined the captain, threw himself upon another couch, covered with various stuffs embroidered in gold, and asked the captain what he wanted.

And the captain told him he was the ambassador of a King of Portugal, who was Lord of many countries and the possessor of great wealth of every description, exceeding that of any king of these parts; that for a period of sixty years his ancestors had annually sent out vessels to make discoveries in the direction of India, as they knew that there were Christian kings there like themselves. This, he said, was the reason which induced them to order this country to be discovered, not because they sought for gold or silver, for of this they had such abundance that they needed not what was to be found in this country. He further stated that the captains sent out travelled for a year or two, until their provisions were exhausted, and then returned to Portugal, without having succeeded in making the desired discovery. There reigned a king now whose name was Dom Manuel, who had ordered him to build three vessels, of which he had been appointed captain-major, and who had ordered him not to return to Portugal until he should have discovered this King of the Christians, on pain of having his head cut off. That two letters had been intrusted to him to be presented in case he succeeded in discovering him, and that he would do so on the ensuing day; and, finally, he had been instructed to say by word of mouth that he [the King of Portugal] desired to be his friend and brother.

In reply to this the king said that he was welcome; that, on his part, he held him as a friend and brother, and would send ambassadors with him to Portugal. This latter had been asked as a favour, the captain pretending that he would not dare to present himself before his king and master unless he was able to present, at the same time, some men of this country.

These and many other things passed between the two in this chamber, and as it was already late in the night, the king asked the captain with whom he desired to lodge, with Christians or with Moors? And the captain replied, neither with Christians nor with Moors, and begged as a favour that he be given a lodging by himself. The king said he would order it thus, upon which the captain took leave of the king and came to where we were, that is, to a veranda lit up by a huge candlestick. By that time four hours of the night had already gone.

[*A Night's Lodging*] We then all went forth with the captain in search of our lodgings, and a countless crowd with us. And the rain poured down so heavily that the streets ran with water. The captain went on the back of six men [in a palanquin], and the time occupied in passing through the city was so long that the captain at last grew tired, and complained to the king's factor, a Moor of distinction, who attended him to the lodgings. The Moor then took him to his own house, and we were admitted to a court within it, where there was a veranda, roofed in with tiles. Many carpets had been spread, and there were two large candlesticks like those at the Royal palace. At the top of each of these were great iron lamps, fed with oil or butter, and each lamp had four wicks, which gave much light. These lamps they use instead of torches.

This same Moor then had a horse brought for the captain to take him to his lodgings, but it was without a saddle, and the captain refused to mount it.[30] We then started for our lodgings, and when we arrived we found there some of our men [who had come from the ships] with the captain's bed, and with numerous other things which the captain had brought as presents for the king.

[*Presents for the King*] On Tuesday [May 29] the captain got ready the following things to be sent to the king, viz., twelve pieces of *lambel,* four scarlet hoods, six hats, four strings of coral, a case containing six wash-hand basins, a case of sugar, two casks of oil, and two of honey. And as it is the custom not to send anything to the king without the knowledge of the Moor, his factor, and of the *bale,* the captain informed them of his intention. They came, and when they saw the present they laughed at it, saying that it was not a thing to offer a king, that the poorest merchant from Mecca, or any other part of India, gave more, and that if he wanted to make a present it should be in gold, as the king would not accept such things. When the captain heard this he grew sad, and said that he had brought no gold, that, moreover, he was no merchant, but an ambassador; that he gave of that which he had, which was his own [private gift] and not the king's;[31] that if the King of Portugal ordered him to return he would intrust him with far richer presents; and that if King Camolim[32] would not accept these things he would send them back to the ships. Upon this they declared that they would not forward his presents, nor consent to his forwarding them himself. When they had gone there came certain Moorish merchants, and they all depreciated the present which the captain desired to be sent to the king.

When the captain saw that they were determined not to forward his present, he said, that as they would not allow him to send his present to the palace he would go to speak to the king, and would then return to the ships. They approved of this, and told him that if he would wait a short time they would return and accompany him to the palace. And the captain waited all day, but they never came back. The captain was very wroth at being among so phlegmatic and unreliable a people, and intended at first, to go to the palace without them. On further consideration, however, he thought it best to wait until the following day. As to us others, we diverted ourselves, singing and dancing to the sound of trumpets, and enjoyed ourselves much.

[*A Second Audience, May 30*] On Wednesday morning the Moors returned, and took the captain to the palace, and us others with him. The palace was crowded with armed men. Our captain was kept waiting with his conductors for fully four long hours, outside a door, which was only opened when the king sent word to admit him, attended by two men only, whom he might select. The captain said that he desired to have Fernão Martins with him, who could interpret, and his secretary. It seemed to him, as it did to us, that this separation portended no good.

When he had entered, the king said that he had expected him on Tuesday. The captain said that the long road had tired him, and that for this reason he had not come to see him. The king then said that he had told him that he came from a very rich kingdom, and yet had brought him nothing; that he had also told him that he was the bearer of a letter, which had not yet been delivered. To this the captain rejoined that he had brought nothing, because the object of his voyage was merely to make discoveries, but that when other ships came he would then see what they brought him; as to the letter, it was true that he had brought one, and would deliver it immediately.

The king then asked what it was he had come to discover: stones or men? If he came to discover men, as he said, why had he brought nothing? Moreover, he had been told that he carried with him the golden image of a Santa Maria. The captain said that the Santa Maria was not of gold, and that even if she were he would not part with her, as she had guided him across the ocean, and would guide him back to his own country. The king then asked for the letter. The captain said that he begged as a favour, that as the Moors wished him ill and might misinterpret him, a Christian able to speak Arabic should be sent for. The king said this was well, and at once sent for a young man, of small stature, whose name was Quaram. The captain then said that he had two letters, one written in his own language and the other in that of the Moors; that he was able to read the former, and knew that it contained nothing but what would prove acceptable; but that as to the other he was unable to read it, and it might be good, or contain something that was erroneous. As the Christian was unable to *read* Moorish, four Moors took the letter and read it between them, after which they translated it to the king, who was well satisfied with its contents.

The king then asked what kind of merchandise was to be found in his country. The captain said there was much corn, cloth, iron, bronze, and many other things. The king asked whether he had any merchandise with him. The captain replied that he had a little of each sort, as samples, and that if permitted to return to the ships he would order it to be landed, and that meantime four or five men would remain at the lodgings assigned them. The king said no! He might take all his people with him, securely moor his ships, land his merchandise, and sell it to the best advantage.

END NOTES

1. Zavra or zabra is a small open vessel, sharp at the stern, with a square sail of matting.
2. The Swahili "dress" their vessels at the feast that follows the Ramadan month.
3. *Alcaide,* from the Arabic *Alkadi,* the Judge.
4. Burton (*Camoens,* iv, p. 241) suggests that this picture of the Holy Ghost may have been a figure of Kapot-eshwar, the Hindu pigeon-god and goddess, an incarnation of Shiva and his wife, the third person of the Hindu Triad.
5. Trigo tremez, corn that ripens in three months. This would be sorghum (the "matama" of the Swahili), which is sent in shiploads to Arabia and the Persian Gulf.
6. The ruins of the ancient town of Malindi lie to the south of the modern village of that name, and are of great extent. They include the remains of a town wall. Persian and Arabic inscriptions have been discovered, but, with the exception of Vasco da Gama's pillar, no traces of occupation by the Portuguese. Malindi Road, or Port Melinda of the Admiralty chart, lies about three miles to the south of the town, but Vasco da Gama anchored off the town, and not in this sheltered road. The anchorage is less than half a mile from the town in four fathoms and a half.
7. *Balandrau,* a surtout worn by the Brothers of Mercy in Portugal.
8. *Lambel,* a striped cotton stuff which had a large sale at the beginning of the African trade.
9. Burton (*Camoens,* iv, p. 420) suggests that they cried *Krishna,* the name of the eighth Incarnation of Vishnu, the second person of the Hindu Trinity, and the most popular of Indian gods.
10. See introductory note, p. 73.
11. The island in question is Kilwa.
12. Alcochete, a town on the left bank of the estuary of the Tagus, above Lisbon.
13. The "Bay" is the Arabian Sea, which the "Strait" of Bab el Mandeb joins to the Red Sea. Cambay (Khambhat), in Gujarat, when the Portuguese first came to India, was one of the most flourishing marts of commerce. The silting up of the Gulf accounts, in a large measure, for its commercial decline since then.
14. Mount Eli (Dely) was probably the land first sighted, a conspicuous hill forming a promontory about 16 miles to the north of Cananor, and named thus from the Cardamoms which are largely exported from this part of Malabar, and are called Ela in Sanscrit (Yule's *Marco Polo,* ii, p. 321).
15. The rains in Malabar begin about April or May, and continue until September or October. They are synchronous with the S.W. monsoon, and are heaviest in June, July, and August. The annual rainfall exceeds 150 inches!
16. Cotta Point, or Cape Kadalur, the "Monte Formosa" of the Portuguese, 15 miles N.N.W. of Calecut.
17. Castanheda and Barros call this place Capocate. It was seven miles N.N.W. of Calecut, at the mouth of the Elatur River.
18. Pandaramy (Pandarani) is Batuta's Fandarain. Barros calls it Pandarane. It is identical

with Pantharini Kollam, the northern Kollam or Quillan, and boasts one of the nine original mosques built on the Malabar coast by Malik lbn Dinar. It is 14 miles N.N.W. of Calecut. The author of the MS elsewhere spells Pandaramy and Pandarin.

19. The visitors thus became at once acquainted with the various castes constituting the population of Calecut, including the *Nairs,* or fighting caste of Malabar, who eat meat (which shows a servile origin), but wear the thread of the Dwija (twice-born), rank next to the Brahmans, and practise polyandry; and the turbulent *Moplah,* who are descendants of Arab fathers and native women. These latter are the "native" Moors.
20. *Bale,* in the Arabic *Wali,* governor. *Alcaide,* in Portuguese, has this same meaning.
21. This river is the Elatur.
22. This "church" was, of course, a pagoda or temple. The high pillar in front of it is used for suspending the flag which indicates the commencement of the Temple festival. It is of wood, but usually covered with copper or silver. The cock, which surmounts it, is the symbol of the War-god Subraumainar. The smaller pillar supports the coco-oil lamps during the festival.
23. *Corucheo,* which literally means spire or minaret; but further on the authors call this sanctuary a chapel, capella.
24. These bells are struck by the Brahmans when they enter the temple, but must not be touched by people of inferior castes.
25. The *"quafees"* are, of course, Brahman priests. The Rev. J. J. Jaus suggests *kaz* (Arabic), meaning "judge".
26. The "white earth" is a mixture of dust, cow-dung, sacrificial ashes, sandal wood, etc., cemented in rice-water.
27. It is just possible that some of the Portuguese doubted whether these Hindu Gods and images represented the saints of their own churches. Castanheda (i, p. 57) says that when João de Sá knelt down by the side of Vasco da Gama, he said: "If these be devils, I worship the true God"; at which his chief smiled. But however this may be, it is equally true that the reports furnished by the heads of the expedition described these Hindus as Christians, and that the king believed them to be so.
28. *Atambor,* a corruption of the Arabic *tambur,* the betel-nut. It is the fruit of Areca Catechu, and is universally chewed throughout India, the Indian Archipelago and Southern China. Its juice discolours the teeth, but is said to make the breath sweet, and to be conducive to health. "Erva" (herb) is quite inapplicable to this fruit. Usually it is cut up into four slices, which are wrapped up in a leaf of Betel-pepper (*Piper Betle*), and chewed with an admixture of lime and catechu.
29. These fruits were the Jack (*Artocarpus integrifolia*) and bananas.
30. It is still the practice in Calecut to ride horses without a saddle, and no slight seems therefore to have been intended.
31. As a matter of fact, Vasco da Gama was very poorly provided with suitable merchandise.
32. Zamorin. It is a title; according to some a corrupt reading of Tamuri Rajah, Tamuri being the name of the most exalted family of the Nair caste, whilst others derive it from "Samudriya Rajah," that is, "King of the Coast."

QUESTIONS

1. What kind of reception do the Portuguese receive from the Moors of Mombaça?
2. How is trust built by the taking and exchanging of hostages by the Portuguese and the people they encounter in East Africa?
3. Why do the Portuguese believe that the people of Calecut are Christians? What do they see in the "churches" there that promotes this belief?
4. How does the captain-major respond to his experiences in Calecut? What gifts does he offer and what do his Indian hosts make of these gifts?